Women's Sports
A History

Women's
Sports

A History

Allen Guttmann

Columbia University Press
NEW YORK

Columbia University Press
New York   Oxford

Copyright © 1991 Columbia University Press
All rights reserved

Printed in the United States of America

CIP data appear at the end of book

c 10 9 8 7 6 5 4 3 2
p 10 9 8 7 6 5 4 3

To Doris

"Dir entgegen knistert meine Liebe,
Durch die blaue Luft"

Contents

Acknowledgments
and Credits

Living as I do in an era of unanswered letters and unreturned telephone calls, I am deeply grateful to the many people who have assisted and encouraged me with this project. Joseph L. Arbena, Paolo Pierangeli, Hajo Bernett, Peter Donnelly, Henning Eichberg, Lars Magnus Engström, Javier Duran Gonzalez, John M. Hoberman, Wray Vamplew, and Leif Yttergren responded to specific requests for information. The staff of the Robert Frost Library performed their usual miracles and obtained books and articles from far and wide. Betty Steele and the staff of the Amherst College Computer Center saved me weeks if not months of tedious labor. The frustrations encountered in the search for visual materials were allayed by Gridth Ablon, Mieko Baba, Hajo Bernett, Richard Cashman, Carl Cone, Wolfgang Decker, Claude Erbson, Sally Fox, Maxwell Howell, Roland Renson, and Eric de Vroude. President Peter Pouncey recklessly assured me that I'd have at least one interested reader.

Portions of the manuscript were read critically by Howell Chickering, Wolfgang Decker, Frederick Griffiths, Rebecca Hague, Margaret Hunt, Donald Kyle, Roberta J. Park, Gertrud Pfister, Joachim Rühl, Thomas Scanlon, and Elizabeth Will. Cindy L. Himes, Richard Mandell, and Kate Wittenberg read the entire manuscript. All these readers made valuable suggestions and saved me from blunders.

For financial assistance, I wish to thank Deans Ralph Beals and Ronald Rosbottom.

For permission to use a number of paragraphs from chapter 10 of my previous book, *A Whole New Ball Game,* I thank the University of North Carolina Press.

I gladly obey the convention that saves the most important acknowledgment for the last: my greatest debt is to Doris Bargen.

Women's Sports
A History

Introduction

There has never been a time, from the dawn of our civilization to the present, when women have been as involved in sports, as participants or as spectators, as men have. Are sports then a "male domain," a "masculine preserve"? Are women like Nadia Comanici, Steffi Graf, and Florence Griffith-Joyner unwelcome intruders? Yes and no. While it is historically true that sports have usually been more important for males than for females, there has never been a time when girls and women were wholly excluded from sports and there have certainly been times and places where their involvement was almost as extensive and intensive as the men's. If the values institutionalized in sports, like physical strength, stamina, swiftness, and skill, are defined as masculine, then one must accept Lois Bryson's assertion that sports are "so thoroughly masculinized that it seems unlikely that [they] can be reclaimed to serve women's interests."[1] If, however, the institutionalized values are thought of as *human* rather than as exclusively masculine, the prospect for women's sports is considerably less gloomy.

Blanket statements about the pre–nineteenth-century exclusion of women from sports are commonly uttered in blissful ignorance of the historical record.[2] (One purpose of the present study is to make such ignorance less blissful.) Statements about exclusion from the "male domain" of sports take into account neither the distinctiveness of times and places nor the complicated ways in which gender has interacted with social class and with the stages of the life cycle. At any given historical moment, some women have indeed been totally excluded from sports while others have been intensely involved. Eighteenth-century English sports, for instance, can be called a strictly "masculine preserve" if one looks only at women of the "middling sort," casting accounts in their husband's shops and dedicating their leisure hours to the perusual of Methodist tracts. One sees a different picture if one turns one's eyes to aristocratic women like the Marchioness of Salisbury, riding to the hounds, or to lower-class women like Elizabeth Stokes, fighting and vanquishing "the famous boxing woman of Billingsgate."[3] In the 1890s, while medical experts debated whether or not strenuous exercises endangered a middle-class girl's capacity to conceive and bear children, working-class women were competing in six-day bicycle races. The historical record for women's sports is frequently sketchy (because Clio has only recently begun to pay serious and sustained attention to her own sex), but the record is much fuller than most people have imagined. My narrative begins with the historian's traditional lament about how little we know; it might have ended with lachrymose comments about an undamable flood of words and images.

In my approach to words and images (and numbers), I remain the eclectic that I have always been. In writing about women's sports before the mid-twentieth century, I have been guided by the archeologists and the historians (themselves a varied tribe, including specialists in women's history, art history, and literary history). In dealing with the present, I have made greater use of the social sciences, especially sociology and social psychology, and of the plethora of data purveyed by journalism. Except for a brief discussion of sports in the ancient Near East, my investigation is limited culturally to what I define broadly as the "West" (I include Australia and New Zealand). I have repressed the temptation to do more than mention Asian and African sports because the materials available for women's sports in non-Western civilizations are largely inaccessible to scholars limited to European languages.

Another limitation must be acknowledged. My focus throughout is upon older girls' and women's sports (as opposed to children's sports). I realize that the social construction of gender begins in infancy and that children's games are a part of every culture, but the sports of older girls and adult women usually reveal more about culture and social structure than the games of young children do. For that reason I have chosen to concentrate on women's sports from the moment when they begin in most times and places to diverge significantly from men's sports. The physical and psychic changes of puberty have always been accompanied by a shift in cultural expectations about the body. Sports have often—but by no means always—been a part of the *rites de passage* that mark the move from boyhood to manhood. For girls, puberty has often—but by no means always—meant the abandonment of sports.

The magnitude of this abandonment is sometimes masked by scholars who mix categories and write of "physical education and sport" or "sport and leisure activities." In my previous work in sports history, I have defined sports as nonutilitarian physical contests. (The competition can be against nature or one's own earlier performance as well as against other persons.) In practice, the historian cannot always determine if runners immobilized in a fresco or swimmers depicted on a Greek vase were involved in a contest or not, but it is nonetheless important to be attentive to theoretical distinctions and to seek as much clarity as possible. While it is necessary to discuss such sports-related topics as noncompetitive physical activities and physical education, it is essential that dancers, acrobats, and fresh-air enthusiasts not be confused with athletes. To rejoice that men and women are equally involved in sports when the men are engaged in a game of rugby and the women are at an aerobics class is to mislead the unwary reader.

This theoretical distinction between sports and noncompetitive physical activities is not trivial because the psychological differences between a competitive activity and a noncompetitive one are immense. Since most sports *do* require at least a modicum of aggressiveness even when their codes of conduct require strict controls on actual physical mayhem, female athletes are likely to be more aggressive than the women engaged in noncompetitive forms of recreation. Croquet may not bring out the "killer instinct," but it comes closer than a stroll among the golden daffodils. Aggressiveness, however, has conventionally been associated more closely with men than with women. It follows, therefore, that a commitment to women's sports has almost always been to some degree problematical—in women's eyes as well as men's. Is it really *feminine* to win at tennis or to hurl a javelin? The role conflict experienced by female athletes has certainly not been a universal phenomenon, but it has occurred in times and places as different as fifth-century Athens and twentieth-century Podunk. In the second part of this book, "The Present State of Women's Sports," I discuss the debate over role conflict and venture some opinions on other contemporary controversies.

Can the demonstrable (and soon to be demonstrated) fact that men have always been more involved in sports than women be attributed to biologically based psychological predispositions? Is anatomy, after all, destiny? Thinking about this possibility, I have taken seriously the work of sports historian Henning Eichberg as well as that of feminist scholars like Nancy Chodorow, Carol Gilligan, and Mary O'Brien, none of whom writes specifically about sports. It may be, as Eichberg maintains, departing for once from his usual emphasis on the cultural relativity of sports, that menstruation, pregnancy, childbirth, lactation, and menopause create a different "structure of time" for women. It may be true that men's "linear time corresponds rather precisely to the temporal configuration of industrial society and modern sports," but I remain convinced that culture—not biology—accounts for most, if not all, of the gender difference that we see everywhere in sports history.[4] When the women of *this* historical moment sit quietly at home with their knitting while the women of *that* time and place battle their muddy way through the travail of a rugby tournament, differences in social structure and in culture offer a more likely explanation than any suggested by physiology. If I have a single proposition to defend, it is that the sheer multiplicity of behaviors revealed by a history of women's sports provides us with yet another reason to distrust even the most beguiling theories of "woman's nature."

I hesitate to sound excessively high-minded. The story of women's sports is one that has—I trust—an inherent fascination quite apart from the abundance of valuable information conveyed about culture and society. The narrative that follows is meant especially for those men and women who enjoy not only doing and watching sports but also thinking about them. A small group, no doubt, but one of which I am quite fond.

PART I

A History of
Women's Sports

ONE

From the Egyptians
to the Etruscans

Surveying the historical record, in which men have traditionally figured as movers and shakers while women have often been dismissed with a few remarks about the domestic sphere, feminist scholars sometimes speak of women's "invisibility." Men stride across the historical stage; women labor quietly behind the scenes. Production matters, reproduction does not. The editor of a recent collection of essays in women's history puts the problem somewhat less polemically when she prefaces her book with the laconic remark, "The documentary evidence for the lives of women in antiquity is fragmentary and difficult to interpret."[1] There is relatively little evidence for a comprehensive history of Greek and Roman women and even less for a discussion of Egyptian, Minoan, or Etruscan women.

The dearth of information becomes almost desperate when one seeks to investigate women's sports before the emergence of Greek civilization. Whether or not ancient women were able to act as priestesses, own property, make wills, testify in court, and divorce their husbands has monopolized the attention of scholars to the point where few of them pause to wonder if women also participated in sports. It is impossible for classicists completely to overlook the panhellenic athletic festivals sacred to Zeus and Apollo, but the games sacred to Hera are commonly ignored. Historians have unearthed hundreds of names of male athletes, from Coroebus, who won the stade-race at Olympia in 776 B.C., to Porphyrius the charioteeer, who was the idol of Constantinople in the sixth century A.D. Perhaps a dozen names of female athletes have been preserved. That physical training and sports were closely related to the man's role in warfare is obvious; that physical training and sports were sometimes associated by the ancients with the woman's role in human reproduction is equally true but much less frequently acknowledged.

Confronted with not only the scarcity of archeological and literary evidence for women's sports but also their colleagues' neglect of what scanty evidence exists, impatient sports historians are tempted to speculate on the basis of analogy. We know a good deal, for instance, about women's sports among African tribes, where pubescent girls often wrestled as part of their ritual initiation into mature womanhood. Among the Diola of Gambia, for example, adolescent boys and girls wrestled (but not against one another) and the male champion often married the female champion.[2] In other tribes, such as the Yala of Nigeria and the Njabi of the Congo, men and women wrestled one another.[3] We know something about women's sports in Melanesia. Exploring the islands of the South Pacific, the eighteenth-century British explorer James Cook was shocked at the sight of female boxers.[4] In British-ruled New Guinea, twentieth-century anthropologists have observed a ceremonial tug-of-war, men against women, performed by moonlight to enhance the fertility of nature and of humankind.[5]

We know even more about women's sports among the Indians of North America, where women played stickball and a number of other games, many of which were clearly courtship or fertility rituals. "Back of each type of game," writes anthropologist Alyce Cheska, "there appeared to be a religious ceremony of which the game was a significant part."[6] The religious element, which was certainly present in the stickball games of the Southeast, can be exaggerated. Not all Indian women's sports were ballgames and not all were as closely related to cult as stickball was. In 1868, John Cremony observed Apache and Navajo girls in a foot race won by one of the Apaches. In 1899, Frederick Miller photographed Crow women in a bareback horserace at a fair in Montana.[7] In neither of these races was there a detectable relation to religious cult.

Does this kind of anthropological evidence of women's sports from many preliterate cultures authorize us to assume then that sports are a cultural universal which appears, in some form or another, in every society? Sports probably *are* universal, for boys and girls if not for grown men and women, but it is the better part of methodological wisdom to hold in check the understandable temptation to argue from anthropological analogy. At the very least, speculations must be plainly acknowledged as such and not disguised as uncontested truths. Meager as it often is, archeological and literary evidence is the only reasonably firm basis for interpretation. A miser's measure of fact is preferable to a feast of fantasy.

Archeological finds from ancient Egypt suggest that men and women of every social stratum, from mighty dynastic rulers to the humblest peasants, mingled freely in their daily lives without the strict segregation by gender which kept respectable Greek women sequestered in their homes. Men and women worked side by side. Stone images of the pharaoh were commonly flanked by images of his consort. Barbara S. Lesko has asserted that "women enjoyed equal rights with men throughout Egyptian history."[8] Although this opinion seems too good to be entirely credible, other Egyptologists have maintained that a woman had the legal right "to own property, retain it on marriage, and dispose of it exactly as she chose."[9] Egyptian women of the pharaonic period were also empowered to act as priestesses, an extremely important role in a culture pervaded by religion. Egyptian women enjoyed sufficient personal freedom for Herodotus and other Greek travelers to Egypt to complain about an "unnatural" reversal of gender roles.

The reversal seems not, however, to have included women's participation in sports. A number of historians, mostly German, have studied the sports of ancient Egypt with Germanic thoroughness. Wolfgang Decker has published a scholarly monograph and edited a collection of documents in which the athletic feats of Thutmosis III and Amenophis II are chronicled and interpreted, but Decker has unearthed very few references to or depictions of their female counterparts. The many scenes of Egyptian sports, painted on the walls of tombs, carved into reliefs, or inscribed upon stone memorials to the dead, are almost exclusively celebrations of male prowess. To prove their physical fitness and testify to their divine right to the throne, pharaohs hunted lions and shot arrows through layered sheets of copper (or were *said* to—we cannot determine if the extraordinary athletic feats attributed to the mighty were actually performed or merely ascribed to them). After thirty years upon the throne, the pharaoh was expected to perform a ceremonial run which demonstrated that he was still physically virile enough to stave off the forces of chaos that continually threaten to overwhelm the universe. The pharaoh's soldiers proved *their* prowess as wrestlers or as stickfighters. The close connection between sports and military preparedness was obvious. Although sports historians sometimes illustrate their texts with depictions of female acrobatic dancers like those carved in relief at the temple of Queen Hatshepsut in Karnak (ca. 1480 B.C.), there is very little unambiguous evidence, visual or textual, for women's sports.[10] When the images are closely examined, most of the scenes of "sports" can just as easily be depictions of a dance, an acrobatic stunt, or a noncompetitive game.[11]

When the scene does unambiguously depict sports rather than some other form of amusement, the female role is usually supportive. A splendid gold and ivory relief from a chest found in the tomb of Tutanchamun (ca. 1350 B.C.) portrays him as an archer. He sits with stretched bow and arrow in hand as a bird, struck through the wing by an earlier shot, drops to the ground. Next to him kneels the queen. She gracefully hands him another arrow and points to a nest of further quarry.[12] On the basis of this and other works of art we can conjecture that royal and aristocratic women sometimes accompanied their menfolk when the hunt was not especially dangerous, but there is—to the best of my knowledge—no Egyptian statue, relief, or fresco in which a female hunter actually bends the bow or flourishes the spear. There is at least one literary text in which women are involved in fowling. They are described at this sport in "The Pleasures of Fishing and Fowling," but here too the translator of the papyrus fragment noted that the women's role was ancillary and supportive: "I believe . . . that the women are rousing the birds from cover for the children to hit them in the air."[13] Girls as well as boys? It is impossible to say.

Egyptian art and artifacts do testify that girls and women swam. The carved body of a nearly nude girl, stretched with slender arms and legs extended, forms the handle of a wooden spoon from the Eighteenth Dynasty. (See Plate 2.) Since the handle of another spoon has the girl holding an elaborately carved duck, the bowl of the spoon, it seems safe to assume that these girls are swimmers. There can be no doubt whatsoever about the women who appear on a lovely plate found in a grave from the 22nd Dynasty; they are surrounded by fish.[14] We can easily imagine that young women sometimes shouted an exuberant challenge and raced to see who was the swiftest swimmer, but the written sources make no reference to such contests. It is also easy to imagine that boats rowed by lower-class women were sometimes propelled in spontaneous races, but races of this sort were beneath the notice of courtly artists and priestly chroniclers. A manuscript papyrus is not the exception it seems to be. It tells the charming story of a bored monarch who commanded that he be rowed upon the Nile by twenty lovely nearly naked maidens, but there is no evidence that anyone ever actually tried this attractive remedy for ennui.[15] What we have in the depictions of swimmers and the tales of rowers are instances of vigorous physical activity—what German scholars call *Körperkultur*—but we cannot call these women athletes.

We have somewhat better evidence for the existence of women's sports when we consider ballgames. The women shown in a relief from a tomb at Sakkara (nineteenth century B.C.) are usually identified as dancers rather than as ball players, but the famous eleventh-dynasty tomb of the Cheti at Beni Hassan, the richest of all sources for Egyptian sports, contains murals showing girls or women sitting astride the backs of other females and tossing balls back and forth.[16] Other paintings from Beni Hassan illustrate females juggling. Archeological treasures of this magnitude have always stimulated speculation. "These ball games . . . were confined almost entirely to women and, as their dress shows, they are mostly professional performers. Yet we can hardly suppose that the games thus represented were not popular also among the young of both sexes."[17] For the assertion about professionalism there is no evidence whatsoever, but the speculation about the popularity of ballgames is plausible. If the young participants also turned their pastimes into contests, as modern boys and girls do, then we have one of the earliest depictions of women's sport, but we must continually remind ourselves that we are in the realm of speculation.

A final illustration of physical activity underlines the difficulty of interpretation. The temple of Queen Hatshepsut in Karnak contains a relief depicting the Queen, who ruled in her own name and took the masculine title of pharaoh, engaged in a ceremonial run. Together with steer-god Apis, whose tiny carved figure accompanies the powerful stone image of the Queen, Hatshepsut runs four times around the sacred precinct. (See Plate 1.) This feat, typical of those performed by Egypt's male rulers (and by those of Assyria as well), symbolized physical vigor, but it was almost certainly not a true sports contest because royal divinity does not deign to compete against mere mortals and the thought of a contest among princely claimants to the throne was devoutly to be avoided.

As this short survey of the evidence indicates, there is hardly a single unambiguous reference to women's sports in the Egypt of the pharaohs. Girls, and perhaps women too, engaged in a number of physical activities of the sort that we in the modern world organize into sports, but there is no way to be sure that Egyptian culture obeyed the same competitive imperatives as ours. We transform almost every sort of game into a contest. Egyptian men seem to have shared this tendency, but their women may well have been dissuaded from such "masculine" behavior. The approved repertory of social roles for respectable upper-class women, as opposed to peasant women and slaves, seems not to have included any sort of strenuous physical activity. If the strenuous physical activity of lower-class women included sports, their literate and artistic contemporaries found these sports unworthy of their notice.

If Egyptian historiography provides shaky ground for speculations about women's sports, Minoan scholarship is a minefield for the unwary sports historian. Sir Arthur Evans, famed discoverer of the "Palace of Minos" at Knossos on the north coast of Crete, contributed mightily to the confusion when he referred to the ivory figure of a Minoan goddess as "Our Lady of Sports." Evans, who admitted that the figure "strikes the eye as of a very different character from that of the girl performers in the Minoan bull-sports as portrayed for us in the frescoes and small reliefs," thought that the "male loin-attire" was enough to justify his reckless attribution.[18]

Of the "bull-leaper" frescoes and reliefs referred to by Evans, the most famous is unquestionably the treasure from the Palace of Minos (ca. 1500 B.C.). The gender conventions of Minoan art are clear enough for most scholars to conclude that females took part in the pictured ceremony. Girls (painted white) boldly grip the horns of the huge bull or wait to catch the boy (painted red) in flight over the bull's elongated back. Evans wrote that the "girl performers were surely of gentle birth," but his evidence is their "fashionably curled locks" and their jewelry. The Czech historian Vera Olivova has confidently added that the bull-leapers were originally hunters and herdsmen who were, in the course of time, replaced by professional acrobats "who underwent special training."[19] Evans also speculated that the three reliefs on the gold Vapheio Cup depicted "a 'drive' of wild or half-wild bulls along the bottom of some wooded glen." The figure "desperately at grips with the horns of the great beast" is "certainly that of a girl, in spite of the sinewy limbs that it displays."[20] There is no evidence for these assertions. The French classicist E. T. Vermeule has shared the conviction, first voiced by Evans, that women hunted. Discussing the fragments found at Tiryns on the mainland, near Argos, he commented,

These are palace aristocrats trained to male sports, the painted counterparts of Atalanta who thrust herself into the Kalydonian boar hunt, of Kyrene who wrestled with lions with such suavity, of Phaidra who on her sickbed tamed imaginary Venetian racehorses.[21]

But the aristocratic female athletes "trained to male sports" are probably as imaginary as Phaidra's hallucinatory racehorses. J. K. Anderson has asked the critical question: "Is the whole scene in fact legendary?"[22] Anderson's sensible implication is that any females who were present at such scenes were either goddesses or, if mortals, merely spectators who waved the men off at the start of the hunt.

The problem, of course, is that the archeological evidence is insufficient for us to know for sure whether the Minoan females in the frescoes and in the reliefs are active or passive participants, nor can we be sure, when the figures seem clearly to be physically active, what their actions meant. Jacquetta Hawkes writes as vividly in *Dawn of the Gods* (1968) as Evans did in his classic works of an earlier generation, but there seems little warrant for her conviction that the "unanimous testimony of so many works of art must express much that was essential in the Minoan experience of life and justify the claim that, more than any other contemporary people, the Cretans expressed the idea of *Homo ludens*."[23] She alludes here to Johan Huizinga's famous book on the role of play in the creation of civilization. Still, Hawkes cannot quite bring herself to assert that the Minoans played for the sake of play (which is what Huizinga identifies as the essence of *Homo ludens*). Despite her obvious desire to emphasize "the grace of life" and the element of play in Minoan civilization, Hawkes agrees with the scholars who have assumed that the bull-leaper's spectacular performance was a part of religious cult, perhaps a fertility ritual.[24]

To say this is not to deny that the ritual may also have been a sports contest. Minoan cult may have been similar to Greek cult as manifested at Olympia, Delphi, and other sites for sports festivals. In that case, Minoan cult did indeed take the form of a sports event with winners and losers. If there *were* winners and losers, how were they determined? By successive leaps which eliminated the unskillful contestants? By subjective judgments about the leapers' performance? The most we can say is that Minoan culture seems to have provided

occasions for extraordinary demonstrations of female physical prowess. Of course, we may carry skepticism to an extreme and argue that
the bull-leaper fresco and other works of Minoan art all depict mythological rather than actual feats, but I am ready in this case to believe
in historicity of the fabulous.

Although the Etruscan language presents too many problems for
scholars to translate inscriptions with any confidence, archeological
evidence is ample enough for us to be sure that athletics were an
important part of Etruscan life. Frescoes like those in the famous
"Tomba delle Olimpiadi" and the "Tomba delle Bighe" ("Tomb of
the Two-Horse Chariots") are a marvelous source of information
about sports. Bronze statuettes and terra cotta reliefs are also invalu-
able. There can be little doubt that Etruscan men threw javelins and
wrestled, ran and jumped, dove and swam. Their favorite sports, if
one judges by the frequency of depiction, were boxing and chariot
racing, both attested by the comments of the Roman historian Livy
as well as by the visual evidence. Whether the athletes were free
citizens or slaves is a matter of scholarly dispute.

The fact that Etruscan women enjoyed considerable personal freedom is quite important. "The Greek woman and the Roman woman,"
writes Jacques Heurgon, "lived in the shadow of their homes; but the
Etruscan woman 'went out' a great deal." And not merely to attend
religious festivals. "In Etruria it was a recognized privilege for ladies
of the most respectable kind, and not just for courtesans as in Greece,
to take part . . . in banquets where they reclined, as the men did
. . . , on the couches of the Triclinium." We see them, for instance,
in the banqueting scene from the "Tomba delle Leopardi."[25] In their
public and their private lives, Etruscan women conducted themselves
with so little inhibition that ethnocentric Greek observers were horrified at what appeared to be sexual depravity. In sharp contrast to
Greek women, who were barred from the Olympic Games even as
spectators, Etruscan women were enthusiasts for chariot races. The
elaborate frescoes of the "Tomba delle Bighe" show wooden stands
in which male and female spectators sit (or recline) together. In the
misleadingly named "Tomba delle Olimpiadi," a fresco shows a
chariot race in which an accident has occurred. A chariot has over-
turned and the driver has been flung into the air. "Three women
watching the event have put their hands to their heads and are screaming
with fright." Not all Etruscan women were as timid as these. One
woman in a scene from the "Tombe delle Bighe" is raising her arms

in what seems to be some kind of signal to the charioteers. She may even be an official of the games.[26]

Physically active females were a common topos of Etruscan art. A typical example can be seen in the bronze figure of a female acrobat. Her slim body, arched backwards in a "bridge," served as the handle of a bronze vessel. Many pictures survive of men and women immobilized by the artist's brush in the contorted poses of ecstatic dances. Were females restricted to such dances and to acrobatic performances or did they also—like Etruscan men—participate in sports? Vera Olivova has ventured a clear answer: "We have statuettes which show women wrestling against men. The statue of a woman cleaning the dust of a match from her body is a further proof of women's active participation in sports."[27] This conclusion may be premature. The scenes may be mythological rather than mimetic, representations of Atalanta rather than of the women of Etruria.

Antiquity's most definite statement about Etruscan women's physical activity comes from the Greek historian Theopompus as quoted in the anecdotal pages of the second-century A.D. historian Athenaeus:

Theopompus in the forty-third book of his Histories says that it is customary with the Etruscans to share their women in common; the women bestow great care on their bodies and often exercise . . . with men, sometimes also with one another; for it is no disgrace for women to show themselves naked. Further, they dine, not with their own husbands, but with any men who happen to be present, and they pledge with wine any whom they wish.[28]

Theopompus does not refer to the element of competition, but his language does imply that competition may have been among the enormities committed by shameless Etruscan women. Unfortunately, modern classicists agree that Theopompus was an unreliable gossip. Jean-Paul Thuillier, author a 700–page book on *Les Jeux Athlétiques dans la Civilisation Etrusque* (1985), warns that this account of naked exercises should be read "with the greatest suspicion." When Theopompus characterized Etruscan women as bibulous, physically attractive, and given to sexual excess, his comments revealed "his own obsessions."[29]

Nonetheless, if we take Etruscan statuettes as mimetic art, that is, as realistic evidence of sports participation, we can conjecture that at least *some* Etruscan women behaved as Theopompus implied they did. In that case, other questions arise. What was the social status of such women? Were they citizens or slaves? Were they specially trained professional entertainers, like the acrobats portrayed in Egyptian art, or were all young Etruscan women expected, like Spartan girls, to demonstrate their prowess as wrestlers? Perhaps, since we seem doomed forever to be tantalized by such questions, it is time to turn our attention to Sparta, to Athens, and to the other cities of the Greek world. The information we have on Greek women's sports in archaic, classical, and Hellenistic times is meager, but, in comparison to what we know about Egyptian, Minoan, and Etruscan women, the evidence startles the fact-starved historian as manna did the ancient Israelites.

TWO

Spartan Girls and Other Runners

The most famous sportswoman of Greek antiquity, Artemis, goddess of the moon, appeared in ancient literature and in art in her guise as huntress. (Millennia later, Ben Jonson sang of her as "queen and huntress, chaste and fair.") When the fourth-century B.C. historian Xenophon described a typical hunt, he noted how important it was for the huntsman to "vow a share of the spoil to Apollo, and to Artemis the Huntress."[1] In antiquity, she was commonly sculpted or depicted on vases with her bow in hand (as she was when Augustus St. Gaudens placed her bronze figure atop New York's Madison Square Garden). She also appeared with her hounds, which she had received from Pan. In Book III of his *Metamorphoses,* the first-century B.C. Latin poet Ovid vividly retold the popular legend of her encounter with the unlucky hunter Actaeon, who discovered the irate huntress–goddess at her bath. Actaeon was forthwith transformed into a stag, and was then torn to pieces by his own dogs. Artemis was not the only immortal huntress. Book II of the *Metamorphoses* contains the tale of the nymph Callisto, who captured the affections of Zeus when he spotted her in hunting dress. When she resisted his amorous attentions, she found herself among the stars, a new constellation.

More athletic still was Atalanta, whom Ovid depicted in Books VIII and X as huntress, wrestler, and runner. Abandoned as an infant and reared by a she-bear, Atalanta was physically the match of any man she met. She joined heroic Meleager in the hunt for the white-tusked Calydonian boar on Mount Parnassus and she was in at the kill. One of the many depictions of this hunt appears as the topmost frieze of a sixth-century mixing bowl by the Athenian artist Cleitias. Sir John Beazley notes that it was

Atalanta who with an arrow drew first blood. Here she has shot already, and is now wielding the spear, but her quiver is at her shoulder. She is dressed in a short tunic, and is the only figure on the vase to wear a wreath.[2]

From the fifth century we have a vase upon which Atalanta prepares for her match with Peleus, the father of Achilles, as male wrestlers did—by bathing and annointing herself with olive oil. "Vase-painters liked to portray their match," observes Mary A. Lefkowitz, "because wrestling in antiquity, as now, had obvious sexual connotations." According to the ancient mythographer Apollodorus, Atalanta vanquished Peleus, but a sixth-century Attic vase, now in the Acropolis Museum, portrays him as the victor.[3]

Atalanta lost another contest that she should definitely have won. Once again, Ovid is the best-known source. Reluctant to marry and confident of her swiftness, Atalanta promises to accept the first suitor who can outrun her. The athletic maiden defeats a number of enamored challengers before she is matched against Melanion, who has been equipped by Aphrodite with three golden apples. Whenever Atalanta begins to leave Melanion in the dust, he tosses one of the apples in her path, a stratagem which tempts her to pause and, of course, to lose the race and her virgin's freedom. Avarice brings the most famous tomboy of antiquity to the marriage bed and, presumably, to a proper appreciation of domesticity.

If the stories told of Artemis and Atalanta were a trustworthy guide to the daily lives of ordinary women, at least in their premarital years, we might safely assert that sports were an important part of a Greek girl's experience. In fact, Artemis and Atalanta captured the imagination of poets and artists, and they may well have played a part in the fantasies of adolescent girls, but their mythic feats of physical prowess were not in accord with the conventional female role. Greek culture—like many others—was always highly ambivalent about women's sports.

Within the confines of the household, girls played ballgames, as Nausicaa does at the seashore in Book VI of *The Odyssey*, but respectable Greek women of the classical period were seldom seen outside their homes except for their participation in religious ceremonies. In the life of the *polis*, married women did appear in public as celebrants and worshippers. During festivals, their daughters joined the chorus of maidens and offered their songs to the gods. Respectable women were, however, excluded from military and political affairs and even from such ordinary domestic activities as a daily visit to the market. (Slaves shopped.) In his famed funeral oration, Pericles paused to address a word to the women of Athens:

> If I am to speak of womanly virtues to those of you who will henceforth be widows, let me sum them up in one short admonition: To a woman not to show more weakness than is natural to her sex is a great glory, and not to be talked about for good or for evil among men.[4]

One way to avoid gossip was to shun social intercourse. To say of a young Greek woman that she knew no men other than her father and her brothers was, therefore, to praise her virtue. If her father died before she was married, and if she had no brothers, she became an *epikleros* and was placed under the care of one of her father's brothers. His avuncular obligation was either to marry her himself or to see that her marriage kept her (and her inherited property) within the family. Normally, however, a girl and her marriage portion passed from her father's house directly to that of her husband. Her new status as a wife was preliminary to the most prestigious role of all: "what marked a woman's definitive passage into the husband's family was not the marriage but the birth of the first child."[5]

Neither maidens nor married women were welcome in the gymnasium, which was as central an institution in the Greek world as the agora and the theater. In other words, the hunts of Artemis and the athletic exploits of Atalanta stood in relation to everyday behavior rather as the bellicose feats of the equally legendary Amazons stood to Greek military reality.[6] What a modern classicist has concluded about the Greek view of the notoriously martial Amazons might well have been averred about the Greek view of Atalanta's mythical athletic prowess: "When men cease to be men, the world ceases to be ordered."[7] For the properly reared Athenian or Corinthian girl, Atalanta's boldly athletic behavior was to be shunned rather than emulated (except, as we shall see, when sports became an aspect of religious ritual).

Psychoanalytic theory suggests, of course, that shunned behavior attracts even those who warn against it. There does, indeed, seem to have been an ambivalence about women's physical prowess. This ambivalence may have been derived from subliminal male fears of female sexuality, as some modern scholars assert, but one should bear in mind that the Greeks were not exactly skittish about sexuality, male or female, heterosexual or homosexual. If the Greek psyche demanded that the Amazons be defeated by Theseus and that Atalanta be brought to the altar by a man cleverer if not swifter than she was, it need not have been because Greek men were frightened by female sexuality. Medusa may well have made men quake and think dreadful thoughts about castration, and the murderous Medea was certainly a woman to be wary of; but Atalanta's suitors were presumably attracted by her swiftness, strength, and courage as well as by her wealth and beauty. The ancient formulations of the Atalanta legend by Apollodorus and Ovid suggest that Atalanta's athleticism intensified her sexual power not to repel but to attract the many men who risked and lost their lives in the vain effort to win her for their marriage bed.

Politics, not sexual politics, lay behind the legendary need to subdue Atalanta and repel the Amazons. Men had always ruled women because most men were stronger than most women. The direct political threat to male dominance posed by physically powerful women was presumably enough to unsettle all but the most confidently masculine men. The defeat of Atalanta by Melanion and the slaying of the Amazon Pentesilia by Achilles reassured Greek men that they had not lost control of their women.

Support for this simpler, more political, less psychoanalytic interpretation can be derived from the fact that the Greeks were by no means totally opposed to demonstrations of female physical prowess if they were institutionalized as an aspect of cult, which they often were. Although the Olympic Games were contested by men and boys, with women excluded even from the spectator's role, the Greeks also celebrated games sacred to the goddess Hera. These athletic festivals —the Heraia—took place quadrennially at Olympia in the spring of the year, approximately a month before the men's Olympic Games. The celebration, which the German classicist Ludwig Deubner thought *older* than the Olympic Games, may originally have been limited to girls from the area around the city of Elis (a few miles from Olympia), but they seem eventually to have attracted girls from the entire Greek world.[8]

One version of the origin of the games attributes them to Hippodameia, whose successful courtship by the hero Pelops was commemorated at the much more famous Olympic Games, but another legend has it that the games were begun by a "council of sixteen venerable women of Elis who, during the sixth century B.C., undertook to bring peace to the land of the Eleans."[9] Almost all of our information about these games comes from Pausanias, whose *Description of Greece,* written in the second century A.D., is also our best literary source for the Olympic Games.

The games consist of foot-races for maidens. These are not all of the same age. The first to run are the youngest; after them come the next in age, and the last to run are the oldest of the maidens. They run in the following way: their hair hangs down, a tunic reaches to a little above the knee, and they bare the right shoulder as far as the breast. These too have the Olympic stadium reserved for their games, but the course of the stadium is shortened for them by about one sixth of its length. To the winning maidens they give crowns of olive and a portion of the cow sacrificed to Hera.[10]

It may be that we have visual evidence for the sort of runners whom Pausanias described. An archaic bronze statuette from Sparta, now in the British Museum, and a marble statue, now in the Vatican Museum, both show running girls in short tunics, with their right breasts bare.[11] (For the former, see Plate 3.) The accuracy of the account by Pausanias is attested by another detail. He notes that the girls raced only five sixths the length of the stadium. We know from the archeological excavations that the dimensions of the temple of Hera at Olympia were smaller by one sixth than those of the temple of Zeus. We can reasonably assume not only that Pausanias listened carefully to his informants but also that the geometrically minded Greeks felt that this six-to-five male-female proportion was somehow derived from nature.

Although Pausanias did not speculate on the significance of the Heraia, some modern scholars are prone to think them part of the girls' coming-of-age rituals or prenuptial rites.[12] Scholars have not, however, indicated why, if the races were female *rites de passage,* they were contested by younger girls as well as by those who had reached puberty. A related theory is that the games for girls were a fertility rite older than the games for men and boys. After all, writes Erwin Mehl, such rites for girls are pervasive in primitive cultures: "At sowing time and at harvesting time, girls run across the fields to make them [i.e., the fields] fruitful."[13] Whether the races were an initiation, a prenuptial ritual, or a fertility rite, they were clearly occasions for mortals to assimilate their behavior to that of the goddesses and heroines of myth. Here, at least, Atalanta was a legitimate model.

Recent excavations at the Temple of Artemis at Brauron near Athens have unearthed evidence of an athletic ritual for the girls of Attica. Close scrutiny of the many shards depicting this ritual has enabled classicists to explain a mysterious reference in the *Lysistrata* of Aristophanes. The play's characters refer to the "Brauron bear" in the life of the Athenian girl. Generations of readers have wondered what the reference meant. Now the archeological evidence from Brauron has provided a clue to the puzzle. Lilly Kahil has observed that black-figured vases unearthed there show dances and "a race of little girls who are either naked, or dressed mostly in short chitons [tunics], holding torches or wreaths in their hands." One of the girls wears a bear-mask. Commenting on fifth-century red-figured Attic vases showing "the sacred race of the girls," Kahil has conjectured that Athenian girls, some masked as the "Brauron bears" referred to in the *Lysistrata,* danced and competed in ritual races in honor of Artemis, goddess of procreation and ritual purity as well as "goddess of the outdoors and of nature." Their dances and their races were "a rite of initiation and, at the same time, of purification."[14] Kahil's views are compatible with Giampiera Arrigoni's interpretation of the ritual as an athletic *rite de passage* symbolizing the girls' transition from savagery (as "bears") to civilization.[15]

The ages of the girls, some of whom were quite young, raises the question asked in reference to the prepubescent girls at the Heraia in Olympia: In what sense were children of nine or ten involved in a prenuptial rite of maturation and initiation? Kahil's answer is an ingenious conjecture: "At the beginning of their novitiate, the little girls, dressed in tunics, performed rites in honor of Artemis, either races or dances; when they attained the age of puberty, in a true *rite de passage,* they performed the same religious acts, entirely nude, for the last time. . . . "[16] If this interpretation is valid, then small girls appeared clothed while older, physically developed maidens appeared naked, a role-reversal from our point of view, which has traditionally accepted public nudity in prepubescent children more readily than in adolescents. Disagreeing with this interpretation, Paula Perlman maintains that the younger girls were unclothed while "those older than thirteen are 'properly dressed' in short chitons," but the semantic and iconographical evidence seems to support Kahil: it was the older girls who were naked.[17] Pierre Vidal-Naquet takes no stand on the question of the ages of the clothed and the unclothed, but he agrees about the ritual transition from wildness to civilization and speculates that a bear may have once been killed in the sanctuary of Artemis, "the retribution for which was at first a human sacrifice and later the ritual substitution performed by the girl-bears." Although one of the vases shows a very youthful looking huntress, classicists have been content to identify the girl as Artemis and seem not to have wondered if archery was also a part of the ritual.[18]

At least one of the nude Brauron runners has the muscular physique and the long stride of a modern athlete, but there is little evidence that Athenian girls were encouraged to train for this or for any other athletic contests, secular or religious.[19] Most scholars infer from the lack of literary reference to such training that young Athenian women did not prepare themselves systematically for any kind of strenuous competition, but Claude Bérard has called attention to an unusual red-figured Attic vase painting in which three young women are depicted in what he interprets as a gymnasium scene. The women, all of them much older than the "Brauron bears," are shown "after their exercise. The one on the left, with a very athletic body, is in the process of cleaning her back with a strigil [to remove oil, sweat, and dust]; above her on the right, one sees the sponge and oil flacon."[20] (See Plate 4.) This vase, argues Bérard, proves that young women as well as young men frequented the gymnasium. If Bérard is correct, assumptions about the place of sports in Athenian women's lives will have to be reconsidered.

At Sparta, the evidence for women's sports is indubitable. Girls were required to train physically and to compete seriously in athletic contests. Fragments from a *partheneion* (chorus for girls) by the archaic poet Alcman describe a Spartan initiation ceremony similar to the *rites de passage* for Athenian girls at Brauron. The ritual included a race.[21] Some eight hundred years later, during his visit to second-century A.D. Sparta, Pausanias learned of a race run by eleven girls as part of the annual Festival of Dionysus Colonatas. An Italian historian has opined that the race, described by Pausanias in Book III of the *Description of Greece,* was the means by which the Spartans selected the priestesses of Dionysus; an American classicist, however, argues in a pair of important essays that the contest was "a prenuptial, initiatory trial."[22]

The sports of Spartan women were dictated by secular motives as well as religious ones. Spartan men, the most stereotypically masculine of all the Greeks, were the most enthusiastic believers in women's sports for eugenic as well as cultic reasons. Ruling over a servile population that greatly outnumbered them, Spartan men were life-long citizen-soldiers. As such, they were also early advocates of fitness and eugenics. That sickly infants, male as well as female, were exposed to the elements and left to die was not unusual. Infanticide was common throughout the ancient world. What *was* unusual was that the Spartans, unlike other Greeks, prized the physical fitness and courage of girls as well as boys. According to Xenophon, who seems to have approved wholeheartedly both of women's sports and of Sparta's armed-camp atmosphere, the legendary Spartans legislator Lycurgus was said to have encouraged girls to run and wrestle:

"Throughout the rest of the world the young girl, who will one day become a mother (and I speak of those who may be held to be well brought up), is nurtured on the plainest food attainable. . . . And in imitation, as it were, of the handicraft type, since the majority of the artificers are sedentary, we, the rest of the Hellenes, are content that our girls should sit quietly and work wools. That is all we demand of them. But how are we to expect that women nurtured in this fashion should produce a splendid offspring?"

Lycurgus pursued a different path. Clothes were things, he held, the furnishing of which might well enough be left to female slaves. And, believing that the highest function of a free woman was the bearing of children, in the first place he insisted on the training of the body as incumbent no less on the female than the male; and in pursuit of the same idea instituted rival contests in running and feats of strength for women as for men. His belief was that where both parents were strong their progeny would be found to be more vigorous.[23]

Plutarch, writing five centuries later, may have drawn on Xenophon for his account in *The Life of Lycurgus,* but he added a number of details (which may or may not be authentic):

He ordered the maidens to exercise themselves with wrestling, running, throwing the discus, and casting the javelin, to the end that the fruit they conceived might, in strong and healthy bodies, take firmer root and find better growth, and withal that they, with this greater vigor, might be the more able to undergo the pains of child-bearing.[24]

The physical education of Spartans girls was, then, intentionally eugenic. Sports, by definition competitive, doubtless contributed as well to the legendary psychological toughness of Spartan women, who were said to have sent their menfolk off to battle with the chilly admonition: "Bring back your shield or be brought back upon it."

As members of the chorus of maidens, Spartan girls sang and danced like other girls in other cities, but in their dances (as in their sports) they performed naked. The commendations and the criticisms of the young men, averred Plutarch, left some of the girls "proud, elated, and gratified" while others were spurred to better themselves.

These public processions of the maidens, and their appearing naked in their exercises and dancings, were incitements to marriage, operating upon the young with the rigor and certainty, as Plato says, of love, if not of mathematics.

For better or for worse, Plutarch's version of Spartan physical education has influenced subsequent generations. It is, for instance, the basis of an early work by Edgar Degas: *Spartan Boys and Girls* (1880).[25]

In their athletic competitions, the girls demonstrated their fitness to bear the hardy sons needed to maintain Spartan military hegemony. As can be inferred from Xenophon's comments on the rigor and certainty of love, the erotic component of the contests was obvious. As Arrigoni remarks, "The races, like the procession of nude girls, took place 'under the eyes of the youths' and were clearly public; moreover, their function was to stimulate the young spectators to matrimony."[26] Those of us inclined to be indignant at this explicit sexual exploitation of women's bodies should be mindful of the fact that Greek sports were a culturally sanctioned occasion for boys and youths to display *their* physical selves as objects of erotic attention. The inequality consisted not in the nakedness but rather in the male's right to choose as compared with the female's right to refuse—if that right of refusal was indeed granted her.

In other ways as well, Spartan women were the exception. There was no word for "horsewoman" in classical Greek. The goddesses depicted in Greek art "often perch insecurely on the bare backs of horses, but, when a mortal female rode, which she rarely did, she was seated awkwardly upon a chair-like saddle or upon a thickly folded blanket." It is possible, however, "that the Spartan girls rode, as the Romans asserted. At least their dress, short and revealing the thigh, would not have prevented them."[27] According to Athenaeus, who cited the *Laconica* of Polycrates as his authority, some Spartan girls were driven in wicker carts at the Festival of Hyacinthus while others "parade in chariots yoked to two horses, which they race, and the entire city is given over to the bustle and joy of the festival."[28]

Married women certainly did not play the role of charioteer, not even at Sparta, but they were the first to compete indirectly in the chariot races that were a part of every major athletic festival. It was a chariot owned by a Spartan princess that ended the male monopoly on Olympic olive branches: an inscription found at Olympia reads, "My father and brothers were kings of Sparta. I, Cynisca, won a victory with my swift-running horses and set up this statue. I claim that I am the only woman from all Greece to have won this crown." Her father was King Archidamus, her brother King Agesilaos. Her victories were most probably won in 396 and 392 B.C.[29]

Inevitably, in our own age of heightened feminist concern, scholars have differed in their assessments of Spartan physical education and its significance for women. Paola Bernardini has charged, rather indignantly, that Spartan policy was "dictated by demographic exigencies and political preoccupations, not by any sort of consideration and respect for the female sex."[30] Paul Cartledge, on the other hand, has written that the "real significance of [Spartan] education, in both its physical and its intellectual aspects, is that it reflects an official attempt to maintain some form or degree of parity between the sexes."[31]

Sparta was not quite alone in its emphasis on women's sports. The colony of Cyrene on the north coast of Africa was also renowned for its female athletes. Its eponym was the huntress Cyrene, whose fabulous exploits were sung by the poet Pindar in his ninth Pythian Ode (478 B.C.). When Apollo observed the "fair-armed" girl vanquish a lion in unarmed struggle, he promptly fell in love and just as promptly had his way with her. The toughest girl had no chance against a god. As Pindar remarked, "Swift is the achievement, short are the ways of the gods, when bent on speed."[32] The mortal maidens of the city were also speedy, and demonstrated their swiftness in foot races.

Sparta and Cyrene were atypical cities. Most Greeks of the archaic and classical periods disapproved of the way that Spartan girls exercised and competed in public. Despite their admiration for the good health and physical beauty of Spartan women, most Greek men determined to deny their own wives and daughters entrance to the gymnasia and stadia they constructed for themselves and their sons. This attitude is illustrated by Euripides, a dramatist often considered rather feminist in his views. Euripides was capable of a sympathetic portrait of the indomitable Medea, who slew her own children to gain vengeance against her faithless husband Jason, but—if Peleus in *Andromache* speaks for the author—he was typically Athenian in his severe disapproval of Spartan women and their sports:

> No Spartan girl
> could ever live clean even if she wanted.
> They're always out on the street in scanty outfits,
> Making a great display of naked limbs.
> In those they race and wrestle with the boys too—
> Abominable's the word.[33]

Similarly, in the *Lysistrata,* it is part of the comic poet's fun that one of the Spartan wives interrupts her antiwar protests to do her exercises. One supposes that sophisticated Athenian audiences found this country bumpkin's leaps and bounds ludicrously provincial.

The dig was characteristic. Aristophanes was no admirer of Sparta. Plato, however, shared Xenophon's admiration of militaristic Spartan customs. In *The Republic,* he proposes that the wives of the guardians join their husbands in gymnastic exercises as well as in battle. (It is difficult to know which suggestion seemed more outrageous to Athenian readers.) Acknowledging that "the sight of women naked in the palaestra, exercising with the men, especially when they are no longer young," will seem ridiculous to the conventional mind, Plato argues that the wise man understands the limits of convention and realizes that "their virtue will be their robe." In his late work, *The Laws,* Plato repeats his convictions about physical education for women. "My law would apply to females as well as males; they shall both go through the same exercises. I assert without fear of contradiction that gymnastics and horsemanship are as suitable to women as to men."[34] The philosopher's contemporaries recognized immediately that the ideal state described in *The Republic* was drawn, in large part, from the Spartan model. This was certainly true of Plato's comments on *gymnastike* as an essential part of the education of both men and women.

Spartan practice may also have left its imprint on the Heraia celebrated at Olympia. As Thomas F. Scanlon remarks,

The race for Dionysus at Sparta . . . resembled the Heraia in its simple program of a race and in the fact that the organizers of the contest, the Leucippides, also had the duty of weaving a robe for a local cult statue. Spartan workmanship in statuettes of female runners and the independent,

Spartan spirit of the Amazon dress suggest particularly strong Spartan influence on the Heraia.[35]

The success of Spartan physical education, defined by the achievement of Spartan eugenic goals rather than by conformity to twentieth-century ethical standards, was unquestionable. They were a rugged lot. Statistics on maternal mortality are obviously unavailable, but we have been told that Spartan wet nurses were sought after throughout the Greek world. Spartan women were, moreover, widely acknowledged to be the most attractive. Helen of Troy was once a Spartan girl. Although Aristophanes poked fun at rustic Spartan female athleticism, the Athenian women in his *Lysistrata* admit that Lampito the Spartan is a robust "out-of-doors" type with "a blemishless complexion" and an enviable physique.[36] The physical beauty of the Spartan girls continued to be legendary in Hellenistic and Roman times.

Greek culture varied with time as well as with place, and the customs of Hellenistic and Roman times were obviously not the same as those of the archaic and classical periods. Political circumstances changed as well. The Greeks who followed Alexander the Great on his career of conquest became the rulers of Asian and African peoples whose cultures were very different from anything they had experienced at home. The life of the ethnically Greek woman in Antioch or Alexandria was similar in many ways to that of the nineteenth-century Englishwoman in East Africa or India. The female role was less restricted than it had been at home, less narrowly domestic, and this relative emancipation of Hellenistic women seems to have occurred to some extent in Greece itself. Scholars disagree about the extent of the liberalization of gender roles. The women who wander about town in Idyll XV of the Alexandrian poet Theocritus are off to participate in a religious festival and are clearly not familiar with the city.[37] Theocritus seems to feel, just as the Greeks of the classical era had, that respectable women had work enough to do at home.

Upper-class Hellenistic women, however, enjoyed considerable freedom of movement. They often controlled considerable wealth, which they sometimes used in ways that brought them into public affairs. One result of relative emancipation from constrictive gender roles was that women's sports were more in evidence during the Hellenistic period than they were in archaic or classical times. Women were, for instance, gymnasiarchs, which probably meant not that they administered the day-to-day nitty-gritty affairs of the gymnasium but rather that they contributed financially to the institution and, perhaps, formulated policy. An inscription on the island of Chios memorializes Claudia Metrodora, four times gymnasiarch and twice benefactor of the games in honor of Heracles, for which games she distributed the oil used by athletes to annoint their bodies. A similar inscription from the colony of Cyrene names Claudia Olympios gymnasiarch for life.[38] Women also served as gymnasiarchs on the west coast of Asia Minor and at Dorylaeum in Phrygia, where "Asclepiades was the gymnasiarch of free men and slaves, while his wife Antiochis was gymnasiarch of the women."[39] That women *had* a gymnasiarch clearly implies that at least some women actually used the gymnasium.

Another sign of political and economic status was the sponsorship of chariots at the Olympic Games and other sports festivals. The celebrated victors in the chariot races had always been the wealthy owners and not the drivers. Women of means were now able to emulate the Spartan Cynisca by winning the fame associated with athletic victories. In the third century B.C., Bilistiche of Magnesia, a concubine of Ptolemy II Philadelphia of Egypt, won at least twice in the four-horse chariot races held at Oxrhynchus.[40] From Cyrene came Berenice II, the wife (and cousin) of Ptolemy III. She was a chariot victor at Nemea (near Sparta) and, perhaps, at Olympia as well. Appropriately, her Nemean victory was won with horses from Cyrene and was celebrated by the poet Callimachus from the same city.[41] In the second century B.C., three of the daughters of Polycrates, the Hellenistic governor of Cyprus, were victors in the chariot races at the Panathenaic Games.[42] A number of women were victors at the Eleutherian Games in Thessaly, where equestrian events were especially important.[43] Cleopatra VII, the last of the Ptolemies, claimed several victories for her chariots; she was also known as a huntress before she set out for bigger game and achieved far greater fame as the paramour of Julius Caesar and Mark Antony.[44]

There is also considerable evidence that Greek girls of the Hellenistic and Roman periods competed in a number of athletic events (but not in the Olympic Games). In Idyll XVIII, an epithalamium for Helen of Troy, Theocritus sang the glories of Spartan girls, among whom Helen is the most glorious:

For here we be, a band four sixties strong,
Maidens all her age, and we race together
By Eurotas' streams, and annoint ourselves like men;
And of all, not one is flawless, compared to Helen![45]

Of course, in imagining Helen running races with the other maidens, Theocritus says nothing directly about what was or was not acceptable conduct in his own day.

Hard evidence of foot-races for Greek girls does, however, appear after the Roman conquest of Greece in 146 B.C. A first-century A.D. inscription found at Delphi informs us that Hermesianax of Tralles in Asia Minor erected statues for his three athletic daughters. Tryphosa he commemorated for winning the stade-race at the Pythian Games, which were contested at Delphi in honor of Apollo, and at the Isthmian Games near Corinth, sacred to Poseidon. She was said to have been the first girl to win the latter race. One of Tryphosa's sisters, Hedea, won the stade-race at Nemea and at Sycion (in Italy). Although the inscription is damaged, one can read also that Tryphosa's other sister, Dionysia, won the stade-race at the Aesclepeia near Epidaurus. This inscription has ignited a lively *Historikerstreit* between those who accept the inscription as evidence for significant participation in girls' sports and skeptics, on the other hand, who argue that Hermesianax was probably a man of such great wealth that he was able to arrange for his daughters to compete in special events that were not a part of the festivals' regular sports programs.[46]

If this inscription were our only evidence, we might agree with the skeptics, but there are other indications, literary as well as archeological, which suggest fairly widespread sports activity for Greek girls and women under Roman and Byzantine rule. Whether married women competed is doubtful, but, as early as 23 A.D., Lucius Castricius Regulus inaugurated Isthmian Games at Corinth which included a contest for maidens.[47] A Corinthian inscription from 25 A.D. states specifically that a contest for *certamen virginum* took place. It was probably a stade race.[48] In the *Deipnosophists*, written about 200 A.D., Athenaeus comments, "on the isle of Chios it's quite pleasant to walk through the gymnasia and on the tracks and see the boys wrestling with the girls in free style."[49] A lost fourth-century A.D. inscription copied in 1491 by Michael Souliardos refers to a statue in parian marble dedicated to Nikegora, "victor on the track in the race for unmarried girls."[50] The sixth-century A.D. historian John Malalas asserted that his native city of Antioch purchased the rights to the Olympic Games early in the third century A.D. and that the games, held at the suburban site of Daphne, included events for virgins: "These women fought against women and the competition was fierce whether in the wrestling, the races or the recitation." Malalas added that the male and female victors became priests and priestesses and remained chaste for the rest of their lives.[51] Unfortunately, the *Oxford Classical Dictionary* describes Malalas as "uncritical, confused, and often childish."[52] We can say with some confidence that Greek girls of the Roman and Byzantine periods competed in foot races and perhaps in other athletic contests, but, beyond that, our picture of women's sports is like the architectural remains at Olympia—fragmentary.

In frustration one can turn, as classicists often do, to literary texts. The *Dionysiaca,* a fifth-century A.D. account of the adventures of the god of wine, was composed by Nonnos of Panopolis, the last of the major Greek poets of antiquity. Like all post-Homeric epics, the *Dionysiaca* contains descriptions of athletic contests that owe more to Homer than to anything Nonnos actually witnessed, but sports historians can nonetheless be faulted for their neglect of Book XXXVII (the funeral games for Opheltes) and Book XLVIII (the god's encounter with not one but two athletic women). Pallene, a doughty maiden cast from the same mold as Atalanta, wrestles against her suitors and defeats them all. She is undaunted by Dionysos. As he approaches, she "stript the clothes off her muscular limbs." But she loses the unequal contest, and with it her virginity. The god lingers by her until he is attracted by Aura, an athletic girl reckless enough to taunt the goddess Artemis:

See what a vigorous body I have! Look at Aura's body like a boy's, and her step swifter than Zephyros! See the muscles upon my arms, look at my breasts, round and unripe, not like a woman. You might almost say that yours are swelling with drops of milk! Why are your arms so tender, why are your breasts not round like Aura's?[53]

Aura's boastful rejection of maternity is not particularly subtle. Artemis obtains revenge for these insults when Eros drives Dionysos mad and he, in his frenzy, rapes Aura, who has imbibed too much wine to resist the god's advances.

The cultural significance of the poem is difficult to assess. Is the fact that Dionysos is sexually aroused by Pallene and Aura a sign that Nonnos and his readers were also attracted by athletic girls or is the defeat of the first and the rape of both vengeful symbolic punishment of their refusal to accept the conventional roles of wife and mother? Like most literary texts of any substance, the *Dionysiaca* resists definitive interpretation. All that we can be certain of is that, for more than a thousand years, Greek poets and artists produced vivid images of Atalanta and her athletic sisters.

THREE

Matrons and Gladiators

With the exception of widows, who in most times and places have had greater freedom of action than other women, the Roman matron of the republican era was almost as strictly guarded and supervised as her Athenian contemporary. As a girl, she bore her father's family's name so that, for instance, a daughter of Camillus was automatically named Camilla. Her brother received not only the family's *nomen* but also a distinguishing *prenomen* of his own. Her father's power, the *patria potestas,* included the right to kill a child. Historical demographers strongly suspect that infanticide was much more common for female than for male infants. When a girl was old enough to marry, her father provided a dowry and suggested the man with whose family he wished to form a political or economic alliance. It is difficult to know what weight was given to a daughter's feelings about a prospective husband. Some historians argue that the father-daughter relationship was especially close and that austere patriarchs were often swayed by a beloved daughter's desires.[1]

In some cases, the prenuptial contract allowed a mistreated bride to return to her father's household and still retain her dowry, but divorce normally left the husband in control of the property and with custody of the children. Young widows were expected to remarry, and their fathers, uncles, or brothers were expected to guide them in the choice of a second husband; but an heiress of thirty-five was obviously better able than a girl of fifteen to articulate her marital preferences and to insist upon them.

During the Republic, a wife's status was legally the equivalent of a child's. The question was: Whose child? Marriage was either with or without *manus*. If married *cum manu*, a bride was completely under the domination of her husband; if married *sine manu*, her father retained certain legal rights (such as the right to put her to death if she dishonored him with an act of adultery). While plebeian women labored in the fields or hawked their wares in the marketplace, respectable matrons were not expected to labor outside the home. They supervised the slaves who did the household work, but their principal function was reproduction, not production. They bore and began to educate the next generation of Roman citizens. Their status was high and their influence was considerable, as numerous moralistic anecdotes from Livy and other historians testify, but their economic role was limited and their political rights were nil.

These legal limitations imply very little about the extent and status of women's sports. A patriarchal society, like Periclean Athens, may restrict its females to minimal participation in athletics while another patriarchal society, like that of Sparta, can encourage female athleticism to the point where a girl's strength and speed are prized as much as a boy's. To understand the place of sports in the life of republican women it is necessary to realize that the Romans were more often sports spectators, at the gladiatorial combats or at the chariot races, than sports participants. Most Romans preferred the spectator's vicarious excitement to the strenuous pleasures of an athletic contest. The lack of references to women's sports is related to the paucity of references to men's sports participation. Roman men certainly believed in physical fitness, a military necessity, but most of them were not, in the republican era, enthusiastic about sports as an end in themselves. Those who were enthusiastic met with disapproval from sterner citizens. The first-century B.C. poet Horace says of his patron in the second satire, Maecenas has "gone Greek"; he plays ballgames and is "averse to rough Roman military drill."[2] Horace obviously thinks this is a dubious choice. It was common for Roman moralists to comment on the military uselessness of Greek sports, to profess horror at the nudity of Greek athletes, and to associate the erotic element in sports with perversity and decadence. One might expect no-nonsense Roman utilitarianism to have implemented women's sports as a eugenic measure, but this did not occur. In his *Tusculan Disputations,* the late-republican orator Cicero, apparently misunderstanding the connection between sports and motherhood, criticized the Spartan girls who spent their days wrestling on the banks of the

Eurotas instead of bearing children.[3] He did not seem to realize that the first activity abetted the second.

While it is clear that the girls and women of the Republic were not encouraged to indulge in sports either as an autotelic activity or as an indirect way to enhance military preparedness, they might—like the girls who competed in Heraia at Olympia—have run races as a part of religious ritual. We have no evidence that they did.

The absence of some Roman equivalent to the Heraia can be explained in part by the relatively secular nature of Roman sports. Roman festivals and religious celebrations did sometimes have an athletic component. There were, for example, footraces at the Consualia (August 15th and December 15th), the Robigalia (April 25th), and doubtless at other festivals as well, most of which were, after all, referred to as *ludi* ("games").[4] The athletic contests were, however, probably less central than was the case among the Greeks. The historian Livy dated events by the names of the two annually elected consuls and not, as was the custom in Greece, by reference to the victor in the stade-race for that Olympiad. In any event, these Roman races were for men rather than women.

Gladiatorial contests, derived from Etruscan or Campanian funeral rites, *were* a part of Roman religious life (a fact which ought to be remembered when optimistic ecumenicists affirm that "all religions teach the same truths"), but not even the Spartans had taken their enthusiasm for women's sports to the point where they staged deadly armed combats. We can be reasonably sure that republican Romans never seriously contemplated the possibility of female gladiators. In short, neither the nearly permanent tutelage of respectable republican women nor the generally utilitarian bias of Roman thought nor the rituals associated with Roman religion were conducive to female athleticism in the republican era. The Spartan example of eugenic sports for girls failed to inspire the Romans to adopt a similar program for similar purposes.

Much changed under the Empire. At Pompeii, the ample archeological evidence for women's involvement in a wide range of political, economic, and religious activities in the first century A.D. has prompted at least one classicist to wonder if a narrow reliance on written evidence has distorted our picture of earlier as well as later women.[5] Under the Caesars, at any rate, respectable women were allowed far greater freedom of movement, literally and metaphorically, than had been granted them under the Republic. The liberalization of sexual mores seems to have troubled many who pined for "the good old days" of stringent chastity. Restrictive laws were sometimes passed, like the *lex julia,* which increased the penalties for adultery, but they were not enforced with that severe attention to duty associated with names like Cato the Censor. To the dismay of historians like Tacitus and poets like Juvenal, high-minded republican austerity and stern devotion to civic duty decayed into what seemed, in nostalgic and moralistic eyes, a riot of shameless hedonism. Senators displayed their wealth at Lucullan feasts and the wives of senators paraded in public with their lovers.

Sports became increasingly spectacular. Gladiatorial games became more grand, more extravagantly expensive, and, if possible, more cruel. Eventually, despite some half-hearted attempts to curtail them, they expanded in amplitude until they involved thousands of combatants and tens of thousands of spectators. Chariot races were at least as popular. Under the Empire, the chariot races of the Circus Maximus in Rome, which accommodated 250,000 spectators, became the model for contests throughout the Empire. The frenzy of the fans, screaming encouragement to the charioteers of the "Blue" and the "Green" factions, became a permanent symbol of hysterically partisan spectatorship.

Once the Greeks fell to Roman rule, some philhellenic Romans became enthusiasts for Greek sports as well as for Greek philosophy. Although Augustus the Imperator was not personally fond of Greek sports, he founded the Actia in 28 B.C. with Greek-style games to celebrate his victory over the naval forces of Anthony and Cleopatra in the battle of Actium in 31 B.C. Self-deluded Nero, who fancied himself a great athlete as well as a superb artist, competed at Olympia and terrified the priestly officials into declaring him victor. In his own honor, he established the Neronian Games, which did not survive him. (And his name was removed from the Olympic records as soon as he was safely dead.) The Capitoline Games inaugurated by Domitian in 86 A.D. were still another symbol of Rome's cultural captivity to its Grecian captives.

Did women compete in the Actia and other games? We have seen that Greek girls like Tryphosa and her sisters were admitted in the Roman era to competition in various Greek athletic festivals. The love poems of Propertius testify that at least *one* Roman poet was enchanted by the bewitching vision of physically active Spartan girls. His extravagant tribute deserves full quotation:

I much admire the Spartan wrestling schools,
but most of all I like the women's rules:
for girls and men can wrestle in the nude
(the Spartans think such exercise is good);
naked they throw the ball too fast to catch,
and steer the creaking hoop in the bowling match,
stand waiting, grimed with dust, for the starting gun,
and bear the brunt of the Pancration,
put boxing gloves on hands so soft and fair,
and whirl the heavy discus through the air,
gallop the circuit, helmets on their brow,
buckling a sword to thighs as white as snow;
with hoar-frost on their hair, they join the chase
as the hounds of Sparta climb Taygetus,
like Amazons, breasts naked to the fray,
who bathed in Pontic streams at the end of day,
like Helen training on Eurotas' sands
with nipples bare and weapons in their hands,
while boxer, horseman, champions to be,
her brothers watched, and did not blush to see.
In Spartan customs lovers may embrace
without concealment in a public place.
Girls aren't afraid, or locked up under guard;
no stern-faced husband makes the going hard;
you need no go-between to pave the way:
speak for yourself, and suffer no delay;
they wear no purple robes to cheat and lure,
no perfumed hair with overworked coiffure.
In Rome your little finger is too large
to make its way through a woman's entourage.
The lover can't get close enough to find
the proper way to ask—he's working blind.
If Roman girls would do as the Spartans do,
then, Rome, I'd have cause for loving you.[6]

If we ignore the fact that the poem is full of historical nonsense, nicely suggested by the translator's intentional anachronism ("the starting gun"), we are left with the problem of representativeness. Did the writer's febrile affirmation of female athleticism meet with widespread male approval or was it a sample of the deviant taste of a quirky philhellenic aesthete?

Although these questions will have to remain unanswered, we know that some girls, and perhaps adult women as well, *did* compete in games as early as the first century A.D. (i.e., a generation or two after Propertius, who died ca. 15 B.C.). The historian Suetonius informs us that there were races for girls at the Capitoline Games.[7] There is strong evidence to indicate that girls also competed at the Augustalia, which were celebrated at Naples, a city that had been founded by Greek colonists and may still, in the first century A.D., have had cultural ties to Greece. The Sebasteia, also held at Naples, probably included races for married women, a departure from Greek custom and a rare occurrence in the Latin parts of the Empire.[8]

Were the girls who ran at the Augustalia and the other *ludi* also the daughters of the Roman elite or were they, like female gladiators (about which more in a moment), plebeians or slaves? At the Sebasteia, a girl named Seia Spes is said to have won the foot race for the daughters of magistrates in 154 A.D. That there *was* a race for magistrates' daughters proves the respectability of the games. How widespread among the daughters and wives of the Roman elite was this taste for Greek athletics? Another bit of evidence, the famed "Bikini Mosaic" of the Piazza Armerina, comes from Sicily, which was also a part of *Magna Graecia* before its incorporation into the Roman Empire. (See Plate 5.) Discussing this fourth-century A.D. work of art in a book originally published in 1962 and still considered a standard work, J. P. V. D. Balsdon insisted that the ten young bikini-clad women are dancers, "not women athletes."[9] Closer and more informed scrutiny on the part of sports historians leads to a different conclusion. The palm branches and other attributes carried by the women symbolize athletic victory. Quite probably, the girls represent a javelin-thrower, a jumper, a discus-thrower, two runners, two ball-players, and three girls with their prizes. Together they form "the most complete and detailed [visual] portrayal of female athletes from ancient Greece and Rome."[10]

We can be sure that the owner of the villa appreciated women's sports; after all, he must have commissioned the mosaic. About his motives—ludic, eugenic, aesthetic, or erotic—we are much less certain. "The owner of the villa is obviously from the Roman upper class. Could his daughters have taken a fancy to Greek athletics?"[11] And, if they had, were they typical of their class, admired and emulated by their coevals, or were they eccentrics, ridiculed and ostracized?

If a significant number of Roman women did train for athletic contests, we must wonder where. The palaestra and gymnasia found in every Greek polis eventually became common throughout the Roman Empire, and at least some of the latter seem to have been open to women; but they were never as popular as the huge public baths that were considered indispensable to civilized life. These Roman baths offer negative evidence of women's sports in that the women's sections "seem never to have had the spacious palaestra, in which men could exercise or lie in the open air, once their bathing was over."[12] At the baths, men often relaxed by playing *harpastum* and other ballgames (whose rules are unknown to us), but an epigram by the satirist Martial suggests that women were not encouraged to join the fun. Philenis, who does play, he calls a tomboy.[13] Perhaps, if sports really were the privilege of the upper class, they were restricted to the grounds of spacious private estates like the Piazza Armerina and to occasional *ludi* like the Sebasteia.

At the other end of the social spectrum from the "bikini girls" at the Villa Armerina were the female athletes who competed in the gladiatorial games. Although our information comes mainly from moralistic historians like Suetonius, men eager to document the depravity of their times, theirs was not the only testimony. There is no reason to doubt that women did enter the arena. Tacitus in his *Annals* asserted that the infamous Nero had commanded aristocratic women to descend into the arena and fight as gladiators. This—like many of Nero's deeds—was scandalous.[14] The scandal was not that women fought but that the wives of senators were forced to violate the conventions of social class. Gladiators, after all, were *noxii*. Dio Cassius in his *Roman History* refers to games staged by Nero in 66 A.D. with male and female gladiators from Ethiopia, a much less shocking departure from the norm.[15] Many of the female gladiators were captives from the north, able-bodied bellicose women of the sort Tacitus described in *Germania*. Domitian too offered the populace the spectacle of female gladiators. Suetonius remarked disapprovingly that he "gave hunts of wild beasts, gladiatorial shows at night by the light of torches, and not only combats between men but between women as well."[16]

A number of scholars have added that Domitian, who rivaled Nero in eccentricity and cruelty, titillated the crowd with a perverse combat between a woman and a dwarf, but this assertion probably derived from a misinterpretation of the poet Statius.[17] The poet, who was Domitian's contemporary, wrote of "women, novices and strangers to battle," who tirelessly wielded "the weapons of men."

In the *Silvae,* however, the "bold battalions of dwarfs" fight among themselves and not against the female gladiators.[18] The taste for these "Amazons" was not confined to the Latin half of the Empire. That it spread to the Greek parts as well is attested by a stele found at Halicarnassus in Asia Minor. The stele, now in the British Museum, pictures two female gladiators locked in combat.[19]

How did the Romans respond to females in the arena? The poet Martial was ironic when women fought beasts at the inauguration of the Colosseum in 80 A.D.:

> That Hercules the Nemean lion slew
> Was thought a mighty deed, a fabled touch.
> Forget that passé stunt! Today our Caesar true
> Shows us that fighting women do as much.[20]

Martial's epigrams are mild compared to the venomous disgust congealed in the lines of Juvenal's *Satires.* Juvenal not only reviled aristocratic women who lusted after gladiators, he also lampooned upper-class women who trained for the arena. That they slashed and battered wooden dummies seemed laughable, but that they dressed themselves in "belts, shinguards, / Arm-protectors and plumes" was utterly absurd. "How can a woman be decent, / Sticking her head in a helmet, denying the sex she was born with?" Some stripped naked to exercise because, as Juvenal comments sarcastically, "Even the sheerest silks are too hot for their delicate bodies." The "degenerate girls" grunted and groaned, sweated and panted, a more repulsive spectacle in Juvenal's eyes than the "gladiator's wench" or the "strip-tease broad." Juvenal was also disgusted by the thought that "women, breasts Amazon-naked, / Face wild boars at the games."[21] These sections of the satires should be recalled by modern physical educators who glibly cite Juvenal's famous words about *mens sana in corpore sano.*

There can be no doubt about Juvenal's attitude toward female gladiators, but the rage that flows through the satires was engendered by the undeniable popularity of the satirized customs. Juvenal was appalled, but Petronius in the *Satyricon* makes it clear that other sports fans were thrilled by the news of girls who fought from chariots.[22] The passion for combative women, like the demand for "bread and circuses," survived Juvenal's frustrated condemnation. What he thought of the "bikini girls" and other aristocratic female participants in Greek sports we shall never know.

FOUR

The Lady Hunts a Stag

In the conclusion of her recent study of *Women in Frankish Society,* Suzanne Fonay Wemple asserts that early "medieval women were far more visible, vocal, and powerful than their sisters in antiquity."[1] Perhaps they were. They seem to have been relatively free to choose their own husbands and to control property as wives and (especially) as widows. Although the birth of a daughter was not the occasion for joy that the birth of a son was, the rate of infanticide, which (almost invariably) meant the murder of girls more often than boys, seems to have declined during the Middle Ages.[2] If there was an improvement in women's lot, however, this improvement did not mean that women were more actively involved in sports. One obvious reason for their relative passivity is that the peasantry lived in "frightful physical wretchedness" that was probably more wretched for women than for men because men considered themselves entitled to a larger share of scarce food.[3] Another reason for women's passivity was that the Christian society of early medieval Europe cared far less for sports than ancient societies had. As Georges Duby and other historians have demonstrated, medieval theologians imagined that earthly society was divided into three orders (*ordines*): the warriors, the worshippers, and the workers (*bellatores, oratores, laboratores*). At that level of idealization, there was no place for the players. Scholastic philosophy had no rubric for them either, and clerical homily routinely condemned earthly entertainments which distracted from an *Imitatio Christi.*

Patristic Christianity was extremely hostile to sports, partly because of their close associations with pagan cult, partly because of

Christianity's dualistic ontology which split the self into mortal body and immortal soul. Tertullian and other Fathers of the Church cried out against the idolatry of the gladiatorial games and the chariot races, both of which were indeed associated with the pagan gods until well into the Christian era. That thousands of Christians met martyrdom in the Roman arena added to the abhorrence felt for the site. The dominant ascetic tradition of Christianity, especially negative about women's bodies, also militated against a passion for sports. In the minds of most theologians, the temptations of the flesh were most tantalizingly present in "the daughters of Eve." In our own age, whose theologians often seek to deny or at least to minimize the asceticism and misogyny of patristic and medieval Christianity, it is easy to forget that the spectacle of athletic women was absolutely anathema to Augustine and his saintly successors.[4] Indeed, the very thought of a confrontation between Augustine and the "bikini girls" of Villa Armerina evokes images of slapstick comedy.

Nor was Christian enthusiasm for women's sports very likely to have been inspired by the tales of physical prowess, at sports and in battle, of a number of pagan women in Germanic literature. Snorri Sturluson's thirteenth-century saga includes the Norse god and goddess Uller and Skadi, who hunt on skis, but the best-known story, by far, is that of the *Nibelungenlied*'s Brunhilde of Iceland. She hurls heavy stones great distances and springs nimbly after them. She is a perfect Germanic parallel to Atalanta who challenges her awed suitors to equal her athletic achievements. Gunther, who hopes to vanquish her in three tests of strength and thus to win her as his wife, loses heart when he observes that it takes three men to carry her spear. His spirits droop even further when he watches twelve men attempting to carry off one of the stones she hefts with ease. Gunther manages to win Brunhilde after all, thanks to the magical intervention of his friend Siegfried. While powerful Brunhilde's defeat at the hands of the still more powerful Siegfried can be read as another sign of the alleged male fear of female sexuality, it seems unlikely that Gunther would seek the hand of a woman whose sexuality frightened him. A less tendentious reading is that strong men like Gunther and Siegfried longed to subdue and domesticate women almost (but not quite) as strong as they were. At any rate, the image of the preternaturally powerful maiden has survived to our day, thanks partly to Richard Wagner's stirring pagan music.

Brunhilde was no model for pious medieval women. Instead of

flexing their muscles in athletic endeavors, they bowed their heads and bent their knees in prayer, emulating the Virgin, whose immaculate life compensated for the eternal disgrace of Eve's sexuality. Many of the most devout women mortified their flesh and devoted themselves to prayerful inactivity. Robust health was no desideratum. The lives of some female saints, writes Caroline Walker Bynum, "have as their sole theme the saint's illness. And many holy women desired to be ill." Although the Beguines of the thirteenth century were not, strictly speaking, members of an ecclesiastical community, their contempt for the flesh was as intense as if they had taken holy orders and become nuns. Like nuns, some Beguines received episcopal permission to immure themselves and thus to suffer what we now refer to as "sensory deprivation." Jutta of Huy, for instance, "had herself enclosed in a cell adjoining the leper-house and spent more than forty years there before she died in 1228."[5] Jacques de Vitry, one of the most notable of thirteenth-century preachers, praised ascetic women for their triumph over the flesh:

They melted altogether in wondrous love for God until it seemed that they bowed under the burden of desire and for many years they did not leave their beds except on rare occasions. . . . Resting in tranquility with the master, they became deformed in body but comforted and made strong in spirit.

Vitry also wrote admiringly of Mary of Oignies (1177–1213) that the contemplation of Christ induced her to cut off pieces of her own body and to bury them in the ground.[6] Historians have, no doubt, sometimes exaggerated this morbid side of the Middle Ages and have written as if a pervasive horror of physicality were a ubiquitous characteristic of the Age of Faith. After all, few women became nuns or Beguines and most of those who did not seem to have been creatures with sensual appetites. Nonetheless, the most saintly, the most often sainted, the most overtly and ostentatiously Christian women despised and mortified their own bodies. And they were obviously the least likely women to be seduced by the pleasures of physical play.

It must be acknowledged that piety was not the sole motive for the nun's vows of celibacy. Medieval convents provided not only a sanctuary for the "bride of Christ" but also a refuge for the unfortunate daughters of noble fathers too impecunious or too miserly to provide them with a suitable dowry. When faith waned and discipline relaxed, which was the case in fourteenth-century nunneries, account rolls began to include sums of money spent on Mayday games. Pious bishops fulminated against lapdogs, fashionable dresses, lutes, and dances. But sports seem not to have tempted the lax new breed of pampered nuns (unless, in unwitting recapitulation of heathen customs, sports were included among their Mayday revels).

Monasticism, whether morbidly ascetic or hypocritically self-indulgent, cannot have been a way of life for very many. Most lives were mundane, and even the most mundane lives had their moments of play. While no medievalist, not even Johan Huizinga, has yet ventured to characterize these centuries as the Age of Frolic, Huizinga and a host of others have established the fact—which never should have been doubted—that the *bellatores* and *laboratores* had occasions for play and even the *oratores*—all but the most fanatical of them— had their pastimes and diversions. Even the darkest ages had their lighthearted moments. At a time when St.Thomas Aquinas was at work on his *Summa Theologica,* Paris had thirteen tennis ball makers.[7]

Inevitably, given the bias of the historical profession, we know much more about men's amusements than about women's, but we are now in the midst of a revolution in historiography. Imaginative researchers like Christine Fell have ascertained, for instance, that some medieval Englishwomen were apparently professional entertainers. Fell admits, "It is not easy to tell whether there was any lighter side to life for the average Anglo-Saxon woman," but there is a mysterious Doomsday Book reference to "Adelina the *joculatrix,*" an appellation that no one quite knows how to translate. Here and elsewhere, we catch a glimpse of the lighter side of a darker time. Commenting on the thirteenth century, Fell notes that the

currency of terms such as "hopster" and "songster" implies that some women worked as entertainers—dancers, acrobats, singers, and perhaps instrumentalists as well; a woman minstrel is recorded in Stratford-upon-Avon, and . . . a "saltatrix" or acrobatic dancer called Maud Makejoy performed several times before the royal court.[8]

Another medievalist informs us that Matilda Makejoy—the same woman?—was popular at the court of Edward I of England. She "appeared at the Christmas feast of 1296 'to make her vaults' for the amusement of the young Edward, and fifteen years later she was amusing his young half-brothers with another performance."[9] Although acrobatics and sports both imply a positive valuation of physical prowess, they are —as I have indicated more than once—clearly not identical. Did Mistress Makejoy and others like her take the leap from the first to the second type of physical activity? Did medieval women compete?

The evidence is scanty. When, in the twelfth century, a somewhat more descriptive cast of mind began to replace the prescriptive categories of the *tres ordines,* commentaries on medieval society referred to *conditio* and *status.* Sports were not among the specific occupational categories mentioned and medieval chronicles, compiled mostly by clerics, have relatively few references to sports—except for tournaments, which are often mentioned despite the Church's official opposition to the bellicose sport. Clerical authors may have disapproved of the knightly passion for playful combat, but they were unable entirely to ignore their patrons' favorite pastime. The young knights, like England's famed William Marshall, who spent several years on what we might anachronistically refer to as the "tournament circuit," were professional athletes in the sense that they specialized in and supported themselves through sports performances.

Early tournaments, which often degenerated into raids to seize valuable goods and capture ransomable hostages, never involved women as combatants. However, as tournaments became less deadly and more theatrical, women took on a variety of supporting roles. At the Smithfield tournament of 1389, sixty richly attired women mounted on palfreys led sixty knights and sixty squires from the Tower of London to the lists.[10] In fifteenth-century tournaments, fanciful allegory was often more important than armed combat, and women were allowed to play the part of lovely maidens in distress whom doughty knights rushed chivalrously to rescue.

While late medieval tournaments were tame affairs compared to the bloody encounters of an earlier time, a fifteenth-century dream book notes that a woman actually *fighting* in a tournament was "as impossible as a king, prince, or knight plowing the ground or shoveling manure," which obviously struck the occult author as extremely unlikely violations of divine order.[11] When medieval documents mention or picture a *Frauentournier,* the reference is usually to a transvestite masquerade or an imaginary event. Masquerades were common. Men sometimes fought in the guise of women just as they sometimes staged a tournament of "Crusaders versus Saracens," with half the company glumly stuck in the role of Saracens. Female tournaments were, moreover, a common *topos* of medieval satire. The *Tournoiement des Dames* by Huon d'Oisi, the *Tournoiement as Dames de*

Paris by Pierre Gencien, and the anonymous fourteenth-century poem, *Der Vrouwen Turnei* are examples of this popular genre. Although some literary scholars have been gullible enough to assume that these poems were based on actual combats by medieval women, the consensus is that they were fantasies. They were probably intended to shame men into volunteering for a crusade to the Holy Land. The patent absurdity of a tournament of women was what gave the poems their coercive psychological force. Whether some men and women were actually attracted by the fantasy of amazon-like behavior is impossible to say.[12]

We enter a similar realm of fantasy when we examine medieval illustrated manuscripts depicting encounters in which women act out forbidden male roles. Robert de Borron's *Histoire du Graal* and the anonymous *Lancelot de Lac* are ornamented with pictures of mounted women, wielding distaffs and spindles, who charge at obviously disconcerted knights and monks. A marginal illustration to Pierart dou Tielt's *Saint Graal* shows a contest between two naked women armed with distaffs, one upon a goat, the other on a ram. The early fourteenth-century *Breviary for Marguerite de Bar* repeats the goat-ram theme with a peasant woman on a goat and a knight about to be unseated from his ram. There is no reason whatsoever to believe that such jousts ever occurred. We can be sure that these scenes were as imaginary as those in which birds waft tilting apes into airborne combat.[13] (Such scenes exist.) These marginalia portrayed a topsy-turvy world in which women, astride notoriously lustful mounts, enacted allegorical roles attributed to them by medieval moralists who were anxious to denigrate sinfulness. Whether or not we wish to believe a scholar who asserts that "the sexual innuendo is . . . turned against chivalry as a sport [sic]," he does seem to be correct about a barely disguised "erotic element," enhanced by pictures of monkeys as attendant musicians and heralds.[14] Although the covert sexual iconography may have attracted some readers it was meant to repel, it is unlikely that anyone was ever demented enough to enact the illuminator's pornographic fantasies with naked peasant girls mounted on rams and goats.

It is, on the other hand, quite probable that the relative absence of written and visual evidence for actual, as opposed to imaginary, women's sports reflects not a lack of involvement but rather the historiographical bias of a truly patriarchal age. We know enough about the formal and informal amusements of humankind to warrant the tepid anthropological conclusion that medieval women were not wholly different from women of other times and places. Fortunately, we are not thrown back entirely upon assumptions about human nature. Now that historians have at long last begun to look for evidence of women's sports, the evidence has begun to appear. Not a great deal of it, but enough to disprove the dismal null hypothesis about play's total absence from the lives of medieval women. The visual record—illuminated manuscripts, stained-glass windows, the carved figures that adorned the great Gothic cathedrals—has proven to be especially important for the glimpses it provides into medieval women's sports.

In a hierarchical society, social status determined who did what. In an agrarian society, the cycle of seasons determined when they did it. As Jacques LeGoff remarks, "rural time was natural time. The great divisions were day and . . . night and the seasons."[15] While it is obvious that peasant women worked too long and too hard to have "disposable leisure time" in the modern sense of regularly recurring hours set aside for whatever one wants to do with them, it is nonetheless true that the medieval calendar included occasions for them to turn from work to play.

In the lives of the lowly, the most striking example is folk football, the medieval free-for-all which eventually evolved into modern soccer. When the game was first played, no one knows. Greek and Roman ballgames seem to have resembled "catch" or dodgeball rather than some form of football. In twelfth-century England and France, folk football was usually played on Shrove Tuesday. Quite apart from the games' Eastertime setting, some of the customs associated with folk football suggest that it may have begun as a religious ritual, perhaps as part of a fertility rite, a way to mark and celebrate the rebirth of vegetation after winter's death. In France, at Boulogne-la-Grasse, the rituals that accompanied the game played on "le jour du mardi gras" survived into the nineteenth century; the symbolism of the day included a basket of eggs and a staff from which a beribboned leather ball was suspended.[16] Since the game was probably derived from a fertility rite associated with the vernal equinox, it may have felt "natural" that women participated.

"A sport had to be very rough indeed before it was too rough for medieval women, who played and disported, as they hunted and worked, alongside the men."[17] This generalization is too grand, but peasant women *did* throw themselves into folk football. They pushed,

shoved, kicked, and frolicked with as much reckless abandon as their
fathers, brothers, husbands, and sons; and they seem to have suffered
as many broken bones and cracked crowns as the men did. The daily
labor of an agrarian economy made them a hardy lot. Although
Renaissance humanists like Sir Thomas Elyot condemned the sport as
"nothing but beastly fury, and extreme violence," there is no evidence
that anyone thought peasant women out of place in the ludic turbu-
lence.[18] Indeed, they were sometimes the only players. In England,
Shrovetide football commonly pitted married women against maidens and spinsters, a traditional division on the conventional basis of
marital status.[19]

In terms of popularity, rite-of-spring football may have been the
medieval equivalent of the Super Bowl, but it was not the only
occasion for peasant women to test their mettle. Milkmaids and other
girls also played Shrovetide stoolball, which resembled modern cricket
and baseball in that a ball was thrown by one player and struck by
another. Sports historian William J. Baker remarks humorously of
this game and its descendents, "Although modern baseball is primarily American, urban, and male, its roots are medieval, English, rural,
and female."[20] Games of stoolball were sometimes played at the great
commercial fairs which periodically enlivened the otherwise dreary
days of medieval peasants. These fairs, often associated with a saint's
day (e.g., Saint Bartholomew's Fair), were welcome opportunities
for drunkenness and rough-and-tumble play. Men wrestled, fought
with staves, lifted barrels, pulled wagons, and ran races. At least the
last of these sports was common among the women, especially but
not exclusively among the maidens.

For prizes such as a smock or a bolt of cloth, girls ran barefoot
across a meadow, cheered on by their families and, perhaps, by their
future husbands. Such contests were clearly not the same as the
prenuptial races run at Sparta, where the maidens displayed the physical fitness that proved them worthy to become the wives and mothers of warriors, but neither can we entirely rule out an erotic element
and a matrimonial function for the smock race. Consider what seems
to have been a medieval version of Sadie Hawkins Day: "In England
on the eve of Hockday [Easter Monday] the women of the village
seized the men and did not release them until they paid ransom, and
on the following day it was the turn of the men to capture the
women."[21] As earth shrugged off winter's shroud, it was time for
men and women to do the same.

It is difficult to say more than this about peasant women's sports without expanding one's definition of sports, which is exactly what many historians are tempted to do. In search of further evidence for women's sports, John Marshall Carter has culled information from coroner's accounts and other medieval legal records of various kinds. In the Wiltshire Eyre for 1249, for instance, he has found reference to a sports-related fatality: "Two strangers were shooting in sport and one of the arrows hit Alice, the daughter of John, and Alice died." In London's records for 1276, Carter discovered that a quarrel disrupted a peaceful game of chess, whereupon David de Bristoll drew his sword and slew Juliana, wife of Richard le Cordwaner. Apropos of such information, Carter remarks, "An investigator can learn a great deal about the social context of sports from such an admittedly laconic source."[22] On the contrary. Carter's admirably assiduous searches add little to our knowledge of women's sports because his examples are almost invariably taken from a loosely labeled grab bag in which sports are jumbled together with other kinds of recreation and with clearly utilitarian activities. Luckless Juliana, slain in a quarrel over chess, should not be memorialized as a sports participant.

As usual, we are somewhat better informed about the top of the social hierarchy than about the bottom. Aristocratic women were expected to be competent managers of their husbands' estates, and some of them proved capable of defending the demesne when armed marauders sought to take advantage of a husband's lengthy absence. Some women were skilled players in the often violent game of medieval politics, but the ladies of the manor and the court kept their distance from folk football and smock races. They favored more decorous, more dignified sports. If one rules out dances (which I do because they are not inherently competitive), then the medieval lady was Diana's daughter. She hunted. Field sports in England were, in fact, reserved to lords and ladies by game laws which remained in force, with various modifications, from 1390 to 1830. Commoners were ordered to desist from killing game on their own lands. Hunting and hawking were, therefore, displays of social status as well as occasions to enjoy the pleasures of physical activity. The well-bred noblewoman was "expected to know how to ride (straight-backed, according to didactic works), to breed falcons and release them during the hunt, to play chess and backgammon, to dance, sing, recite poetry and tell stories."[23] Philippa of Hainault, wife of Edward III of England, was famed for her falcons. Joseph Strutt claimed in *The*

Sports and Pastimes of the People of England (1838) that "the ladies had hunting parties by themselves," but it is unlikely that they were entirely on their own even when the men of their own class were otherwise occupied.[24] Male retainers accompanied, assisted, and protected them. It is often said, by Strutt and many later historians, that Dame Juliana Berners wrote the *Boke of St. Albans* (1486), a disquisition on hunting, hawking, and heraldry, but, here too, skepticism is in order. The attribution of authorship is very doubtful.[25]

Illuminated manuscripts—such as Marguerite de Bar's *Breviary* and the "Tenison Psalter"—abound with illustrations of noblewomen hunting stags or handling falcons.[26] In the beautifully illustrated, justly famous *Très Riches Heures du Duc de Berry,* the scene for the month of August includes mounted ladies with their hawks.[27] (See Plate 6.) In a strictly hierarchical society, everyone had the kind of falcon most appropriate to his or her status. Royalty sported with the gerfalcon, earls with the peregrine, ladies with the merlin.[28] Literary evidence reassures us that the depictions of falconry, unlike male-female goatback-ramback jousts, mirrored medieval reality. In his *Policraticus,* John of Salisbury opined that women actually bred falcons more skillfully than men, but he meant no compliment. He explained female superiority by commenting that "the weaker sex tend more to rapaciousness."[29] This grouchy opinion was not shared by the anonymous poet who wrote lyrically about his knightly patron's bride, a girl who rode and hawked,

> Petites mamelettes,
> Corps bien fait et moulé,
> Dures comme pommettes,
> Blanches comme fleurs de pré.
>
> (Small breasts,
> A body well made and shaped,
> Firm as little apples,
> White as wild flowers.)[30]

Illustrated manuscripts also depict aristocratic women who hunted with the longbow (but not, apparently, the crossbow). The huntresses of medieval allegory had unimpeachable motives. They captured unicorns, proof of their virginity, and slew fabulous beasts, symbolic of Satan. Ordinary noblewomen joined the chase for ordinary reasons, i.e., the fun of it. If there was any religious significance to their exploits, it was attenuated beyond our recognition.

And what of the *bourgeoise?* She was unquestionably her husband's helpmate. Craftmen's wives worked in the shop and merchants' wives often handled complicated economic transactions when their husbands were away on other business. The skills and expertise of many widows were such that they were sometimes allowed to continue as artisans or merchants after their husbands' deaths. This active participation in economic life did not, however, mean that middle-class women joined their husbands at play. They seem neither to have participated in folk contests like medieval football nor to have hunted nor even—as a rule—to have taken an active part in the archery contests that were the special joy of medieval townsmen.

These archery contests were organized by guilds formed as early as the fourteenth century. They were often grandly staged intercity matches planned months or even years in advance, attended by the entire community, and accompanied by considerable uninhibited revelry. The wives of craftsmen and merchants certainly joined in the communal festivities of a crossbow contest—as spectators. In northern France and the Low Countries, they were sometimes accepted as auxiliary members of the archers' guild, but they rarely stepped up to the mark and drew the bow and sent the arrow or the bolt to the butt. Their role was to prepare the feast and grace the banquet. There were, however, exceptions to this rule. In 1496, Job Rorbach reported an archery contest for women. He made it clear, however, that these daughters of Diana were not engaged in an official match. In medieval Paderborn, the *Schützenkönigin* ("queen of the archers") usurped the administrative functions of the *Schützenkönig* ("king of the archers"), but she did not seize his bow along with his authority. Theo Reintges, a modern historian of medieval archery, believes that women never shot in official guild-sponsored contests.[31] Although archery contests were a favorite subject for medieval artists, I know of no print in which women appear other than as spectators.

In the late Middle Ages, the complicated game of court or royal tennis came into favor. In England, royal decrees of 1388 and 1410 forbade the game to servants and laborers. Played at first by princes, the game eventually attracted middle-class enthusiasts. In France, the *jeu de paume* eventually became extremely popular among the bourgeoisie. As courts proliferated throughout the city of Paris, competition became intense. Most of the players were, of course, men, but the *Journal d'un Bourgeois de Paris* provides us with another possible exception to the rule that middle-class medieval women never engaged in formal sports contests. Writing in 1427, the Parisian burgher noted that a certain Margot of Hainault, twenty-eight years old, had come to town and had outplayed the men at their favorite game.[32] He could not have known, as he made this entry in his journal, that Margot was a portent.

PLATE I. Queen Hatshepsut of Egypt and the Steer-God Apis performing a ceremonial run. *Collection: Wolfgang Decker*

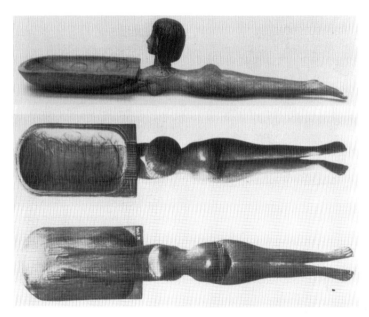

PLATE 2. A swimmer as the handle of an Egyptian spoon. *Musée du Louvre*

PLATE 3. Archaic Greek bronze statue of a running girl (probably Spartan). *The trustees of the British Museum*

PLATE 4. Red-figured Attic vase with young women after exercise. *Museo Cívico (Bari)*
PLATE 5. The "bikini girls" mosaic (detail), Piazza Armerina, Villa Romana del Casale. *Scala/Art Resource*

PLATE 6. Pol de Limbourg, falconing scene (from *Les Très Riches Heures du Duc de Berry*, early 15th century. *Musée Condé (Chantilly) and Giroudon/Art Resource*

le donne L'abitanti i lidi circostanti a Ven.ᵃ concorrono parimente a cosi fatta festa uogando insieme,
et contendendo i premij con uniuersal piacere de riguardanti

Giacomo Franco fo: Con Priuilegio

PLATE 7. Regatta of Venetian peasant women (from Giacomo Franco, *Habiti delle Donne Venetiane*, 1610. *The Spencer Collection, New York Public Library*

PLATE 8. John Collet, *The Ladies Shooting Poney* (1780). *The Yale Center for British Art*

PLATE 9. The Marchioness of Salisbury clearing a gate (from *The Sporting Magazine*, June 1794).
PLATE 10. A.-C.-H. Cham, *Wrestlers from Rouen* (1868). *Serge and Françoise Laget*

PLATE 11. Winslow Homer, American, 1836–1910, *Croquet Scene*. Oil on canvas, 1866, 15 7/8 x 26 1/16 inches. Friends of American Art Collection, 1942.35 Photograph © 1990, The Art Institute of Chicago. All rights reserved. *The Art Institute of Chicago*

PLATE 12. Cyclists in the Bois du Bologne (from *Harper's Weekly*, December 19, 1868).

PLATE 13. William Powell Frith, *The Fair Toxophilites. The Royal Albert Museum, Exeter*

PLATE 14. Fernard Khnopff, *Memories* (1889). *Musées Royaux des Beaux-Arts, Brussels*

PLATE 15. Charles Dana Gibson, *The Coming Game: Yale versus Vassar* (1896). *Collection: Sally Fox*

PLATE 16. Senda Berenson coaching basketball at Smith College (1904).
Sophia Smith Collection, Smith College Archives

PLATE 17. Lacrosse at Lord's (London), Oxford versus Cambridge (1914). *Archives of Lady Margaret Hall, Oxford*

PLATE 18. British and French runners contesting the 800–meter race at the Jeux Féminins (Monte Carlo, 1921) *Institut für Sportwissenschaft und Sport, Universität Bonn*

PLATE 19. Suzanne Lenglen and Helen Wills before their match at Cannes (February 1926). *Collection: Larry Engelmann*

PLATE 20. Mildred "Babe" Didrikson in her Olympic uniform (Los Angeles, 1932). *The Bettman Archive*

PLATE 21. Sonia Henie practicing at St. Moritz (1933). *AP/Wide World Photos*

FIVE

A Renaissance for Women's Sports?

Did women have a Renaissance? Ever since Joan Kelly-Gadol asked this provocative question, historians have differed over the correctness of Kelly-Gadol's answer. She asserted that women of the Renasiance, in comparison to women of the Middle Ages, "experienced a contraction of social and personal options." In her pessimistic judgment, courtly love, which might have seemed to raise the status of women, was actually an extension of vassalage from politics to the domain of love. The Neo-Platonic visions of Dante and Petrarch spiritualized the Idea of Woman but did little to improve the status of ordinary women. "All the advances of Renaissance Italy, its proto-capitalist economy, its states, and its humanistic culture, worked to mold the noblewoman into an aesthetic object: decorous, chaste, and doubly dependent—on her husband as well as the prince."[1] Restrictions on her physical movement were the last link in a golden chain of privileged captivity.

Husbands and princes, on the other hand, were expected to be men of vigorous action. For them, masculine *virtù* was no passive virtue. Renaissance Man, that vital figment of the historian's imagination, was unquestionably competitive and ambitious. Indeed, almost every notable Renaissance figure seems to have entered into the fierce struggle for power and glory. The struggle took place most obviously in the political arena, where names like Borgia, Medici, and Sforza still summon up images of ruthless grandeur, but artists like Michelangelo and Rubens and writers like Rabelais and Shakespeare were also driven by the desire to surpass their rivals. The emulation of antiquity was obviously one means to that glorious end.

Memories of the Olympic games began to germinate. Virgilius Polydorus mentioned them in *De Inventoribus Rerum* (1499) and Conrad Celtes drev· an inaccurate map of Olympia in 1508. Eight years later, in Venice, Pausanias was printed for the first time—in the original Greek. The French poet Robert Garnier referred to the Olympic Games in 1574 in a play that the Elizabethan dramatist Thomas Kyd then translated into English as *Pompey the Great* (1595).[2] In the years just before the outbreak of the Civil Wars, the English gentleman Robert Dover actually instituted "Olympick Games" in the Cotswolds of Gloucestershire. Despite their name, however, they consisted not of Greek athletics but rather of traditional English sports.[3]

Although artists and writers seemed almost enthralled by classical civilization, there was no real effort to revive the Olympic Games. Except for the singular instance of Robert Dover, there is little evidence that Renaissance humanists were inspired to leave their studies and actually do as the Greeks had done. Having little in the way of actual sports to refer to, sports historians who have written on the period have concentrated on theoretical works like Nicolas Wynman's *Colymbetes* (1538) or on spokesmen for physical education, like Hieronymus Mercurialis, whose *De Arte Gymnastica* appeared in 1569. Neither book had much to do with sports. The first encouraged readers to learn to swim, a useful skill, thought Wynman, for those who fall into the water; the second book advocated mild exercise but warned against athletic contests because they are useless and make one lethargic.[4]

This lack of enthusiasm for sports might seem strange when one considers that historians since Jakob Burckhardt have characterized the Renaissance as an intensely agonistic age. The explanation for this relative neglect of sports is that most humanists tended to believe that physical activity should be either utilitarian, as in work and warfare, or aesthetic. In their writings, the human body reappeared as the object of admiration and wonder that it had been for the Greeks (and that it most emphatically had *not* been for the medieval cleric). The most obvious symbol of this new humanistic attitude toward the embodied self is doubtless Leonardo da Vinci's familiar geometrical sketch of a male figure with outstretched arms and legs. That the sketch is geometrical, that the beautifully symmetrical figure is inscribed within a circle and a square, is immensely suggestive of the Renaissance attitude toward physicality. Geometry was the mathematical key, not arithmetic; it was the form of one's movement that mattered, not some quantified result. "Exercises were regularized and rationalized, but without simplification. They were, on the contrary, complicated. The ideal that one sought in everything was a complex regularity."[5] For the Renaissance, the much-mocked adage might even have been true: it was not whether one won or lost but how one played the game.

This attitude can be seen in the evolution of the tournament from the bloody mêlée of twelfth-century combat to the allegorical pageantry of the sixteenth-century spectacle. The early tournament involved scores if not hundreds of knights energetically engaged in a free-for-all the purpose of which was to capture and, simultaneously, to avoid captivity. Spectators were rare, rules were minimal, and bloodshed was an accepted if not a positively welcomed part of the game. In the fourteenth century, the pageantry that grew up around the combats began to overwhelm them. By the sixteenth century, the entire tournament had become a lavish spectacle in which theatrical costumes, colorful processions, extravagant sets, and allegorical figures were far more important than the jousts, which were often inept and nearly always harmless. Spectators, who flocked to the venue in order to see and be seen, filled the elaborate stands. Grace and decorum counted for more than physical prowess. At no point in history was sport closer to dance.

This transformation of *agon* into art can also be observed in the most important conduct book of the entire Renaissance, Baldesar Castiglione's *Book of the Courtier* (1528), which quickly became the standard Renaissance authority on appropriately courtly behavior. Queried about the deportment of the courtier when engaged in a tournament, Duke Federico of Montefeltro, in whose palace at Urbino *The Courtier* is set, replies as follows:

If he happens to engage in arms in some public show—such as jousts, tourneys, stick-throwing, or in any other bodily exercise—mindful of the place where he is and in whose presence, he will strive to be as elegant and handsome in the exercise of arms as he is adroit, and to feed his spectators' eyes with all those things that he thinks may give him added grace; and he will take care to have a horse gaily caparisoned, to wear a becoming attire, to have appropriate mottoes and ingenious devices that will attract the eyes of the spectators even as the loadstone attracts iron.

Earlier in the discussion, Count Ludovico da Canossa acknowledges the martial usefulness of running, jumping, swimming, and throwing stones, but he too emphasizes elegance as opposed to prowess and praises court tennis as "most suitable for a man at court" because it "shows off the disposition of the body, the quickness and litheness of every member, and all the qualities which are brought out by almost every other exercise."[6]

Horses, once selected for the strength necessary to carry an armored knight in warfare or in the mock battle of the tournament, were trained in the Renaissance to pirouette and gallop in intricate patterns. "Beauty, delicacy, and position—these were the foundation of courtly equestrianism."[7] This choreographic tendency reached its zenith in the *Rossballett* ("ballet of stallions") performed in Vienna in 1667 for the delight of Emperor Leopold I.[8] In this period, the modern sport of dressage had its origins.

Meanwhile, the knight dismounted from his warhorse, unbuckled his armor, and exchanged his heavy two-handed sword for the rapier. Brute strength was replaced by agility and finesse. The very extravagance of the Renaissance tournament prohibited its occurrence except for grand occasions of state, such as coronations or royal weddings, but the art of fencing was relatively inexpensive. It became the favorite sport of the aristocracy. Fencing masters learned their lessons in Italy and France and passed them on to the Germans and the British, both of whom acknowledged the Latin influence in their adoption of Italian and French terms. Traditionalists resisted the innovation. George Silver complained in 1599 about "these Italianate weake, fantasticall and most divellish and imperfect fights."[9] In vain. Cut-and-slash swordplay gave way to thrusts. Treatises on the sport emphasized its aesthetic appeal. "For the Renaissance fencer, the charm of his sport clearly lay in the exercise of every spatial and positional possibility."[10] At the court of Louis XIV, the ceremonial bow, the *révérence,* became an essential part of the sport. Fencers' manuals, like Camillo Agrippa's *Trattato di Scientia d'Arme* (1553) and Girard Thibault's *L'Académie de l'espée* (1628), were illustrated by diagrams of the appropriate positions to take before, during, and after the match. Such manuals looked like textbooks in geometry.

A similar transformation can be seen in the evolution of football. The tumultuous seasonal game played by the medieval peasantry became the stately entertainment of the Renaissance aristocracy. As one might have expected, the "civilized" version of football first appeared in northern Italy, where it was known as *calcio*. As described by Giovanni de' Bardi in his *Discorso sopra il Gioco del Calcio Fiorentino* (1580), the game was played by two teams of twenty-seven youths, "gentlemen, from eighteen years of age to forty-five, beautiful and vigorous, of gallant bearing, and of good report." Looks counted, and "he who appeareth badly clad maketh but an ill show and acquireth evil report thereby."[11] Play might have been rough, but ruffians were not allowed to play.

Typical of French pedagogic institutions was the school established by Antoine Pluvinel in 1594, where aristocratic youths learned to ride, dance, fence, and do mathematics, including geometry. At one such academy, at Angers, George de Villiers, Duke of Buckingham, learned the arts of the Renaissance courtier.[12] A 1649 account of the famous *Ritterakademie* in Tübingen (founded in 1589) provides another glimpse of the transition from medieval to Renaissance conceptions of physical exercise. As if they were medieval squires, the scholars at the academy learned to joust, wrestle, and shoot with the crossbow, but they also acquired the Renaissance courtier's ability to dance, fence, play court tennis, and handle the primitive firearms of the age.[13]

Given this intensely aesthetic approach to sports, one might expect that Renaissance women, at least those of the aristocracy, were welcomed into the world of sports as graceful and elegant participants. They were not. Once again, Castiglione seems to have best articulated the common wisdom of the age. In the Third Book, entirely devoted to women, Gaspar Pallavicino asks about the "bodily exercises proper to a Court Lady." The poet Unico Aretino comments that it was the custom of ancient women to wrestle naked against the men. To this remark, based upon a misinterpretation of Plato or Plutarch, Cesare Gonzaga adds, "And in my time, I have seen women play tennis, handle weapons, ride, hunt, and engage in nearly all the exercises that a cavalier can." At this point, Giuliano de' Medici sets everyone straight:

Since I may fashion this Lady as I please, not only would I not have her engage in such robust and strenuous manly exercises, but even those that are becoming to a woman I would have her practice in a measured way and with that gentle delicacy that we have said befits her.[14]

He continues to describe his ideal and to attribute to her not only elegance and grace but also magnanimity and fortitude of spirit.

Before long, everyone has offered tribute to unusual women who ruled cities, led armies, and in other ways proved themselves the equals of men. But not, it seems, in sports. Male hands grasped the fencer's foil and male feet propelled the football.

At least a few humanists disagreed with Castiglione's courtiers on the question of women's—or at least girls'—sports. At his Casa Giocosa ("House of Joy") at Mantua, Vittorino Da Feltre encouraged the aristocratic girls under his tutelage to run, ride, swim, leap—and play ballgames. It is unclear whether or not these games included football, but the girls were thought hardy enough to be indulged in snowball fights. Da Feltre's pupils were not the only females to be introduced to the joy of sports. Antonio Scaino, a propagandist for ballgames, observed that some girls and women were quite skilled at handball and racquet games.[15]

Renaissance women were welcome as tournament spectators who were supposed conventionally to motivate the love-struck knights to deeds of valor, but the only women actually to gallop into armored combat were poetic characters like Bradamante in Ludovico Ariosto's *Orlando Furioso* (1532) and Britomart in Edmund Spenser's *Faerie Queen* (1596). Women were an essential part of tournament pageantry, but they appeared as the maidens to be rescued rather than as the noble knights who rescued them. In honor of women like Katharine of Aragon, the first of Henry VIII's numerous wives, a tournament was staged at Westminster in 1511, but her part was played before the tournament began; she bore Henry a son and provided the occasion for the men to preen, which is exactly what they seem to do on the thirty-six vellum membranes of the Great Tournament Roll of Westminister.[16] "The most usual active role of women in [English] tournament pageantry was that of leading in the *tenants* to the field." At Smithfield in 1390, for instance, "the ladies led their knights to the lists by means of a golden chain. . . . The use of a chain rather than a bridle was a particularly effective way of stressing the allegorical chains which bound the lover to his mistress and her service."[17] When René of Anjou staged a *table ronde* and took the part of King Arthur, his consort played Guinevere, who inspired but did not participate in the jousts. It has been said of Italian women of the Cinquecento that they *did* participate in tournaments, which were harmless spectacles, but these—if they occurred at all—were clearly exceptional events.[18]

Information on women's sports in Spain and Portugal is scanty, and comparatively little research has been done even for the modern period, but a Spanish historian refers to a female bullfighter in 1654 and assures us that many women followed her into the arena.[19] It is nearly certain that these *toreras,* like the overwhelming majority of their male counterparts, came from the peasantry. An illustration in the *Habiti d'Homini e di Donne* (1610) shows finely clad Italians of both sexes participating together in what is called bull-hunting (*"caccia toro"*) but what looks more like bull-baiting. They restrain the bulls by means of ropes twisted around or tied to the bulls' horns, but the elegance of the men's and women's attire seems incompatible with the physical effort demanded to control bulls under attack by dogs. Lower-class women may have aided their men in the rough and dangerous work of controlling the bulls, but the picture is a pleasant fantasy of brute nature effortlessly tamed.[20]

There were some occasions for upper-class women to enjoy the pleasures of athletic activity. In terms that might have been taken from Castiglione's *Courtier,* Dame Juliana Berners affirmed in *The Boke of St. Albans* (1486) that hunting, hawking, fowling and fishing were "absolute parts of Musicke which make perfect the harmony of a true Gentleman."[21] And a true gentlewoman as well. As an awareness of classical antiquity became more widely disseminated, women with a passion for hunting imagined themselves as avatars of Atalanta, whom Peter Paul Rubens painted in the act of slaying the Calydonian boar. Another painter of mythological scenes, Lucas Cranach the Elder, went "modern" and portrayed Sybil, Duchess of Saxony, hunting deer with a crossbow.[22] Diane de Poitiers, mistress of Henri II, loved to pose with bow and arrow and to remind her admirers of "the ancient goddess whose name she bore."[23] Her splendid portrait as Diana hunting, by an anonymous painter of the School of Fontainebleau, is owned by the Louvre.

Queen Mary of Scotland hunted at Athole, where, in 1564, some two thousand Highlanders were employed to drive the deer from the woods to the glen where the royal party waited. Two years later, the Scottish Privy Council passed an ordinance to dissuade the poachers whose depredations threatened to ruin the queen's pleasure. Mary was also—like Katherine of Aragon—an avid golfer.[24] Her rival, Elizabeth I of England, was notorious for her life-long inability to withstand the temptation of field sports. George Turberville's *Book of*

Faulconrie or Hawking (1575) showed the queen with her hawks.[25] In the summer of 1591, Elizabeth visited Sussex and hunted in the company of the Countess of Kildare.

Her highnesse tooke horse, and rode into the park, at eight o'clock in the morning, where was a delicate bowre prepared, under the which were her highness [*sic*] musicians placed; and a cross-bow, by a nymph, with a sweet song, was delivered into her hands, to shoote at the deere; about some thirty in number were put into a paddock, of which number she killed three or four, and the countess of Kildare one.[26]

The members of her court marveled at her passion for field sports. Rowland White wrote to Robert Sidney that the queen was "exceedingly disposed to hunting, for every second day she is on horseback, and continues the sport long." Visiting Kenilworth in the Queen's company, Robert Dudley, Earl of Leicester, sent the same message in an epistle to William Cecil, Lord Burghley, "Even by and by Her Majesty is going to the forest to kill some bucks with her bow, as she hath done in the park this morning. God be thanked, she is very merry and well-disposed now."[27] "Elizabeth's hunting," comments one historian,

could be an expensive and destructive activity, when she and her huge train of unruly courtiers swept about the country on the royal progresses, devastating many a lord's deer park or chase, but the activity did help to bind her to her great subjects, furthering the image of the royal mistress, a living Diana.[28]

The royal hunt was clearly a political act as well as a sport. It was a grandly destructive display of privilege and power.

In *Antony and Cleopatra,* composed a few years after Elizabeth's death, Shakespeare imagined the Egyptian queen as an angler:

> Give me my angle, we'll to the river there,
> My music playing far off, I will betray
> Tawny-finn'd fishes, my bended hook shall pierce
> Their slimy jaws; and as I draw them up,
> I'll think them every one an Antony,
> And say, "Ah, ha! You're caught."

This tells us nothing about the historical Cleopatra, but it does suggest that Shakespeare may have thought fishing an appropriate activity for an activist queen in his own day as well as Antony's.

Elizabeth's father, Henry VIII, was quite an athlete in his youth, before his greatly expanded girth reduced him to sedentary amusements. As a young man he was fond of royal tennis, but his love of female companionship did not impel him to mixed singles (at least not on the tennis court). Aristocratic women seem not to have emulated Margot of Hainault, the fifteenth-century tennis player. Elizabethan and Jacobean literature had many references to the game and the artists of the Renaissance have left us a profusion of illustrations of courtiers at play, but neither the literary nor the iconographical evidence reveals females other than as spectators.

From the favorite sport of the male bourgeoisie, archery, most Renaissance women were excluded. Rank, however, had its privileges and royalty sometimes bent the bow. Anne Boleyn was such a passionate disciple of Diana that Henry VIII complained unchivalrously about the costs of her archery.[29] Elizabeth I was also said to have been "much praised" for her skill with a crossbow.[30] As a crossbow huntress, she made the most of her royal advantages. "In 1591, while musicians played, she shot deer from a paddock."[31] The wife of Ferdinand II of Tyrol won a silver beaker at a crossbow contest held in the summer of 1570, but her victory may have been arranged in acknowledgment of her status.[32] Isabella of Brabant shot at the popinjay (a wooden bird mounted on a tall pole) at Brussels in 1615 and at Ghent in 1618. In a woodblock print by Lucas Hoorenbault she is shown surrounded by the supportive males of Ghent's famous guild of St. George.[33] The noble women of France were also known to have drawn the bow. Whether or not they were entirely serious about the sport is an open question. The *grandes dames* of France carried "little crossbows made especially for them." These "elegant weapons were inlaid with pearls and ivory and sculpted, cut, carved, and adorned with heroic or amorous scenes."[34] These bows were probably purely symbolic—like the gilded armor worn by the men on state occasions.

The exclusion of middle-class women was not total. In Flanders, northeastern France, and along the Rhine, where Renaissance archery guilds proliferated, women were often enrolled as auxiliary members, useful for the many social functions of the guild, and they were occasionally accepted as participants in the sport, especially in the guilds that evolved under ecclesiastical rather than military auspices. In some guilds the "queen" who presided over the annual championship match was simply the wife of the "king" who had triumphed the previous year, but in other guilds—like the guild of St. Sebastian at Kappelen in Flanders—the *gildezusters* competed, bow in hand, for the title of *koningin*. Contests for women were also held at Hooger-heyde. In this period of transition from traditional folk games to modern sports, there were no standard rules and regulations applicable to all guilds. In the archery guild of St. Anthony at Olen, the women sought to hit the popinjay not with arrows or crossbow bolts but with sticks that they threw by hand.[35]

As this quaint custom suggests, Renaissance archery matches were not merely contests in toxophilic skill. Planned months or even years in advance, they were grandly elaborate festive occasions for all sorts of diversion—oratory, pageantry, theatrical performances, eating, drinking, and whoring. Although the archers were members of the highly restrictive middle-class guilds, their matches were usually accompanied by a diversified program of sports for the lower classes who flocked to town to watch the archery. Peasant youths and urban apprentices wrestled, cast stones, and ran races, and there was commonly at least one event for women. At Augsburg in 1470, there were horse races and sprints for journeymen, apprentices, and women. The match held at Herrenburg four years later included a footrace for the archers and two events for "all good wives": a one-legged triple-jump and a two-hundred-yard race.[36] A ceremonial archery target from Zickau, a figured copper plate dated 1573, depicts an archery match accompanied by a footrace for women.[37] During the celebrations of the archers' guild of St. Nicholas in Willebroek in Flanders, the women played ballgames.[38] In England, France, and the Low Countries, the game of "Trou-Madame," which required the players to roll a ball through an aperture in a wooden plank, was often played by the men and women gathered at a festive archery match.[39]

The densely populated, splendidly animated canvases of Hendrick Avercamp and other Dutch and Flemish genre painters provide us with scenes of popular winter sports. Avercamp's *Winter Landscape,* for instance, painted in the early seventeenth century, shows the erstwhile sober Dutch at exuberant hibernal play; the women join the ice skaters but they are not involved in the exclusively male game of *kolf* (a precursor of both golf and ice hockey). In a drawing by Romeyn de Hooghe, elegantly attired female skaters wear masks to protect their delicate features from the cold wind. They are probably wives of the mercantile middle class. It is difficult to imagine them in a helter-skelter race across the ice. The social class of Avercamp's skaters and *kolf*-players is hard to determine, but the variety of their clothing suggests that the frozen canals tempted just about everyone to frolic if not actually to compete in a lively game of *kolf*.

Specialists in Renaissance history, like Carlo Ginzburg, can be quite gloomy about the paucity of information on the lower classes:

> The state of the documentation reflects, obviously, the state of the relationship of power between the classes. An almost exclusively oral culture such as that of the subordinate classes of preindustrial Europe tends not to leave traces, or, at least, the traces left are distorted.

This pessimistic generalization may be true for the spheres of politics and religion, but the discrepancy in information about the classes is less pronounced for the realm of Renaissance sports.[40]

In the Renaissance as in the Middle Ages, the young women of the lower classes, those most accustomed to physical labor, were the women most likely to be involved in holiday sports. In England, girls and women competed at stoolball, a primitive game with family resemblances to cricket and baseball. German and Scandinavian women played similar kinds of bat-and-ball games. All over Europe, peasant girls and married women competed in foot races. The races run as a "side show" to the great archery contests of northern Europe have already been mentioned. Sebald Bechem's woodblock print, *Die grosse Dorfkirchweih* (1539), shows the processions, feasts, sports, dances, and fistfights that were commonly a part of the dedication of a village church in Germany. In the rear of the picture, five peasant girls are running a footrace.[41]

There were also numerous races for the lower-class urban women of northern Italy. We know, for instance, that women ran races in Florence in 1325, in Brescia in 1444, and in Rome in 1519. The merchants of fourteenth-century Ferrara offered prizes for two races for men and one for women. Women raced in sixteenth-century Verona, perhaps for the same green cloth which Dante, two centuries earlier, named as the Veronese men's prize. In addition to the usual footraces, the carnival in Florence may have included female fencers, presumably girls or women of the *popolo*.[42] Carnival was, of course, a liminal time to do whatever was, in the normal course of events, *not* done.

Despite the classical appellation given them by seventeenth-century poets, Robert Dover's famed "Olympick Games" in the Cotswolds of Gloucestershire were actually traditional pastimes of the

English countryside. At Dover's games, which took place on King-combe Plain the Thursday and Friday before Easter, men ran, jumped, threw, and wrestled, but they also danced, sang, mimed, performed in masques, and did acrobatics. The range of women's activities was narrower, but there may have been races for girls and women in Dover's day as there were a century later. These events

attracted much attention from the few early commentators, as they doubtless did also from the spectators. The usual prize was a smock (hence, "smock races") which, at the Cotswold Games . . . was displayed on a tall pole before the event; the "panting rivals" waited in line for the start and the course must have been over some distance since the runners soon "left the field behind."[43]

In the traditional English Michaelmas sport of cross-country follow-the-leader, women "of less scrupulous character" joined the men in their dashes, jumps, and clambers across the fields and streams.[44]

Remarks of this sort which impugned the character of the female participants were common. When the upper classes stepped in as sponsors, they frequently arranged contests for marginal groups whose social status was already too low to be lowered by rough-and-tumble sports participation. Like modern tourists who toss coins into the sea for native divers to retrieve, Renaissance courtiers offered prizes to stimulate the poor to acts of physical prowess. When the French essayist Michel de Montaigne visited Rome in 1580–81, he observed the Shrovetide races: "Along the Corso, which is a long street . . . that gets its name from this very thing, they race, now four or five boys, now some Jews, now some old men stark naked, from one end of the street to the other." (Meanwhile, gentlemen, mounted on fine horses, ran at the quintain, a target to be touched by the lance.)[45] Montaigne did not mention a race for Roman women, but earlier accounts tell of Carnival-time races for Jews, old men, donkeys—and women. Ferrara, Florence, and a number of other Italian cities had contests for prostitutes. In 1501, Pope Alexander VI, a member of the Borgia family and not exactly a spoil-sport, hosted one such race at Saint Peter's basilica in Rome.[46] When Castruccio Castracani of Lucca wished to humiliate the besieged citizens of Florence, he ostentatiously staged a series of sports events, including a race for prostitutes, before the walls of the city. After his death, the Florentines repaid the insult and sent *their* city's prostitutes to race before the gates of Lucca.[47] Needless to say, the aristocratic Italian patrons of the arts who commissioned and admired Guido Reni's painting of Atalanta, bending voluptuously to gather a golden apple, were adamantly opposed to footraces for women of their own class.[48]

Races for prostitutes were also common north of the Alps. Sometimes the *"gemeine Weiber"* ("common women") ran in the same race with their untainted sisters, as they did in Noerdlingen in 1442, and sometimes the fallen women had the field to themselves, as they did at Augsburg in 1454.[49] In Basel, the women ran 250 paces for the prize: a piece of cloth worth a gulden and a half. The surviving evidence does not indicate whether the prostitutes of Basel competed separately or together with the "honorable wives."[50] Commenting on the carnival-time prostitutes' races of Switzerland, Walter Schaufelberg remarks that the scantly clad women were more likely exemplars of *Liebesübungen* than *Leibesübungen* ("exercises in love" rather than "exercises of the body").[51] In the south of France, races for prostitutes were mentioned in conjunction with saint's day's festivities at Pernes (in 1458) and at Arles (in 1557). The "public women" of the former town competed after the archery contest and before the footraces for children.[52] Throughout the period, such races were probably regular occurrences to which we have only scattered references. These races were often rituals of degradation. When prostitutes competed, often for cash prizes rather than articles of clothing, it was considered good sport for the male spectators to trip them and send them sprawling to the ground. The mood was Rabelaisian and rowdy. In the latter part of the sixteenth century, Protestant reformers grimly curtailed the more tumultuous and licentious aspects of such sports festivals as were still allowed. The women's races were discontinued.[53]

In Venice, where boats were the standard means of transportation and nautical sports were important, one of the most exciting events was the annual boat race for peasant women:

Understandably, the women's regatta enjoyed special popularity. The participants were peasant women of the area—especially from Pellestrina—who had plenty of practice thanks to weekly boat trips to the market in Venice. . . . It is probable that the spectators were more attracted by the charming country costumes than by the sports performance. At any rate, Antonio Gabellico reported of the first official women's regatta in 1493, to celebrate the arrival of Beatrice d'Este, that the fifty competing peasant maids in their

short linen skirts made a strong impression and that the spectacle, as unfamil-
iar as it was charming, greatly diminished the effects of the men's regatta
which followed.[54]

Here, too, it is impossible not to wonder about the motives of the
spectators. Innocent delight in the colorful costumes and admiration
for the strength and endurance of the women probably mingled with
elitist condescension and male voyeurism. All in all, a familiar combination. (See Plate 7.)

While folk football continued to be popular in villages north of the
Alps, the urban populace of fifteenth-century Italy threw itself enthusiastically, and sometimes murderously, into a kind of ludic street
warfare. In Lucca, Orvieto, Pavia, Perugia, Pisa, and a number of
other cities, thousands of men and women played a bellicose game
whose rules, such as they were, allowed them to fight with fists,
stones, and staves, often for the possession of a bridge or gate that
linked two quarters of the city.[55] A charming fourteenth-century
fresco from the Castello del Buonsiglio in Trento depicts an aristocratic man and two smiling women engaged in a friendly snowball
fight, but the bloody mayhem of street fighting was quite another
matter.[56] When the game began, the urban nobleman withdrew to his
palazzo, barred his doors and windows, and gave thanks that the
mob's energies were expended in this form rather than in protests
against their lawful rulers. It was a brutal aspect of Renaissance life
that the modern scholar, enchanted by the delicate pastel artistry of
Botticelli or intrigued by the Neo-Platonic poetry of Petrarch, tends
to forget.

SIX

Cricketeers on the Green and Viragos in the Ring

1. From Traditional to Modern Sports

Although sports of one kind or another seem to be a human universal found in every known culture, for children if not for adults, most historians agree that the formal-structural characteristics of modern sports are fundamentally different from those of earlier periods. The emergence of the modern can be seen most clearly in England because the Interregnum of Puritan rule came as a great divider between the traditional sports of the early seventeenth century and the very different, incipiently modern sports that came with the Restoration. Admittedly, to draw a line and say, "Here begins the modern," distorts the complexity of historical processes. Although one can find intimations of the modern in antiquity and many traditional sports have survived into the twentieth century, modern sports are best understood as the result of those processes of secularization and rationalization classically described by Max Weber in *Wirtschaft und Gesellschaft*. In ideal-typical form, modern sports are secular rather than an aspect of religious ritual. They are open to all on equal terms rather than reserved on the basis of ascriptive characteristics like race, sex, or religion. Modern sports are also specialized, rationalized, bureaucratically organized, and—most distinctively—marked by a kind of mania for quantification and the records that quantification makes possible.[1]

For example, races against time became common in England during the Restoration. Times were recorded ever more precisely. "In 1721," writes Henning Eichberg, times were measured in seconds. In 1731, stopwatches were used. In 1757, times were taken to the half second. . . . From the end of the eighteenth century the most important English horseraces were officially timed as a matter of course. By the early nineteenth century these times began to appear as a regular feature of the racing calendar."[2]

Needless to say, the process of modernization did not roll along like a train on a track nor do sports as we experience them always assume their ideal-typical form. Nonetheless, the abstraction—modern sports—is a benchmark by which to measure departures from the ideal type.

How did sports in general and women's sports in particular evolve from premodern to modern forms? At the highest level of abstraction, materialist historians have discussed industrial capitalism as the force behind the transformation while "idealists" influenced more by Weber than by Marx have suggested that the scientific revolution of the seventeenth century shaped industrial capitalism *and* sports *and* every other aspect of the modern world.[3] At a somewhat lower level of analysis, there is more of a consensus. Early modern times witnessed extraordinary changes in patterns of work as Europeans and then Americans moved away from the natural rhythms of the agricultural year. To speak of "leisure" in reference to antiquity, the Middle Ages, or the Renaissance makes no sense except for those few privileged members of society who had significant amounts of "disposable time" with which to do as they wished, but there had always been occasions for holiday celebrations, ritual festivities, and other activities set apart from the labors necessary to sustain existence. "Most wakes, fairs and parish feasts came at times of slack in the agrarian work calendar, with a particular concentration in the lull between spring sowing and the summer harvest and also in the post-harvest break."[4] These were also times for sports. The shift from a predominantly agricultural to a predominantly industrial economy disrupted this seasonal pattern.

The daily tempo mattered too. On the whole, work in the preindustrial age was much "more intermittant than it is today; for most workers there was no such thing as a regular working week or even a regular working day."[5] The line between work and play was seldom precisely drawn and an easy movement between work and play was typical of preindustrial culture. All this changed as men and women were subjected, by their employers or by their internalizations of "the Protestant ethic," to a stricter as well as a more abstract work discipline. Increasingly men's and women's lives were divided into time at work and time not at work. Employers who purchased a worker's time frowned upon his or her "playing around" while on the job. Peasants at work in the fields often sang to lighten their labors; factory workers were usually compelled to silence.

The Industrial Revolution was also accompanied by spatial differentiation. There had always been peasants, like those of Sicily, who trudged long distances from their village homes to the fields they worked, but industrialization and urbanization made it necessary for most men, and for many women, to "go to work" in a different sense. And it became increasingly difficult, at least until the development of modern corporate-sponsored recreational complexes, to transform the workplace into a venue for ballgames or other sports.

The larger transformation of rural and urban space also influenced the transition from traditional to modern sports. The enclosure of common lands and the preemption of large stretches of coastal or riparian land by private owners limited opportunities for traditional pastimes. Urbanization increased at an explosive rate, and it was a rare city whose farsighted magistrates thought to reserve parks and other open spaces for public recreational use. When planners began in the nineteenth and early twentieth centuries to introduce playgrounds into crowded urban space, when entrepreneurs began to build ballparks, rinks, courts, and other sports facilities, the separation between the spaces reserved for work and those designed for play probably became greater than at any time in history.

Although many of the changes associated with industrialization reduced opportunities for traditional amusements, the economic historian Wray Vamplew has commented insightfully on the enhancement of opportunity that occurred when Europe's more efficient economic system increased the available food supply and thus provided more of the energy that is a prerequisite for sustained sports participation.[6] Since the men of preindustrial Europe and America had tended to consume more of whatever food was available than the women did, often to the point where wives and daughters were reduced to the verge of starvation, a substantial increase in the food supply was an important factor in the development of women's sports.

To the degree that traditional (mostly lower-class) sports offended modern (mostly middle-class) sensibilities, such sports became contested cultural terrain. They were, and still are, occasions for class conflict. English working-class defenders of animal sports, for instance, fought in the 1840s to preserve bull-runs in Derby and other towns; cockfight enthusiasts still flock to mains even though cockfights have long been illegal in most modern societies. When the struggle to preserve the old forms against the encroachment of the new went badly or was wholly lost, antiquarians, folklorists, and ethnologists have nonetheless lovingly collected what evidences of traditional culture survived into the nineteenth and twentieth centuries.[7]

Assiduous sports historians have combed through seventeenth-century diaries and eighteenth-century newspapers and magazines in order to reconstruct the rise of modern and the decline of traditional sports. Thanks to their research, we have a much more complete documentation of sports than was possible for earlier periods—for England. For the European continent, the documentation is poor for men's sports and worse for women's. While numerous specialists in the history of physical education have utilized the readily available published works of Jean-Jacques Rousseau, Christian Wolff, Heinrich Pestolozzi and other educational reformers to trace the development of high-minded theories of health and hygiene for girls as well as for boys, almost no one has investigated the archival and published materials in order to discover what early modern upper-class and middle-class girls and women actually *did* under the rubric of physical education, and even fewer historians have troubled themselves about girls' and women's *sports* (as opposed to calisthenics).[8] Once we leave England and cross the Channel, sports historians are confronted with another example of women's oft-lamented "invisibility." We know more about the sports of Roman women in the first century A.D. than in the seventeenth and eighteenth centuries.

Since the evolution of *men's* sports from traditional to modern forms began in England and spread to the continent, with the French and the Germans quicker to adopt the innovations than were the Italians, the Spanish, or the Slavic nations, one can hypothesize that the evolution and diffusion of modern sports for women followed the same path. Since European men were much more quickly swept up by the processes of political and economic modernization than women were, one can also hypothesize that the pace of modernization for women's sports was considerably slower than that for men's sports. This was certainly the case in the nineteenth century, which is when the vast majority of monographs on European sports history begin. I have tried to avail myself of whatever historiographical help is available, but the present chapter is, faute de mieux, mostly an account of women's sport in England from the mid-seventeenth to the early nineteenth centuries.

2. Smock Races and Boxing Matches

The return of Charles II in 1660 signaled the restoration of a modicum of hedonism for weary survivors of a decade of high moral purpose. The Puritans had not—to put it mildly—encouraged sports participation of any sort. Their attitude toward women's sports can be gauged from Thomas Hall's *Funebria Florae* (1660), which traced England's traditional May-Day revels back to 242 B.C., when a Roman prostitute named Flora allegedly bequeathed funds for these impious amusements. "By sound of trumpet," wrote Hall, "all the whores were called to their sports, where they danced naked about the streets with trumpets blown before them."[9] Puritans like Hall had been delighted when Robert Dover's Cotswold Games were halted in 1642, one year before Parliament officially condemned the "Declaration of Sports" promulgated by James I in 1618 and reaffirmed by Charles I in 1633. During the Restoration, the Cotswold Games were revived.

The Cotswold Games were rather special, but fairs and wakes were common throughout the year. The latter were "a community's own petty carnival." Wakes should not be confused with the festivities that accompany an Irish funeral.

A wake normally included several of the familiar sports and pastimes of the period: wrestling, or boxing, or cudgelling; perhaps donkey racing, a wheelbarrow race (while blindfolded), a smock race for the women; contests might be arranged in hot hasty-pudding eating, grinning through a collar (the funniest won), chasing a greased pig, running in sacks, or smoking pipes of tobacco; at some wakes, bull-baiting, cock-fighting or badger-baiting, were featured.[10]

Rural festivities of this sort were durable enough to last into the late nineteenth century, where their traces survive in the works of amateur ethnologists and in the novels of Thomas Hardy.

Smock races were often part of the entertainment available at a fair or a wake or—especially in the eighteenth century—at a cricket match. These races are frequently attested by ballads, such as this one from Yorkshire:

> Four Virgins that supposed were,
> A Race did run I now declare,
> Sure such a race was never seen
> As this at Temple Newsham Green:
> In half shirts, and Drawers these maids did run,
> But Bonny Nan the Race has won.[11]

One motive of the virgins was to win the smock or ribbon offered as a prize. The fact that "the female competitors were often encouraged to come lightly clad" strongly suggests that the spectators were motivated by something more than an interest in the girls' unhindered movements.[12]

One's suspicions about voyeurism are confirmed by an account in *Mist's Journal* for October 23, 1725:

Vast Numbers of the lower class of Gentry attended on that Occasion, expecting that they [two young damsels] would have run in puris naturalibus [i.e., naked]; but that was over-ruled, and they were clad in white Waistcoats and Drawers, but without Shoes or Stockings.[13]

Most of these smock races were contested by rural maidens, but London's Pall Mall was the site of an October 1733 race when some "absurd persons" offered a Holland smock, a cap, clocked stockings, and laced shoes "as prizes to any four women who would run for them at three o'clock in the afternoon." The anecdotal chronicler James Pellor Malcolm reported that the races "attracted an amazing number of persons, who filled the streets, the windows, and balconies."[14]

The *Penny London Morning Advertiser* for June 11, 1744, recorded a race run by "two jolly wenches, one known by the name of The Little Bit of Blue (the Handsome Broom Girl) at the fag end of Kent Street, and the other, Black Bess, of the Mint." The erotic element came to the fore in the *Advertiser's* comment that the girls were "to run in drawers only, and there is excellent sport expected."[15] As attested by comments in the *Marylana Gazette* for June 14, 1753, Englishmen who migrated to the colonies continued to be interested in "well-legged" girls running races at local fairs.[16] Thomas Rowlandson's etching, *Rural Sports: Smock Racing* (1811), offers another glimpse into the carnival mood. Bare-breasted, long-skirted girls race while uninhibited male and female bumpkins cavort and brawl.[17] In eighteenth-century England, as in ancient Sparta, the demonstration of female physical prowess was sometimes an enticement to courtship. A correspondent in *The Spectator* (September 4, 1711) noted that "nothing is more usual than for a nimble-footed Wench to get a Husband at the same time she wins a Smock."

Visitors from the continent often took notice of these smock races in a way that suggests surprise and curiosity. J. B. LeBlanc, for instance, wrote in 1747 that the rural parts of England were often the scene of sports like those of ancient Sparta. (The parallel was one he explicitly acknowledged.) The "young damsels are to be seen contending for the prize at a course. They are uncommonly strong robust country girls, who run with surprising swiftness." His countryman, the Abbé Prévost, was puzzled at what we can now see was the incipient modernization of a race he witnessed. The women were weighed, as if they had been jockeys, and the lighter runners were handicapped although, as Prévost correctly pointed out, it is not body weight that determines a runner's speed.[18] The Abbé might have had even greater cause for wonder had he observed a contest which took place fourteen years later. On May 11, 1749, an eighteen-month-old girl

was to walk the whole length of the Mall (half a mile) in 30 minutes. Considerable sums were staked upon this novel race against time, which the backers of the little one carried off, for the infantine Atalanta "walked over the course in 23 minutes, to the great admiration of thousands," say the papers.[19]

With this grotesque scene in mind, one wonders if there was an actual incident behind an episode in Fanny Burney's popular novel *Evelina* (1778). The upper-class characters stage a foot race between two female octogenarians and jeer at the feeble old women when they collide and collapse. In their efforts to escape boredom, upper-class men were accustomed to using lower-class women almost as they willed. In this instance, the sponsors of the race callously demand a new start because one hundred pounds have been wagered on the outcome. In the absence of modern soccer pools, Englishmen were ready to court Fortuna in whatever guise she might appear.

Tests of swiftness were far more common than feats of strength, but women who worked alongside their menfolk in the fields had to be physically equal to the task, and there were occasions for them to display their ability to lift, carry, or throw. The strength and courage displayed during the Civil Wars, when a few women like Anne Dymoke fought in the ranks, may have given the impression, as Antonia Fraser has remarked, "that women were 'stronger grown.' " Evidence of women competing in tests of pure strength is rare before the eighteenth century, but we catch a glimpse of such competition when *The Spectator* relates, with "polite" middle-class condescension, a rural conversation: "The young maids . . . were . . . engaged in some Diversion, and upon my asking a Farmer's Son of my own Parish what he was gazing at with so much Attention, he told me That he was seeing Betty Welch, whom I knew to be his Sweet-Heart, pitch a Bar."[20]

At the end of the century, the fishwives of Scotland tried their hands at golf. The records for Inveresk observe that the women of Musselburgh "do the work of men, their manners are masculine, and their strength and activity is equal to their work." The men of the Royal Musselburgh Golf Club took note of the women's improvised holiday games of golf and resolved

to present by Subscription a new Creel and "shull," with consolation prizes of two of the best Barcelona silk handkerchiefs, to the best female golfer who plays on the annual occasion of the next January 1 to be intimated to the Fish ladies by the officer of the Club.[21]

We do not know how the "Fish ladies" responded.

Eighteenth-century Londoners seemed more drawn to a less pastoral version of female physical prowess. References to female pugilists occur with surprising frequency. The sources, mainly newspapers and travelers' accounts, were seldom precise about the promoters of the bouts, but they were presumably men. It was unlikely that women's options included this kind of entrepreneurship. The women who fought were almost certainly extremely poor and they were probably sexually disreputable as well. They had little to lose from what seems, in many instances, to have been a ritual of degradation similar to the prostitutes' races of the Middle Ages and the Renaissance. The female boxers, however, appear to have felt pride in their prowess rather than shame at the ignoble uses to which they were put. When the German traveler Zacharias Conrad von Uffenbach visited London in 1710, he attended a boxing match and was told by a rowdy female spectator that she herself "had fought another female in this place without stays and in nothing but a shift. They had both fought stoutly and drawn blood, which was apparently no new sight in

England."[22] If it *was* a new sight, it soon became a familiar one. John Trenchard's *London Journal* for June 23, 1722, refers to a battle between "two of the Feminine Gender" who "maintained the Battle with great Valour for a long Time, to the no small Satisfaction of the Spectators." A year later, a forthcoming match was publicized with fanfare reminiscent of twentieth-century hype: "There has not been such a battle for these twenty Years past, and as these two Heroines are as brave and as bold as the ancient Amazones, the Spectators may expect abaundance of Diversion and Satisfaction, from these Female Combatants." Martin Nogüe's *Voyages et Avantures* [sic], published in 1728, reported matches between girls and grown women "stripped to the waist." James Pellor Malcolm's *Anecdotes of the Manners and Customs of London* collected numerous references to female pugilists at Hockley in the Hole (a traditional venue for combat sports) and at James Figg's famed "Amphitheatre."[23]

Women fought with blades as well as fists. César de Saussure commented in 1725 on a fencing match between an Englishwoman and an Irishwoman, probably the same combat as the one reported in *Mist's Journal* for November 20, 1725. The versifier James Bramston wrote of "Figg's new Theatre" where "cocks and bulls and Irish women fight." Female fencers, however, were not nearly as popular as the boxers. What motivated the male and female spectators is hard to say. As was the case with the smock races, it is impossible to disentangle male and female voyeurism from the desire to place a bet, to admire raw courage, or just to mingle with the crowd.[24]

The flavor of the times can be detected in the bravado of two women who publicly challenged each other in the *Daily Post* for October 7, 1728. Ann Field of Stoke Newington, an ass driver, announced herself ready to take on Elisabeth Stokes, "styled the European championess." The "championess" was more than willing to enter the ring:

I, Elisabeth Stokes, of the City of London, have not fought . . . since I fought the famous boxing woman of Billingsgate 9 minutes, and gained a complete victory, which is six years ago; but as the famous Stoke Newington ass woman dares me to fight her for 10 pounds, I do assure her I will not fail meeting her for the said sum, and doubt not that the blows which I shall present her with will be more difficult for her to digest than any she ever gave her asses.[25]

The frequency of references to Irishwomen in the prize ring cause one to wonder at William Rufus Chetwood's 1749 remark that an Italian woman was applauded in England for her acrobatic feats of strength while the Irish found her "masculinely indelicate."[26] The shocked Dubliners must have led sheltered lives. They were obviously unused to the daily struggle for existence waged by their impoverished countrywomen.

William Hickey, a Hogarthian rake fond of eighteenth-century low life, wrote memoirs that include a vivid account of a ferocious fight at Wetherby's in Drury Lane. Hickey found two women

engaged in a scratching and boxing match, their faces entirely covered with blood, bosoms bare, and the clothes nearly torn from their bodies. For several minutes not a creature interfered between them, or seemed to care a straw what mishap they might do each other, and the contest went on with unabated fury.[27]

This fight may have been simply a bar-room brawl, but the *London Times* continued to publish accounts of regular matches conducted under the same rules as men's fights. The tone of the reports changed, however, early in the nineteenth century when pugilism began to seem intolerable to middle-class sensibilities. When Betty Dyson, a vendor of sprats, met Mary Mahoney, a market woman, the *Times* (March 24, 1807) commented that the "Amazons" fought for over forty minutes and were both "hideously disfigured by hard blows." It was a sight that "afforded the most disgust."[28]

Another match, which took place in 1822, fifteen years before Victoria's ascent to the throne, signaled a sea-change in British manners. It pitted Martha Flaharty against Peg Carey. As was often the case, the promoters of the bout counted on English-Irish antagonisms to increase the crowd's excitement. The social class of the two participants was obvious: they fought for a prize of nearly eighteen pounds; they began at 5:30 A.M., before the fighters and the spectators had to be at work; and Flaharty consumed half a pint of gin before she stepped into the ring. Perhaps the gin deadened the pain of the blows she received. She won despite severe injuries.[29]

The sight of female pugilists, stripped or not, surprised French visitors. A seventeenth-century Breton ballad relates the story of a peasant girl who challenged a young nobleman to a wrestling match and defeated him (and won his heart), but the great urban fairs of eighteenth-century Paris seem never to have featured the female combatants who were such a striking part of London life. Although the singers, dancers, pantomimists, acrobats, and mountebanks of Saint-

Germain, Saint-Laurent, and Saint-Ovide provided plenty of *spectacles,* the closest thing to women's sports was apparently a 1754 exhibition of strength by *"les femmes fortes,"* who supported great weights on their stomachs while stretched supine with their heads on one chair and their feet on another.[30]

While lower-class London women battered each other in the ring, their rural counterparts managed to find a less violent way to amuse themselves and their spectators. Instead of reports of pugilism, which, of course, might have occurred unreported, we come upon poetic references to stoolball and pastoral accounts of cricket. The former game was "more properly appropriated to the women than to the men, but occasionally it was played by young persons of both sexes indiscriminately."[31] One bit of evidence for this assertion by the antiquarian Joseph Strutt is the tetrameter couplets of "Stool-Ball, or The Easter Diversion," an anonymous poem from the late seventeenth or early eighteenth century. The poem narrates a match between the youths and the maids:

> Set at the goal Pulcheria stand
> And grasp the board with snowy hand!
> She drives the ball with artful force
> Guiding through hostile ranks its course.
>
> Where does the shame or crime appear
> Of harmless romping once a year?[32]

Stoolball, however, was on the decline; cricket was on the rise. By the end of the eighteenth century, cricket had become the English gentleman's favorite ballgame, and it was surprisingly popular among the women. The first female players were as socially humble as they were athletically bold. The earliest recorded game seems to have been played on July 26, 1745. It was, according to the *Reading Mercury,* the "greatest cricket-match that ever was played in the South part of England." On Gosden Common, near Guilford in Surrey, eleven maids of Bramley met a team from Hambleton

dressed all in white. The Bramley maids had blue ribbons and the Hambl]sic] maids red ribbons on their heads. The Bramley girls got 119 notches and the Hambleton girls 127. There was of bothe sexes the greatest number that ever was seen on such an occasion. The girls bowled, batted, ran and catched as well as most men could do in that game.[33]

Only two years later, the *London General Advertiser* (July 14) referred to a kind of tournament at the Artillery Ground, Finnsbury, to which women's teams from several Sussex villages were invited.[34] While the teams in this instance represented their villages, an older division between the maids and the married women was also common, as can be seen in a notice from 1765:

A few days since, a cricket match was played at Upham, Hants, by eleven married against eleven maiden women, for a large plum-cake, a barrel of ale and regale of tea, which was won by the latter.[35]

Sometimes, both kinds of representation were involved. The *Times* (June 20, 1793) reported:

A match of cricket was played last week on Bury Common . . . by females, the married women against the maidens; it was won by the married women, who had 80 notches more than the nymphs. So famous are the Bury women at this game, that they have challenged all England.[36]

The rhetorical difference between the reports of female pugilism in the metropolis and women's cricket in the countryside is enormous. The reports of the latter are obviously a version of pastoral that escaped the eye of William Empson.

A very curious match of cricket was played [in 1792] by eleven girls of Rotherby, Leics., against an equal number of Hoby, on Thursday on the feast week. The inhabitants of all the villages adjacent were eager spectators of this novel and interesting contest; when after a display of astonishing skill and activity, the palm of victory was obtained by the fair maids of Rotherby.

The spectators, said *Sporting Magazine,* were "the honest rustics of the first-named village." Victory was "a matter of exultation."

The bowlers of the conquering party were immediately placed in a sort of triumphant car, preceded by music and flying streamers and thus conducted home by the youth of Rotherby, amidst the acclamations of a numerous group of pleased spectators.

This kind of idyll was eventually captured in the pages of Mary Russell Mitford's novel, *Our Village* (1824–1832), which includes a charming account of a rural cricket match. The blowzier side of the women's game appears in Thomas Rowlandson's lively etching, *Rural Sports: A Cricket Match* (1811–12).[37]

The pastoral associations of the game did not always overshadow the incipient modernizaton of the sport. In every sport in which points are scored, at least some quantification is necessary and the potential for the conscious pursuit of a sports record is present. It may be that the potential was realized in eighteenth-century women's cricket. The first recorded "century" (one hundred runs in a single match) was scored by a certain Miss S. Norcross on July 11, 1788.[38] What we do *not* know, however, is whether or not her teammates on the Maids of Surrey understood the significance of the achievement, thought about it in relation to their own scores, and determined to better it. If they did, then the Maids of Surrey helped to give birth to the modern concept of the sports record.

3. The Sports of the Middle and Upper Classes

"In contrast to the numerous accounts of working-class women playing cricket," writes Shirley Heather Reekie, "it seems that relatively few games of cricket were played (or at least reported) among upper-class ladies."[39] For the entire eighteenth century, only one game is known. We should not be surprised. Although our perception of cricket is that the leisurely game is the chosen sport of the English upper classes, played at country estates, at Eton and Harrow, at Oxford and Cambridge, cricket actually evolved from folk games and did not become identified with the English elite until the late eighteenth century. When the gentry and nobility finally discovered the pleasures of cricket on a summer day, a few of their wives joined the fun. The first cricket match known to have been played by aristocratic women occurred in 1777 when the Countess of Derby and a bevy of other women of wealth set up their wickets at the Oaks, a private estate in Surrey. A famous drawing by the Duke of Dorset, who was one of the spectators, appeared two years later (and is now the property of the Marylebone Cricket Club). At this match, the Duke of Hamilton fell in love with the top scorer, Elizabeth Burrell, and successfully courted her. This was obviously a newsworthy event. The *Morning Post* for January 22, 1778, reported that the Duke "fell in love with Miss Burrell at the cricket match at the Oaks last year." The writer, at this point, began to mix romance and statistics: Miss Burrell "took bat in hand" and "her Diana-like air communicated an irresistible impression." She got more notches in the first and second innings than any lady in the game. The Duke was so charmed by his beloved's physical activity that he urged other women to turn to cricket. He sounds, in fact, almost like an early feminist: "Let your sex go on and assert their right to every pursuit that does not debase the mind. Go on, and attach yourselves to the athletic."[40]

One form of "the athletic" which attracted aristocratic women was archery, a sport "peculiarly adapted to the gracefulness of the female form," and one with properly classical associations.[41] The fact that yeomen no longer went to war with longbows in their hands liberated archery from immediate martial (and lower-class) associations. At the same time, archery contests of the early modern period had an aristocratic sheen heightened rather than dimmed by memories of English bowmen at Crécy, Poitiers, and Agincourt. Robin Hood's exploits also lay far enough in the past for upper-class archers to identify with the legendary outlaw. The lords and ladies paid homage to him when they dressed in Sherwood green.

The Toxophilite Society (1781) was simply a group of upper-class men and women in love with bows (Greek = *toxon*) and arrows (Greek = *toxa*). The Royal British Bowmen admitted women to *their* society in 1787. On October 17, 1788, they awarded their first prize to Miss Harriet Boycott.[42] Archery's aristocratic ambiance can be glimpsed in a lovely 1794 aquatint by Robert Smirke and John Emes. *A Meeting of the Society of Royal British Archers in Gwersyllt Park, Denbighshire* shows the ladies shooting while the gentlemen gallantly assist and admire. The feathery leaves of the stylized trees add to the pastoral charm.[43] The daughters of the rising manufacturing class eventually joined their sisters from the ranks of the gentry. The granddaughter of pottery manufacturer Josiah Wedgwood wrote of *her* daughter that she "went with us to the Archery and was much admired; and what is more, she got the first prize, a beautiful pair of earrings."[44] Although Donald Walker's *Exercises for Ladies* (1836) condemned archery for women because it caused an asymmetrical physical development, he had apparently changed his mind by the time he published *Games and Sports* in 1837. Archery for women was now among his recommendations.

How serious were these female archers? The women who participated in the extravagantly anachronistic "medieval" dress-up tournament at Eglinton in 1839 were said to be "a society probably more elegant in costume than proficient in archery." This comment may have been fair—or it may have been one of those perennial male disparagements of women's accomplishments. *Some* women must have been fairly serious about the sport. Five years later, at the second Grand National Archery Meeting, eleven women, shooting at targets sixty yards away, vied for the national championship.[45]

Archery contests were also popular in the smaller courts of central Europe. In 1721, for instance, at the summer palace of Ludwigshafen near Stuttgart, the son and daughter-in-law of Duke Eberhard Ludwig of Württemberg joined him in a splendid match designed to reflect glory on the ruling house.[46]

Archery attracted many well-to-do Englishwomen, but the most popular recreation for upper-class women remained what it had been for centuries—field sports. The Restoration of the Stuarts in 1660 led to a restatement of the game laws. An act of 1671, which remained in force for the next century and a half, limited the chase for game to those with freeholds of one hundred pounds a year or leaseholds of one hundred fifty pounds. Farmers were not even permitted to shoot the crows that devastated their crops. "Field sports . . . were more than a recreation. They were a symbol to English country gentlemen of the virtues of their class."[47] Participation in field sports was unquestionably a pastime in which social class mattered more than gender. Fox hunting and other vigorous out-of-doors activities were what allegedly set hearty British lords and rosy-cheeked British ladies apart from effeminate French aristocrats who dwelled in Paris and knew not the thrill of hound and horn.[48] While some women rode with the pack to see the hounds dismember the fox, others, like those who appear in John Collet's 1780 mezzotint, *Ladies Shooting Poney,* dispatched their quarry with firearms. (See Plate 8.)

Roger Longrigg probably exaggerates when he writes that Miss Ann Richards, a determined spinster, was "a rare 18th-century example of the sporting female squire." Her stamina was certainly extraordinary. Accompanied by her greyhounds, she coursed for hares on the Berkshire downs and was said to have walked as far as twenty-five miles a day.[49] But her choice of avocation and her passion for it were by no means unusual. It was actually quite common for an upper-class English girl to learn to ride and to join the men as they galloped across the moors, cleared ditches, and sailed over fences. John Wootton's fine picture, *Lady Henrietta Harley Hunting with Harriers* (ca. 1740) depicts Lady Henrietta galloping in the company of a party of male hunters and grooms. There was good reason to expect her to have been a skilled horsewoman. Her father, the Duke of

Newcastle, had been Charles II's Tutor to Horsemanship.[50] Woot-ton's picture was unusual only in its quality. The mounted huntress was, in fact, a popular theme for English painters throughout this period. While most of Diana's avid disciples hunted in the company of men, who usually stepped into the leading role, one extraordinary woman, the Marchioness of Salisbury, actually became the "Master" of the Hatfield Hunt in Hertfordshire in 1793. Her ardor impressed a contributor to *The Sporting Magazine:*

if she was not the founder of the Hatfield Hunt, she presided for a long series of years over the destinies of that Pack . . . ; and this she continued up to her 70th year; when, with a spirit unsubdued by advanced life, she was heard to say, if she could not hunt a pack of fox-hounds, she was still able to follow the harriers. Her Ladyship's ardour in the chase was excessive; and a friend who sits at our elbow assures us that he was a constant attendant of the Hunt for eighteen successive years, during which she was seldom absent a day from the covert side. She was an elegant and accomplished horse woman, and rode with as much intrepidity as judgment: no day was too long for her, and she was ever anxious to give good sport to the field.[51]

She remained in the saddle until she gave up the sport at the age of seventy-eight.[52] (See Plate 9.)

The redoubtable marchioness was a woman of impeccable charac-ter. Her younger contemporary, Laetitia Lade, whom George Stubbs painted sidesaddle on a splendid horse, was made from a different mould. She had been the mistress of a highwayman who ended on the scaffold before she married the "equally notorious Sir John Lade, who . . . picked her up in a brothel."[53] From their elegant portrait, one would never guess that either Laetitia or John had had a shady past.

Some women responded to the impulse to test themselves and their horses in a race. This seems to have been especially true in the American colonies, where necessity placed many women in the sad-dle, and the less restrictive customs of the frontier allowed a broader definition of women's roles. The French traveler Ferdinand Bayard noted in 1791 that the women of the Virginia backcountry were accustomed from childhood to travel on horseback. Since they "de-scended steep mountains, crossed rivers, and were exposed at the tenderest age to the mettle of very swift horses," they became "skill-ful and intrepid" riders who often challenged one another to races. Like his fellow countrymen who were astonished to see London's female pugilists batter one another, Bayard was clearly taken aback by what he saw. His assumptions about appropriate gender roles were revealed in his puzzled comments. How was it that these young women who raced their steeds and "seemed made more for the fatigues of Diana than the games of Cupid" were nonetheless obedient "to the laws of this master of gods and of men"? Bayard was clearly intrigued that a hard rider might yet be a soft mistress.[54]

A few English women were as bold as their colonial cousins and as ready to race their mounts. Colonel Thomas Thornton of Falconer's Hall in Yorkshire had a beautiful twenty-two-year-old wife, Alicia, who won an impromptu race against her sister's husband, Captain William Flint. Injured pride impelled the defeated military man to challenge his sister-in-law to a more formal race. The stake was a thousand guineas. A huge crowd gathered to see the contest on August 25, 1804, but the drama turned farcical when Alicia's horse broke down and the captain cantered across the finish line. Alicia's husband refused to pay the thousand guineas, which led to some nasty verbal exchanges in the *York Herald*. Captain Flint, feeling his honor impugned, horsewhipped Colonel Thornton and was sent to prison for assault. A year later, the unchastened Alicia challenged Francis Buckle, a professional jockey, a five-time Derby winner, to a two-mile race for 700 guineas and a gold cup. The race was run at the York racecourse, where the amazing Alicia, riding sidesaddle, won by half a neck. She was the toast of the town until it was discovered that Alicia was actually nobody's wife. She was the unmarried daughter of a Norwich clockmaker. Society's reaction was predictable. Her reputation suffered; her lover's did not.[55]

A few equestrian women rode in time trials and thus contributed even more than Alicia did to the rise of modern sports. *The Idler* for May 20, 1758, reported a woman's attempt at what appears to have been a sports record. She attempted to ride a thousand miles on the Newmarket track within as many hours, a feat of endurance that seems hardly to have tested her ability because she finished in twenty-eight days, about two-thirds of the time allotted her.[56]

This was an unusual event. On the whole women's sports were much less likely than men's to become rationalized and take on the other formal-structural characteristics of modernity. This can be explained in part by the fact that women of all classes (but especially of the middle class) were less likely to be involved in any kind of sports. When women *did* participate, it was more often than not in traditional sports. In the decades that saw the development of a fairly high level of quantification in foot races for men, women continued to compete in untimed smock races. Was it because women were felt to be closer to "nature" and thus less appropriately involved in the new systematic approach to athletic achievement? Given the present stage of research into women's sports, one can only speculate.

SEVEN

The Victorian Age: Debility and Strength

1. Debility

In Nathaniel Hawthorne's *Blithedale Romance* (1852), the hero, a rather effeminate poet named Miles Coverdale, falls in love with the frail Priscilla rather than the robust Zenobia. Priscilla's diaphanous veils attract him erotically as her voluptuous sister's "garb of Eden" does not. Is it significant that Coverdale's heart is won when Priscilla, tempted in an exuberant moment to run, stumbles and sprawls weakly on the grass? Can we take this scene as an indication that Hawthorne and his contemporaries idealized female weakness and debility? Was there, as Stephanie Twin has recently asserted, a mid-nineteenth-century "cult of ill health in which women proved their femininity with invalidism"?[1]

It is certainly true that the nineteenth century was dominated aesthetically by Romanticism and that one important strain of Romanticism idealized debility as a form of symbolic protest against the vulgar health of bourgeois society. European and American artists did produce "images of women in stages of abject physical degeneration." A number of writers did exhibit a penchant for pale, sickly, lovelorn maidens. The wraith-like damsels of pre-Raphaelite art were not, however, more typical of their era than the sturdy peasant women painted by Jean-François Millet or the rubicund nudes of Auguste Renoir. Not all the women of Victorian literature were as delicate as Hawthorne's Priscilla or the ethereal heroine of Coventry Patmore's saccharine poem, *The Angel in the House* (1854). Physically powerful heroines were created not only by Hawthorne, whose regal Zenobia should not be forgotten, but also by writers as different as J. K. Huysmans and Edward L. Wheeler, authors, respectively, of the symbolist masterpiece *A Rebours* (1884) and the dime-novel thriller *Bob Woolf, the Border Ruffian; or, The Girl Dead-Shot* (1878). In the first book, Miss Urania, a muscular acrobat, physically dominates the hypersensitive sissy. In the second book, Hurricane Nell is shown to be athletically superior to the men of her frontier town.

When the hero, a handsome Philadelphia lawyer, hires her as a guide, she lassoes a mustang for him and rescues him from the Indians in a scene that reverses a vast tradition. As the hero's horse tires, Hurricane Nell seizes the man about the waist, raises him high overhead "by the power of her wonderful arms," and deposits him on the back of the wild stallion.

Another reversal of convention occurs when the gun-shy hero bets a thousand dollars that the crack-shot heroine will win a rifle match. She does.[2]

At a rather more exalted level, Hawthorne's contemporary Walt Whitman sang "the body electric" and wrote lyrically about robustly athletic women. In "A Woman Waits for Me," he was positively ecstatic about them:

> They are not one jot less than I am,
> They are tann'd in the face by shining suns and blowing winds,
> Their flesh has the old divine suppleness and strength,
> They know how to swim, row, ride, wrestle, shoot, run, strike,
>   retreat, advance, resist, defend themselves,
> They are ultimate in their own right—they are calm, clear, well-
>   possess'd of themselves.

If there was a "cult of invalidism" in Whitman's America, he was not a part of it.

Whitman's "barbaric yawp" was nearly devoid of classical allusions, but Atalanta made a strong appearance in nineteenth-century English poetry. She figures in Algernon Charles Swinburne's *Atalanta in Calydon* (1860), Walter Savage Landor's "Hippomenes and Atalanta" (1863), and William Morris's "Atalanta's Race" (1870).[3] Clearly, not all British writers were mesmerized by the vision of feminine frailty that attracted Coventry Patmore and some of the pre-Raphaelite painters. Alluding to Homer's rather than to Ovid's classic example of a physically active girl, Charles Kingsley's "Nausicaa in

London" (1873) extended the campaign for "muscular Christianity" to include sports for women.[4]

The classically educated sportsmen of Moses Coit Tyler's novel, *The Brawnville Papers* (1869), are also admirers of athletic women. Judge Fairplay contrasts delicate American ladies to the rugged women of ancient Sparta and he wishes in his homespun way that the former were more like the latter. "in justice to my fair countrywomen, I must declare, that if they were as strong as they are beautiful, if they were as vigorous as they are lovely, why—I don't know what would happen!" The judge, clearly excited by the indeterminate prospect, goes on to recommend that the town of Brawnville construct a gymnasium "to give us a race of pretty girls!"[5]

Always mindful that he was an *educated* adventurer, Clarence King also tapped the springs of classical antiquity in *Mountaineering in the Sierra Nevada* (1872) when he described a teen-age girl he met during one of his many geological excursions through the wilderness. She was the strapping daughter of an itinerant ne'er-do-well hog-raiser.

In the region of six feet, tall, square-shouldered, of firm iron back and heavy mould of limb, she yet possessed the suppleness which enabled her as she rose to throw herself into nearly all the attitudes of the Niobe children. . . . I could not fail to admire the magnificent turn of her shoulders and the powerful, queenly poise of her head. Her full, grand form and heavy strength reminded me of the statues of Ceres.

Nonetheless, King was made uneasy by a "fighting trim" that suggested some of the swagger of the prize ring. Eros, beguiled a moment, vanished quickly when the girl's father sought to tempt the young geologist to holy matrimony: "Thet—thet—thet man what gits Susan *has half the hogs!*" King did not rise to the bait, but his qualified admiration of this particular embodiment of female strength was probably closer to the typical nineteenth-century response than the extreme timidity of Hawthorne's Coverdale or the extreme exultation of Whitman's poetic persona.[6]

Relying on medical history rather than on aesthetic expression, G. J. Barker-Benfield and a number of other historians have suggested that nineteenth-century doctors, European and American, sought to control women's bodies in order to consolidate the power of patriarchal society. John S. and Robin M. Haller admitted in *The Physician and Sexuality in Victorian America* (1974) that chronic illness served as an alibi for the woman who hoped to excuse "her lack of achievement." Nonetheless, their harshest words are for the medical profession: "Concealing their punitive moralism in the guise of medical prognosis, doctors maintained the facade of the disinterested professional when faced with the open discontent of the woman seeking to fulfill her potentialities as a human being."[7] This interpretation of medical motives has become the conventional wisdom of revisionists. "It is clear," writes Helen Lenskyj, "that doctors' interests were served by women's alienation from their bodies."[8] In an extreme version of this accusation, Barbara Ehrenreich and Deirdre English insinuate a kind of metaphoric rape: "The medical profession threw itself with gusto on the languid figure of the female invalid."[9] In reply to the charge that women's health suffered at the hands of the male-dominated medical profession, Edward Shorter has argued in his *History of Women's Bodies* (1982) that the nineteenth century brought dramatic improvements in women's health, which had been wretchedly poor, and that these improvements were directly attributable to two related factors: advances in medical research and the nineteenth-century husband's heightened concern for his wife's welfare.

Shorter's views have been widely ignored. Discussing nineteenth-century British women, Jennifer Hargreaves has given a Marxist accent to the argument about women's health. She has alleged that "middle-class women with affluent husbands made ideal patients who, in addition, supported the economic status of doctors."[10] While it is true that many doctors were well paid for their services, the plausibility of this economic interpretation is diminished when its adherents apply it to explain radically dissimilar behaviors. It is difficult to believe that the physicians' economic interests dictated female invalidism in the middle years of the nineteenth century and female physical activity in the eighties and nineties. Yet this is exactly what Patricia Vertinsky has maintained. She asserts that "medical explanations initially supported the idea that women were naturally small, frail and weak until physicians found it expedient . . . to join forces with moral physiologists and support female physical education and other health reforms which fortified the female frame." The new stance was motivated by the desire to "generate good business" and to "counteract female independence and the weakness they believed was caused by too much brainwork." Orthodox physicians now worked "to renovate the female body and fortify a lady's will to be a good mother."[11] Vertinsky's subtle interpretation I find difficult to accept because it is too readily applicable to *whatever* the medical profession did.

More plausible than the theory that doctors changed their opinions because they were profit-maximizers and agents of social control is the likelihood that most Victorian medical professionals shared their culture's preference for "refined" women. "Refinement," like the "conspicuous leisure" satirized later in the century by Thorstein Veblen, was what distinguished middle-class ladies from "coarser" women, but *invalidism* was never a widespread ideal. When the results of fashionable inactivity persuaded Victorian doctors that the languid life was positively unhealthy, they responded quickly to the evidence of induced debility by advocating some kind of moderate exercise. There is no reason whatsoever to assume that this advice was less sincere or less popular than Dr. S. Weir Mitchell's notorious "rest cure" (which undoubtedly *did*, by its sensory and intellectual deprivations, sometimes produce the physical and psychic disaster described in Charlotte Perkins Gilman's classic story, "The Yellow Wallpaper"). In fairness, it ought to be acknowledged that even Mitchell altered his views on exercise and inactivity. "When I see young girls sweating from a good row or the tennis field," he wrote in 1887, "I know that it is preventive medicine."[12]

Did middle-class husbands caution against a good row or an afternoon on "the tennis field"? Did they prefer debility to strength? Were they so insecure in their masculine roles that they petitioned the medical profession to give them the additional props of sickly wives and daughters? These are, in fact, among the charges in the indictment. Barbara J. Berg asserts that the "flower-like creatures who languished through the pages of antebellum literature enhanced the male self-image; weakness in women bolstered men's feelings of strength."[13] Elizabeth Fox-Genovese takes the same tack when she comments that the Southern planter's "emphasis on female delicacy and frailty implicitly recognized the positive value of male strength." It is impossible to prove or to disprove such assertions about conscious and unconscious motivation. Since, however, healthy men are, on the average, stronger than healthy women, husbands hardly needed debilitated wives in order to indulge themselves in feelings of physical superiority.[14] Deborah Gorham has probably given the most reasonable response to the theory that Victorian men prized female weakness.: "Those who gave advice to the middle classes . . . were aware that . . . middle-class girls would grow up with tasks too difficult and too essential to permit chronic invalidism."[15] Eve healthy was a better helpmate than Eve bed-ridden with a nervous breakdown.

In their concern for women's health, Victorian men were supported by women's-rights advocates like Amelia Bloomer (for whom "bloomers" were named). *The Lily,* which she edited, urged women to greater physical activity, and Bloomer tried valiantly to popularize a new form of dress designed to make such activity easier. In *Harper's Monthly* for October 1850, the English reformer Harriet Martineau asserted that girls should climb trees, walk briskly, run, leap, row, and swim. Similar advice appeared in reformist publications like the *English Woman's Journal,* founded in 1858 by Bessie Raynor Parkes. Magazines aimed at a more conventionally middle-class audience, like *The American Farmer* and *Godey's Ladies' Magazine,* expressed the same sentiments. In "The Ladies Department," the first periodical encouraged women to remove the tight corsets that constricted their lungs and to travel by horseback rather than by coach and carriage. An unsigned article of November 9, 1827, proclaimed that "no absurdity is greater than that which associates female beauty with great delicacy of body and debility of constitution. . . ." At mid-century, *Godey's* advised its readers not only to dance, at a time when most religious fundamentalists considered dances un-Christian, but also to swim in the summer and skate in the winter.[16]

The campaign to improve women's health did not, however, mean that middle-class women were encouraged to do sports. In Britain, the most influential of the early nineteenth-century books on female physical education was Donald Walker's *Exercises for Ladies* (1836), which advised movement but warned emphatically against overexertion. Kathleen E. McCrone's wry account of Walker's phobia deserves quotation:

Owing to the "excessive shocks" running and leaping communicated, and the "one-sidedness" produced by archery, these Walker discouraged, while horseback riding in particular he considered anathema because it coarsened the voice and complexion, twisted the body, bestowed a masculine air and "produced an un-natural consolidation of the bones of the lower part of the body, ensuring a frightful impediment of future function, which need not be dwelt on."[17]

The fears about the delicately unspecified "future function" were not fully allayed for another century.

Americans confronted the same dilemma: how were women to become more physically active without the negative consequences, mostly imaginary, of strenuous physical activity? For many middle-class women, Catharine Beecher seemed to have the answer. As early as 1832 she offered her readers *A Course of Calisthenics for Young Ladies.* She responded sympathetically to the miseries of sedentary married women and warned in her very popular *Treatise on Domestic Economy* (1841) that lack of exercise produced "softness, debility, and unfitness." To remedy the situation, she advised in her *Letters to the People on Health and Happiness* (1855) that "every man, woman, and child . . . ought to spend one or two hours every day in *vigorous* exercise of *all* the *muscles.*" Her concerns were hygienic rather than athletic. She thought that housework was the best form of exercise. For women with servants, calisthenics were her recommended substitute for the mop and the wash tub. By no stretch of the imagination can she be said to have been an enthusiast for women's sports.[18]

Lydia Sigourney was slightly bolder in an 1838 essay published in the *Southern Literary Messenger,* and Lydia Maria Child was positively daring in an appeal for girls' sports that she included in *The Little Girls' Own Book* (1847):

Walking and other out-of-door exercises cannot be too much recommended to young people. Even skating, driving hoop and other boyish sports may be practised to great advantage by little girls provided they can be pursued within the enclosure of a garden or court; in the street, of course, they would be highly improper. It is true, such games are rather violent, and sometimes noisy, but they tend to form a vigorous constitution; and girls who are habitually lady-like, will never allow themselves to be rude and vulgar, even in play.

Her views, slightly more advanced than Beecher's and Sigourney's, were nonetheless a not unusual mix of brave determination and prudish caution.[19] A more radical approach to physical education was adopted, with little fanfare, by the abolitionists Theodore Weld, Angelina Grimké Weld, and Sarah Grimké at their Eagleswood School at the Raritan Bay Union, an offshoot of the North American Phalanx at Red Bank, New Jersey. At the school, which opened in 1853, Emerson and other Transcendentalists occasionally lectured. An admiring war time visitor observed that "young women were found educating their limbs in the gymnasium, rowing in boats, and making 'records' in swimming and high diving."[20] Needless to say, the school was unusual if not unique. At a time when most proponents of physical education for females still hesitated to encourage sports, the Eagleswood girls competed and set records.

In Germany, where physical education for girls had been widely instituted decades before most British and American schools were ready for such an innovation, there was the same hesitation about the move from exercise and hygiene to sports. In 1829, Phokian Clias published *Kalisthenie*, the source of our modern term "calisthenics" (from the Greek for "beauty" and "strength"). Although Clias favored moderate exercise, he rejected ballgames because they were thought to require the excessive use of a girl's shoulder and breast muscles. Ironically, at the very time that Clias was working on his book, the greatest of German writers, Johann Wolfgang von Goethe, recorded in his notebooks the appearance in Weimar of Rosa Baglioni, an Italian fencer whose shoulder, breast, and arm muscles held up very well as she outfought a number of students on the stage of Weimar's court theater.[21]

Germany's pedagogues were less open to unconventional views than the aged poet, but, in 1834, Johann Adolf Ludwig Werner took a hesitant step and allowed, in *Gymnastik für die weibliche Jugend,* for nearly the full range of gymnastic activities then known—in the coinage of Friedrich Ludwig Jahn—as *Turnen.* Werner's pupils ran, jumped, threw, swam, balanced on wooden beams and clambered up poles. A gymnastics club for girls was opened in Magdeburg in 1843; four years later a club for grown women was formed in Mannheim.[22]

Competition, however, was discouraged because it was "unwomanly" and because it led to overexertion which led to total physical collapse. On the crucial question of overexertion, a congress of pediatricians, meeting in Berlin in 1880, was as conservative as the educators of the previous generation: "After the age of ten," they concluded, "girls should no longer do gymnastic exercises with equipment [such as the horizontal bar and the balance beam] because they are scarcely decent and are often injurious." As late as 1908, German schoolgirls were cautioned by some of their teachers not to run for more than five minutes, not to sprint, not to throw, not to jump higher than 50 centimeters. "Distance and height are not the point," they counseled, "but a steady and attractive performance."[23] French educators may have disagreed with their Teutonic rivals on most scores, but not on this question. When, in 1882, the official governmental rules for girls' physical education called for three 30–minute sessions a week, the apprehensive instructions to the teachers "made it clear that it was absolutely necessary to avoid fatigue."[24]

The clear supposition behind the attempts to restrict young women to gentle exercise and graceful motion was that vigorous sports are essentially masculine. Young boys were strongly encouraged to run, jump, throw, climb, and wrestle, but tomboys were merely tolerated. With the onset of puberty, boys were expected to display physical prowess as a symbol of virility and dominance; girls were expected to do just enough calisthenics to remain healthy while they developed the domestic skills and the feminine wiles needed to attract potential husbands. On both sides of the Atlantic, the Cult of Domesticity and the Doctrine of Separate Spheres confined middle-class women to the home and garden.

One might imagine that the pervasive Darwinism of the late nineteenth century influenced educational theory, and it did. The Darwinist slogan, "survival of the fittest," implied that competition was an essential part of human life. Sports for boys and men were, therefore, an ideal preparation for life's grimmer struggles. The logic of Social Darwinism, however, exempted the female of the species from the battle for survival. Luther Gulick, an influential leader in American physical education, was convinced that human nature is the product of evolutionary development and that primitive man was "a hunter and a fighter." Primitive woman was not.

> Boyhood and manhood have . . . for ages long been both tested and produced by athletic sports. . . . The case is very different for women. They were not predominantly the hunters or fighters. They cared for the home.[25]

For them, exercise is necessary but not "serious, public competition." Nurture is not a contest. The Boy Scouts earned Gulick's approbation; he saw no need for modern girls to master woodcraft. Juliette Low disagreed. She founded the Girl Scouts of America in 1912, put them in vaguely military uniforms, and set them to doing calisthenics, hiking through the woods, and playing basketball. Such direct emulation of the Boy Scouts was too much for Gulick, who swiftly countered by organizing the Camp Fire Girls, whom he dressed like demure Indian maidens and encouraged to sing songs around a suitably domestic campfire.[26]

In the application of Darwinism to physical education, British opinion was like American. In *C. B. Fry's Magazine,* an "Oxford

Blue" expressed the common conviction that the evolutionary process steered men towards sports.

Man has been, is, and will be easily first in athletic sports and games because in the first place he has a natural instinct for them, which is the primitive combative instinct of the warrior and the hunter watered down to suit modern civilization; in the second place, he has the physical formation which is in every respect perfectly adapted for such pursuits, and was meant by nature to be so; and in the third place, he has the right temperamental qualities. . . . Women fail in all three particulars.[27]

In Great Britain as in the United States, there was agreement. The virtues of strenuous athletic competition were increasingly extolled as a means to prepare the male animal for the breadwinner's struggle, but the female animal was destined to comfort and to nurture. While clouting a baseball and dribbling a soccer ball were thought to be a useful preparation for careers in industry and commerce, middle-class women were excluded from these branches of endeavor, and few mid-Victorian moralists imagined a connection between ballgames and childcare. Not until the end of the century did Darwinists—at least some of them—begin to advocate the Spartan eugenic ideal of physically trained and athletic womanhood.

Arguments against women's participation in sports were based on aesthetic ideals as well as on conceptions of woman's "natural" role as supportive wife and nurturant mother. Hugo Rothstein, advocating the Swedish rather than the German system of gymnastics, agreed with his rivals, in 1853, that "an amazon-like education runs diametrically opposite to the true concept of female worth and grace."[28] Moritz Kloss, who represented the mainstream of *Turnen* (with the apparatus that the Swedish system had dispensed with), seconded Rothstein on this point. In *Die weibliche Turnkunst* (1855), Kloss continued to preach the gospel of calisthenic drill and insisted that his exercises were appropriate because they emphasized "the aesthetic element; girls in general desire to appear delicate and graceful." Physical education, argued Kloss, should not sacrifice "tender femininity" for the sake of "Spartan toughness."[29]

In a curious way, the aesthetic ideals espoused by European and American writers on women's physical education were quite Darwinistic, in that a woman's beauty was considered to be an important weapon in her struggle for survival, i.e., the capture of a husband. Calisthenics enhanced a girl's attractiveness and improved her prospects. Sports, however, were thought by many to spoil a girl's looks, to diminish her charm, and thus to hamper her in the all-important race to matrimony.

Numerous Victorians—British, American, and European—feared that the athletic girl who beat the odds and caught a husband was liable to have damaged her reproductive organs and thus to have been rendered permanently infertile. Although Arabella Kenealy held a medical degree and might have been expected to challenge the old wives' tales that passed as conventional wisdom, she mounted one of the most intemperate attacks against women's sports. Her 1899 essay on "Woman as an Athlete," published in both *Living Age* and *Nineteenth Century,* described the foolish athleticism of a young woman named Clara. Once unable to walk two miles without fatigue, Clara now plays tennis and field hockey and tours the countryside on her bicycle. While a hasty judgment of Clara's achievements might be positive, Kenealy begs her readers to ponder the fact that Clara has lost her gentleness, warmth, and sparkle.

In her evening gown she shows evidence of joints which had been adroitly hidden beneath tissues of soft flesh, and already her modiste has been put to the necessity of puffings and pleatings where Nature had planned the tenderest and most dainty of devices. Her movements are muscular and less womanly. . . . Her voice is louder, her tones are assertive.

Behind Kenealy's critique lay the mechanical theory of fixed force. Clara is wasting her portion of energy on pulmonary and muscular development and jeopardizing her brain and her reproductive organs. Nature groaned at the sight of athletic women because "Nature knows . . . it is the birthright of the babies Clara and her sister athletes are squandering." The rider of bicycles and swinger of tennis rackets also risks madness and an early grave. "Athletes die proverbially young. Lunatics and other diseased persons frequently exhibit muscular strength which seems almost superhuman."[30]

Kenealy herself showed almost superhuman perseverance as she continued, for another twenty years, her unbalanced diatribes against athletic women whose infatuation with sports doomed them to "abnormal sex transformation," i.e., the "obliteration of the secondary sex-characteristics." Convinced that muscular arms and legs sapped the strength of the internal organs, she warned that obstetricians required forceps to deliver the babies of athletic women. Of a "well-known" women's college she wrote despairingly, in 1920,

Here are seen, absorbed in fierce contests during the exhausting heat of
summer afternoons, grim-visaged maidens of sinewy build, hard and tough
and set as working women in the forties; some with brawny throats, square
shoulders and stern loins that would do credit to a prize ring.

The progress of the race was threatened more by sports than by "too
close an application to intellectual pursuits."[31]

   Neither the sneer at working women nor the hint of anti-intellec-
tualism was unprecedented among those who decried women's sports,
but Kenealy was a quotable fanatic whose views should not be cited,
as they sometimes are, to prove that all middle-class opinion was
utterly benighted. Professor Dudley A. Sargent, director of Harvard's
Hemenway Gymnasium, a prestigious physical educator with a national reputation, was a more representative—as well as a more
enlightened—spokesman. Sargent was convinced that not only calisthenics but also sports were physically and psychologically beneficial
for both sexes, and he discounted the common fear that all sports
masculinized. Progressive as he was, he nonetheless had qualms about
strenuous competition for the allegedly weaker sex. He deprecated
female boxers, wrestlers, and ballplayers.[32]

2. Strength

   Historians differ over the degree to which feminine debility was
admired by the Victorian bourgeoisie in its heyday. There is agreement that physical frailty has never been much prized by the men and
women of the lower classes. In England and America, Irish girls
worked hard as domestics and as factory hands. Black women, slave
and free alike, performed heavy agricultural tasks of the sort that
European peasant women had done for centuries. No one proclaimed
this fact more eloquently than the eloquently named ex-slave Sojourner Truth. At a woman's rights convention in 1851, she responded to
a clerical speaker who thought women too weak and helpless to make
their way to the ballot box:

The man over there says women need to be helped into carriages and lifted
over ditches, and to have the best place everywhere. Nobody ever helps me
into carriages or over puddles, or gives me the best place—and ain't I a
woman? Look at my arm! I have ploughed and planted and gathered into
barns, and no man could head me—and ain't I a woman? I could work as

much and eat as much as a man—when I could get it—and bear the lash as well! And ain't I a woman? I have born thirteen children, and seen most of 'em sold into slavery, and when I cried out with my mother's grief, none but Jesus heard me—and ain't I a woman?[33]

Pride in her strength doubtless led more than one female worker not only to protest against allegations of weakness but also to test her strength and her speed against others, just as men did.

Necessity forced Sojourner Truth—a slave—to labor in the fields, and necessity required thousands of middle-class white women to adopt conventionally male roles when they went West on the Oregon and the Santa Fe Trails. As they drove wagons, herded cattle, and learned to handle a rifle, many of them, especially the younger ones, discovered the pleasures of physical competence. Some of them took to the sports of their fathers and brothers. Four young Southern women, for instance, joined Thomas Potter's overland company, hunted for the group, shared in the governance of the company, and "even put on a shooting demonstration for a band of Snake Indians." Annie Oakley, one of the sure-fire pistol-packers of Buffalo Bill's Wild West show, was unusual, but she was no anomaly.[34]

Annie Oakley, who performed in the 1880s, was among the exceptional women who earned their livelihood by exhibiting their physical skills—or simply by displaying their powerfully developed bodies. Among the most famous of them was Adah Isaacs Menken. Born in 1835 in the vicinity of New Orleans, Adah Bertha married Alex Isaacs Menken but quickly left him to fly into the brawny arms of John C. Heenan, the foremost Irish-American pugilist of the day. Abandoned by him, she took to the stage and made a successful career for herself as actress, dancer, and acrobatic performer. Her most flamboyant role was in *Mazeppa,* an 1861 melodrama based on Byron's romantic poem. Dressed in flesh-covered tights, strapped to the back of a runaway horse, she thrilled her mostly male audiences. Among her admirers was Walt Whitman, who acted as best man when she married her second husband, the theatrical impressario Robert H. Newell ("Orpheus C. Kerr"). With Newell beating the drum, she became the nineteenth-century equivalent of a superstar. Even then, in those pre-Andy-Warhol days, celebrities attracted one another. Menken met Bret Harte and Mark Twain in San Francisco, Charles Dickens and Gabriel Dante Rossetti in London, and Napoleon III in Paris. By the time she died in 1868, she had divorced Newell, married Captain James Berkley, and returned to the Judaism of her childhood.[35]

Menken was not, strictly speaking, an athlete (because she did not participate in sports contests). She was soon followed by women who were. Among them was Etta Hattan, who took the stage name of Jaguarina and was billed as the "Ideal Amazon of the Age." From 1884, when she was twenty, to the end of the century, Jaguarina challenged and defeated numerous men in mounted broadsword contests. When she overwhelmed Sergeant Owen Davis in 1887, the humiliated champion of San Francisco's military post charged and threatened the hapless referee. He was neither the first nor the last man to find defeat by a woman intolerable.

Hattan retired just as Bernarr Macfadden, an entrepreneur and publicist more successful than Robert Newell, began to broadcast his message of strength, health, and sexual attractiveness.[36] In 1899 Macfadden took over a struggling magazine, *Physical Culture,* which had a meager three thousand readers, and in two years raised the journal's circulation to more than a hundred thousand. The magazine's covers frequently featured a picture of an attractive young woman in some sort of athletic endeavor. In the June 1899 issue, Macfadden proclaimed his creed: there "can be no beauty without fine muscles." Women need not fear masculinization. "To illustrate the absurdity of such a fear, one has merely to call attention to the rounded, smooth and symmetrical development of most professional women athletes, though under this beauty there are muscles of steel."[37] In . . . another issue, he lauded tomboys for the "beautiful symmetry of [their] muscles."[38] The lyric espousal of female athleticism continued in subsequent issues of *Physical Culture.*

Macfaddan's planned "Physical Culture Show" in New York's Madison Square Garden on October 9, 1905, was threatened when Anthony Comstock arrested him four days before the performance. The show went on, however, and the posters of shapely young women in union suits drew an audience of 20,000. Macfadden's search for the world's most perfectly developed female included not only the kind of poses later made famous by the Miss America Pageant but also a strenuous program of athletic contests. In order to win her title, Marie Spitzer had to compete in a weight-lifting contest, in the high jump, and in six races over distances varying from fifty yards to three miles. The title of Mrs. Macfadden, however, was won by a lucky girl whom her husband publicized as "Great Britain's Perfect Woman."[39]

The French, too, were captivated by the combination of physical prowess and sexual appeal. During the *belle époque* that brought the century to a close, a number of women, known by such names as "Sandwina" and "Apollina," performed feats of strength and bravado. An Irish girl, Kate Roberts, astonished the men of the *Haltéro-phile Club de France* by hoisting a 120–pound barbell to her shoulders and then lifting it overhead with one hand. As "Vulcana: La Femme Athlète," Roberts, flexing and observing a very impressive right arm, appeared on the cover of *La Santé par les Sports*.[40]

Throughout nineteenth-century France, in circuses, in music-halls, and at fairs, French women of the working class boxed and wrestled. Although eighteenth-century London had been the preferred venue for female pugilists, it was from London to Paris that Lydia Harris fled in 1872 when the ferocity of her blows injured her opponent and brought in the police. Some forty years later, Francis Carco's novel, *Jesus la Caille* (1914), narrated the exploits of female boxers at the famed Moulin Rouge, where Henri de Toulouse-Lautrec had once sketched his beloved Jeanne Avril.[41]

A Daumier-like drawing by Amadée-Charles-Henri Cham, comte de Noé, published in 1868, caricatured a pair of tubby wrestlers as they pulled and tugged at each other before a crowd of grinning male spectators. (See Plate 10.) Twenty years later, a certain Couturier, who might have been any one of several artists of that name, visited the Elysée-Montmartre and sketched two bare-breasted young wrestlers. Another minor artist, Henri-Gabriel Ibels, portrayed two of the era's grappling women in *Lutteuses* (1895). Five years later, a young man who was to become one of the century's greatest sculptors, Aristide Maillol, produced a bronze statue with the same title: *Les Lutteuses*. With an eye, perhaps, on the Spartan girls painted by Edgar Degas in 1880, Emmanuel Croisé exhibited *Les Jeunes Filles de Sparte* (ca. 1903), a conventionally sylvan scene with no fewer than three sets of wrestling adolescents. In a photograph taken at a fair at Neuilly, in 1905, a crowd of men and women are gathered before an outdoor stage to stare at a group of wrestlers. From the stage, in the second row, almost unnoticed, a beefy female glares her challenge. The French wrestlers were numerous, but the most famous of the female grapplers may have been the Russian Masha Poddubnaya. Married to the champion wrestler Ivan Poddubny, she was one of several claimants to the title of women's champion.[42]

The novelist Frantz Reichel, writing in the sporting magazine *Le Vélo* in 1899, published a verbal sketch of the wrestlers at the Salle du

Nouveau Concert. Although he claimed to have been initially skeptical of this form of entertainment, he was quickly converted: "Supple
and feline, the female wrestlers combine the brutality of their holds
with an elegance . . . that pleases and captivates!" The atmosphere of
one of these bouts can be sensed in the vivid words of sports journalist Max Viterbo. He recalled a 1903 visit to a dive *("boui-boui")* on
Rue Montmartre. Although there was music to mollify the waiting
crowd,

> the room was wild with impatience. The stale smell of sweat and foul air
> assaulted your nostrils. In this overheated room the spectators were flushed.
> Smoke seized us by the throat and quarrels broke out. . . . a lubricious gleam
> came to the eyes of old gentlemen when two furious women flung themselves
> at each other like modern bacchantes—hair flying, breasts bared, indecent,
> foaming at the mouth. Everyone screamed, applauded, stamped his feet.

The classical reference to the *modernes bacchantes* does not do much to
elevate the tone of the passage.[43]

If the English assumed that they had to visit Paris for such a sight,
they were mistaken. In rural England, women wrestled in barns and
in back rooms for a handful of coins tossed upon a plate. On at least
one occasion, witnessed by the French painter Jean Veber, the wrestlers were naked and the spectators at the degrading scene were
predominantly female.[44]

Was Dudley Sargent's high-minded deprecation of female boxers
and wrestlers a sign that American women actually punched and
grappled as British and French women did? Polite opinion hoped they
did not. As early as 1793, *The Lady's Magazine* dismissed American
women who sought a greater measure of equality with gibes about
"Mesdames Humphries and Mendoza." (Richard Humphries and
Daniel Mendoza were two of the era's most famous pugilists.) In
1852, a writer in *DeBow's Review* asked sarcastically if the ladies were
"ready for a boxing match?"[45] The *ladies* were not, but American
women of the lower classes were hardly exemplars of restrained
gentility. When New York's slum-dwellers fell out, the women "lit
into each other, usually with their bare hands—scratching, pummel-
ing and tearing each other's clothes." On these occasions, a ring of
spectators quickly gathered. It was not long before entrepreneurs
realized that gawkers might as well be mulcted for the sight of female
pugilism as for the oddities exhibited in P. T. Barnum's American
Museum. On March 16, 1876, an excited crowd assembled to watch

Nell Saunders outbox Rose Harland at Hill's Theater in New York (a well-known pugilistic venue). Saunders won a silver butter dish.[46]

By 1891, the *Police Gazette* was ready to sponsor a "championship match" between two female wrestlers. Dressed in tights, with short hair (to prevent pulling), Miss Alice Williams took on Miss Sadie Morgan. Some of the less publicized events were positively raunchy. In his *Recollections of an Old New Yorker* (1932), Frederick Van Wyck looked back on his youth and recalled how he escaped from his upper-class home in order to spend "a night with Tommy Norris and his attractions." The attractions offered by Mr. Norris, who owned a livery stable, included a match between two female boxers stripped to the waist.[47] On the whole, however, American accounts of female pugilism have few references to half-naked combat and few apologetic allusions to Greek antiquity. No *modernes bacchantes* in *our* prize rings!

There were, of course, less sensational competitions. In the last decades of the century, a number of inventors devised ways to modify the extremely hazardous "ordinary" bicycle and to make it safe for women. It seemed, in the 1880s and 1890s, as if *everyone* had a "wheel," a *Rad*, or a *Vélo*. In 1893, sixteen-year-old Tessie Reynolds of Brighton, wearing "rational" dress, rode a crossbarred bicycle to London and back, a distance of some 120 miles, in eight and a half hours, a feat which touched off a month of controversy in the cycling press. Should feats of this sort be encouraged or not? In 1888, American women competed in a six-day bicycle race in Pittsburgh. Some 1500 spectators paid to watch them race to the point of exhaustion. This, too, provoked controversy, but the races continued. In 1895, sixteen-year-old Frankie Nelson won a six-day race in New York and went on to compete in Europe.[48]

Victorian conservatives like Miss T. R. Coombs disapproved of these commercial competitions and advocated in their stead healthful cycling tours of the countryside. How, she asked,

can we admire a girl, however beautiful she may be, whose face is as red as a lobster, and streaming with perspiration, whose hair is hanging in a mop about her ears whose hairpins are strewn along the race-course, and whose general appearance is dusty, untidy, and unwomanly?

A writer for *Cycling* (London) agreed that a woman who raced to set a record was indeed "an object of ridicule." Since the swiftest female cyclists were young women of the working class, there was surely a modicum of elitist bias in the preference for leisurely tours rather than hectic races.[49]

Owners of British cycling tracks lost their licenses if they permitted women to race. French promoters, unimpeded by the law, were more than willing to meet the spectators' demand for the newest spectacle. In 1868, French girls raced in the Bois de Boulogne before a cheering crowd of *mesdames et messieurs*. (See Plate 12.) In 1869, the Olivier brothers, who manufactured bicycles, and *Le Vélocipède Illustré,* which propagandized for the new sport, sponsored a dash from Paris to Rouen. Four intrepid Frenchwomen joined the men. (The winner, James Moore, averaged 7.5 mph.) Paris soon boasted of several velodromes, of which the most famous were *Le Vélodrome de la Seine* and *Le Vélodrome Buffalo,* both operated by Toulouse-Lautrec's friend Tristan Bernard. In the nineties, Hélène Dutrieu became the world champion. In 1895, she set a record of 39.19 kilometers in an hour-long trial. (Her sponsor, Simpson Lever Chain, commissioned Toulouse-Lautrec to do its advertisements.) Dutrieu was outdistanced by a young Bretonne, Amélie LeGall, but she never lost her spunk. In 1913 she became an aviator. LeGall, riding under the name of "Lisette," went on to triumph in a series of six-day and eight-day races. A high point of her career came in 1896 when she won a 100–kilometer race against the celebrated Scottish professional, Clara Grace. Lisette's time was two hours forty-one minutes twelve seconds. Having vanquished most of the women, she began to challenge the men. With the help of a four-kilometer head-start, she defeated Albert Champion in a 25–kilometer race. In these years of international velomania, two Danish girls, Johanne Joergenson and Susanne Lindberg, gleefully broke a number of cycling records set by their chagrined countrymen.[50]

Paris was a center for swimming as well as cycling. In the summer of 1885, lithographed *affiches* were posted on the city's kiosks to invite male and female swimmers to a *Grand Concours de Natation* between the Pont de Passy and the Pont de Grenelle. Avowing that the proceeds were destined for charity, the poster enticed contestants by picturing a young female swimmer, floating down the Seine with bare calves, bare arms, and an incongruous pair of shoes. In swimming as in cycling, the mixture of "athleticism and femininity" was exciting.[51]

How many Parisian women actually competed as cyclists or swam in the *Grand Concours* can no longer be ascertained, but we are told that 2500 Parisian shopgirls participated in the most famous footrace of *la belle époque,* which took place on October 25, 1903. Setting out from the Place de la Concorde, the girls ran to Nanterre. A mostly male crowd of 20,000 turned out to cheer and jeer (but not to leer — the girls ran in their work clothes or in their Sunday best). The winner, a *modiste* named Jeanne Cheminel, covered the twelve kilometers in an hour and ten minutes. Her reward was the opportunity to perform at the celebrated Olympia music hall.[52] Exactly two weeks later, some 250 Parisian shopgirls competed in a series of 300–meter races in the Parc des Princes.[53]

The following spring, the Germans organized races for *their* girls. At Carnival time, it had long been common to stage *Juxlaufen* ("comic races") for girls and women (like the broom-in-hand race at Leipzig in 1869). Now the Germans wanted to be as *au courant* as the French. At Berlin, in 1904, seventy girls competed in a *Damensportfest* that included 400–meter heats and a 500–meter final. A large crowd, mostly if not entirely male, cheered Gertrud Furkert's victory. Like the French girls, the *Fräulein* were dressed so that no bare arm or leg offended the canons of public decency. Such precaution failed to prevent some of the newspapers from complaining about sensationalism.[54] By 1909, at the latest, middle-class women, like the members of Dresden's *Verein für Turnen und Bewegungsspiele* ("Club for Gymnastics and Games of Motion"), were also involved in modern track-and-field sports. A photograph shows nine of the Dresden women leaping forward at the start of a 1000–meter race. Hajo Bernett notes in his caption to the picture that "the handsome sports dress freed their arms and legs" (from the elbows and the knees).[55]

Although most of the lower-class female athletes were celebrated for their individual feats of strength, endurance, or combativeness, there were also sporadic attempts to commercialize the appeal of women involved in team sports. Anticipating the Women's Basketball League (1978) by nearly a century, an American entrepreneur named Harry H. Freeman attempted in the 1880s to launch a team of female baseball players. He was thwarted by rumors that he wanted to recruit the "buxom beauties" for prostitution. One irate New Orleans father sued the entrepreneur and charged that his dark-haired daughter had been whisked from town in a blonde wig. A number of women had careers as amateur or semiprofessional baseball players and one or two of them appeared briefly on all-male professional teams, but none of the women's teams was able to tour successfully. The

Blondes and the Brunettes played in New York and several other cities in 1883, but they were stranded in Chicago and had to rely on charitable donations to return to their homes in the Philadelphia area.[56] English enterprise foundered too. William Matthews and S.B. Lohmann hired twenty-two young women to form two cricket teams, a Red eleven and a Blue eleven. An advertisement promised that the players would be "elegantly and appropriately attired" and that their reputations would be protected by pseudonyms. Press comment was favorable. The *Illustrated London News* for May 26, 1890, found them "a social novelty illustrative of the disputed notion that women can, may and will do everything quite as well as men."[57] At the Police Athletic Ground in Liverpool, 15,000 spectators came to see the match. Unfortunately, the girls were more skillful with bats and balls than with tills and ledgers. Matthews and Lohmann absconded with the profits and the enterprise collapsed.[58]

Were these and other women the victims of commercial exploitation? Since most of these women were sponsored, managed, or employed by men, they suffered the same disadvantages as other women who sold their talents (and sacrificed their respectability) in the entertainment marketplace. It should not, however, be forgotten that they also reaped the same benefits: a modicum of fame and fortune. Much more difficult is the question of the spectators' motivation. The men who attended Menken's performances, Macfadden's contests, and the combats of French female boxers and wrestlers were certainly not motivated simply by the disinterested desire to inform themselves about the wonders of human movement. On the other hand, however one interprets the men's motivation, one must admit that their interests were aroused by physically robust rather than delicately frail specimens of the opposite sex. Macfadden himself practiced what he preached. He was a physical culturalist inspired by the example of the famous strongman Eugene Sandow, whom he first observed at Chicago's Columbian Exposition of 1893. Macfaddan's message of "vim, vigor, snap and energy" was delivered to men as well as women, and his third wife allowed that Macfadden was "a superb male specimen."[59] There is no reason to doubt that he and others like him genuinely admired the "most perfect" women of their age. This possibility seems at least as plausible as Donald J. Mrozek's speculative assertation that the men's attitudes were determined by their sexual fears of strong women.[60]

In the absence of their own testimony, we can only conjecture what sort of satisfaction the women themselves took from the roles they played in the male-dominated world of entertainment. They *seem* to have been proud of their strength and combativeness. Miss Vulcana certainly looks self-satisfied as she contemplates her impressively developed biceps on the cover of *La Santé par les Sports*. Was she any less proud, was she any more commercially exploited, than Eugene Sandow or John L. Sullivan? It seems reasonable to assume that she and other female athletes had a sense of accomplishment denied to less physically active women. To think otherwise, to insist that her pride came from the deplorable internalization of patriarchal values, is to reduce the complexity of history to a monotonously doleful tale of man's oppression of woman.

EIGHT

The Victorian Age: From Swedish Drill to Field Hockey

1. Schools and Colleges: British and American Women

While most members of the Victorian middle class remained committed to the Cult of Domesticity, while most lower-class women were too overwhelmed with physical labor inside and outside the home to have much time or energy for regular sports participation, the seeds of change were sown in the elite schools and colleges. Timidly at first, then with greater self-confidence, British and American women took control of girls' and women's physical education and began the transition from calisthenics to sports.

Among the "foremothers" was Dorothea Beale, principal of Cheltenham Ladies' College from 1858 to 1906. (The "college" was actually a private secondary school modeled on England's famous "public" schools for boys.) Miss Beale required calisthenics and eventually introduced Swedish gymnastics in 1890 but, as was typical of her generation, she steadfastly opposed ballgames because she disliked competition in any form. It is doubtful that she understood what sports are about. When she observed a game of field hockey, she ordered, "The children will hurt themselves if they all run about after one ball. Get some more balls at once." Pressure from the students and from the younger mistresses eventually caused Miss Beale to compromise. At the time of her death, Cheltenham had twenty-six tennis courts, two fives courts, a two-acre playground, and facilities for fencing, riding, and swimming. She presided over these facilities, but she never became reconciled to interscholastic contests. "I am most anxious," she wrote, "that girls should not over-exert themselves, or become absorbed in athletic rivalries, and therefore we do not play against other schools."[1]

Her successor, Lilian Faithfull, had other ideas. Having been a games enthusiast at Somerville, one of Oxford's newly founded women's colleges, she was ready to spread the good news. Miss Faithfull introduced athletic trophies and school colors. She broadened the athletic roster to include badminton, netball, and lacrosse, and she introduced interscholastic matches in cricket, field hockey, and tennis. She became president of the All-England Women's Hockey Association.[2]

Miss Beale's close friend, Frances Mary Buss, also differed from her friend on the question of sports. At the North London Collegiate School for Ladies, which she founded in 1850, the girls endured the inevitable dreary calisthenic drills and were then rewarded with the opportunity to swim, skate, and play field hockey and other games. North London's gymnasium went up in 1880, nine years before Cheltenham's.[3]

When she left Girton College, Cambridge, to found St. Leonard's School (1877) in St. Andrews, Scotland, Louisa Lumsden included a drill mistress in her original staff and allowed the girls ninety minutes a day for cricket, field hockey, rounders, golf, and tennis—despite protests from the scandalized townspeople. The school offered challenge cups for thrice yearly competitions in fives, golf, and tennis. "Sports were a virtual passion at St. Leonard's by the turn of the century," and the students' newspaper "devoted more space to games than to any other subject." Lumsden's successor, Jane Frances Dove, was also a graduate of Girton College, where women's sports had become extremely important. To the customary defense of sports as a necessary and healthful diversion from study, she added the same imperialistic justification for games as her colleagues at boys' schools: sports were a means to ensure "the supremacy of our country in so many quarters of the globe."[4]

Sports were, if possible, more important still at Roedean School, which Millicent, Penelope, and Dorothy Lawrence opened at Brighton in 1855. The aim of the school, the sisters announced, "will be to give a thorough education, physical, intellectual, and moral. Special pains will be taken to guard against overwork, from two to three hours daily will be allotted to outdoor exercise and games."[5] They were as good as their word. Field hockey was played from the start, despite local condemnation. The girls rode, ran, swam, cycled, competed at archery, and played tennis, rounders, fives, lacrosse, and netball.

On the whole students were games mad. Entire student bodies turned out for major house and school matches . . . . Militant school songs . . . were sung with religious fervor. A plethora of trophies were objects of grail- like devotion, as were the colors awarded to outstanding athletes who themselves were virtually worshipped. Photographing of teams for posterity was an annual rite, and sporting language conjuring up masculine images was considered smart.[6]

There were the inevitable complaints from outsiders that sports were too strenuous for girls in the midst of puberty, and there were the usual fears that delicate reproductive organs might be damaged, but the Lawrence sisters were undeterred. In justification, Penelope offered the opinion that cricket was "a strong social bond between the mother country and the colonies, between class and class, and race and race."[7]

Organizationally, girls' and women's sports followed the same path as boys' and men's sports. Impromptu matches led to clubs, and clubs joined together, first in local and then in regional, national, and international organizations. The All-England Women's Field Hockey Association was born in 1895. Lacrosse was less popular than field hockey, but alumnae from Wycombe Abbey, Roedean School, and Prior's Field School formed the Southern Ladies' Lacrosse Club in 1905. In 1912, Audrey Beaton (an Old Roedeanian) formed the Ladies' Lacrosse Association. A year later, seven clubs and seventy schools were members, and Oxford played its first lacrosse match against Cambridge. The Cambridge team wore knee-length tunics and knickerbockers; the Oxford team wore skirts.[8]

In *The Games Ethic and Imperialism* (1986), J. A. Mangan has traced the diffusion of men's sports from Oxford and Cambridge to the most distant parts of the empire. A similar process led to the diffusion of girls' sports from English schools to those of Canada, Australia, and the colonies. The Australian case was typical. Field hockey was brought to Adelaide in 1899 by graduates of Cheltenham Ladies' College. The girls of Unley Park School (founded in 1855) had cricket games before the end of the century.[9] At Merton Hall (Melbourne), which Mary and Edith Morris founded in 1898, calisthenics preceded sports just as they had at most English schools. A third Morris sister, Gwynneth, was sent back to England in 1904 specifically to study the Swedish system of physical education (which had been adopted by English educators of the previous generation). Gwynneth Morris disliked the notion of strenuous competition and condemned the win-at-all-costs attitude that seemed always to accompany sports, but Australian schoolgirls were no fonder of Swedish drill than their counterparts in the home country. Before her return from England to Australia, the students had begun to play in a Girls' Hockey Association. With a sigh, she accepted the *fait accompli*.

The girl who played cricket and other sports at North London Collegiate School, at St. Leonard's, or at the Roedean School was unlikely to relapse into sloth upon entering the university. In 1869, when Emily Davies opened what eventually became Girton College, Cambridge, the students were encouraged to walk and swim and to play croquet and a version of cricket. In 1877, the college erected its first gymnasium. When the girls began to play soccer football, Davies intervened: "It would certainly shock the world if it were known."[10] In 1878, Girton women competed in tennis against the women of Newnham College, Cambridge, which also traced its origins back to 1869, the year Anne Jemima Clough helped to launch a lecture series for young women seeking the equivalent of a university education. Five years later, the two Cambridge colleges competed in tennis against the two women's colleges of Oxford—Lady Margaret Hall and Somerville (both founded in 1879). The students provided most of the impetus for a series of clubs in various sports. Girton women, for instance, formed a field-hockey club in 1890 and played against Newnham in 1892. The club became a charter member in the All-England Women's Hockey Association (1895).

What did the young men of the middle and upper classes make of their sisters' enthusiasm for sports? The male students of Oxford and Cambridge seem on the whole to have been positive about female athleticism. There was little controversy because of the care taken not to violate behavioral rules, the generally inoffensive type of games played, the undoubted femininity of the players, and the fact that for years play was virtually invisible within the protected confines of college or private grounds, where it was completely separate from and no challenge to men's sport.[11]

The Chaucerian scholar F. J. Furnivall coached a sculling club and "did as much as he could to get women out in boats." In Jessie

Curie's memoir of the good professor, she recalled how she moved into a studio in Primrose Hill and was accosted by the previous tenant: "Let me introduce you to Dr. Furnivall. He will ask you if you can scull. If you say 'No,' he will take you up the river to teach you. If you say, 'Yes,' he will take you up the river to keep you in practice." Another sign of men's approval of women's sports, at least among the educated, was the publication of Grant Allen's popular novel, *Miss Cayley's Adventures* (1899). The impressively competent heroine is a Girton graduate who rows while at college, wins a trans-Alpine bicycle race against male competition, and shoots a tiger in India.[12]

The graduates of the newly founded women's colleges at Oxford and Cambridge—women like Faithfull, Lumsden, and Dove—were vitally active in bringing sports to the girls' schools, but the most important single person in British physical education for women was surely Swedish-born Martina Bergman-Osterberg. In order to understand her contribution to British physical education, one must understand the role played by Per Henrik Ling and the "Swedish system" that he invented. At the Royal Gymnastics Institute of Stockholm, which he founded in 1814, Ling taught a complicated system of calisthenics designed to develop every part of the body. Ling and his followers insisted that theirs was the only scientific approach. Ling's theories, which dominated Scandinavian physical education and found adherents throughout northern and western Europe (and in North America), were hostile to the competition inherent in sports. What has been written about Finland's gymnastics union (founded in 1896) can be applied generally to the many organizations created by Ling's numerous disciples:

Esthetics, harmony, health and beauty were the corner stones on which women built their gymnastics; they assumed a very critical attitude towards competitive sports and the craze for records and medals, which they considered typically male.[13]

Bergman-Osterberg, a product of the Stockholm Institute, was a perfect exemplar of this noncompetitive philosophy.

She arrived in London in 1881 to replace Concordia Loefving (also from Sweden) as the second Superintendant of Physical Education for the city's public schools. By 1886, she had trained some 1300 teachers in the methods of Swedish gymnastics. A year later, she departed to devote her enormous energies to the Hampstead Physical Training College, which she had founded in 1885 (the year of her marriage). In 1895, she moved the institution to suburban Dartford and proudly renamed it the Bergman-Osterberg Physical Training College. Although she always prized the Ling system, which claimed to train the entire body in the most scientific manner, she sadly accepted the fact that sports motivated students as scientific drill did not. She saw to it that her graduates were able to instruct their pupils in cricket, basketball, and other games. An awesome disciplinarian, Bergman-Osterberg was respected rather than loved, but she seemed not to mind that she was less motherly than dear Miss Buss and dear Miss Beale had been. She was, in fact, a female Darwinist. "I try to train my girls to help raise their own sex, and so to accelerate the progress of the race; for unless the women are strong, healthy, pure, and true, how can the race progress?"[14]

Among her most influential graduates was Rhoda Anstey, who founded her own College of Physical Training and Hygiene for Women Teachers in 1897. She was "an intense and eccentric woman who dressed in sandals and an arab-style djibbah, ate no meat and was so devoted to astrology that she was inclined to admit any Sagittarian."[15] An ardent feminist as well (like Madame Bergman-Osterberg), Anstey was a founder of the Gymnastic Teachers' Suffrage Society. (When the women bravely marched to demand the vote, hecklers shouted, "Here come the elastic teachers. Let's see their biceps.") Despite her aggressive political stance, or perhaps because of it, her emphasis as a teacher was on grace and harmony rather than on muscular strength. Nonetheless, her young charges played cricket, lacrosse, netball, field hockey, and tennis. When they gathered for festive occasions, they sang the high-spirited college song:

> To Swedish gymnastics now,
> Our youth and strength we bring
> To build up healthy bodie
> After the laws of Ling.
> For we ourselves the sculptors are,
> And we ourselves the clay,
> When mind and will and spirit
> United hold their sway.[16]

Their motto might well have been: "Be your own Pygmalion!"
Another of Bergman-Osterberg's enterprising disciples, Margaret

Stanfeld, founded the Beford Physical Training College (1903). She ran the school for forty-two years, helped to found the Ling Association, and served as that association's president from 1910 to 1920.

The influence of Ling was felt in the United States as well. His system completely eclipsed that of Dioclesian Lewis, who had advocated gymnastics for women as early as 1862.[17] The Boston School Board voted in 1890 to adopt Ling's system. A year earlier, Amy Morris Homans and the philanthropist Mary Hemenway established the Boston Normal School of Gymnastics with Nils Posse to drill the students in the Swedish manner. A number of Harvard and MIT professors, including the famed philosopher Josiah Royce, lectured at the BNSG. In America as in England, the girls were impatient with repetitive drills and eager for sports, which the curriculum soon broadened to include. The catalogue for 1899–1900 referred to "games." By 1908, the school boasted of instruction in basketball, fencing, field hockey, tennis, and track and field. Like the formidable Madame Bergman-Osterberg, Amy Morris Homans was an authoritarian teacher. She ordered Mabel Lee, later to be one of the leaders of American physical education, to gain ten pounds; Miss Lee heaped her plate with meat and potatoes until she tipped the BNSG scales at an acceptable weight. It is symbolic of the influence of Miss Homans that three-fourths of the first intercollegiate basketball rules committee were graduates of the Boston Normal School.[18]

The future of women's sports did not, however, lie with schools devoted exclusively to physical education. Cindy L. Himes has written that the coeducational colleges of the West "pioneered the area of intercollegiate sports for women." [19] There are certainly grounds for this assertion, especially at the University of California, where a Young Ladies Lawn Tennis Club was organized in 1890. The university hired Genevra Magee in 1896 as an "Assistant in Physical Culture." [20] Hearst Hall, donated by feminist millionaire philanthropist Phoebe Apperson Hearst, included a women's gymnasium in which Magee was able to conduct her classes. "Athletic clubs for tennis, boating, and fencing followed, as the women now had a place to meet and store equipment." In 1901, Hearst, whom we should perhaps refer to as a philogynist, presented the coeds with an outdoor basketball court—surrounded by a twelve-foot fence.[21]

Despite the importance of developments at Berkeley, the transition from calisthenics to sports can best be followed in the women's colleges of the East. By the last decade of the century, sports flourished in these elite institutions just as they did at Girton College and Lady Margaret Hall. In fact, Vassar College, which constructed a gymnasium for its students in 1865, can claim to have anticipated the British colleges in physical education and sports. The name of the Calisthenium proclaimed that building's noble function. The college catalogue informed the prospective student that a "suitable portion of each day is set aside for physical exercise and every young lady is required to observe it as one of her college duties."[22]

Students at Vassar were originally drilled in the calisthenic system designed by Dioclesian Lewis for the Normal Institute for Physical Education which he had founded in Boston. In the quarter century after 1875, Vassar women were introduced to archery, baseball, basketball, rowing, tennis, and track. The Laurel Base Ball Club with twelve members and the Abenakis Base Ball Club with eleven were both founded in the spring of 1866. A few years later, in 1875, there were at least three clubs: the Sure-Pops, the Daisy-Clippers, and the Royals. When a student broke her leg playing baseball, the college's authorities did not react in panic; they decided that the accident could have happened on the dance floor (and shortly after, a similar accident did). Baseball continued. At some of the women's schools, students sought to legitimize their athletic aspirations by wearing sweatshirts blazoned with the emblems of Harvard, Yale, and Princeton. Not at Vassar. "A pink V on a Vassar girl's sweater," wrote Alice Fallows in *Century* magazine, "means she has broken a [school] record." Among the records were Agnes Wood's time of 30.6 seconds for 220 yards, set in 1903, and Fanny James's 6.2 seconds for 60 yards, set a year later. When Dorothy Smith exceeded the school's records for both the high jump and the baseball throw, in the spring of 1911, the *New York Herald* sent an intially skeptical reporter to investigate. Smith demonstrated her abilities and he was "amazed." He reported that she was an attractively modern girl, "not marred by overdeveloped muscles, but so well trained that every bit of her strength counts."[23]

The athleticism characteristic of Poughkeepsie raised some eyebrows and set Charles Dana Gibson's pen in skillful motion. In 1896 he published a drawing, *The Coming Game,* in which several determined Vassar girls are about to tackle a very worried football player from Yale. (See Plate 15.) In response to criticism of Vassar's athletic program, Sophia Foster Richardson summoned up the ever-useful classical comparison: "The daughters of Sparta were handsomer and more attractive than the more delicately nurtured Athenians." When voices were raised to accuse the young women of hoydenish behavior, Vassar's Director of Physical Training, Harriet Isabel Ballintine, responded boldly:

If refinement and quietness are but the results of weakness and inactivity, and a pronounced manner must necessarily be the outcome of a more vigorous life, we must be willing to sacrifice the former feminine attributes for the more precious possession of good health.

When she wrote these words in 1898, Ballintine was still doubtful about intercollegiate competition and the quest for records, but she eventually altered her opinions and decided that some women were rugged enough for a more strenuous approach to sports. She was probably influenced by the redoubtable Constance Applebee, whom she met at Dudley Sargent's Harvard Summer School in 1901. The British-born Applebee, a life-long (and long-lived) enthusiast for field hockey, joined Ballintine in introducing the game at Vassar.[24]

The enthusiasm of the students can be perceived even today in old issues of their undergraduate publications and, perhaps even more keenly, in their letters to parents and friends. In 1866, long before sports had ousted calisthenics as the main form of physical education, Vassar student Martha Warner reassured her anxious mother that exercise was not dangerous: "Isn't it good that I am so strong, and have learned to take such long walks?" Five years later, Josephine Jewell reported excitedly about a baseball game in which she had dashed from third base to home plate. Thrilled by her introduction to sports, she expressed determination "to cultivate my muscle this summer by hook or by crook."[25]

When Smith College opened its doors a decade after Vassar, calisthenics were required. The earliest catalogues noted that regular gymnastic exercises were prescribed under the direction of an educated lady instructor. Like Vassar, Smith initially relied on teachers trained by Dioclesian Lewis. An alumna, Edith Naomi Hill, looked back on the dreary regimen. The students, "in their twilled flannel with long drawers, their ankle length skirts and high collars," exercised "to slow music with dumbells and Indian clubs, wands and chest weights.". . .
Like their sisters at Vassar, the students at Smith were eager to drop their boring Indian clubs and get on with the ballgame. In the spring of 1878, Minnie Stephens organized a baseball team and, needing equipment, attempted to make off with a bat owned by a group of Northampton boys. When they pursued her, she fled. Securing "balls

and bats in the accustomed manner," by purchase, she and her friends began to play the game on the lawn in front of Hubbard House. The college banned the game, but it was revived in 1892. When President L. C. Seelye was asked if he did not think it "unladylike" for the students to play like men, Seelye urged the concerned inquirer to observe a game. "Then," he added, "you wouldn't say they played like men.[26]

The "Smithies" were fortunate at this time to have an innovative graduate of the Boston Normal School of Gymnastics, Senda Berenson, arrive upon the scene. Within a few months of the invention of basketball at nearby Springfield, Massachusetts, in the winter of 1891, Berenson adapted the game for her students. "Equipped with the memory of long and tedious hours spent at dull gymnastic work, she viewed basket ball as a sport that would develop healthy women while allowing them the fun of moderate competition." Berenson modified the rules to eliminate roughness and to minimize the danger of overexertion. She divided the court into three zones and stationed two players in each of them so that no player had to dash breathlessly from one end of the court to the other. Her adaptation was a huge success. The students flocked to the court and were ecstatic when Miss Berenson invited them, with a personal handwritten note, to play for their class team. The players were chosen soon after Christmas and practiced faithfully for the big game, which occurred in the spring. The seniors coached the sophomores, the juniors the freshmen.

In order to protect the players from the embarrassment that might be caused either by the bloomers and black stockings that they wore . . . or by the nature of the exertion demanded in the game of basket ball, all men aside from President Seelye, who was expected to give the game an air of dignity, were barred from the gymnasium on the day of the game. Lines formed outside of the gymnasium as early as an hour before the game was to start. The audience filed in in an orderly fashion. Every inch of the gym was occupied. The supporters of each class sat on opposite sides and wore their team's chosen colors. Because cheering was "not included in the present scheme of womanliness," the audience took to enthusiastically singing songs.

Despite Miss Berenson's efforts to prevent an excess of partisanship, rivalries were fierce. Grace Whiting, who played on an intramural team in 1894, wrote that she and her friends were "very much excited over basket ball as there is a match to come off soon between '96 and '97."[27]

Berenson was content, for the moment, to promote intramural rivalries between the classes. Meanwhile, the first intercollegiate game was played in Berkeley between the University of California and Stanford on April 4, 1896. The hosts insisted that male spectators be barred from Armory Hall. The *San Francisco Examiner* reported that a luckless male who approached a window was driven away by the hisses of the assembled women. A month later, the *New York Journal* for May 17th ran a headline: BASKET BALL—THE NEW CRAZE FOR ATHLETIC YOUNG WOMEN. The illustration showed Vassar girls "in their Field Day game of basket ball."[28]

At Wellesley, the transition from calisthenics to sports occurred more slowly, perhaps because of the proximity of the Lingians at the Boston Normal School of Gymnastics (which was eventually merged with Wellesley College). The college catalogue for 1876–1877 boasted of a large gymnasium "where the students are instructed in Calisthenics." Faithful to Ling's system, the faculty and administration "frowned on intramural games, and adamantly opposed interscholastic sports." The annual regatta known as "Float Day" was judged, as late as 1898, on the basis of good form and gracefulness rather than by speed. That year, however, Abbie Carter Goodloe noted in *Scribner's* that the students had trained hard with rowing machine when poor weather prohibited practice on the lake. Carter detected a new seriousness: "In their dark blouses and bloomers, the muscular young rowers of to-day present a very different appearance from those of other years, when the formation of a crew was almost a social affair, and those who composed it were elevated chiefly for their good looks." The students expressed their strong preference for real competition. When the faculty relented and introduced basketball, the 1898 yearbook exulted "The grimy and generally disheveled appearance of the players, as they emerge from the fray, fills our athletic souls with pride."[29]

Martha Carey Thomas, president of Bryn Mawr, probably had greater scholarly ambitions for herself and her students than did the presidents of the other "Seven Sisters," but her conception of the "New Woman" was not exclusively intellectual. Writing to her close friend Mary Garrett in 1884, ten years before she assumed the presidency of Bryn Mawr, Thomas described a visit to Wellesley College's gymnasium and marveled at "the girls in trowsers swinging on rings, twirling on bars, a newer race of athletes—ushers in of a new day." Another letter to Garrett, written in 1899, painted a vivid picture of intense class rivalry in Bryn Mawr sports. At the junior-senior supper that followed the fiercely fought match, "The wounded heroes were carried in on stretchers and hobbled in on crutches." There were injuries of another kind as well. At all the women's colleges, the susceptible girls were often "smashed" by (i.e., in love with) athletic classmates.[30]

With their programs in physical education, the women's colleges were able emphatically to disprove the hysterical claims of medical men like England's Henry Maudsley and America's Edward Clarke, both of whom had warned that cerebration during puberty was an extremely dangerous expenditure of a girl's fixed supply of nervous energy. The move from calisthenics to sports alarmed many who were otherwise well disposed to the new ventures in higher education for women. Complaining about Smith's athletic program in *Godey's Lady's Magazine* in 1895, Winifred Ayres portrayed a student who had gone overboard for the outdoor life. Not only was she tanned, her "arms were bare also, and the muscles were so developed they appeared in lumpy protuberances, just as those of the professional athletes are wont to do." To such expressions of distaste, Berenson had a feminist answer. Now that "all fields of labor and all professions are opening their doors" to her, a woman "needs more than ever the physical strength to meet these ever increasing demands." Lucille Hill, the Director of Physical Education at Wellesley, went further and linked "the delights of athletics" with the "desirability of possessing a strong and beautiful body for both use and ornament." It is reductionist to argue, as some historians have done, that comments like Berenson's and Hill's unwittingly reveal a bourgeois instrumentalist conception of the female body as an object to be used. Men's and women's bodies were indeed used instrumentally, as they must be in any society; they were also perceived as vehicles for self-expression. The female educators of the elite women's colleges and of the coeducational universities may have been daughters of the bourgeoisie, but they were unmistakably ready to defy middle-class convention and proclaim ideals of physical activity that flew in the face of earlier shibboleths about delicacy and decorum. They redefined what it meant to be a lady.[31]

2. Clubs and Country Houses: British Women

The British women who had fallen in love with sports while at Girton or Lady Margaret Hall were reluctant simply to abandon them upon graduation. They played at English country houses and at continental spas. In the African colonies, in the Japanese port of Kobe, along Argentina's Rió de la Plata, wherever a nucleus of British colonial administrators, soldiers, or businessmen was to be found, their wives and daughters displayed their ardor for sports.[32] Of course, they had to be sports of the right kind. In the antipodes as in England, "women of the upper classes rode to the hunt, played croquet and tennis and participated in archery, but all other sports were considered 'manly' and thus unbecoming for colonial women." When a "Ladies' Race" was announced in 1859, the Adelaide (South Australia) *Register* condemned it and thought no decent female would "exhibit herself for the vulgar delectation." The race was cancelled.[33] In New Zealand, where Englishwomen hunted, played tennis, and cycled, it was a projected 1891 tour by a team of female rugby players that caused the line to be drawn. Public outcry forced cancellation of the tour.[34]

Archery, which had for centuries attracted a number of aristocratic women, seemed on the verge of a new wave of popularity. Pierce Egan, the first of the great sportswriters, thought that he had identified a trend as early as 1828, nearly a decade before Victoria mounted the throne:

Archery is equally open to the fair sex, and has these last thirty years, been the favourite recreation of a great part of the female nobility, the only field of diversion they can enjoy without incurring the censure of being thought masculine.

A year later, the *Young Lady's Book . . . of Elegant Recreations, Exercises and Pursuits* commented on matches held by noble archers of both sexes and noted that "the attitude of an accomplished female archer . . . at the moment of bending the bow, is particularly graceful."[35] Classical associations with Artemis-Diana were doubtless one of archery's attractions for women. Another was that the stationary target obviated the need for quick movement on the part of women whose clothes effectively immobilized them.

Clubs like Lancaster's John O'Gaunt's Archery Society were quite exclusive. The thirty men and twenty women admitted to John O'Gaunt were representatives of the nation's elite.[36] Since archery was one of the few sports which captivated Queen Victoria, occasionally pictured with a bow in her hand, the women of John O'Gaunt's doubtless felt a special bond with their young monarch. The upper-class archers' milieu was preserved for us in 1872 when three "fair toxophilites" (the artist's daughters) were painted by the highly skilled realist William Powell Frith. The fairest of the three, portrayed in sharp profile, draws her bow against the background of a country estate. In the distance are hills clouded in wisps of morning fog. (See Plate 13.) With such women as these in mind, the Grand National Archery Society initiated national championships for women in 1880, but the sport's appeal was limited even within the leisure class. It provided very little exercise and most people found the mediated competition of an archery contest rather tedious.[37]

In the 1850s and 1860s, the croquet match, which afforded opportunities for moderate exercise in mixed company, became one of the most popular pastimes of the upper class. An All-England Croquet Club, with male and female members, was formed in 1869. "Throughout most parts of the country," wrote Mayne Reid,

there were "croquet clubs," exclusively under the direction of ladies, each consisting of ten or a dozen families, the "best," of course, who lived within driving distance of one another, and whose grounds, as well as tables, afforded the necessary accommodation.

The reference to "tables" requires a moment's thought. Reid referred to the ostentatious repast that was a socially necessary adjunct to the upper-class croquet match. It was common, he noted, for the host to offer "a cold champagne dinner for nearly a hundred guests." By the mid-1870s, the musicians were able to enliven the party with a rendition of C. H. R. Marriott's "Croquet Schottische."[38]

Although we, who have endured televised images of female mud-wrestlers, are prone to think of croquet as the most innocent of games, nineteenth-century participants responded to the game's undercurrent of sexual excitement. James Tissot's painting, *Croquet* (1878), portrays a young woman holding her croquet mallet behind her back as if it were a gymnastics wand. The wanton pose accentuates her breasts, whose shape is clearly visible beneath her shawl.[39] By the end of the century, occasions for dalliance were so many that prudery counterattacked: "Who takes the mallet in his hand," intoned one scandalized contributor to *Living Age,* "has grasped naked vice; and who passes through the treacherous wire portal leaves virtue, honor and charity behind."[40] This assault, in an article entitled "The Immorality of Cricket," may have been tongue-in-cheek. Citing the article, taking it at face value, a modern art historian has made the game's latent sexual imagery manifest. In the act of "croquet," a manoeuvre allowable after one player's ball touches another's, the first player places his foot firmly on his own ball and uses his mallet to strike it. The shock thus transmitted to his opponent's ball sends it spinning away. The historian concludes that this deed, when performed by female players, was tantamount to symbolic castration.[41]

For women who found croquet, with or without the alleged sexual element, too mild an exercise, field sports beckoned. Fox hunting became more difficult as woods and fields were destroyed by urban growth or by the demands of agriculture, yet the difficulty itself became part of the sport's attraction because it accentuated the social status of those who could afford the increasingly expensive use of scarce resources. As noted earlier, medieval game laws reserving field sports for the upper class remained in force until 1830, when the domain of play had its version of the famous Reform Act of 1832 (which effectively opened Parliament to the middle class). The revision of the law spurred socially ambitious tradesmen to learn the hunter's code. The wealthy cockney grocer Mr. Jorrocks, the beloved comic character invented by R. S. Surtees, took awkwardly to the saddle. Jorrocks wasn't the only *arriviste*. Some of the exclusive glitter of field sports was tarnished when Jem Mason invited Catherine Walters, a notorious prostitute, to join the Quorn, the most prestigious English hunt. "If you go on like this," complained Miss Walters after her mount had cleared some fences, "my bloody arse will be as red as a beef-steak."[42]

Although they generally avoided such colorful language, a number of aristocratic women seemed to share some of the combative instincts of the prostitutes, washerwomen, and butchers' wives who fought and wrestled in the nether corners of the Victorian underworld. To strip to the waist and pummel each other before a drunken mob was obviously out of the question for upper-class women, but quite a number of the ladies released their aggression with fencing foils in their hands. Clubs were formed in London, Leeds, and Oxford, and their members achieved a modicum of success in international competition. The best of them, however, were usually outclassed by their continental rivals recruited "from the aristocratic circles of Vienna, Budapest, Rome, Madrid, and Paris." It was the custom for the European clubs to have special sections for female fencers.[43]

The upper-class female archers, croquet players, fox hunters, and fencers were soon outnumbered by the tennis players and the golfers.

The first of these new games required a good deal of carefully tended space and the second even more. Both sports required expensive lessons and both allowed sexually mixed play. Young men and women who had begun to mingle on the lawn with croquet mallets in their hands quickly discovered that it was possible to combine the pleasure of social intercourse with more serious athletic competition. In 1877, the All-England Croquet Club renamed itself the All-England Croquet and Lawn Tennis Club. On its courts at Wimbledon was played the first national championship for women, in 1884. In the finals, Maud Watson, an Anglican clergyman's daughter, defeated her older sister Lilian. She won again in 1885 and was then overshadowed by the first female tennis star, Blanche Bingley, who married the club's general secretary and then competed successfully as Mrs. G. W. Hillyard. The use of one's husband's name signaled social status undreamed of by the women who called themselves "Sandwina," "Miss Vulcana," or "Lisette." Bingley's great rival, Charlotte Dod, won her first championship at fifteen. It was an advantage for Lottie Dod that she was young enough to play in short skirts and race after balls that her hobbled opponents were unable to reach. Another early player, Dorothea Katherine Douglas (later Mrs. Robert Lambert Chambers) combined a string of seven national championships with an enthusiasm for badminton, field hockey, and golf.[44]

In Scotland, the Royal Musselburgh Golf Club had, as we have seen, offered occasional prizes to female golfers as early as 1810. By the end of the century, Scottish women golfers comprised as much as a third of the membership of organizations like the Aberfoyle Golf Club and the Tillcoultry Golf Club. In central Scotland, at least thirteen of thirty-one golf clubs are known to have had women members. Contrary to what many historians have asserted, these Scottish women preferred real competition to simply putting on the green. In the 1897–98 season, for instance, the Stirling Ladies' Golf Club sponsored twenty-two separate competitions for its members. In 1900, the ladies played seven matches against rival clubs. The game came into its own south of the border when the Westward Ho! and North Devon Ladies' Golf Club was organized in 1868. At first, the women merely putted, but the insipidity of this decorous pastime failed to hold their attention for long. By 1890, the *Illustrated London News* pictured women whose long sleeves and bustles failed to keep them from rough terrain. With the help of the men, the women established the Ladies' Golf Union in 1893. That summer, thirty-eight women from England, Ireland, and France played in the first national tournament, won by Lady Margaret Scott (who repeated her triumph in 1894 and 1895). When the Ladies' Golf Union asked in 1901 to be allowed to hold their annual tournament at hallowed St. Andrews, the club refused its permission, but the men relented seven years later—with the stipulation that the lockers and the lounge remain sacred to the male sex. In 1894, a year after the Ladies' Golf Union's first championship, and a year *before* the first national tournament for Australian men, the women of New South Wales and Victoria held a national championship at Geelong (Victoria). Within five years of its founding in 1891, the Royal Melbourne Golf Club had 132 female members.[45]

Although British women of various social classes had played cricket in the eighteenth and early nineteenth centuries, the first mention of the game at a girls' school occurred in 1868. By 1873 the game had become popular enough for *Punch* to chuckle condescendingly:

IRREPRESSIBLE Woman is again in the field. "Ladies Cricket" is advertised to be followed, there is every reason to apprehend, by Ladies' Fives, Ladies' Football, Ladies' Golf, etc. It is all over with men. They had better make up their minds to rest contented with croquet, and afternoon tea, and sewing machines, and perhaps an occasional game at drawing-room billiards.

When the Birmingham Teachers' Association debated the case for girls' cricket, in 1881, the *Birmingham Daily Mail* decreed grandly that cricket "is essentially a masculine game. It can never be played properly in petticoats." The newspaper went on to shudder at the possibility that female students might begin to box and to become "horney-handed, wide-shouldered, deep-voiced . . . and with biceps like a blacksmith's. . . . Let our women remain women instead of entering their insane physical rivalry with men."[46]

Schoolgirls and teachers were easy targets for the editorial satirists, but it was harder to laugh when the women of the aristocracy returned to the game that they had begun to play, intermittently, in the eighteenth century. Informal country-house cricket led to the formation in 1887 of the White Heather Club, founded at Nun Appleton in Yorkshire by eight socially prominent women, one of whom, Lucy Ridsdale, later married Prime Minister Stanley Baldwin. *Cricket,* a magazine whose readership undoubtedly came from the upper echelons of British society, managed to be supportive: "The New Woman is taking up cricket, evidently with the same energy which has characterized her in other and more important spheres of life."[47]

Cricket, still played by a number of female enthusiasts, lost ground to field hockey, destined to become the rage with the young women of the upper middle class. The women of Alexandra College (Dublin) started a club in 1892 and, two years later, invited the students of Newnham College to a tour of Ireland. (The Irish won every match, which must have been a small boon to the nationalists of the day, angry at their inability to win political home rule.) When England's Hockey Association refused to accept women as members, the female players promptly formed the Ladies' Hockey Association (1895). The women of Wales and Scotland followed suit in 1898 and 1900. In October 1901, the LHA began publishing *Hockey Field*, "the first periodical devoted entirely to women's sport." The social status of the early hockey players was never in question: "Practices and matches were during the day in mid-week, which excluded working women; and club subscription fees and the cost of uniforms and travel to matches were an additional guarantee of class distinctions." If these disincentives were inadequate, there was always the amateur rule, then construed to bar participation by anyone who worked with his or her hands. Predictably, opponents of the game were vocal, complaining that its "fierce excitement destroys the serene, tranquil beauty of the features, and its spasmodic climax is most injurious to the fine, keen nervous temperament of women." The proponents' strategy was to allay suspicions by "emphasizing the grace and femininity of female hockey players."[48]

The roughness of soccer football and the fact of its growing popularity with miners, dock workers, and factory hands inhibited efforts to popularize the game among the women of the upper classes, but the *Illustrated London News* printed a drawing by Richard Wright of English girls chasing a soccer ball. The girls were said to belong to the upper classes.[49]

3. Clubs and Country Clubs: American Women

By the end of the nineteenth century, athletic clubs were a fairly common feature of urban American middle-class life, but most of them closed their doors to girls and women. A few hardy creatures refused to be excluded. Some women responded to closed doors by forming their own clubs—like the Ladies Club for Outdoor Sports (Staten Island, 1877) or the Crescent City Archery Club (New Orleans, 1870s).[50] In 1881, young Charlotte Perkins Gilman persuaded a gymnasium owner in Providence, Rhode Island, to open an establishment for women, and she personally rounded up the women for the initially skeptical proprietor. Gilman was, of course, exceptional. As she noted in her autobiography, she had a "life-long interest in physical culture" and she was determined to develop "a fine physique." She ran a mile a day while a student at the Rhode Island School of Design, boasted of her ability to "vault and jump, go up a knotted rope, walk on my hands under a ladder, kick as high as my head, and revel in the flying rings." She was "absurdly vain of [her] physical strength and agility." As a mature woman, she played basketball with her teenage daughter.[51]

It was, however, the summer resort and the country club, not the urban athletic club, that became the preferred venues for upper-class women's sports. In the United States as in Great Britain, the game of croquet became immensely popular with the women of the leisure class. Between 1865 and 1869, the young Winslow Homer painted no fewer than five oils in which men and women are shown playing the game. Fourteen of the seventeen depicted figures are young women, all dressed in the period's billowing skirts and rather diminutive hats. The scenes are all pastoral, with none of the sexual tension that allegedly characterized the game in the 1870s and after.[52] (See Plate 11.) Croquet, which seemed ideal for displaying a summer dress, failed to liberate women from the material constraints of Victorian clothing. The physical demands of croquet were minimal. The game's vogue was short-lived. The same can be said of the Scottish sport of curling on ice, an activity that brought a few warmly clad young women to the frozen streams of New York's Central Park.[53]

Tennis did more than any other sport to revolutionize the clothing worn by upper-class sportswomen. In 1893, the arbiter of the cosmopolitan social set, Caroline Astor, was defied by her daughter-in-law, Ava Willing Astor, who appeared on the tennis courts of the Newport (Rhode Island) Casino—in bloomers. A year later, the Amherst-educated man of letters, W.C. Brownell, announced in Scribner's that the summer resort had given birth to a new ideal of physical beauty—the female athlete.[54] Inevitably, women like the young Mrs. Astor were likened to the icon of the new woman, the

Gibson Girl, created in 1890 by the artist Charles Dana Gibson. His creation was destined to dominate American aesthetic ideals for a quarter century. Tall, slim, with long arms and legs, she was definitely athletic. Although she was frequently portrayed with a bicycle, her favorite sports were golf and tennis. Speaking as one of the foremost feminists of the age, Charlotte Perkins Gilman was enthusiastic about her; the Gibson Girl was "braver, stronger, more healthful and skillful and able and free, more human in all ways."[55] Although Gilman did not expressly make the point, informed readers knew that the Gibson Girl, unlike the the heroine of Gilman's story, was not likely to go mad from inactivity.

Braver, stronger, more healthful, skillful, able, and free, the Gibson Girl was also richer. She belonged to the same social class as the "lovely archeresses" of Newport, whom Edith Wharton remembered in her autobiography. Wharton drew upon her memories of Newport's "almost pagan worship of physical beauty" when she created May Welland, the heroine of her retrospective novel of fin-de-siècle New York, *The Age of Innocence* (1920).[56] Like the Gibson Girl, May is a sports enthusiast who loves to swim, ride, row, sail, and play tennis. Skilled at archery, she is frequently compared—like many of her real-life contemporaries—to the goddess of the hunt. When May enters a room, she looks "like a Diana just alight from the chase." When she competes in Newport's archery contest, everyone pauses to admire:

She had her bow and arrow in her hand, and placing herself on the chalk-mark traced on the turf, she lifted the bow to her shoulder and took aim. The attitude was so full of a classic grace that a murmur of appreciation followed her appearance.

Not sharing Diana's legendary hostility to men, May marries a wealthy sportsman, Newland Archer, whose name is presumably meant to call further attention to his wife's athleticism. He is thrilled by "the nymph-like ease of his wife, when, with tense muscles and happy frown, she bent her soul upon some feat of strength." Wharton's portrait of the heroine is not, however, uncritical. While emphasizing May's physical attractiveness, Wharton remarks upon her intellectual shallowness: "She had just been for a row on the river. . . . As she walked beside Archer with her long swinging gait her face wore the vacant serenity of a young marble athlete."[57]

There was no hint of mental vacancy in Elizabeth Cynthia Barney's 1894 *Fortnightly Review* article, "The American Sportswoman," which joyfully proclaimed the arrival of a new athletic female. In the immediate post–Civil War years, the American girl "was supposed to live on candy and novels, and too often sink into a nervous invalid before she was thirty," but a "generation has sufficed to effect a complete change." The modern American sportswoman was a creature of "strong, active physique, erect carriage and energetic spirit." She was "aglow with the ruddy color of physical health and energy." She was also, quite emphatically, a member of the leisure class. Barney dwelled admiringly on the exclusive sports clubs of the elite. She was, for instance, complimentary about the national ladies' tennis championships held in Philadelphia:

The Philadelphia Country Club ranks with the foremost in tone and social standing, and every thing that it does is in the best style. Consequently the tournaments . . . are social functions of the highest class, and none enter their names but those of assured social position. As a matter of fact, all our first lady tennis players belong to the best families.

To exclude the hoi polloi, invitations to the tournament were issued only to socially acceptable women. It was appropriate that the first winner, Ellen Hansell Allerdice, took up the game after observing a match at John Wanamaker's posh suburban estate. It is also suggestive that tennis was brought to the United States from Bermuda in 1874 by Mary Ewing Outerbridge, a charter member of the Ladies' Club for Outdoor Sports, and that one of the earliest tournaments was held at the socially exclusive Staten Island Cricket Club.[58]

Among the most successful of the early tennis players was Eleonora Sears. A Boston Brahmin of impeccable lineage, she was also a descendant of Thomas Jefferson, uniting in one person the elite traditions of Beacon Hill and Monticello. Flouting convention, Sears rode astride and played polo in jodhpurs. Although the closest she came to a national title in singles tennis was her 1912 loss in the finals to Mary K. Browne, she won five championships in doubles and mixed doubles. She was also the first national champion in the even more exclusive game of squash. In these and other sports she accumulated some two-hundred forty trophies. She "lived the athletic Gibson Girl image to its limits and beyond."[59]

A similar receptivity to women's sports (of the right kind) characterized the Canadian elite. In a 1896 paean to "The Canadian Girl," Reginald Gourlay painted a verbal picture of high society:

The Canadienne has, as a rule, magnificent health, the reward (as is much of her beauty) of her fondness for the open air. She is as happy on the tennis court or golf ground, as in the ballroom; as much at home in the canoe, or the saddle, as in the opera box or at five o'clock tea.[60]

It is easy to imagine Thorstein Veblen fulminating at this or at the even more egregious document published in 1901 as *The Book of Sport*. This lavishly illustrated volume, which only the wealthy were able to purchase, ignored popular pastimes like baseball and concentrated on the sports of the leisure class. Photographs of well-dressed women graced the book's chapters on women's golf and tennis. Similar photographs appeared in *Outing*, a kind of nineteenth-century *Sports Illustrated*. The journal included articles on baseball, football, and track and field, but there was a pronounced emphasis on upper-class recreation.

The editors of *Outing* clearly felt that women ought to be involved in sports. In the eighties and nineties, Margaret Bisland wrote a series of *Outing* articles devoted to a variety of women's sports. An advocate of rowing, she scorned the timid souls who advised that light boats were best for women's "meagre muscles" and she reassured her readers that excessive muscularity was not a real danger:

By some happy provision of kind Nature, no matter if the woman's biceps grow as hard as iron and her wrists as firm as steel, the member remains as softly rounded, as tenderly curved, as though no greater strain than the weight of jeweled ornaments had been laid upon [it].[61]

In a 1902 *Outing* article entitled "The Athletic Girl Not Unfeminine," Christine Terhune Herrick waxed lyrical about "the joys of the track with its competition and chance to make or break a school record."[62] In a 1905 issue of *Harper's*, which appealed to the same upper-middle-class audience, the Coca-Cola company published its first advertisement. Attractively posed were a man with golf clubs and a girl dressed for tennis with a racquet in her hand. Long before the arrival of the sports-mad "Pepsi generation," Coca-Cola had discovered the country-club set.[63]

The country club was the upper-class American equivalent of the English country house and the French chateau. Whisked away by the newly constructed commuter rail lines from the city and its immigrant throng, wealthy Americans withdrew to the suburbs. While snobbery was unquestionably a motive, the rich were also unsettled by their fear that lower-class spectators were not only unsavory but also rather dangerous. Sports spectators *were* often a rowdy bunch. In 1886, when the New York Caledonians, a perfectly respectable middle-class organization for Scottish immigrants, added a 220–yard race for young women to its annual athletic festival, the spectators went wild. The New York *Times* reported that the race "excited immense enthu-siasm, and the ropes were broken down in several places by the eagerness of the crowd to get a good view."[64] After reading such an account, the affluent sportsman was likely to write out his check for membership in Peter Lorillard's Tuxedo Park, which opened that year.

At Tuxedo Park and other country clubs, sports were an important attraction for both sexes. Indeed, an *Outing* article by Robert Dunn emphasized the fact that women were more than welcome to join in country-club sports. At a time when it was almost as unusual for a woman to watch as to play a game of baseball, the wives and daugh-ters of the wealthy were devotees of golf and tennis. In the protected country-club environment, isolated from the urban masses by social as well as geographical distance, literally shielded from vulgar eyes by fences and hedges, women who had participated in sports while at Mount Holyoke, Smith, Vassar, and Wellesley were able to ride, swim, row, swing their golf clubs and their tennis rackets, and bend their bows in graceful emulation of Diana. Writing in *Harper's Weekly* on "Country Club Life in Chicago," H. C. Chatfield-Taylor an-nounced with approval, "There are fewer sallow complexions than formerly, more bright eyes and rosy cheeks, fewer pinched-in waists, and more broad shoulders and well-browned arms." Chatfield-Tay-lor was probably aware, at least subliminally, of the inverse relation-ship between the work of lower-class women and the leisure of the rich. When women labored in the fields, a pale face was the sign of high status; when factory girls bent over their machines in stuffy lofts and dank basements, a "well-browned" arm signaled freedom from material necessity.[65]

It is undeniably true that money mattered and that golf and tennis were attractive to the country-club set because they required costly lessons, expensive equipment, or extensive tracts of land, i.e., because they were *exclusive,* but it is also true that many of the most favored sports were popular because they were considered appropriate for both men and women. Since none of the popular country-club games allowed for physical contact and most were played in modest (and cumbersome) dress, men and women were free to play in mixed groups. In his sports, the Robber Baron demanded social, not sexual, segregation.

4. Chateaux and Clubs: European Women

In this quest for social rather than sexual segregation, the Robber Baron was rather like the real barons whom he often took as his role models. With a touch of exaggeration, one might say that prerevolutionary French hunters were divided not into males and females but into aristocrats and poachers. Feudal privileges were abolished in 1789, but hunting remained an important element in the nobility's self-image. Hunting was "the preserve of a politically disinherited elite clinging tenaciously to social pre-eminence."[66] *La duchesse* hunted in the forest of Rambouillet and *la baronne* had her hounds blessed yearly on St. Hubert's Day (June 11th). *La Comtesse de La Martinière* preferred to hunt grouse in Scotland. For a fourteen-year-old girl like the future Comtesse de Pange, the moment when she was allowed to mount her first horse was *"le grand évenement"* of her life.[67] When the *petit bourgeois* and even the peasantry began to purchase hunting licenses, the aristocracy either withdrew within the borders of their estates or barricaded themselves behind the exclusive rules of their hunting clubs.

Under the protective auspices of a club, upper-class and upper-middle-class European women felt free not only to ride to the hounds but also to participate in a wide variety of other sports. Among the oldest and most prestigious clubs were the archery guilds patronized by St. Sebastian. Many of these clubs traced their origins back to the late Middle Ages. This was the case for Dresden's *Schützenverein,* which awarded Princess Amalie of Saxony the 1851 prize for the most accurate crossbow shot. At the court of Napoleon III, the Vicomtesse de Gillyd was envied for her skills as an archer and a fencer. For her and other aristocratic sportswomen, Empress Eugenie constructed an archery grounds at the summer palace at Compiègne. When the Second Empire was succeeded by the Third Republic, the prolific Jean-Alexandre-Joseph Falguière and a number of other late nineteenth-century sculptors produced bronze and marble statues of Diana as archer-huntress. Asked why he returned again and again to this subject, Falguière replied, "I create a Diana because Dianas are successful." Her lithe figure adumbrated a new aesthetic ideal.[68]

After young Englishmen introduced the game of lawn tennis to the vacationers at fashionable Bad Homburg on July 28, 1877, aristocratic Germans of both sexes quickly organized tennis clubs noted for their steep entrance fees and their aura of *Snobismus*. The prestige of tennis became still greater when Kaiser Wilhelm began to take lessons.[69] At Bad Homburg's annual tennis tournament, courtside seats were reserved for royal spectators.[70] As a prelude to courtship, tennis quickly overshadowed croquet. In 1885, a prominent member of the Prussian legislature noted with satisfaction that modern youngsters are as likely to fall in love on the tennis court as on the ballroom floor.[71]

As the leisure class took delightedly to the tennis courts, artists who found it difficult to imagine Atalanta or Diana rushing to the net with racquets in their hands took their cue from the magazine illustrators and began to produce images of modern sportswomen. The work of profounder artists was often a meditation on what it all meant. A group portrait of female tennis players, painted in 1889 by the most famous of the Belgian Symbolist painters, Fernand Khnopff, is probably the finest of the many depictions of *fin de siècle* sportswomen. (See Plate 14.) Entitled *Memories* (in English), the somberly painted picture shows seven elegantly clad women with tennis racquets in hand but no tennis court in sight. Each seems lost in thought; each gazes into some world of her own. It is a haunting suggestion that the emancipation of the individual had its costs.[72]

The rowers on European rivers and lakes had somewhat less status than the hunters, archers, and tennis players, but the women of St. Petersburg's exclusive Yacht Club were doubtless the talk of the Czarist capital when they held a regatta in 1865.[73] These aristocratic Russian women may well have been inspired by women enrolled in German clubs, which were (and are) Europe's most numerous and best organized. The elite status of Germany's *Rudervereine* was unmistakable. As Henning Eichberg notes in reference to the late nineteenth century,

Rowing displayed the typical profile of an upper-class sport. Organized on English models and with ties to the navy, sponsored by government agencies and by royalty, exclusively amateur, it was the sport of "the better sort," of businessmen and students.

In Copenhagen, where cultural ties to England were also quite strong, twenty-seven Danish women organized a rowing club in 1890. Despite the women's protests, male colleagues judged the women's "races" on the basis of style rather than speed.[74] In 1895, one of Berlin's many rowing clubs, the *Touren-Ruderer Verein,* held a widely publicized canoe race for women on the Oberspree. A club exclusively for the city's women was organized in 1901, four years before forty Oslo women organized Norway's first rowing club. A decade later, Berlin alone had three clubs for female "oarsmen." A year after that, under German influence, Warsaw got its first rowing club for women. Finally, in 1919, German women organized nationally and founded a *Damenruderverband.*[75] The cover of *Le Figaro Illustré* for 1890 pictured an enticingly bare-armed young woman seated in a racing scull. Enticement failed. Middle-class French women were not as quick to take to the sport as German women were.[76]

When German women began to swim competitively, they confronted the inevitable moral problem: was the relative undress of the swimmers an incitement to male voyeurism? The *Verein Nixe Charlottenburg,* founded in 1893, announced plans to organize races for its "nymphs." The club's announcement of the *Schwimmfest* caused consternation in the press. Moralists were placated when the club agreed to ban male spectators. An exception was made for the starter, whose professionalism was thought to protect him from improper thoughts. At subsequent meets, the band was seated discreetly behind a curtain and the spectators were placed no closer than thirty meters from the swimmers.[77]

Social historians sometimes refer to the bicycle as an inexpensive way for the men and women of the working class to obtain a modicum of spatial mobility. Posters painted by none other than Henri de Toulouse-Lautrec encourage us to imagine the young *ouvrière* touring and even racing on her *vélo.* As we have seen, a number of working-class girls like Hélène Dutrieu and Amélie LeGall had careers as professional cyclists. The female members of the *Touring Club de France* (1891), however, were definitely middle-class. As the club's name indicates, these cyclists used their costly vélos for excursions, not for races. Compared to the women who crowded British and American highways and byways, these middle-class Frenchwomen were very few in number. Fourteen, to be exact, of a total club membership of 1138. It may be that prudish resistance to the "rational" dress necessary for safe cycling was stronger in France than in the English-speaking world. In *most* sports, the *bourgeoise* seems to have lagged behind her American, British, and Germans counterparts while upper-class and lower-class Frenchwomen kept pace or took the lead.[78]

Many of the athletic events for middle-class European women were sponsored by gymnastics clubs. Despite their commitment to pageantry and to mass displays of agility and strength, despite their persistent doubts about the value of competition, the German *Turnvereine* often held contests in what were referred to as *volkstümliche Leibesübungen* (i.e., "physical exercises of the common people"). In a contemporary illustration of a girls' race at a gymnastics festival in Markgroeningen am Neckar in 1861, one can see the flags and banners and the crowd of attendant dignitaries. The event was thoroughly *bürgerlich,* very proper, very different from the smock races of earlier times or the commercially sponsored shopgirl races of a later date.[79]

There were, of course, also clubs for *Wintersport.* One of the earliest club-sponsored races for female ice-skaters was held in Hamburg in 1885. It was probably a good idea to have club sponsorship; as late as 1851, Maria Weigel was stoned for appearing on skates. (She survived.) In the last decade of the century, ski clubs began to organize serious competitions for women. In 1893, in Mürzzuschlag, a certain Mizzi Angerer won a 400–meter "cross-country" race. Twelve years later, on a hillside near Lilienfeld, she won an early form of the slalom.[80]

In France and Germany as in Great Britain and the United States, there was acrimonious debate between those who welcomed the prospect of women's sports and those who feared that female athletes jeopardized their anatomical destiny as wives and mothers. In the *Revue des Revues* for July 1900, the poet René François Armand Sully-Prudhomme expressed his *"horreur"* at the athletic woman's tendency to "borrow from men the virile qualities that denature her and negate her charm." The novelist and intrepid political activist Emile Zola strongly disagreed. He was receptive to "whatever physical exercises can contribute to woman's development —as long as she doesn't abuse them." Zola denounced the tyranny of received opinion and refuted the argument that sports masculinize the female athlete.[81]

It is impossible to say just how serious these leisure-class women of *la belle époque* were about athletic competition. They were often ridiculed in the contemporary press for their alleged "dilettantism." More recently, Marxist historian Jennifer Hargreaves, has belittled them by maintaining that these women were passive rather than active. Their approach to sports was on a par with "playing the piano, singing, drawing and painting, reciting poetry and doing needle-work."[82] No doubt there were tight-laced corseted ladies who daw-dled at croquet and breathlessly murmured lines from Tennyson, but the evidence suggests dedication as well as dilettantism. Diligent scrutiny of *Womanhood*, an upper-class British journal published from 1898 to 1906, has convinced Cartriona M. Parratt that Hargreaves badly underestimated the fin-de-siècle female athlete. Parratt quotes a typical report of women's field hockey: "Vigorous, vivacious young womanhood is certainly seen at her athletic best when taking part in some keen struggle with the sticks between the goals."[83] That upper-class Americans were as ready to give their utmost can be seen in an account of the finish of a race at Vassar College. "With brain of fire, throat of parchment, feet of lead, she makes a last spurt into the arms of her friends beyond the tape, and breaks the record."[84]

Doubts about the seriousness of the women should be allayed by the fact that they began, in the last quarter of the century, to organize national and even international competitions for female athletes. By 1900, when Margaret Abbot of the Chicago Golf Club came home from Paris with Olympic gold, European and American women had national championships in archery, golf, and tennis. While these women may not have demonstrated the obsessive drive of today's elite female athletes, there is no reason whatsoever to believe that they were not serious about their titles and their trophies.

To the accusation of dilettantism some radical feminists have added the graver charge of sexual exploitation. In "The Sexual Politics of Sport," Helen King quotes an 1895 article that urged young Austra-lian women to do various sports to maintain their "trim, well knit and muscular figures." King criticizes this instrumentalization of sports for the sake of health. Were not the benefits of health and hygiene misused to restrict women to the "anatomical destiny" of mother-hood? This is clearly the opinion of Patricia Vertinsky when she charges that the women of North America were encouraged by male medical professionals "to hone their bodies to a machine-like effi-ciency through modest and sociable sport and exercise in order that they might better secure the biological future of the race."[85] There is certainly an element of truth in such sharply worded assertions. No historian can deny that male (and female) reformers were motivated by a concern for health, hygiene, and prospective motherhood. It is, however, reductionist to conclude from the evidence that this was the only motive. One might also ask if giving birth with "machine-like efficiency" to a healthy child is not preferable—for those women who want children—to dying in the middle of prolonged and difficult delivery.

Summing up the feminist debate over the repressive versus the emancipatory elements in nineteenth-century women's sports, Kathleen E. McCrone admits that the sports participation of English women was "hedged in . . . by compromises with the social system," but she goes on to conclude, quite reasonably,

> The emergence of the Victorian sportswoman was part of the same broad movement for social transformation that saw middle-class women contradict received definitions of their sex's true nature and challenge a system that restricted opportunities for development to males. . . . In its own way sport was just as significant to the ultimate goals of feminism.[86]

While no statistically minded historian has attempted to study the relationship of sports participation in the women's colleges and subsequent involvement in political reform, England's Rhoda Anstey, America's Charlotte Perkins Gilman, and a number of others can be cited as suggestive instances of a positive correlation. Alice Paul, for example, excelled in basketball while a student at Swarthmore (class of 1902) and went on to found the National Women's Party (1917) and to lead the stubborn fight for an Equal Rights Amendment.[87] Another way to think about the matter is to look at the politics of those who *opposed* women's sports.

After all, if the advocates of women's sports had been as repressive as historians like King, Hargreaves, and Vertinsky maintain they were, then truly sexist voices, like that of Arabella Kenealy, would not have wailed as they did at the unconventional behavior of athletic women. Perhaps the last word on the turn-of-the-century social transformation should be given to someone who participated in it. Assessing the "athletic girl" for a 1901 issue of *Munsey's Magazine,* Anne O'Hagen concluded, "With the single exception of the improvement in the legal status of women, their entrance into the realm of sports is the most cheering thing that has happened to them in the century just past. . . . The revolution meant as much psychologically as it did physically."[88]

NINE

Play Days and
Muscle Molls

1. The Alternative to Competition

Early-twentieth-century expectations that the female athlete was about to asssume her rightful place in the sun were disappointed. In the popular imagination, the twenties were the Jazz Age, the years when flappers bobbed their hair, donned their shorts, grabbed their tennis rackets, played three furious sets against F.Scott Fitzgerald, and danced all night. The twenties are remembered as "The Golden Age of Sports." In reality, women's sports entered a period of stops and starts (and were thus like the "woman's movement" generally, which lost most of its momentum after the triumphant achievement of the ballot in 1920). The women who were firmly in charge of physical education for schoolgirls and college students developed an ideology remarkably similar to the nineteenth-century doctrine of "separate spheres." They abjured competition. Women's sports were sponsored in the 1920s and 1930s by industrial leagues or by the Amateur Athletic Union rather than by the educational institutions which had once nurtured them.

It was not just that female physical educators had changed their minds about sports. In the twenties, American educational institutions reconceived their purpose and reorganized their curricula. Unprecedentedly large numbers of women attended the nation's colleges and universities, but they were less likely than their mothers and grandmothers had been to prepare for and enter the professions.

Barbara Harris has rightly emphasized the crucial difference between the flapper and the career woman:

The whole significance of the 1920s is epitomized by the fact that the symbol of the decade was not the emancipated career woman, but the flapper. Although she was sexually liberated and had greater social freedom than her predecessors, the flapper fit easily into a society that saw women in predominantly sexual terms. When her dancing and drinking days were over, she settled down as wife and mother. [1]

The flapper was certainly not averse to sports, nor were the men who courted her unaware of the erotic appeal of an athletic body, but the message incessantly drummed into her consciousness was that women who were *too* competitive, *too* serious about either physical or intellectual achievement, were likely to finish last in the race for a husband. What other contest mattered?

Female physical educators emphasized the same values as their colleagues in more academic disciplines. What Catherine E. D'Urso calls "the ideology of educated motherhood" led to the proliferation of college-level courses in domestic science and, simultaneously, to programs of physical activity designed to improve health while avoiding overexertion and the dread spectre of exercise-induced infertility. [2]

The revived doctrine of "separate spheres," which emphasized motherhood almost to the exclusion of any other concern, dictated fundamentally different sports programs for male and female students. An additional influence on the women who controlled physical education at the colleges and universities was the appalling corruption that they witnessed in men's intercollegiate athletics. By the twenties, men's programs had already been through a series of crises brought on by the perceived need for victory at all costs. When the Carnegie Commission reported on the sorry state of men's intercollegiate athletics in 1929, there was an already familiar litany of subterfuge and special treatment. Not only did the second generation of female coaches and athletic directors know what they wanted; they also had a vivid sense of the distortions and abuses they were determined to avoid.

Idealistically, they labored to provide a more humane alternative for women. Although their predecessors had defied convention and experimented boldly with intercollegiate athletics, the younger generation opted for moderation. The result was more often than not an outright ban on intercollegiate contests or their transformation into "play days" or "telegraphic meets." In the first, young women from different schools were assigned to mixed teams so that, for instance, a single basketball team might include students from Mount Holyoke, Wellesley, and Smith. Since no team represented a school, identification with *alma mater* was practically impossible and athletic ineptitude was easily excusable. Fun and games were followed by tea and cookies. Competitiveness was not rewarded. "Telegraphic meets" were suitable only for highly quantified individual sports like track and field and swimming. The students of one college put forth their best efforts and then wired their times and distances to their rivals at another school. Such meets were inexpensive and unmarred by the tumult and disorder that often accompanied men's sports. They were also dull. The thrill of immediate head-to-head competition vanished and the complex frame of an entire sports-centered weekend—with all the attendant excitement, with train trips, dances, bonfire rallies, cheers, jeers, post-game parties—was gone.[3]

If they are to prevail, ideologies require institutional structure. Ever since the creation of the American Physical Education Association in 1885, women had formed a committee within the APER. Now the threat of "excessive" competition spurred them to more effective organization. The immediate stimulus occurred when President William Prout of the Amateur Athletic Union proposed that the AAU send a team of young women to compete in international competitions to be held in Paris in the summer of 1922. Speaking at an AAU meeting at New York's McAlpin Hotel, Prout went further: "I agree that the women of America should be put upon the same physical basis as the women of other countries. We don't want them to get too far ahead of us."[4] The members of APER's Committee on Women's Athletics were "incensed."[5] They "issued two statements, one denying any affiliation with the AAU and a second disapproving of sending a representative women's team to Paris."[6]

Dr. Harry Stewart, who accompanied the team to the games, defended a girl's right to compete. "Let the girl have the joy of competitive athletics under proper restrictions and develop to the utmost her physical powers."[7] Anne Harwick, a student at Florida State College for Women, was expected to be the star of the American team, but she overtrained, did not compete in the javelin and shot put, and failed to reach the finals of the 300–meter sprint. Dr. Katherine Montgomery, chair of Florida State's Department of Physical Education, had helped in raising money to send Harwick to Paris;

now, disappointed by Harwick's poor showing and upset by stories of extreme exhaustion, she became an adversary of intercollegiate competition for women.[8]

The AAU had more faith. Voting in January of 1923 to accept women in track and field, swimming, gymnastics, basketball, and handball, the organization also ruled that all committees dealing with women's sports had to have at least one female member and that all clubs with women's teams had to have at least one female officer or official.[9] The angry members of the APER's Committee on Women's Athletics were not placated. They met in Washington in April of 1923 in order to do something about the "lamentable failure to safeguard the physical and even moral well-being of the girls of the country in their athletic contests."[10]

The outcome of the emergency was a new organization, the Women's Division of the National Amateur Athletic Federation, and a sixteen-point "Athletic Creed." The principles of this creed included the belief that "the motivation of competitors in athletic activities should be play for play's sake" and not for the sake of prizes or awards. In line with this belief, the Women's Division advocated participation for all and not just for the talented few. ("A sport for every girl and every girl in a sport.") The Women's Division condemned the "exploitation [of female athletes] for the enjoyment of the spectator or for the athletic reputation or commercial advantage of any school or other organization."[11]

The original set of sixteen resolutions did not include a prohibition against intercollegiate contests, but the Women's Division realized almost immediately that such competitions, especially when they culminated in national championships, spawned precisely the kinds of abuses that the organization wished most ardently to eradicate. Quite apart from the dishonesty and hypocrisy which plagued men's intercollegiate athletics, there was the fear of what the physical and psychic strain of intense competition might do to adolescent girls. Bryn Mawr's Louisa Smith, speaking for an earlier generation, had said, "Life is one long competition, so why not prepare for it in the gymnasium?"[12] The Women's Division thought otherwise. Less than a year after the formation of that division, Mabel Lee—their most influential spokeswoman—summed up the case for and against intercollegiate competition, and concluded that the dangers far outweighed the benefits.

It seems impossible that the "many" would not suffer neglect for the "few." No school has sufficient staff or equipment to carry out a correct program for both the "many" and the "few." The many girls neglected are sure to be the very girls who need the most training for their physical welfare. They would not have their legitimate share of athletic and department funds spent upon their training, so high would be the expense of intercollegiate teams.[13]

To this concern for equity, Ethel Perrin added the theme of female modesty, which played a larger role in the debates over intercollegiate sports than one might have thought. Perrin warned that a respectable woman should "never be seen by the opposite sex when she is likely to forget herself," a precept which, if taken literally, severely limits women's sexual lives.[14] Mabel Lee was also moved to worry about endangered modesty. On the topic of athletic costumes, she was quite strict. She quoted with approval a businessman whom she persuaded to change his mind about what was or was not appropriate in sports clothing: "You know," he bashfully admitted, "I am a little bit old-fashioned, I guess, and if I had a daughter, I should hate to have her go on a gymnasium floor wearing an abbreviated costume before a mixed audience."[15] If the colleges and universities restricted women's sports to intramurals, the possibility that someone's daughter might appear in short pants or lose her composure in the heat of the contest would be greatly reduced. And most men would stay away. The Women's Division asked that competition be restricted to intramurals. Young women who competed for AAU-affiliated sports clubs were barred as if they were professionals from what little intercollegiate competition the Women's Division was willing to countenance.[16]

Small wonder that the physical educators of the Women's Division felt themselves menaced by the Olympic Games. After the introduction of women's track and field at the 1928 Olympics, the Women's Division repeatedly petitioned the International Olympic Committee not to repeat the dangerous "experiment." Frederick R. Rogers shared the convictions of the Women's Division and supported them in a 1929 *School and Society* article entitled "Olympics for Girls?" Explaining that "men are more animal-like, mobile, energetic, aware, while women are more plant-like, more closely attached to the soil," Rogers answered his own rhetorical question with a resounding negative: "Intense forms of physical and psychic conflicts . . . tend to destroy girls' physical and psychic charm and adaptability for motherhood."[17] Writing in *Scientific American,* Donald A. Laird did without the animal-vegetable imagery but came to the same unscientific conclusion. Although medical research had clearly demonstrated the opposite, he announced that "feminine muscular development interferes with motherhood."[18]

The campaign to end intercollegiate contests and national championships was fairly successful. In 1924, Mabel Lee conducted a survey of fifty colleges from almost every part of the nation and found that only 22 percent of them sponsored intercollegiate athletics; the rest felt that such contests were harmful to their women students. Lee reported that 24 percent of the program directors believed that sports were physically beneficial, 28 percent thought them mentally beneficial, and 42 percent admitted that they were socially beneficial, yet fully 60 percent of those surveyed indicated their belief that women were harmed physically by intercollegiate competition.[19] Seven years later, after the Women's Division of the National Amateur Athletic Federation had had more time to propagandize for its views, Mabel Lee conducted another survey and found that an overwhelming 79 percent of those queried felt that the effects of intercollegiate sports were detrimental to their physical-education programs. Only 12 percent of the schools surveyed allowed intercollegiate contests.[20]

Meanwhile, the students had their own ideas. If Wellesley was at all representative, the students' views were starkly opposed to those of their physical-education teachers. In 1924, the undergraduates voted 237–33 in favor of intercollegiate athletics. The response of the editors of the *American Physical Education Review* was to deplore such benighted attitudes.[21] The desires of the students, which had been crucial during the nineteenth-century transition from calisthenics to sports, were ineffective when they came into conflict with the dictates of an entrenched educational bureaucracy.

Since Swedish drill was no longer an acceptable substitute for intercollegiate sports, the physical-education instructors turned to intramural competitions (encouraged by three schools in Lee's 1931 survey), to "telegraphic meets" (which 39 percent of the schools allowed), and to "Play Days" (endorsed by 53 of the 98 schools in the study). Lee was clear about her own preferences. "Play Days" were impromptu and informal; they required none of the intensive practice "which is one of the greatest evils of intercollegiate athletics." An essay by Helen N. Smith, "Evil of Sports for Women," added that "Play Days" were an opportunity for "spontaneous fun which is unspoiled by the tension of an overexcited audience and an oversti-mulated team."[22] The dominant view of the twenties and thirties was summed up by Agnes Wayman: "What is sauce for the gander, is *not* sauce for the goose!"[23]

Ignored by most spokespersons for women's physical education and by most surveyors of the collegiate scene was Alabama's Tuske-gee Institute. At that Afro-American school, athletic director Cleve-land Abbott promoted women's track and field (as well as a variety of men's sports). Under Abbott's tutelage, Tuskegee's women's team won the 1937 Amateur Athletic Association championship. They repeated their victory in ten of the next eleven years. Alice Coach-man, star of the 1948 team, won the high jump at that year's Olympic Games. In 1944, Abbott's daughter Jessie, a member of the 1937 team, became the women's track coach at Tennessee Agricultural and Industrial (now Tennessee State), a school whose teams were to include Wilma Rudolph and a number of other world-class runners. Tuskegee was, however, an exception even among black colleges.[24]

The Great Depression and the war years brought massive changes to women's lives, driving some women from the work force in the 1930s and then bringing millions of women to wartime assembly lines and government offices. Despite the massive transformation of the economy, attitudes towards women's sports changed slowly. In 1938, the International Olympic Committee had to deal—once more —with a petition from the Women's Division of the National Ama-teur Athletic Federation. The women asked—once more—that women's track and field be removed from the Olympic program. The IOC rejected the petition.[25]

Gladys Palmer of Ohio State University, calling for "excellence of play" and "admiration of excellence for its own sake," tried to per-suade her peers in the profession to abandon their opposition to intercollegiate competition. She sent out an open letter to that effect, suggested the formation of a Woman's National Collegiate Athletic Association, and invited like-minded colleagues to a conference on the OSU caompus in the summer of 1941. In vain. Hers was "a voice crying in the wilderness." In 1942, the Women's Division, along with the AAU, the YWCA, the YWHA, and seven other national groups opposed competition at the district or county levels. The 100–yard dash was also discouraged as too strenuous for female athletes. A 1945 article by Gladys Scott reported on a replication of the earlier sports-participation surveys by Mabel Lee. Of 227 institutions polled, only 16 percent participated in intercollegiate athletics.[26] In 1956, the Division of Girls' and Women's Sports, as the organization was then known, continued to urge that extramural competition "not lead to county, state, district or national championships." As late as 1957, the DGWS called once again for "Play Days" instead of intercollegiate encounters. Varsity sports were not accepted until the 1960s, when the second wave of American feminism finally overwhelmed the spokeswomen for "separate spheres."[27]

2. Industrial Sports

The Division of Girls' and Women's Sports never had the opportunity to stifle the competitive instincts of most American girls because most American girls never went to college. Whether they graduated from high school or dropped out without a diploma, they were likely to work for wages, marry young, have several children, and return to the workforce. For very few working women was there time or money or energy enough for a serious commitment to regular sports participation. European women of the same social class had at least the opportunity to join a sports club affiliated with one or another of the workers' sports federations that were to be found in Germany and most other European countries, but the American equivalent of Germany's *Arbeiter Turn- und Sportbund* was available to a mere handful of working-class women.

In the late nineteenth and early twentieth centuries, when recreational opportunities for upper-class and middle-class girls and women expanded, their working-class counterparts were more likely to spend their scant leisure hours at dance halls than at sports events.[28] In these years, the YWCA and YWHA provided some facilities for some sports activity. Boston's YWCA held athletic contests for girls as early as 1882 and opened a girls' gymnasium in 1894. The "Y," however, found it difficult to attract working-class girls. Settlement houses were successful in offering sports to the sons of the new immigrants, but immigrant parents were often adamant about the "indecency" of their daughters' playing in bloomers or in short skirts and long stockings. Settlement-house leaders like Jane Addams helped found the Playground Association of America in 1906, but few girls were attracted to urban playgrounds, and those who were were predominantly middle-class. Newspapers took up part of the slack when they sponsored sports events that they then reported. In the 1930s, for instance, the *Chicago Evening American* organized bowling tournaments that brought thousands of working-class women to the sport. The *Philadelphia Tribune* sponsored a basketball team for black women. (The team included Ora Washington, star of the all-black American Tennis Association, winner of seven consecutive national singles titles from 1929 to 1935.) Most newspapers preferred the newsworthy tournament format to the expensive sponsorship of regular leagues and year-round play.[29]

The brightest light in this rather bleak landscape was the industrial league. Motivated by enlightened self-interest, a number of American corporations began to offer their employees the extensive benefits of "welfare capitalism." Among the amenities whose purpose was to ameliorate if not to eliminate class conflict was the sports club. At Western Electric's Hawthorne plant, for instance, the recreational program included fourteen different sports. Any employee was eligible to participate after three months on the job. Although the Depression forced many companies to curtail or to eliminate their programs, a study done in 1940 found that 38.3 percent of the 639 firms surveyed continued to sponsor sports for their employees. The most popular activities for women were bowling and softball, but women's tennis, surprisingly, was offered in 10 percent of the programs. When John J. Glenn of the Illinois Manufacturers' Association visited the Chicago plant of the Calumet Baking Powder Company, he was impressed by a noonhour game of baseball: "Those girls were pitching curves, catching hot ones and sliding to bases with all the joyous abandon of youth."[30]

"On balance," writes Cindy Himes, "the industrial programs probably served their intended audience more effectively than school and college athletics did theirs." At the first two national championships for women sponsored by the Amateur Athletic Union, in 1923 and 1924, teams from the industrial leagues dominated the track and field events. Sociologists have failed to provide us with good data on the number of women who joined the companies' clubs and played on the companies' basketball or volleyball or softball team, but we do know that the industrial leagues reached a much larger number of women than the colleges and universities did (partly because higher education was still a restricted privilege).[31]

The level of competition was often quite high. One of the most

famous of American athletes—Texas-born Mildred "Babe" Didrikson—competed for the Employers Casualty Insurance Company of
Dallas rather than for the University of Texas. Shortly before her
birth on June 26, 1911, Didrikson's parents came to the United States
from Norway. She was born in Port Arthur, the youngest of seven
children, the only one born in this country. Growing up in Beau-
mont, Texas, where her father worked as a furniture finisher, she was
the prototypical tomboy, preferring boys' games to girls.' When her
mother attempted to put her into a party dress, she romped away in
her overalls. As a child, she asked the neighbors to clip their hedges
to the height she was able to hurdle. "My goal," she wrote in her
autobiography, "was to be the greatest athlete that ever lived." [32] She
did not say the greatest *female* athlete. After her triumph at the 1932
Olympics she told an interviewer, "I don't worry about the races
with girls." [33] In high school, she played baseball, basketball, volleyball, golf, and tennis. And she swam. Her athletic career might have
ended when she dropped out of high school had she not been fortunate enough to attract the attention of Melvorne Jackson ("Colonel")
McCombs of Employers' Casualty insurance company. McCombs
was a shrewd eccentric who believed in women's basketball (and
married one of the players on the company's team). He outfitted the
"Golden Cyclones" in shorts and jerseys and beamed as attendance
soared from under 200 to some 5,000 a night. [34] In 1930, McCombs
hired Didrikson, ostensibly as a stenographer, for $75 a month. A
year later, she led the company's basketball team to the AAU national
championship.

Didrikson and several of her teammates requested that the company sponsor a track team, and McCombs complied. On July 7,
1930, at the AAU's national championships, Didrikson broke three
world records. At the 1932 meet she won six gold medals and set
four world records, all within a space of three hours. Alone, she
outscored the twenty-two women of the Illinois Women's Athletic
Club, which came in second. Although the Olympic rules limited her
to three events, the 1932 games, held in Los Angeles, were the
occasion of another triumph. In her first effort in the javelin competition she exceeded the world record by more than two meters. She
had serious competition in the high jump from Jean Shiley, a physical-education major from Temple University (who had not been allowed to train on college grounds). [35] When the two women tied for
first place, at record level, the judges awarded the medal to Shiley on

the grounds that Didrikson dove over the bar. The possible unfairness of that decision was matched by the possible unfairness of the decision in the 80–meter hurdles. Although Evelyne Hall had a welt on her neck, from breaking the tape, Didrikson threw up her arms in the victor's gesture, and she was given the medal. Both runners finished in 11.7 seconds, a new world record.

Didrikson also garnered most of what meager newspaper and magazine space was devoted to the women at the games. Although it has been said that "the boys of the press felt at ease with her," their coverage was not always flattering. Referring to her appearance and her origins, the *Los Angeles Times* described her as "a lanky, homely longhorn." In the same frontpage story, the *Times* for July 30th called Jean Shiley "the prettiest girl of the American track team." An obsession with the looks of the female athletes was, in fact, typical of media coverage of the 1932 Olympics. "In the *Los Angeles Times* . . . there was a decided tendency to publish pictures of women Olympians posed like beauty queens."[36] Eleanor Holm, winner of the 100–meter backstroke in world-record time, was referred to as a "beautiful little New Yorker" (July 17th), a "beautiful young lady" (August 10th), and the "most beautiful girl athlete" at the games (August 14th). While Didrikson tended to be abrasive in her public statements, Holm soothed the apprehensive:

It's great fun to swim and a great thrill to compete in the Olympics, but the moment I find my swimming is making me athletic looking, giving me big, bulky muscles, making me look like an Amazon rather than a woman, I'll toss it to one side.[37]

The wonder is, given the temper of the times, that the American media gave Didrikson as much favorable attention as they did. She had few admirers in the press corps. Paul Gallico's notorious remarks were typical:

She was the muscle moll to end all muscle molls, the complete girl athlete. . . . She was a tomboy who never wore make-up, who shingled her hair until it was as short as a boy's and never bothered to comb it, who didn't care about clothes and who despised silk underthings. . . . She had a boy's body, slim, straight, curveless, and she looked her best in a track suit. She hated women and loved to beat them. She was not, at that time [1932], pretty. . . . She had good, clear, gray-green eyes, but she was what is commonly described as hatchet-faced. She looked and acted more like a boy than a girl, but she was in every respect a wholesome, normal female [i.e., she was not a lesbian]. She was as tough as rawhide leather.

Gallico meanly attributed her athletic ambition to her inability to "compete with women at their own and best game—man-snatching."[38]

Long before the disputes at Los Angeles, Didrikson's arrogance had made her intensely unpopular with her teammates, who "came to detest her."[39] There was little sympathy for her, from men or from women, when the AAU briefly suspended her, shortly after the 1932 games, for appearing in an advertisement for Dodge automobiles. The manager of the agency which marketed the advertisement, allegedly without her permission, became Didrikson's agent when she did subsequent commercials and went on the vaudeville circuit. (She raced on a treadmill, sang in her strong Texas accent, and played the harmonica.) In 1933 and 1934 she barnstormed as a baseball player, first with "Babe Didrikson's All Americans" and then with the bearded team from the House of David. After deciding in 1933 to become a golfer, she toured with Gene Sarazen. She was spectacular. In 1946 she won seventeen tournaments in a row.

To the surprise of many, she married George Zaharias, a "professional" wrestler, whom she met at the Los Angeles Open of 1938. When he gained weight and lost his looks, the romance lost its bloom, and her assessment was typically blunt: "When I married him, he was a Greek god, now he's nothing but a goddam Greek."[40] Her animosity intensified when she learned of his love affair with her friend Betty Dodd. Mildred Didrikson Zaharias was sticken by cancer in 1953 and died on September 27, 1956, at the age of forty-five.

3. Respectable Heroines

Except for the brief vogue of "pedestrianism" in the early nineteenth century, track-and-field sports have never been as popular in the United States as in Europe, and women's track and field had to wait until the Olympic Games returned to Los Angeles, in 1984, to win a modicum of attention from the American media. In the twenties and thirties, of the handful of American women who made front page headlines because of their sports achievements, three were probably better known than Didrikson: Gertrude Ederle, Amelia Earhart, and Helen Wills. All three were certainly more acceptable in Middletown than Didrikson was.

Like Didrikson, Ederle was the child of immigrants, but her father, a German-American butcher, was more successful, in an economic sense, than Ole Didrikson. Although Ederle could have attended the City College of New York, like thousands of other second-generation Americans, she dropped out of high school and might have disappeared into anonymity but for the intervention of Charlotte Epstein of the Women's Swimming Association of New York. Epstein was a remarkable woman. Giving up on the colleges and universities, she had persuaded the Amateur Athletic Union to register female swimmers and to sponsor meets. This occurred in 1914, after the death of AAU President James Sullivan, an adamant opponent of women's sports. In the twenty-two years of Epstein's leadership, the swimmers of the Women's Swimming Association claimed fifty-one world records and comprised thirty national championship relay teams.[41] Ederle was encouraged by her older sister, Margaret, who also swam successfully for the Association. She also had sympathetic, if somewhat old-fashioned, parents. "Gertrude's mother often attributed her daughter's physical strength and athletic success to the regimen of household chores and the strict sense of discipline she encountered at home."[42]

In 1922, Ederle defeated fifty-one other women in a 3 1/2 mile race across New York Bay. Two years later, at the Olympic Games in Paris, she won bronze medals in the 100–meter and 400–meter freestyle races and a gold medal as a member of the 400–meter relay team. That year the seventeen-year-old held eighteen world records. In an otherwise admiring account of her achievements, *The Literary Digest* was unable to resist the snide suggestion that physical prowess was detrimental to feminine allure:

Gertrude declares she can polish off a large steak, rare, and consume more ice-cream than any girl she knows. A strapping, wholesome, fun-loving young creature is Gertrude, with muscles of steel and a great chuckle in her throat and honest wide-set brown eyes that would never lure a good sailor-man on the rocks when there were a a wife and children waiting for him on shore.[43]

She was, it seems, a Lorelei with principles.

When the *Literary Digest* printed this article, Ederle was still comparatively unknown despite her Olympic medals. Two years later, in the summer of 1926, she became the first woman to swim the English Channel. Her time from Gris-Nez to Kingston was fourteen hours thirty-one minutes. Accompanying her in a tugboat, her father and sister emphasized a patriotic motif. They led the journalists on board in a continual round of American songs, including "The Star-Spangled Banner." Back home, the family shop was draped in red, white, and blue. When New York's mayor welcomed her back to the city, she announced, "It was for my flag that I swam and to know that I could bring home the honors, and my mind was made up to do it."[44] The British press, belittling her achievement as tugboat-assisted, played into the hands of her American promoters. Chauvinism was a rich lode to mine. "Movie, stage, and commercial offers poured in." Ederle's lawyer and promoter, Dudley Field Malone, claimed that he had received contract offers for $900,000, including a $125,000 offer for a twenty-week engagement on the stage, but $200,000 seems a more reasonable estimate. The sum equaled a skilled workman's lifetime earnings.[45]

The nationalistic note was acompanied by a feminist one. After all, Ederle's time was a new record.

In response to the fact that Ederle beat the record time of the five previous male Channel swimmers by approximately two hours, the press engaged in a debate over the validity of the old dictum that women are the "weaker sex." American journalists gleefully ridiculed a London Daily News article declaring the incontrovertible physical inferiority of female athletes; the article had gone to press too late to prevent its publi- cation on the same day that news of Ederle's Channel swim hit the headlines.[46]

Ederle seemed for the moment to be an ideal representative of the physically liberated American flapper. She was hailed by *The Literary Digest* as "the bob-haired, nineteen-year-old daughter of the Jazz Age." Paul Gallico, who had nasty comments to make about the "muscle molls," called her "the greatest girl or woman athlete that ever lived, certainly the greatest of our time."[47] Her fame did not last. As she toured the United States and Europe, the emotional strain of public life proved harder to endure than the physical effort of swimming the Channel. Less brazen than Didrikson, who was ready with a tart response to any criticism she heard, Ederle suffered a nervous breakdown in 1928. Slipping into the obscure role of swimming instructor, she was soon overshadowed by a woman who seemed even more than a tugboat-assisted swimmer to be an appropriate symbol of the new technological era.

PLATE 22. The Olympic fencer's victory ceremony (Berlin, 1936): Ellen Preis (Austria), Ilona Elek-Schacherer (Hungary), Hélène Mayer (Germany). *Author's Collection*

PLATE 23. Amelia Earhart (1937). *AP/Wide World Photos*

PLATE 24. Poster for the Third Worker's Olympics (Antwerp, 1937). *Archiv voor Ret Turnweren, I.-L.O., K. V. Leuven*

PLATE 25. Dawn Fraser. *Collection: Maxwell Howell*

PLATE 26. Wilma Rudolph winning the 4 x 100 relay (Rome, 1960). *AP/ Wide World Photos*

PLATE 27. Billie Jean King, ca. 1965. *Patrick DeLuca*

PLATE 28. Ludmilla Tourescheva on the Balance Beam (Munich, 1972).
AP/Wide World Photos

PLATE 29. Rosi Mittermeier competing in the World Cup (Copper Mountain, Colorado, 1976). *AP/Wide World Photos*

PLATE 30. Kornelia Ender with her fourth gold medal (Montreal, 1976).
Nationales Olympisches Komitee der Deutschen Demokratischen Republik

PLATE 31. Nancy Lieberman playing for Old Dominion University. *Old Dominion University*

PLATE 32. Nancy Lopez. *The Ladies' Professional Golf Association*

PLATE 33. Zola Budd and Mary Decker Slaney moments before the fall (Los Angeles, 1984). *The Bettmann Archive*

PLATE 34. Kelly McCormick in springboard competition (Los Angeles, 1984).

PLATE 35. Model posing for a Lifecycle advertisement. *THE SHARPER IMAGE* (April 1989).

PLATE 36. Kim Ablon on Woodland's Snapdragon. *Judith S. Buck*

PLATE 37. Katarina Witt as "Carmen" (Calgary, 1988). *Nationales Olympisches Komitee der Deutschen Demokratischen Republik*

PLATE 38. Florence Griffth-Joyner winning a 200–meter heat (Seoul, 1988).
The Bettmann Archive

Amelia Earhart was certainly not the first "aviatrix." After the Wright brothers became the first men to fly, European women took to the air with more alacrity than their American sisters. Raymonde de Laroche, a French actress-artist, acquired a pilot's license in 1910 and Germany's famed Melli Beese learned to fly in 1911.[48] America's Harriet Quimby also secured her license in 1911. She successfully flew the English Channel, west to east, on April 16, 1912, but her daring brought her "little publicity" and she was "virtually forgotten."[49]

Earhart, "America's winged legend" was luckier. She was the most famous female pilot of her time. She was born in 1897, in Atchinson, Kansas, into what was then a comfortably middle-class home. Unfortunately, her lawyer-father became an alcoholic and her childhood was lonely and unsettled. Nonetheless, it was he who paid for her first flight, at an airshow in Long Beach in 1920. The experience convinced her that she wanted to become a pilot. After only two and a half hours of instruction, she impetuously decided she needed her own airplane. She went to work for a telephone company and saved her money. Her mother contributed $2,000 and Earhart purchased a Kinner Canary, a small, experimental airplane with an unusual air-cooled engine. Within weeks of her first solo flight in 1921, she set a women's altitude record of 14,000 feet. She became "a familiar figure on the dusty runways and in the tin airports of southern California." When she lost the altitude record to Ruth Nicholas, she attempted immediately to outdo her rival, and nearly crashed when she became disoriented in a fog bank. Recklessness became her trademark.[50]

Ironically, this eminently activist woman became famous for a wholly passive achievement. In 1928, a year after Charles Lindbergh's dramatic solo crossing in the *Spirit of St.Louis,* she became the first woman to fly the Atlantic. The irony is that she was merely a passenger. Wilmer Stultz was the pilot of *Friendship* and Louis Gordon was navigator. Any courageous female might have done what Earhart did, but she was the right woman at the right time. It was a stroke of luck that she *looked* amazingly like Lindbergh. She was also fortunate to have a skilled publicist as her promoter and then, when she finally surrendered to his repeated proposals, as her husband. George Palmer Putnam, who had published Lindbergh's *We,* admired Earhart's independent spirit and agreed with her egalitarian views of marriage. "Please," she wrote to him just before the wedding, "let us not interfere with [each] other's work or play. . . . " Their relationship was "as much a business arrangement as a marriage."[51]

Feeling a moral obligation to earn the fame that she enjoyed, Earhart took off from Newfoundland on May 20, 1932, and piloted her own plane across the Atlantic. She hoped to reach Paris as Lindbergh had, but engine trouble and icy wings brought her down in an Irish pasture. "I've come from America," she said to the startled owner. Londonderry was surprised and London went mad.

Amelia was showered with honours. She met the Pope, Mussolini, and the King and Queen of Belgium. Three aircraft dropped flowers on the liner *Ile de France* as she left Europe from LeHavre. In America, she was guest of honour at a formal dinner at the White House.[52]

Working as an editor at *Cosmopolitan* and *McCall's,* speaking at dinners, counseling coed students at Purdue University, she urged women to seize their opportunities for autonomy and adventure. She helped to found and served as president of the Ninety-Nines, an international organization of women pilots. She supported the political efforts of the National Woman's Party, the most aggressively feminist organization of the period.[53]

Fame fed ambition. In 1935 she flew from Honolulu to Oakland. That same year, she flew nonstop to Mexico City, where she received a heroine's welcome. She decided to circle the globe. Her twin-engine Lockheed Electra was redesigned for long distances. Her projected flight was nonetheless extremely hazardous. Flying west, she and her three-man crew landed safely in Hawaii, only to crash when they attempted to take off again. She repaired the plane and made new plans. The risk of death seemed to entice rather than deter her: "When I go," she said to her husband, "I'd like best to go in my plane. Quickly."[54]

She and Frederick Noonan, her navigator, tried again. Taking off from Miami, flying east, she reached the most dangerous leg of the flight. Between Lae, New Guinea, and tiny Howland Island, 2556 miles away, the only visual checkpoints were the USS *Ontario*, cruising midway between the two points, and the Coast Guard cutter *Itasca*, near Howland Island. Earhart had left her flares in California. She had no emergency portable radio. She did not inform the *Itasca* of her radio frequency and she was unaware that Howland's field had a high-frequency direction finder. She and Noonan took off on June 30, 1937. The *Itasca* picked up a radio message referring to cloudy and overcast conditions. Another message, six hours later, sounded "anxious and uncertain: 'We are on a line of position 157 dash 337. Will repeat this message on 6210 kilocycles. We are running north and south.' It was not repeated."[55] That was the last that anyone heard from her. Her Icarian flight prompted H. I. Phillips to write a poem in which he compared her to "Sparta's ancient women."[56] The comparison was apt.

Of America's athletic heroines of the twenties and thirties, Helen Wills was probably the best known and most typical. She was born in Centerville, California, on October 6, 1905. She was respectably upper-middle-class. Her father was a surgeon, her mother had a B.A. in education but preferred not to work outside the home. At the Berkeley Tennis Club, in 1920, young Helen Wills caught the attention of a distinguished visitor, Hazel Hotchkiss Wightman, four times national champion in singles tennis.

She was about fourteen years of age, very pretty and prim in her pig tails. She hit the ball with definite skill and earnestness that stamped her as far superior to the others. Her figure, her concentration, her poise were remarkable in a child so young.[57]

Wightman prolonged her visit by three weeks in order to nurture the young talent.

In 1921, Wills became the state champion. A year later she played in the national finals against Norwegian-born Molla Bjursted Mallory. She lost that match, but she won the doubles championship with Marion Jessup as her partner. The spectators marveled. Calm, methodical, conventionally beautiful, she was "a goddess in the form of an American girl."[58] The mostly middle-class tennis fans were doubtless reassured that she also professed a serious interest in art and poetry.

Her ability to write and to draw was obviously not in conflict with her ability to serve and volley. In 1923, she crushed Molla Mallory 6–1 and 6–2—in thirty-three minutes. She won six more U.S. championships in the next eight years (1924–25, 1927–29, 1931). At her first Wimbledon, she was the doubles champion (with Hazel Wightman) and the singles runner-up (against Kitty McKane). She went to France in the summer of 1926 in order to challenge the most famous female athlete of the era, the highly temperamental Suzanne Lenglen. When the two finally met at the Carlton Club at Cannes, the Wills-Lenglen match was bigger news than the 1924 Olympics had been.

Rumor had it that exclusive film rights had been sold for $100,000. Extra stands were built to accommodate the expected crowd, but demand outstripped supply and scalpers asked $44 for tickets—twenty-two times the price of a seat at the U.S. Championships at Forest Hills. Lenglen won the first set but was hard pressed in the second when a disputed line call angered Wills. A not wholly impartial biographer has written that there were "delightful squeals of triumphant ecstasy from Suzanne's sycophants and camp followers."[59] Lord Charles Hope, the linesman, then indicated that he had not called the ball out. Lenglen was gracious, but Wills had lost her composure. Fifteen minutes later she had also lost the match.

Since appendicitis forced Wills to drop out of the French championships and one of Lenglen's mysterious "illnesses" struck her at Wimbledon, the return encounter was postponed. When Lenglen turned professional in the fall, the United States Lawn Tennis Association refused to sanction a Wills-Lenglen match.

Wills suffered another kind of rebuff in 1927 when she attempted to begin a second career as an actress. Although the admiring Mexican artist Diego Rivera chose her as the model for the central figure in his mural for the San Francisco Stock Exchange ("She represented my ideal of the perfect type"), a Hollywood screen test found that "her limbs were too developed" to appeal to the American movie-goer.[60] She responded to Hollywood's bias with the calmness expected of "Miss Poker Face." She made a campaign film for Herbert Hoover. That year, 1928, she won the French, the British, and the American championships. At the peak of her career, Helen Wills Moody (as she was known after marrying stockbroker Frederick Moody) was generally admired rather than loved. Like the young Christine Evert, unlike the flamboyant Lenglen, she seemed too cerebral, too controled, too mechanical, an "Ice Maiden" with whom it was difficult to identify. She seemed beyond "the plaudits of others" because she had "her own vision of perfection."[61] As a consequence of the 1934 singles at Forest Hills, Moody became even less popular. After losing the first set against Helen Jacobs, her archrival, Moody suffered a back injury and forfeited the match. Many fans, remembering Lenglen's histrionic behavior, doubted the authenticity of Moody's injury (which was real). When Jacobs was injured during their last encounter, at Wimbledon in 1938, Jacobs continued despite the pain and she graciously accepted the defeat and thereby won the affection that had always eluded "Queen Helen."

Nonetheless, more than any other woman of this "Golden Age of Sports," more than Earhart and much more than Didrikson and Ederle, Helen Wills Moody seemed to embody the athletic ideals of the era. Physically gifted, properly educated, dedicated to her sport but not obviously, crassly, materialistically aggressive, she was a superior athlete who remained conventionally feminine.

TEN

The Europeans Take
the Lead

1. Fantastic Athletes

In the twenties and thirties, while American physical educators decried women's sports and sought to channel their charges' energy into "Play Days" and other forms of mild exercise, their European counterparts were somewhat less negative about athletic competition. The pattern of positive and negative opinion varied from country to country and from region to region, but the more urbanized (and urbane) parts of the continent were distinctly in advance of the United States.

The resistance to women's sports did not disappear overnight, not even in the most advanced countries. The churches, especially the Roman Catholic Church, were at best ambivalent about girls' and women's sports. Clerics approved of cloistered calisthenics, and they tolerated some gentle sports as an aspect of physical education; but they fretted constantly about "excess" and "indecency." A conference of German bishops, meeting in Fulda in 1913, strongly condemned public gymnastics contests.

It would be extremely regrettable if women's physical education were cultivated to the point that the emotions were disturbed, the feminine sense of self-control weakened, and the aptitude for quiet domestic labor lessened. Most reprehensible is female [sports] attire, which has become—for both children and adults—shameless.

In 1927, the German bishops cancelled a women's gymnastics festival in Neuburg an der Donau because they feared that male spectators would be present. Four years later, they repeated the ban on public displays of women's gymnastics. Compared to French, Italian, and Polish prelates, however, German Catholics were quite permissive.[1]

In Europe as in America, there was also resistance from medical authorities who continued to maintain that sports endangered a woman's health and jeopardized her ability to give birth to normal children. Prejudices published as if they were the results of scientific study were widespread even in Germany, but they were not unopposed. Feminist doctors like Germany's Alice Profé cited more objective data and waged a brisk counteroffensive on behalf of women's rights to untrammeled physical activity. Ironically, the prejudiced men who propagated old wives' tales about nervous prostration and "stiffened pelvic musculature" accused their female opponents of "unscientific partisanship."[2]

Influenced by clerical and medical authority, most European school systems hesitated to stress girls' sports within their physical-education programs. This hesitation did not retard European women to the degree that American women were held back by American educators because modern European sports have usually been institutionalized by private clubs rather than in the public or parochial schools. The Roman Catholic Church and some of the Protestant sects had their own sports federations, which were inhospitable to women's sports, but most federations were secular and, except for the tradition-bound *Deutsche Turnerschaft,* most were more positive about women's sports than were the schools, the churches, and the medical establishment. Many British, French, and German clubs were eager to promote serious competition. The men and women who acted as coaches and trainers (and ideological inculcators) were mainly volunteers whose commitment of time and energy was motivated by their own personal involvement in and enthusiasm for sports. While many of these coaches and trainers continued to think of aggressive competition as typically masculine rather than feminine, female athletes received much more encouragement than their American counterparts did. Eduard Spranger, probably the most prestigious German physical educator of the period, actually championed women's sports as an aspect of what he termed "eternal Spartan-ness" (*"ewiges Spartaner-tum"*).[3]

The work of writers and artists cannot be taken as simple mimetic reproductions of reality, but the contrast between Europe and the United States is nonetheless suggestive. Major European artists were less inclined than American painters and sculptors to ignore women's sports. While American artists like Thomas Eakins and George Bellows became famous with pictures of oarsmen and boxers, the croquet pictures of Winslow Homer and John Sloan remained isolated examples of women's sports as an artist's (as opposed to an illustrator's) motif. Far more active than Sloan's staid pair were the female rowers and tennis players of Marcel Gromaire's *Les Bords de la Marne* (1925) and *Tennis devant la Mer* (1928), the runner of Willi Baumeister's *Die Läuferin* (1927), and the straining ballplayers of Ossip Zadkine's *Les Joueuses à la Balle* (1928).[4] The major American writers were as aloof as the artists. They seldom mentioned a female athlete. When they did, the athlete—like Jordan Baker in F. Scott Fitzgerald's *The Great Gatsby* (1925)—was often shown in a negative light. (Jordan cheats.) European novelists, however, were fascinated by female athletes, some of whom they extolled as the epitome of strength and beauty. Two examples should suffice.

In 1924, Henry de Montherlant admitted that women's bodies had been an aesthetic disappointment to him until he saw "the athletically trained young girls in the stadium. . . . What a revelation!" Dominique Soubrier, the heroine of Montherlant's novel *Le Songe* (1922), is one of these athletically trained girls. Driven by "the ideal of the Amazon," she is "a strong girl, with broad shoulders, a helmet of hair, heroic hands that hurled the javelin across the field." She has "a chaste and savage soul." The imagery is intentionally martial (the "helmet" of hair) and the sports are those originally associated with warfare. Although Romantic convention generally avoids anatomical exactness, Montherlant places Dominique before her mirror and allows her to indulge in a narcissistic admiration of her own physical perfection:

Without changing her pose, she contracted her muscles across the length of her body. . . . Her entire body was like a thing of delicately hammered metal. . . . The lateral ridges of her abdomen flexed, mounted, slid smoothly one above the other beneath her breasts.

Despite the poses, Dominique is not a body-builder whose physical development has become an end in itself. She is an impassioned track-and-field athlete. Running, she experiences an ecstatic sense of pure exhilaration that culminates when she throws herself to the ground and enters a mystic state of absolute transcendence. Montherlant was obviously attracted to his heroine, but he distanced himself from her by remarking that her face stiffened with the exertion of a race until it took on a "splendid unattractiveness." The phrase adroitly captured Montherlant's ambivalence. It seemed that the splendor of the body somehow meant "the annihilation of the mind and the heart." Physical perfection becomes, paradoxically, a kind of imperfection in that neither Dominique nor her lover can overcome their sense that sexual intercourse is tantamount to violation.[5]

This is certainly not a problem for the heroines of Kasimir Edschmid's novel *Sport um Gagaly* (1928). The action takes the classical form of the erotic triangle. Cesare Passari, a wealthy industrialist with a passion for sports, runs, rides, plays tennis, and races his Fiat against his rival's Peugeot. He becomes romantically involved with Gagaly Madosdy, a mature married woman, and with Contessa Pista Tossuth, an unmarried adolescent. Athletic physicality is emphasized throughout the novel (his as well as theirs). Gagaly's legs are "perfectly beautiful, muscular, curved and firm but nonetheless graceful." Pista's "steel-slim body" has a "wonderfully elastic form," revealed when she lifts her head and tosses her mane of hair. Her body seems to be made "of thin bronze." Cesare admires her flat belly but concludes that her "thighs were not entirely mature." This rhetoric of metallic physicality is typical of Italian Fascism. Indeed, Edschmid writes that his hero's conception of sports resembled Mussolini's view of the state. *Der Sport um Gagaly* parts company from Fascism and its obsessive insistence on *normalità* when Edschmid anatomizes and affirms the lesbian attraction which develops between the two women. At moments, they seem more in love with each other than with their athletic boyfriend. However, when Gagaly kisses Pista to celebrate Cesare's lucky escape from an automobile crash, the women decide not to consummate their affair. "From this kiss on, the two loved him in each other." Rather than resolving the erotic triangle into the conventional form of a happy couple and a rejected loser, the three athletes continue as a triad. What is more, "The passions of the three gave them tripled strength—and not only in love." It was not until 1982, when Jennifer Levin published *Water Dancer,* that an American novelist imagined a female athlete physically comparable to those of Montherlant and Edschmid.[6]

2. The Goddess of Tennis

Suzanne Lenglen, the most famous female athlete of the 1920s, was born in Compiègne on May 24, 1899. Her father was a wealthy man, able to provide his family with vacations on the Riviera. In the summer of 1910, Charles Lenglen bought his daughter a tennis racquet. That autumn, at the Nice Tennis Club, he taught her the game. When he realized her athletic potential, he began systematically to train her at a level of intensity uncommon for the period. At a time when most players were quite casual about their physical fitness, he had her swim, jump, and sprint. He taught her the aggressive serve-and-volley style characteristic of men's tennis. He praised her successes, he ridiculed her failures. "She became athletically formidable and emotionally tattered."[7] In 1914, when she was just fifteen years old, Suzanne Lenglen won not only the local tournament sponsored by the prestigious Carlton Club of Cannes but also the international competitions held at the Stade Français in St. Cloud.

Papa decided she should wait a year before she went to Wimbledon for her inevitable triumph, but the war intervened and it was not until 1919 that Lenglen faced the forty-year-old seven-time winner, Dorothea Lambert Chambers, in the Wimbledon final. Chambers served underhand and returned the ball from baseline. Lenglen won, 10–8, 4–6, 8–6, in those days before tiebreakers.

To the fame she harvested by her skill was added the celebrity garnered by her flair for bold movement and brash gesture. Although she was what the French call *jolie laide* ("ugly but beautiful"), her movements on the court were ballet-like. Her spectacular leaps made her seem almost airborne. On the court and off, she dressed as if to dare anyone to call her less than beautiful. Older spectators were shocked to see her appear for a match in a short pleated skirt designed by Jean Patou. She played in a sleeveless blouse and wore "two yards of brightly coloured silk chiffon wound tightly around her head." She bobbed her hair and she was the first player to appear on court in full makeup. Bill Tilden thought her 1921 costume was a cross between a prima donna's and a streetwalker's. Her arrogance was monumental. When she played at Forest Hills in 1921, she demanded wine before her matches and the Volstead Act fell to her imperious will. At Wimbledon in 1926, she lost her temper because Queen Mary had asked that a match be rescheduled for royal convenience. Lenglen sulked in the women's locker room until her teammate Jacques Borotra entered, blindfolded, and persuaded her to emerge. The British spectators, resentful that the Queen had been insulted, watched in silence as she won for the sixth time.[8]

Lenglen was also notorious for sudden inexplicable illnesses that came just as she was about to lose a match. Claiming poor health, she defaulted at Forest Hills and escaped defeat by Molla Mallory. That evening she went dancing. Her mother, Anais, explained the inconsistent behavior, "Suzanne est coquette toujours."[9]

Coquette or not, she went from championship to championship and lost exactly two sets in seven years of play. From 1919 to 1926 she won 269 of 270 matches. The German novelist Kasimir Edschmid, whose heroines bear some resemblance to Lenglen, wrote that Lenglen was "for the unpoliticized world . . . almost the only visible public representation of France."[10] Bill Tilden, best-known male player of the era, admitted ruefully that Lenglen was a greater draw than he was.[11] She decided to cash in on her popularity. Shortly after her 1926 victory over Helen Wills at Cannes, she signed a contract with C. C. ("Cash and Carry") Pyle and went on the road as a tennis professional. "People," she remarked blithely, "will pay to see anybody they hate."[12] After the tour opened at Madison Square Garden, she dined with Jack Dempsey and Georges Carpentier. As a professional, she made a second fortune to add to her inherited wealth. She died of pernicious anemia on October 28, 1939. It is said that all of France mourned her.

3. Workers' Sports

Suzanne Lenglen was certainly the most flamboyant and the best-known female athlete of the era, but French women were numerically less likely than German women to be seriously involved in sports either at their schools and universities or in the private clubs which were—and are—the favored organizational form for European sports. We have seen that a few upper-class and middle-class women began to compete in international sports competitions as early as the turn of the century. In the 1920s and 1930s, the period the cynical French call *entre deux guerres,* these competitions became much more frequent and attracted a far greater number of female athletes. They have also attracted more than a few historians. "Women at the Olympics" is, for instance, an inevitable topic (and this study will be no exception to the rule). Much less attention has been given to the less socially advantaged European women who were, after all, the vast majority. They too began to compete in the vast international sports festivals which have come to be a hallmark of the modern age.

In 1893, German socialists organized their own national sports federation, the *Arbeiter Turnerbund* (ATB). Initially, few working-class women joined. In 1895–96, the first year for which data are available, women were a mere 2.0 percent of the ATB membership. By 1912, the number had risen to only 8.9 percent. As Gertrud Pfister comments, it was always difficult "to bring women's sections to life and then to keep them alive." In the 1920s, tenacity and determination were still required to bring women into the ranks of the working-class *Sportler*. Germany, spared the military devastation that wasted much of northeastern France, was a nation ravaged first by a catastrophic inflation and then by a catastrophic depression. Working-class women had bleak lives. Yet, despite their hardships, 95,000 women joined the renamed *Arbeiter Turn- und Sportbund* (ATSB). They were 14.5 percent of the total membership and another 45,000 women made up some 12.3 percent of the membership of the federation of workers' cycling and motorcycling clubs. In Berlin, the women may have been as many as one-third of the total membership. Since women were 23 percent of the national membership of the closely allied *Sozialdemokratische Partei Deutschlands,* it is evident that—except for the Berliners—their sports engagement lagged behind their political commitment to socialism, but no other nation in Europe, probably none in the world, had a higher percentage of working-class women involved in organized sports. Despite the political and economic conditions, there was reason for optimism. In comparison to the ATB's 11,944 female members of 1895–96, the 100,000 of the late 1920s were a throng.[13]

Their rhetoric was idealistic. They demanded that their bodies be as free—and as ready for life's struggles—as their minds.

We want to bathe our bodies in light, air, and sun, to do our sports while as lightly clothed as possible, and everyone is welcome to observe us when we . . . take to the swimming pools and the sports grounds to refresh our bodies and make them elastic enough for us to return on the morrow, with renewed strength, to the struggle for existence.[14]

Brave words. They were spoken with more conviction by the young and single than by the married and middle-aged. With marriage, working women's participation dwindled much more rapidly than men's because women had less time for sports than men did after their work inside and outside the home. Socialist rhetoric about equality sometimes made domestic inequality hard to bear. Clara

Zetkin was among the radical women who thought that the socialists' treatment of women was glaringly unjust. She proclaimed as early as 1889 that women were subjugated by men just as the workers are by the capitalists, and she predicted that this subjugation would continue as long as women were economically dependent upon men. Hers was a message that working-class husbands, struggling to survive, were reluctant to hear. [15] Despite the ATB's official commitment to equality, the organization's women were scarcely better treated than the women of the ultra-conservative *Deutsche Turnerschaft*. It was not until 1930 that the leaders of the workers' organization placed a woman in charge of women's sports at the national level. [16]

By 1933, some working-class women had grown very impatient with the men's remarks about ineptitude in sports and incompetence in administration. "First," shouted Luise Vierke, "they cut off our eagle's wings so that we can't fly, and then they call us stupid hens." It is, therefore, remarkable how many of these socially handicapped women were involved in sports. Remarkable too is their enthusiasm for the bit of freedom they enjoyed. Wilma Köhler remembered her years in the ATSB with fondness. "We really lived only when we were on the playing fields. They were the best years of my life." [17]

Some of these women were world-class athletes and, like other ambitious women conscious of their prowess, they wanted competition. By the 1920s, the *Arbeiter Turn- und Sportbund* had more or less overcome its initial antipathy to competition, which it had once disdained as "capitalistic." The *Arbeitersportler* were ready not only to compete among themselves but also to challenge the International Olympic Committee with a series of "Workers' Olympics." At the *Arbeiter-Olympiade* held in Frankfurt in 1925, German women broke the world record for the 4 X 100–meter relay with a time of 51.3 seconds. [18] There was obvious pride in this achievement despite the repeated disavowal of "record-seeking," which was held to be characteristic of "bourgeois sports." [19] At a time when the International Olympic Committee still harbored doubts about the suitability of track and field for female athletes, the official poster for the third *Arbeiders Olympiade* (Antwerp, 1937) showed a sinewy young woman about to let her discus fly. [20] (See Plate 24.)

The women of the ATSB also published their own journal, *Die Freie Turnerin,* the masthead of which featured a drawing of a naked girl. Frieda Drechsler defended this "indecency" in a 1921 article. Lauding the figure as "a free maiden, with a joyful sense of her

strength and her trained body, whose nakedness is unashamed because it is natural," she dismissed the journal's small-minded critics.[21]
Sigrid Block, the historian of women in the ATSB, laments that these
women suffered discrimination even within this egalitarian organization, and they did; but Block's accent might well have been placed on
the tenacity of the factory girls and sales clerks who persevered
despite the daunting obstacles placed in their path.

Germany was not the only European country where workers organized their own sports federations. The Finnish case is also instruc-
tive. In the twenties and thirties, middle-class opinion deprecated
strenuous competition by female athletes. Leading journalists and
physical educators like Martti Jukola, Lauri Pihkala, and Hilma Jal-
kanen joined physicians like Kaarina Kari in a chorus of opposition to
women's contests. Finnish women were not sent to compete in the
track-and-field events introduced at the 1928 and 1932 Olympic Games.
At the same time, however, the workers' sports clubs sent a small but
highly successful women's team to the *Arbeiter-Olympiade* held in
Frankfurt in 1925. The five track-and-field athletes and four swimmers returned with one gold, seven silver, and two bronze medals.[22]

In Great Britain and in France, a small number of women competed in sports contests organized by the British Workers' Sports
Federation and the *Fédération Sportive et Gymnastique du Travail*. If the
figures reported by nineteen British clubs in 1930 were representative,
then some 18 percent of the BSWF's 6,000 members were women. In
England and in France, there were sharp words of criticism for
"bourgeois" sports organizations. In *Sport,* the journal published by
the *Fédération Sportive et Gymnastique du Travail*, verbal volleys were
aimed at the official *Fédération Française des Sports Féminins*, which
received government funding, and at the commercial press, which
allegedly featured women's sports in order to merchandise facial
creams and other cosmetics. Like their German sisters, the British
and French women were sometimes unhappy about their status within
the organization. Gladys Keable of the Red Star netball team complained of working-class sportsmen "who regard women as a bit of a
nuisance." The ambivalence of the men may have inhibited British
and French women's participation in workers' sports.[23]

Germany's ATSB remained much the largest and best organized
of the various national federations that joined together in Lucerne in
1921 to form the *Internationale Sportive Ouvrière Socialiste*. In 1927, the
Germans were over 70 percent of the eighteen-member organization's

1.3 million members. The Austrians comprised another 11 percent of the ISOS and Czechoslovakia's 153,188 members included a large number of ethnic Germans. When the Nazi regime destroyed the ATSB and its Austrian and Czech counterparts, working-class women lost an important part of their lives.[24]

4. Women on the Road to Olympia

When Pierre de Coubertin summoned the youth of the world to participate in the revival of the Olympic Games at Athens in 1896, his conception of *jeunesse* definitely excluded young females. Not a single woman competed in the 1896 games. If Coubertin had had his way, the games would have remained sexually segregated, with women restricted to the role of awed admirers of male prowess. "Coubertin had not planned for the admission of women, did not want women to be admitted, and fought against their admission for more than thirty years."It was not that Coubertin was wholly opposed to women's sports; it was just that he disapproved of women's involvement in *public* competitions, "for the spectators who gathered for such competitions don't show up to look at sports."[25]

Although the early records of the International Olympic Committee have been kept secret, we can conjecture that Coubertin must have faced some opposition on this question because the games celebrated in Paris in 1900 included women's golf and women's tennis. In 1904, the games were held in St. Louis and the American organizers, led by the redoubtable James Sullivan, seem to have been more than ready to humor the French founder in his antipathy to women's sports. Sullivan was, in fact, extremely hostile to women's sports— except for the purpose of recreation and diversion. In his clouded view, sports were "morally a questionable experience for women."[26] At St. Louis, archery was the only sport in which women were allowed to compete (and all the contestants were Americans). Tennis, archery, and figure skating were on the program in 1908, in London, where most of the participants were British. In that less specialized age, England's Lottie Dod was able to add a silver medal in Olympic archery to her five Wimbledon trophies.

During these Olympics, enthusiasts for swimming met at the Manchester Hotel and organized the *Fédération Internationale de Natation Amateur*. FINA made women's swimming one of its priorities and the sport was introduced at the 1912 Olympics in Stockholm. Not everyone was pleased. Reluctance to disclose female bodies to male eyes motivated Australia's ardently feminist Rose Scott to resign from her post as president of the New South Wales Ladies' Swimming Association. The immediate cause of her resignation was that the NSWLSA's Sydney club planned to send Sarah "Fanny" Durack and Wilhelmina "Mina" Wylie to Stockholm. "I think it is disgusting," said Miss Scott in reference to the women's events, "that men should be allowed to attend."[27] Men were allowed to attend and they cheered vociferously as Durack, Wylie, and 39 European women competed in the 100–meter and 400–meter races and in platform diving. The Australian women finished first and second in the 100 meters. There were no American swimmers at the 1912 games because Sullivan, who had prevented AAU sponsorship of national championships for women, managed also to block the path to Stockholm.[28]

In addition to the swimmers, divers, and tennis players, there was a team of 236 Scandinavian gymnasts who staged a splendid exhibition that may have persuaded some skeptics to alter their views about female frailty and indecent exposure. AAU Secretary Everett C. Brown, whose impulses were clearly much more generous than Sullivan's, was delighted by the women: "I personally saw the competitions at Stockhom and if there was any criticism there, it might have been brought about by foul minds." [29]

World War I intervened to prevent the Olympic Games of 1916, which had been scheduled for Berlin, and the first postwar games, held at Antwerp in 1920, limited women to tennis and the aquatic events. While the Americans boycotted the tennis tournament in a dispute over the rules, American women dominated swimming and diving, winning all but one of the events. (Sullivan's death on September 16, 1916, had removed the main impediment to their participation.) After fencing was introduced in Paris in 1924, the next real breakthrough came when the International Olympic Committee decided, in an unrecorded vote, to allow track and field and team gymnastics at the 1928 games in Amsterdam.

The International Olympic Committee's decision was made possible, in part, by Coubertin's retirement as president of the committee. After the Olympic Congress held in Prague, in 1925, he stepped aside and Comte Henri Baillet-Latour of Belgium succeeded him. Another factor in the IOC's decision to open the door a little wider was the pressure brought upon the committee by European women who were determined to have international competitions, with the IOC if possible, without it if necessary. These women acted as individuals and, more importantly, through their clubs and national and international federations. It was unquestionably the continental Europeans, not the British or the Americans, who battered down the gates that barred the path to Olympia. The transition from calisthenics to modern sports for women had—as we have seen—occurred in schools and colleges of Great Britain and the United States, but British and American physical educators were hesitant to take the next steps, which led to national and then to international competitions.

German women might have been expected to lead the way. They had become increasingly active in the thousands of sports clubs open to them in the 1920s. The *Berliner Sport-Club,* for instance, inaugurated a *Damenabteilung* in 1919. Its most successful athlete, Margarethe Rahel Henoch, set several official and unofficial world records in the early twenties.[30] National championships for German women were inaugurated in 1920. Six hundred German women participated in the *Deutsche Kampfspiele* held in Berlin in 1922 at a time when American colleges were beginning to substitute "Play Days" for intercollegiate sports. Nine thousand German women went to Munich in 1923 for the national *Turnfest.* In Berlin, Carl Diem welcomed female students to the newly founded *Deutsche Hochschule für Leibesübungen* ("German Sports University").[31] In fact, Diem married one of these athletic girls, who later recalled, "We were ready for anything—from weight-lifting to pole-vaulting. We had black and blue bruises from diving from the 10–meter platform, and we were the best rowers in the club."[32]

Unfortunately for Liselott Diem and the other female athletes of the Weimar Republic, the British and the French bitterly resented the devastation wrought by German armies during World War I. For most of the twenties, German athletes were barred from international competition. It was, accordingly, the French sports clubs and federations that moved to the fore and led the way first to international and then to Olympic competition.

Among the socially exclusive sports clubs catering to young Parisian women of the leisure class were *Fémina-Sport* (1911) and *Academia* (1915). Despite the ravages of World War I, *Academia* staged the first track meet for French women at the Stade Brançion on May 1, 1915.

Fémina-Sport, which fielded a team of female soccer players on April 28, 1918, won the national soccer title from 1926 through 1932. In 1922, intrepid club members tried rugby football, but the experiment was premature and it was not until 1970 that a women's rugby association was founded.[33]

The women of *Fémina-Sport* also played a decisive role in the long campaign to persuade the International Olympic Committee to open its games to female track-and-field athletes, but it was a man, Camille Blanc, Mayor of Beaulieu and president of the socially exclusive International Sporting Club of Monaco, who took the first step. He realized that the tiny principality on the Riviera was an ideal place to gather a number of these upper-class *femmes sportives*. He set up an eight-man organizing committee and invitations went out for the first *Olympiades Féminines* of the modern age. The games that began on May 25, 1921, took place at the *Stand du Tir* built in 1896 for the pleasure of English marksmen. Athletes came from England, Italy, Norway, and Switzerland as well as from France. The twenty-five women from the London Polytechnic Club greatly raised the level of competition, and the presence of the world's fastest female sprinter, Mary Lines, gave additional panache. (She had done 100 yards in 11.8 seconds.) Track-and-field competition and a basketball tournament were the central events, the latter won by the English, who defeated *Fémina-Sport* by a score of 8–7. The spectators were especially enthusiastic when Irene Popard and her dance students performed *"gymnastique harmonique"* at the closing ceremonies. As Hajo Bernett has remarked, "The artistic frame represented the organizers' realization that track and field and ballgames alone were not an adequate embodiment of the Olympic idea."[34]

The French press covered the games and laudatory articles appeared in *Le Miroir des Sports, Vie au Grand Air,* and the *Revue de la Riviera Illustrée.* The games were repeated a year later as the *Jeux Internationaux Féminins.* Blanc was once again the principal organizer, but Henri Pathé, national commissioner of physical education, was the honorary president. Whereas five nations had sent 300 athletes in 1921, the contests held in 1922 attracted some 600 women from nine countries. The competition, which lasted from April 15 to 23, included swimming events, dominated by the Swedes and the Dutch, as well as basketball and track and field. French honor was upheld by Madelaine Bracquemond, who won the high jump at the height of 1.37 meters, and by Violette Gouraud-Morris, who repeated her victory in the shot put. Popard's troupe performed again at the closing ceremonies, and Justinien de Clary represented the International Olympic Committee at the final banquet.[35]

Although the games at Monte Carlo were repeated in 1923, the baton of women's sports passed into the hand of Alice Milliat, organizer of the *Jeux Internationaux* held in Paris on August 20, 1922. (It was to these games that the first American contingent came despite the outraged opposition of the Committee on Women's Athletics of the American Physical Education Association.) Milliat, a member of *Fémina-Sport,* had been first treasurer and then president of the *Fédération des Sociétés Féminines Sportives de France* (founded in 1917). This organization had successfully staged national championships in field hockey, soccer, basketball, and swimming. On October 31, 1921, only five months after the games at Monte Carlo proved the viability of international competitions for women, Milliat founded the *Fédération Sportive Féminine Internationale.* Her program for Paris was comprised of eleven events, including a 1000–meter race, a distance then considered to be an enormous challenge. The games, at which two world records were set, were dominated by the British victors from the Monte Carlo competitions and by the Americans (who were carefully chaperoned by Winifred Merrill of the Oaksmere School in Mamaroneck, New York). Britain's Mary Lines won three gold medals, a silver, and a bronze. "For the first time, perhaps," writes Mary Hanson Leigh, "a women's sports event was reported with the same mixture of respect, admiration, and mystic fervor as the 'real' (i.e., male) Olympics."[36] According to the *Miroir des Sports,* the twenty thousand spectators in Le Stade-Pershing, mostly men, were interested only in "naked legs and thighs," but this sour note was unusual. Most reporters seemed impressed by how fast the naked legs and thighs could move.[37]

The success of the *Olympiques Féminines* left the International Olympic Committee unmoved. Although the aristocratic men who still dominated the committee decided to admit female fencers to the 1924 games (celebrated in Paris as a favor to Coubertin), their reluctant acceptance of this sport practiced by their wives and daughters did not mean that they were quite ready to embrace a plebeian sport like track and field.[38]

Milliat was deterred neither by undue concern for the spectators' motives nor by worry about the IOC's slowness in opening the games to women. She planned to continue her *jeux internationaux* on the Olympic model, with games every four years. The second games, which took place in Gøteberg, Sweden, in 1926, were another resounding success. France's Marguerite Radideau did the 100 yards in 11.8 seconds, but the sensation of the day was Kinue Hitomi, who defied custom and became the first Japanese woman to represent her people in an international sports competition. She won gold medals in the long jump and the standing long jump, a silver medal in the discus, and a silver medal in the 100–yard dash. When the ban against German women was lifted in the 1930s, the broader basis of their sports participation enabled them to dominate the games. In 1934, they won nine of the twelve events—a portent for the 1936 Olympic Games.[39]

Milliat was by no means content merely to stage athletic events for women. Between 1921 and 1936, she was the main force behind no fewer than nine international conferences on women's sports (held in Paris, Gøteborg, Amsterdam, Prague, Vienna, London, and Berlin).[40] Her bold initiatives compelled the International Amateur Athletic Association, formed in 1913 to administer track and field, to reconsider its rather detached position in regard to women's sports. Originally, the International Amateur Athletic Federation had acquiesced in Pierre de Coubertin's refusal to grant women's track and field entrance to the Olympic Games, but the *Fédération Sportive Féminine Internationale* had become a real embarrassment. Although Sigfrid Edstrøm, founder and president of the organization, was unhappy about the FSFI and its *Premiers Jeux Olympiques Féminins du Monde,* he opted for compromise and persuaded Milliat, in 1926, to drop the word *Olympiques* and to accept IAAF rules and regulations (revised for women when necessary). In return, Edstrøm officially recognized the FSFI and allowed its affiliates to join the IAAF. The IAAF then asked the International Olympic Committee to include women's track and field in the program for the games scheduled for Amsterdam in 1928. The IOC complied with the request from this most powerful of international sports federations.

It was a partial victory. Together with the swimmers, the divers, and the fencers, the newly invited gymnasts and track-and-field athletes comprised 9.6 percent of all the Olympians at Amsterdam. While this was a considerable improvement from 1912, when the women were a token 2.2 percent, the gymnasts were limited to team competition and only five track-and-field events were on the program: the 100–meter and 800–meter races, the high jump, the discus, and the 4 x 100–meter relay race.[41] The British women, who had dominated both the Monte Carlo competitions and the first *Jeux Féminins,* felt that five events were a paltry token. They stayed home.[42] In their absence, the Canadian women were the leaders, with gold medals for the high jump and the relay and silver and bronze for the 100 meters. In winning the high jump, Ethel Catherwood set a world record of 1.59 meters. Unfortunately, a storm of controversy broke out over the 800–meter race. Germany's Lina Radke won in world-record time (2:16.8), but the *New York Times* responded hysterically to the fact that some of the breathless women lay down after their effort. "At the finish six of the runners were completely exhausted and fell headlong to the ground." According to the *Times,* "eleven wretched women" were strewn upon the cinder track. There was now a clamor of voices, including those of American physical educators, calling for the reversal of the IOC's "reckless" decision to include women's track and field in the Olympic program. In panic, the IOC voted in 1929 to drop women's track and field from the 1932 games in Los Angeles. This decision left the field open, once again, for Milliat's federation. The FSFI's third games were held in 1930, when 214 athletes from seventeen countries gathered for a three-day celebration at Prague's Letna Stadium. Although the American universities continued to boycott the games, the University of British Columbia sent a basketball team which defeated the French to win the gold.[43] The brightest star of the individual events was Poland's Stanislava Walaciewicz, subsequently known in the United States as Stella Walsh. She won three gold medals for races over 60, 100, and 200 meters. (Decades later, alas, an autopsy revealed that Stella Walsh was a man.)[44]

At this point in the prolonged struggle over women's Olympic participation, Gustavus Kirby, president of the AAU and the American representative to the International Amateur Athletic Federation, entered the fray. He threatened a boycott of *men's* track and field at the 1932 Olympics in Los Angeles if the International Olympic Committee did not reverse its discriminatory decision. His resolve was strengthened when he attended the Olympic Congress held in Berlin in 1930 and had an opportunity to observe some particularly impressive athletic demonstrations by female members of German sports clubs. Kirby wrote to a friend,

I personally saw groups of young girls in the scantiest kind of clothing, trotting around the fields or running tracks, engaging in 100 metre runs, taking part in the broad jump, and hopping about in all kinds of athletic and gymnastic movements; and to my direct statement as to whether or not such character of exercise was not bad for them, the answer invariably was that on the contrary, it was good for them.

Like many middle-class Americans, Kirby had his doubts about the nudity that was fairly common among the German *Naturfreunde*. He worried aloud about "whether or not this intermingling of the sexes in a nude condition did not make for immorality," but he was informed that it did not. "Irrespective of the moral question," he concluded, "there is no gainsaying the fact that the boys and girls and youth of Germany are today to a large extent well developed and bronzed." Although Kirby's close friend, Avery Brundage, has often been accused of narrow-minded hostility to women's sports, he joined the debates on Kirby's side and argued for the continued inclusion of women's track and field. "Anyone who observed the exhibitions put on by girl athletes in connection with the Olympic Congress in Berlin would be a strong advocate for sports of all kinds for girls under proper supervision."[45] When the program for the 1932 Olympics finally came to a vote at the 1930 Congress, the delegates endorsed women's participation in track and field by a margin of 17–1. The motions for team gymnastics, swimming, tennis, and ice skating all carried by 26–1, and fencing passed by 19–8. As it turned out, the exploits of Mildred "Babe" Didrikson were the most memorable events of the l932 Olympic Games. Her accomplishments helped to dim the memory of the faltering 800–meter runners of 1928.

The IOC's reversal of its decision to drop women's track and field was an important victory, but it probably doomed the independent women's federation to a slow death. The FIFS-sponsored fourth Women's World Games took place at London's White City on August 9, 1934, with nineteen countries represented. Germany, which had taken the lead at the third games, now garnered more points than the next three countries combined. At the IAAF's 1936 congress, the IAAF agreed officially to recognize world records registered by the FSFI and to advocate a fuller women's track-and-field program for the 1936 Olympics in Berlin. The men's promises were not kept. Some records were registered; others were not. The women's track-and-field program for the 1936 games was not expanded. When Milliat responded to the breach of faith by staging the fifth in the series of FSFI-sponsored quadrennial celebrations in Vienna in 1938, the IAAF refused to recognize these games except as its European championships. The embittered women were compelled for a time to abandon the unequal struggle.

In these years of controversy, Milliat often served on IAAF committees with Avery Brundage. His opposition to women's sports has been greatly exaggerated, but Brundage was certainly less enthusiastic about them than Milliat was. Had Milliat lived long enough, she might have been amused by Brundage's annoyed reminiscence: "She was active for years and she demanded more and more. She made quite a nuisance of herself." [46] Indeed she did.

ELEVEN

Women's Sports and
Totalitarian Regimes

1. Women's Sports in Communist Society

Russian women of the Czarist era had been members of aristocratic organizations like the Imperial Yacht Club (1846), originally limited to 150 noblemen, but there were relatively few sports clubs of any sort outside of Petersburg and Moscow. In rural Russia, when the grain was safely harvested and seasonal celebration was in order, peasant women ran races just as women did in the rest of Europe, but modern sports for women were, on the whole, restricted to members of the aristocracy and the bourgeoisie. Men, needless to say, were more active in modern as well as traditional sports.

Before the Bolsheviks overthrew Kerensky and established the Union of Soviet Socialist Republics, eliminating the disparities between men's and women's sports was not a part of their crowded agenda. They assumed that inequality between men and women would disappear once Communism had eliminated the inequalities of class engendered by capitalism. Lenin and Trotsky never expected that equality could be achieved overnight but, once they came to power, they and their comrades were eager to begin the work of creating "New Socialist Man." They quickly developed a sports program along the lines that Marx and Engels might have desired if Marx and Engels had ever given much thought to sports (which they hadn't). On May 7, 1918, less than a year after the October Revolution, the government set up a Central Board of Universal Military Training, known as *Vsevobuch,* to supervise physical training throughout the Soviet Union. This organization was provisional and was disbanded in 1923, a year after the establishment of the Supreme Council of Physical Education.

Initially, many of the Soviet leaders imagined a program that combined gymnastic drill and sports. Modern sports were, however, perceived by the more ideologically motivated as contrary to the ideals of the new regime.

Competitive sport bred, in some people's minds, attitudes alien to socialist society. . . . Doubts were cast on the social value of competitive sport— above all, on attempts to attain top-class results, which were considered an unjustified drive to break records.[1]

Like the German socialists of the *Arbeiter Turn- und Sportbund,* the Soviets tended to associate sports contests with the ruthless competition of laissez-faire capitalism.

Accordingly, from 1921 to 1929, Soviet sports officialdom advocated a program of physical culture, i.e., physical education, based more on the noncompetitive model of German and Swedish gymnastics than on the imperatives of modern sports. Within the system, there were debates over the precise degree of danger from "bourgeois" sports. "While the 'hygienists' admitted the possibility of the usefulness of some 'bourgeois' sports, the 'Proletkul'tists' made no such concessions."[2] Although the Soviets were surely unaware of the fact, the "Proletkul'tists" of the USSR agreed with the Women's Division of the National Amateur Athletic Federation of the USA—the excesses of competition and commercialization were to be avoided at all costs. The difference, of course, was that the "Proletkul'tists" wanted to restrict men's sports as well as women's. For nearly a decade, these opponents of modern sports had the upper hand.

By 1930, however, it was clear to almost everyone that the men— and, to a lesser degree, the women—who participated in physical-culture programs were unhappy about the restrictions placed on serious competition. No more than the students of British and American colleges were they enraptured by repetitive drill. In 1928, the government departed from "Proletkul'tist" orthodoxy and held the first Spartakiad, a national sports festival named in honor of Spartacus, the Roman slave who led antiquity's most famous servile rebellion. Some 4,000 male and female athletes competed in the finals of what was clearly meant to be a socialist alternative to the "bourgeois" Olympics that took place that summer in Amsterdam.

In 1930, the Supreme Council of Physical Education was replaced by the All-Union Physical Culture Council, which was attached to the Central Executive Committee of the Communist Party. One of the first initiatives of the Council was to insist that all sports clubs be organized at the workplace, i.e., through factories, offices, schools, or military and police units. Beginning in 1931, the Council adopted the German practice of awarding badges for specified physical achievements such as running, jumping, throwing, and swimming. A hierarchy of ranks was established to classify athletes as they rose, achievement by achievement, to become Merited Masters of Sport of the USSR. National championships in soccer were held in 1933, and in other sports soon after. Although officials loved to condemn the commercialism of "bourgeois" sports and to proclaim their loyalty to the ethic of amateurism, elite athletes were paid for their performances. On October 22, 1945, *Pravda* published the details of the monetary awards given for setting national and world records. Nina Dumbadze, for instance, received 25,000 rubles when she set a new European record in the discus.[3]

The acceptance of the "bourgeois" model brought with it some not unexpected consequences. Gifted athletes were recruited with offers of an excellent job (that required no time at all), an apartment (for which ordinary citizens waited years), an automobile (at a time when only Communist Party bigwigs had them). Newspapers occasionally exposed the misdeeds of pampered athletes whose arrogance and irresponsibility had exceeded even the generous bounds allotted them.

In a system where sports clubs are organized through the workplace so that, for instance, all transportation workers are eligible to join *Lokomotiv,* some occupational groups have distinct advantages over others. Recruitment of gifted athletes is simply easier for *Dinamo,* the club for the secret police and the border guards. At the 1972 summer Olympics, *Dinamo* members comprised one third of the entire Soviet team and collected twice as many medals as the next strongest team (the army's). Ludmilla Tourescheva competed for *Dinamo* and Olga Korbut for the army; it is unlikely that either of them spent much time in any uniform other than that of the highly successful women's gymnastic team.[4]

Once the Soviet Union entered the Olympic Games, in 1952, the

All-Union Council (and its variously named successor organizations) made no attempt to disguise its goal of athletic superiority over the decadent capitalists. In order to attain this ideologically motivated goal, the USSR expanded its system of specialized sports schools, which soon existed at every level from the elementary grades to the university. In 1975, there were 4938 such schools with 1,633,132 children enrolled.[5] At these schools and at the sports universities, elite athletes are trained to win championships and set records, which they do. It should be noted that the students are also vocationally trained so that they can begin second careers when they are no longer able to function as elite athletes. In this instance, at least, Soviet educators are more enlightened than those American coaches whose concern for their student-athletes lasts only as long as the student's eligibility for intercollegiate competition.

Although officials boast of sports participation by one-third of the entire population between the ages of ten and sixty, microstudies indicate that the number of Soviet citizens who actually participate twice a week for six months a year is closer to one-tenth, and even this figure is attained by defining "sport" to include chess and a number of noncompetitive physical activities like hiking.[6] In the city of Taganrog, for instance, officials claimed sports participation by 27 percent of the population, yet survey data showed that only 5 percent of the manual workers and 8 percent of the office personnel were active—and only 2 percent of the city's women.[7]

Taganrog's three-to-one ratio of male-to-female participation is emblematic of a problem endemic to the entire system. At the national and international levels, elite female athletes are prized as highly as elite male athletes, which partially accounts for the many victories of Soviet women in the Olympics and in other international contests, but the frequently and loudly proclaimed goal of equality between the sexes has not been realized except for this tiny elite. Sonia Kovrova's career can illustrate the fate of Russian athletes who fall short of the elite level. In love with basketball, she trained at her club but failed to make the team. She was expelled from the club. After she told her story to a French journalist, he concluded sententiously that "the pleasure of feeling one's body vibrate is forbidden the mass of female athletes in the USSR."[8] Kovrova's case may have been unusual. She may, indeed, have misrepresented it to this sympathetic foreign journalist. But the statistical data on women's sports participation seem to underscore the message that ordinary women have found it difficult to take advantage of the USSR's sports facilities—just as ordinary students have found it difficult to gain access to varsity facilities on American campuses.

Throughout the Soviet Union and the similarly organized societies of Eastern Europe, women's recreational sports simply have not been emphasized to the degree that men's sports have been. Empirical investigations have repeatedly belied official rhetoric about a society where "New Socialist Man" has been liberated to pursue the goal of physical as well as intellectual development. Communism has proven to be less potent than capitalism as a solvent of gender inequality in sports. A brief statistical survey of sports participation in Communist societies is in order, but I must admit in advance that the lag between surveys and publication is often so long that some of the most recent available data come from the 1960s and 1970s.

A national study of Czech industrial and agricultural workers, published in 1968, found that women employed in factories spent only 0.2 percent of their weekday free time in "physical training." On Sundays, the percentage rose to 1.5 percent. For women who worked on farms, the figures were even lower: 0.15 percent and 0.95 percent. Sports participation, broadly defined, occupied 4.7 percent of the Sunday hours of female workers and 5.5 percent of male workers—for a suspiciously low m/f ratio of 1.17.[9]

In Poland, the position of the Roman Catholic Church and the prevailing attitudes of a traditional peasant society both militated against a serious commitment to women's sports. In the first congress devoted to women's physical education and sports, held in 1928, the majority concluded that the emphasis for women should be on "good technical performance and factors related to beauty" rather than on strenuous competition and the quest for records. Poland's leading physical educator, Eugeniusz Piasecki, strongly opposed competition. Writing in 1936, he feared for "the loss of one of the most precious virtues of women, namely the feeling of shame." He noted with obvious alarm that

school sports fields and sports stadiums are under the overpowering influence of nudist shows at dances, variety shows, cinemas and theaters. As long as the chorus girls from the stages and screens continue unpunished to arouse the instincts of the young, they are bound to be the model for sports activities for thousands of girls.

The new regime came to power in 1945, but old attitudes died hard. While nude chorus girls were no longer deprecated as role models for impressionable female athletes, serious competitors were still thought to jeopardize their chances for a good marriage, and most women engaged in sports seemed to "fear . . . deformation of the body, excessive development of the muscles and loss of 'feminine' looks." That these fears were most prevalent in rural areas can be surmised from table 11.1, published in 1973. Although the men as well as the women came disproportionately from the "intelligentsia," the disproportion was even greater for the women (and the likelihood of peasant origins was even smaller). Finally, the life of the female athlete was made more difficult still by the fact that many Polish men were appalled by "the idea of the possible physical superiority of their female partner."[10]

Despite the barriers keeping Polish women from sports, their membership in sports clubs increased rapidly during the 1960s. At the beginning of the decade, only 371,400 women were enrolled in clubs; in 1968, the numbers had more than doubled to 809,600. The ratio of men to women, however, remained at more than three to one. The number of female club members who participated actively in sports is uncertain.[11]

The Hungarian situation was similar. In Hungary as in Poland, men have been much more positive about sports than women have been. Eleven percent of the total population were sports club members at the end of 1973, a total of some 1,146,079 members in 4302 clubs, but 46.8 percent of them were "supporting" members who sat on the sidelines and encouraged the athletes to give their all. Of all the members, active and inactive, only 29.3 percent were female, which yields a male/female ratio of 2.44.[12]

A commitment to egalitarian "socialist physical culture" was a repeated theme in the speeches of East German political leaders like Walter Ulbricht and in the writings of physical educators like Ingeburg Wonneberger.[13] East Germany's success in international competition was spectacular. Although the population of the former German Democratic Republic at the time of reunification was only one-

TABLE 11.1.
Class Origins of Polish Elite Athletes
(In percent)

	Peasantry	Working Class	Intelligentsia
Male	80.8	71.5	45.3
Female	19.2	28.5	59.7

fifteenth that of the United States, the GDR's female athletes won
more Olympic and world championships than the women of any
other country. They were the nation's heroines.[14] (Whether such
extraordinary achievements are now things of the past, as Katarina
Witt fears, remains to be seen.) For ordinary women "socialist physical culture" was rather a disappointment. The statistics gathered in
1965, are best presented in tabular form. (See table 11.2.) Although
the categories are not entirely clear, the under-representation of women
is quite obvious, especially as members of sports clubs, where the
male/female ratio was a disheartening 5.70. If one looks at the data
for specific recreational sports and physical activities, one finds that
East German women were almost as likely as men to go to the beach
and that they were more likely than the men to do "morning exercises," but real sports competition was rare.[15] Nine years later, in
1974, when the number of female sports-club members had risen to
631,103 and the male/female ratio had dropped to 3.0, most of the
women still continued to shun strenuous competition.[16]

A "striking discrepancy" in male versus female rates of sports
participation has been characteristic of the Soviet Union as well.
Between 1959 and 1969, there was an increase in the percentage of
men and women who reported that they were involved in sports and
the male/female ratio declined from 2.13 to 1.84. (See table 11.3.)
Other survey data from the early 1970s indicated that, on the average,
"men spent five times more time on sport than women." The disparity is most striking in the Islamic parts of the Soviet Union where
cultural barriers to women's participation have always been much
higher than in Russia or the Baltic states. In Tashkent, in 1921, for
example, a woman was murdered when she called upon Islamic

TABLE 11.2.
Organized Sports Participation: German
Democratic Republic
(In percent)

	Men	Women
Membership in sports clubs	13.7	2.4
Training near the home	10.0	5.1
Training at work	3.7	0.8
Training somewhere else	2.9	1.0
Mass sports near the home	9.1	2.4
Mass sports at work	4.8	0.7
Compensatory calisthenics	2.5	2.4

TABLE 11.3.
*Participation in Organized Sports
in the Soviet Union*
(In percent)

	1959	1969
Soviet Men	—	37.0
Soviet Women	5.6	14.1
Women's Share		
of Participants	31.9	35.2
Male/Female Ratio	2.13	1.84

women to compete in the Central Asian Games. Persistent efforts by Communist modernizers have slowly modified traditional attitudes. The percentage of Uzbek women involved in sports rose from 3.6 percent in 1959 to 10.8 percent a decade later. Still, the Islamic areas lagged far behind the rest of the USSR. In Lithuania, for instance, the comparable figures for 1959 and 1969 were 16.4 percent and 41.2 percent. The Olympic gymnasts Elvira Saadi and Nelli Kim, both of whom came from Islamic families, were exceptional.[17]

The problem, ironic in societies officially committed to "dialectical materialism," is that the Soviet Union and the other regimes of Eastern Europe have never been willing to create the material conditions necessary for ordinary women to enjoy the equality constitutionally granted them. Of the typical woman "under Communism," Barbara Wolfe Jancar writes, "She cannot choose not to work and she cannot choose not to have children." Analyzing the empirical studies that document a persistent pattern of inequality in politics and economics, Jancar notes that "a three-child family makes it impossible for a woman to spend the time necessary to work for advancement to the higher echelons of any professional category."[18] Since child-care facilities are inadequate and husbands are generally too traditional in their attitudes to share in the burdens of housework, most women work the notorious "double shift" and have too little time and energy for regular sports participation. They content themselves with hurried calisthenics—if that. They consider themselves lucky if a brief vacation on the Black Sea or the Baltic coast includes a few hours of volleyball.

Had Jancar's wide-ranging study touched upon sports, she might have commented that the spectacular successes of the elite female athletes of Eastern Europe are the predictable results of professionalization. For these women there is no disabling opposition between sports and work because sports are their work. Women with other occupations, i.e., over 99 percent of those gainfully employed, are often nominal members of sports clubs who remain on the sidelines while their menfolk play. In the 1960s and 1970s, in no country of Eastern Europe did women have the same opportunities for sports participation that they enjoy in Western Europe and in North America. Whether the gap was closed in the 1980s is debatable. A number of Eastern European sports sociologists have reacted angrily to the allegation that their system has privileged an athletic elite and neglected recreational sports for the masses. Andrzej Wohl, for instance, claimed in 1983 that such allegation were slanderous. In fact, he wrote, 30 percent of the entire population of the USSR was enrolled in sports clubs and 40 percent of these sports-club members were women (male/female ratio = 1.5). Wohl also maintained, incredibly, that the level of participation in the Asian republics was actually *higher* than in the rest of the Soviet Union. Similarly, Krěsmir Petrović proudly claimed a male/female ratio of 1.5 for Yugoslavs engaged in "physical culture," but "physical culture" included picnics and a number of other pleasantly noncompetitive activities. For East Germany, Heidi Bierstadt made similar claims with similar unpersuasive evidence. Until better evidence is provided that ordinary "women under Communism" have had something approaching equal opportunity in sports, skepticism is in order.[19]

2. "Il Duce Wants Female Athletes!"

Of all the political leaders of the 1920s and 1930s, Benito Mussolini was the one most determined to project an image of superb vitality and exuberant physical strength. His sycophants raved about him as a "man of sports" with "imposing torso and athletic arms." He was said to be an example of perfectly harmonious physical and intellectual development. *Popolo d'Italia* and other Italian newspaper printed photograph after photograph of *Il Duce* performing exemplary feats of physical prowess. The most famous image is surely that of the Fascist leader as barechested skier. This exhibitionist athleticism was in line with Fascist theory, which made a fetish of masculine physicality. F. T. Marinetti, for instance, proclaimed in *Teoria e Invenzione Futurista* the necessity of "pride in one's own body, in one's own physical health, in one's own lovely musculature."[20] The British approach to sports was denigrated as "pure personal satisfaction" while the Italian path was celebrated as a way to prepare young men for service to the state.[21] Italy had had compulsory physical education in its schools since 1878, in theory; in practice, the law was generally ignored before the Fascists came to power in 1922. Once they were in control of the educational system, they demanded that Italy's schools produce vigorous athletes rather than ungainly (and politically unreliable) intellectuals.

A youth organization, the *Opera Nazionale Balilla,* was created in 1926 to supplement the work of the schools. Sports were an important part of the ONB's program. From 1934 on, boys competed in national championships while girls were encouraged "in a lighter and less agonistic way than the boys" to dance, to swim, to compete in archery, and to perform in mass gymnastic exercises.[22] Young adults were organized in *Gioventù Italiana del Littorio,* which also staged sports events. In 1940, GIL's 2,720,941 young women were 32.2 percent of the organization's total membership. While the men boxed and competed in track and field, the women swam and competed in archery contests.[23] Still another Fascist organization, the *Opera Nazionale Dopolavoro,* provided "after-work" recreation. The OND recommended that women dance, do mild gymnastics, play tennis, and ski, but the organization did "little or nothing to provide the special facilities for those pastimes judged proper for women." The task of the OND was made harder when the Roman Catholic Church accused it of "kindling eroticism" by means of women's sports.[24] The Church had its own sports clubs for girls, as an aspect of *Azione Cattólica,* but watchful nuns carefully shielded the maidens from the public's morally destructive gaze.[25]

As the various programs for girls and women suggest, the ideologues of the Fascist regime were not of one mind on the question of women's sports. On the one hand, Italian women were constantly urged to be "exemplary wives and mothers" and eugenic theory demanded physical fitness in order to improve the Italian "race." On the other hand, the Fascist state was irresolute about implementing the theory. Calisthenics were boring, serious competition was deemed to be unwomanly, and the public display of women's bodies in athletic attire was contrary to new Fascist doctrines as well as to traditional Roman Catholic values.[26]

Writing on "La donna italiana e lo sport" in the journal *Lo Sport*

Fascista, Romeo Panti concluded that it was better to lose points in international competition than to sacrifice modesty and decorum. *Atlética Leggera,* the track-and-field journal, published occasional reassuring photographs of female athletes who had fulfilled their patriotic obligation and become happy mothers. They were the ones who had wisely shunned soccer and unfeminine field sports like the discus and the javelin.[27] A few ardent believers in women's sports swam against the current. In *La Scuola Fascista,* Augusto Turati saw no reason why girls should not experience "the joy of running with bare legs and trying to go faster." Such an experience, thought Turati, made the girls braver, happier, and—of course—prepared them to be healthier mothers.[28]

When Italian women did well in international meets, as they did in the *Jeux Féminins* in Prague in 1930, their photographs were captioned to underline the fact that they were not only exceptionally athletic but also thoroughly feminine, the very image of Italian *bellezza.*[29] When the Fascist Grand Council decided in 1930 to continue its hesitant endorsement of women's sports, it asked the doctors of the sports medicine federation and the officials of the National Olympic Committee to oversee the athletes to ensure that they were adequately protected "in their natural and fundamental mission: maternity."[30]

Dissidents advocating strenuous competition had a hard row to hoe. They faced nearly insurmountable cultural obstacles in a country still overwhelmingly Roman Catholic. It was difficult for them to motivate young women to engage in physical training of any sort. Peasant women, the majority, were especially resistant to Mussolini's vision of an athletically revitalized nation. Most of those who represented the Fascist regime in international sports came from the less traditional, less religiously devout strata of Italian society. It was an additional annoyance for the Fascists that Jewish women were numerically overrepresented in Italian sports (partly because Italian Jews were on the average more urban, better educated, and more affluent than Italian Catholics).

Traditional barriers to women's sports combined, therefore, with Fascist reluctance to condone public competition. While the 101 male representatives of Fascism performed very impressively at the 1932 Olympics in Los Angeles, winning twelve gold, twelve silver, and eleven bronze medals, Italian women brought home no medals because there *were* no women on the Italian team.[31] Fascist dictatorship had achieved for Italy what voluntary organization had failed to accomplish for the female physical educators of the United States—an all-male Olympic team.

3. *Kraft Durch Freude*

The slogan "Strength through joy" is often taken to be symbolic of the National Socialist approach to sports, but the slogan referred to only one of many programs of physical culture, and sports were only one aspect of the "Strength through joy" program. In fact, Hitler and the other ideologues of the Nazi regime had serious reservations about sports. What most offended the author of *Mein Kampf* was not competition, which he endorsed as the very essence of "Aryan" manhood. Hitler objected because modern sports are organized on the basis of universalistic criteria. In a game of soccer, the alleged purity or impurity of an athlete's blood is irrelevant. Another irritation for the Nazis was that modern sports are an international phenomenon. Unlike *Turnen,* they cannot be extolled rhapsodically as a unique expression of the German *Volk.*

In many of their early statements about physical culture, the Nazis seemed almost to echo the propagandists of the *Deutsche Turnerschaft.* The gymnasts of that extremely nationalistic organization had initially refused to participate in the first modern Olympics and had condemned modern sports as "a passionately pursued form of physical exercise as alien to German behavior as their name, for which there is no German word." [32] In 1917, in the *Monatschrift für das Turnwesen,* a spokesman for the *Deutsche Turnerschaft* emphasized the aesthetic element in German *Turnen* and condemned English sports as "thoroughly individualistic and egoistic." [33] By the 1930s, however, the *Deutsche Turnerschaft* had abandoned much of its earlier opposition to competition even as it maintained an undiminished commitment to traditional nationalism and an equally undiminished opposition to individualism. Indeed, by 1933, the *Turner* were ready to affirm the spirit of struggle—the *Kampfgeist*—as a collective expression of the German soul.

It was, therefore, no surprise when Edmund Neuendorff, the rabidly chauvinist chairman of the *Deutsche Turnerschaft,* proudly proclaimed the organization's fealty to Hitler. When the gymnasts met in Stuttgart in the summer of 1933 for what proved to be their last hurrah, the swastika was displayed along with the *Turnerschaft's* traditional insignia. Hitler was the guest of honor, and Neuendorff announced that the entire gymnastics movement was marching side by side with Hitler's Storm Troops. [34]

Hitler had other ideas. The *Deutsche Turnerschaft*, incorporated into the state bureaucracy, lost its autonomy. The other sports federations fared no better, although many of their leaders had hoped opportunistically to win favor by quickly declaring their full allegiance to the Nazi regime and by hastily expelling their Jewish members even before new legislation required them to. The sports federations' hopes for at least partial autonomy were naive. It was Hitler's intent to combine physical culture and ideological indoctrination within a wholly revamped system of sports federations and youth organizations like the *Hitlerjugend* and *Bund Deutscher Mädel*. For the workers, there was the "Strength through joy" program.

In all of these organizations, young men were encouraged to do sports and to develop toughness and combativeness (*"Kampfgeist"*) while young women were instructed to prepare themselves for motherhood. [35] Unambivalent about maternity and about physical education as a means to that glorious goal, theorists engaged in heated debate over the proper means: Were sports an appropriate preparation for maternity? Opinions varied just as they did in Fascist Italy. Karl Ritter von Halt, head of the national track-and-field federation, president of the National Olympic Committee, and a member of the International Olympic Committee, affirmed the superiority of mild competition over noncompetitive exercise. He opined, however, that female athletes had no need for strenuous training because their achievements were "the natural fruit of joyful and untroubled activity." Another Nazi, Hans Möckelmann, expressed deeper doubts about the value of women's sports. Writing in *Die Leibesübungen der Mädchen* (1934), he was exuberant about the "combative forward thrust, the attack," that characterized men's sports, but he felt that women's sports should be restricted to "exercises compatible with woman's maternal destiny." [36] Hans von Tschammer und Osten, Hitler's new *Reichssportführer*, was also critical of women's sports and referred to the 1928 Olympics and the horrors of the endlessly controversial 800–meter race, but Heinz Cavalier, editor of *Der Leichtathlet* bravely disagreed with Tschammer und Osten on this issue. [37] He thought the distance might be covered by a trained athlete. Margaret Knipper was another who resisted the effort of the minority to "protect" women from the rigors of modern sports. She urged women to struggle against timidity, to use sports as a means to achieve "cour-age, toughness, hearty self-confidence, tenacity, and strength of will."[38] These were the attributes of the "Aryan" mother. With such senti-ments as hers in mind, a French scholar has recently observed that "the Fascist woman modeled herself after the Spartan woman."[39] The observation is close to the mark. Nazi theory came increasingly to resemble ancient Spartan eugenics, a resemblance that many Nazis proudly acknowledged. World War II made the similarity even more striking. In 1941, the guidelines for girls' physical education and sports called for schooling in toughness and courage.[40]

Sports were prominent in many of the organizations the Nazis created to divert and indoctrinate the German people. In the *Bund Deutscher Mädel,* established in 1933 for all "Aryan" girls aged ten to eighteen, sports were given pride of place. Baldur von Schirach, the man in charge of both the BDM and also the *Hitlerjugend,* decreed that two-thirds of the girls' time should be devoted to physical edu-cation and sports. The typical BDM program consisted of a five-minute run, twenty-five minutes of gymnastics, then forty-five min-utes of track and field followed by another forty-five minutes of games. Achievement was stressed. "The point was always to be faster, better, braver and more skillful than the others."[41] From the age of fourteen, girls were required to earn the bronze badges awarded for sports achievements. In all these activities, there was great empha-sis on willpower.

From the *Bund Deutscher Mädel,* which became compulsory in 1936, the girls graduated to the *Glaube und Schönheit* organization, established in 1938 for girls up to the age of twenty-two. Sports were one official path to this "Faith and Beauty." Gymnastics were an-other. From their seventeenth through their twenty-fifth year, young women were also required to work for the state in the *Reichsarbeits-dienst,* which also included an elaborate program of recreational sports. Female students at German universities were required to take four semesters of physical education, the avowed purpose of which was to produce "strong-willed" women determined to give birth to healthy progeny. Girls whose appetite for competition was not satisfied by this interlocking array of organizations were encouraged to join a sports club, where official competition was permitted for "Aryan" girls who were also members of the *Bund Deutscher Mädel.*[42]

Although Hitler's totalitarian regime aspired for absolute control of the entire population, not even the Nazis were able to achieve that impossible goal. Women who survived the twelve years of Nazi rule have testified that they thoroughly enjoyed the opportunity for sports and other forms of physical expression during their schooldays, but Nazi ideology, they now claim, never interested them. Looking back on this shameful period, these German women frequently assert that their teachers were also resistant to Nazi doctrine. "For the physical-education instructors, sports obviously had a meaning quite different from that described in the official propaganda. They did sports not for '*Volk und Vaterland*' but for sociability and engagement." The credibility of such disavowals depends, of course, on the political background of the women who now portray themselves and their teachers as immune to Nazi propaganda. It cannot be that *no one* was taken in by the delusions of the Nazi regime. If volunteer work on behalf of the regime's youth organizations can be interpreted as an indication of ideological commitment, then women physical-education teachers were more ardently Nazi than their male colleagues; according to figures cited by Hajo Bernett, 12.5 percent of the female instructors were active in the *BDM* while 5.8 percent of the males took on roles in the *Hitlerjugend*. On the other hand, incredulity in the face of the women's claims can be carried too far. The rhetoric of political leaders and the pompous instructions of educational bureaucrats cannot be taken at face value as a reliable guide to what actually happened when the girls changed into their sports uniforms and joined their teachers in the gymnasium and on the track.[43]

On the whole, German women were certainly much quicker to participate in sports than Italian women were (even though Germany's Roman Catholic bishops were nearly as antagonistic to women's sports as their Italian counterparts). German women had done well at the first Olympic Games to allocate a significant part of the program to women's sports. In 1928, Lina Radke won the notorious 800–meter race and the German team had placed third in the 4 x 100–meter relay. Hélène Mayer won a gold medal in fencing. German women far outdistanced their British and French rivals at the third and fourth FSFI-sponsored *Jeux Féminins* held in 1930 and 1934.

For the Nazi regime, the 1936 Olympic Games, scheduled for Berlin, posed a political dilemma. On the one hand, there were lingering doubts about modern sports in general and especially about strenuous sports competition for women. The Olympics were still perceived by many Nazi ideologues as a symbol of liberal internationalism. And a number of German Jews had "infiltrated" the Olympic movement and its organizations. On the other hand, the games were a splendid opportunity to publicize the new Germany and to propagate the belief in "Aryan" physical superiority. As it happened, the opportunity for propaganda was too great to be resisted. Rather to the surprise of the Olympic officials who had expected the Nazis to decline to host international sports festival, Hitler and Goebbels gave their approval. Once that approval was given, it was necessary to persuade the International Olympic Committee and the various National Olympic Committees of the democratic states to the west that the exclusion of German Jews from sports clubs and from public sports facilities did not constitute a violation of the Olympic Charter. Even as they lied to the IOC, the Nazis worked to put together the most powerful Olympic team the world had ever seen.

The desire for a propaganda coup overrode the instinctive conviction, still cherished by many, that women should be restricted to *Kinder, Kirche, Küche* ("children, the church, the kitchen"). German women trained for the games. In order to blunt the threat of a boycott and mollify those who demanded that the Olympic rules be followed, the Nazis arranged for Hélène Meyer, who had won the gold medal at the 1928 Olympics, to fence for Germany even though she was a "half-Jew" and a resident of the United States. No doubt it was a point in her favor that she was a statuesque blonde who looked beautifully "Aryan." Germany's best high jumper, Gretel Bergmann, was less fortunate. Dark-eyed, dark-haired, Jewish, she was kept from the team even after she set a national high-jump record of 1.60 meters. Germany was represented by Elfriede Kaun and "Dora" Ratjen, who was actually a man. Perhaps Bergmann found some consolation in the fact that the event was won by Ibola Csak, a Hungarian Jew.[44]

The German women did, on the whole, outperform their rivals. Among the most impressive athletes at the games was Gisela Maurmayer. She had begun to do track and field as a thirteen-year-old member of the *Turn- und Sportverein Neuhasen-Nymphenburg*. She began to compete in the discus and participated in Madame Milliat's *Jeux Féminins* in 1930. At the Women's World Games in London in 1934, also sponsored by the FISF, she won the first-ever women's pentathlon competition. Now, before the eyes of her delighted *Führer,* she won the discus with a throw of 47.63 meters.[45] Tilly Fleischer threw the javelin 45.18 meters for another gold medal while the runners and jumpers won a silver medal and two bronzes. The swimmers and divers also won several silver and bronze medals, and the gymnasts won a gold in team competition (which was all there was). Photographs of suitably flaxen-haired German victors, their hands raised in the Nazi salute, appeared everywhere. Hélène Mayer, who placed second in foils, raised her arm too in deluded tribute to the man who was soon to send women like her to the gas chambers.[46]

To win in team gymnastics, which had been placed on the program in 1928 and removed in 1932, the German women outperformed the Czechs and Poles. The rather mediocre American gymnastics team was composed entirely of German-American women from the *Turner* movement because the colleges and universities continued to disapprove of international competition for women. The best-known woman on the American team was the veteran swimmer Eleanor Holm Jarrett, who had won the 100–meter backstroke in record time (1:19.4) at Los Angeles in 1932. She qualified easily for the 1936 team and sailed with the rest of the athletes on the S.S. *Manhattan*. Feeling that a married woman needed less chaperonage than the adolescent girls who made up most of the team, Jarrett danced, drank, and ignored reprimands. The American Olympic Committee expelled her from the team and the American press plunged eagerly into the controversy in order to side with the lovely "water nymph" against the bureaucratic meanies. Avery Brundage, never one of the reporters' favorites, was pilloried for his rigid adherence to the rules.[47]

All in all, the legacy of these games probably mitigated some of the aversion against international women's competitions. A French historian of track and field has written that even Hitler was "apparently subdued by the virile beauty" of Helen Stephens, the American winner of the 100–meter dash. Hitler gave her his autograph.[48] Hitler may have been subdued but Pierre de Coubertin was not. Before his death in 1937, the founder of the modern Olympic Games uttered his last word on the subject of women's sports: "Let women do all the sports they wish—but not in public."[49]

TWELVE

Evolutionary Change

1. Participation: From 1945 to the Early Seventies

For European and American women, the immediate postwar decades were a medley of confusing and conflicting tendencies and countertendencies. World War II had mobilized millions of European and American women in roles conventionally thought of as male. Women entered offices and factories, and women entered the armed services, although rarely as combatants. They managed at home because they had to. When the war ended, many women gave a sigh of relief and hastened back to the more comfortable roles of wife and mother. Others were reluctant to surrender their newly discovered sense of competence and autonomy (not to speak of their pay checks). Millions of women were widowed and had meager hopes of finding another husband in the decimated ranks of the men. Most of them became heads of a household whether they wanted to or not. They had little choice but to remain in the work force. With much of the European continent in ruins, there was more than enough work at hand.

Slowly at first, then with accelerating rapidity, in both Europe and America, the nature of work was transformed. The shift from the industrial to the postindustrial age, from steam to electricity, was as great as the earlier shift from farms to factories and, within agriculture, to mechanized production. The relative decline in heavy industry and the relative increase in the service sector brought middle-class women into the labor market in unprecedented numbers and often kept them on the job after marriage and even, in many cases, after child-bearing. More work, paradoxically, did not mean a greater psychic commitment to the work ethic. As the middle classes approached the affluence long enjoyed by the leisure class, the work ethic, with its emphasis on self-denial and material accumulation, was mitigated. Participant sports consumed much of the physical energy formerly expended in hard labor. Spectator sports began to appear on television. Sports of all kinds stimulated and excited minds dulled by routine work or fatigued by the need for mental concentration.

What did all of this mean for *women's* sports? No simple answer is possible, but there is some truth in Mary Leigh's comment, "The hardships European women withstood as a result of World War II made American objections to women's competition in sports appear ridiculous."[1] Men who had observed women working as truckdrivers and welders were somewhat less amenable than they had been to the notion that sports were too strenuous for "the weaker sex." The "feminine mystique," which dictated wifehood and motherhood for middle-class women in Europe as well as in the United States, discouraged professional careers for women, but the roles of middle-class wife and mother included much more sports participation than had been the case in earlier generations. The suburban wife in her thirties and forties was expected to remain physically attractive, and sports were seen as one way to stay forever youthful.

The change in attitudes can easily be exaggerated. In both Europe and the United States, there were still, in these first postwar decades, defenders of sports as a purely masculine domain. There was still considerable resistance to the notion of women as serious competitors. In 1958, for example, when thirty Norwegian women took to their skis for a 10–kilometer cross-country race, the newspaper *Dagdbladet* was outraged. The winner, Ingrid Wigernes, arrived with her make-up intact, but the others—breathless, sweaty, with clumps of ice in their mussed hair—fell exhausted to the ground. *Dagdbladet* writers and other opponents of women's sports did not rely solely on arguments about aesthetics. Girls were still warned that sports might endanger their reproductive organs. Yves Brossard, for instance, warned French coaches and athletes "to take account of the natural suppleness and fragility of the feminine organism. It is necessary to respect the role of the future *maman* so that sports do not become an occasion for suppressing or damaging this role."[2] This opinion, widely shared even in the 1960s, appeared in a series entitled *vues chrétiènnes*.

Widely shared, but no longer the sentiment of the majority. Despite opposition to women's sports on the part of those who cherished visions of demurely noncompetitive perspiration-free damsels, despite the misguided concern about supposedly endangered motherhood, positive attitudes prevailed. Girls were encouraged to do sports by parents, older siblings, friends, teachers, and coaches.[3] Athletes, together with rock musicians and film stars, ousted political leaders, writers, artists, and scientists as the idols of the young. The girl who once dreamed of Eve Curie or Virginia Woolf had visions of herself as another Helen Wills or—if she was ready to resist the residual prejudice—another Althea Gibson.

The change in self-conception was strikingly evident when sociologists asked American high-school students how they wished to be remembered. When James Coleman conducted his famous study of the American high school, he found—in the 1950s—that boys were more likely to want to be remembered as athletic stars than as brilliant students or as members of "the leading crowd." When Coleman put similar questions to the girls, he did not think to offer them the option of indicating that they, too, preferred to be remembered for their sports achievements rather than their aptitude for poetry and mathematics. Adding the category of sports to her 1970s replication of Coleman's study, Deborah L. Feltz discovered that more than a fifth of the girls longed to be remembered as athletic stars.[4] In a similar study, Canadian sociologists discovered, contrary to what might have been expected, that athletic girls had significantly higher peer-group status than girls who did poorly in sports. They were admired by boys as well as by other girls.[5]

American colleges were, as we have seen, still generally unwilling in the immediate postwar years to sponsor intercollegiate sports for women, but physical educators did preach the gospel of "moderate exercise" and many students were eager converts to sports. Adult women, reluctant to give up an activity that they had found pleasurable and that society told them was good for them, bombarded with news of sports events and with appeals to purchase sports equipment, were more likely to remain active than their mothers and grandmothers had been.

There is, indeed, evidence that the women's *desire* to remain active

exceeded the capacity of the available facilities. The discrepancy between supply and demand was especially severe in Europe. Many of
Europe's sportsgrounds and gymnasia had been devastated by the
war. They were not rebuilt in the immediate postwar years when
food and shelter took priority over inessentials. In all of Great Britain,
in 1950, there were, for example, only 195 cinder tracks (compared
to 730 in Finland).[6] Officials anxious to revive postwar sports in
France looked enviously at Sweden, unravaged by war. They noticed
with chagrin that there were 110 tracks and 60 swimming pools for
every million Swedes; the French had five tracks and two pools for
every million citizens.[7] It was not until 1959 that West Germany's
local, state, and national governments joined to forge the "Golden
Plan" for sports development and to launch an ambitious program
for constructing new facilities. Since sports for men and boys continued to be favored even by those who were positive about sports for
girls and women, scarce resources were seldom equitably shared.

Fields, tracks, halls, pools, courts, rinks, and links were built.
Enough of them were made available enough of the time for women's
sports participation to increase in Europe as in the United States.
Unfortunately, it is impossible to state the exact degree of the increase. Researchers began in these years to amass quantified information on sports participation, but their publications were and often still
are frustrating. One source of frustration is that many surveys report
aggregate results for the whole adult population and fail to break the
data down by sex (or age or social class). Incongruent definitions are
another endemic problem. Government surveys of leisure often ask
respondents whether or not they participate in "sports or other outdoor activities." Three gardeners, a bird watcher, and a basketball
player are counted as five "sports participants."

Pollsters are similarly imprecise and sociologists, who might be
expected to be more careful with the concepts they utilize, often
employ an implicit definition of sport which includes such noncompetitive activities as hiking and wading. Loose definitions lead to the
conclusion that almost every American "goes to the beach," which
tells us nothing about the number of them who actually swim. (Surveys have revealed that most of the swimsuits sold never enter the
water.) When we are informed that over 90 percent of all teenagers
are cyclists, we can be sure that they sometimes race each other on
their way to school, but they are clearly not cyclists in the sense that

Jacques Enquetil and Eddy Merckx were. Realizing that peddling to the *lycée* by the dawn's early light is rather different from contesting the *Tour de France,* the *Miroir du Cyclisme* commissioned a scientific survey of French cyclists and found that only 2 percent of them raced and only 3 percent of them toured.[8] One study reported that elderly Finns showed an astonishingly high rate of sports participation; our astonishment grows less when we realize that the sociologist who conducted the survey included berry picking among Finland's popular "sports."[9] Researchers in Illinois came to similarly surprising conclusions about the vim and vigor of the elderly when they included gardening in their list of "sports."[10]

Political factors can also perturb the data. A study of "Daily Participation in Sport across Twelve Countries," conducted in 1965–1966, concluded that the women of the Soviet Union were from three to fifteen times as likely to participate in sports as the women of eleven other Communist and non-Communist countries.[11] This wildly improbable conclusion, which has been repeatedly contradicted by empirical work done by Soviet sociologists, can best be explained as the result of ideologically motivated wishful thinking.

Although pre-1960 numbers are not very reliable and the pre-1970 numbers are not a great deal better, certain sociological patterns do come into reasonably clear focus. In Europe and in America, investigators confirmed some not very surprising hypotheses. They found that young women participated more than older women, that single women did more sports than married women with young children, that the affluent and the well educated were more involved, actively and passively, than the economically and educationally disadvantaged, that Roman Catholic, Greek Orthodox, and Islamic faith diminished the likelihood of a woman's engagement in sports, that ethnic minorities were often underrepresented in sports clubs, and that excellent facilities in close proximity are a stimulus to participation. It may, however, surprise some readers to discover that women who worked outside the home were more rather than less likely than housewives to make time for sports. Needless to say, there was some cross-cultural variation, to which we shall turn in a moment, but the differences were less striking than the similarity of the pattern encountered in country after country. While this kind of quantified sociological information is not everyone's cup of tea, it is essential that the historian's more impressionistic surveys be cautiously supple-

mented by whatever numerical data are available. In the data that
follow, most ratios are expressed decimally without a second term,
e.g., as "3.65" rather than "3.65 to 1."

Thanks to Germany's long tradition of sports sociology, thanks
also to generous funding by the federal government and the national
sports federation, German statistics were generally good and the data
on sports-club membership were excellent. A study conducted in
1965, based on interviews with 936 men and 1,077 women aged
sixteen and over, found that 22 percent of the men and only 7 percent
of the women were club members.[12] The numbers may seem low,
but they were a dramatic improvement from the situation in 1959,
when men were seven times as likely as women to be members.[13]
The men sampled in this 1965 study were also more likely to obtain
the popular achievement badges awarded by the *Deutscher Sportbund,*
but the number of male badge-winners began to decline in the early
seventies while the number of women was on the rise.[14] Critiques of
the "achievement motivation" (*"Leistungsmotivation"*) provided radical men with a socially acceptable reason to drop out of sports even
as raised feminist consciousness gave radical women new justifica-
tions for participation in activities formerly reserved for men.

Although comparable numbers of the sampled men and women
cite health as a motive for doing sports, 18 percent of the men and
only 8 percent of the women welcomed the opportunity "to measure
themselves against others."[15] Since behaviors often diverge from
attitudes, it is no surprise that an EMNID survey conducted in December 1972 and January 1973 reported that men were in practice *six*
times more likely than women actually to compete in sports contests.[16]

The importance of social class as a determinant of sports-club
membership can hardly be overstated. At this time, approximately 50
percent of the German population was designated as lower class, but
only 35.5 percent of sports-club members, aged fifteen to twenty-
five, came from that segment of society. As was almost invariably
the case, lower-class women were even more drastically underrepresented than the men.[17] Of the German women engaged in skilled
blue-collar work (*"Facharbeiterinne"*), 7 percent claimed to be active
in sports; 17 percent of the female white-collar workers (*"Angestellten"*
and *"Beamte"*) made the same claim.[18]

The situation was not very different on the other side of the Rhine.
A French national poll published in 1967 asked about sports partici-

pation, a formulation which invariably produces higher percentages than questions about club membership. Broken down by ages, the figures were as shown in table 12.1 The very low male/female ratios can be explained by the fact that "sports" were defined, as usual, to include a variety of noncompetitive activities. The lowest ratio of all —1.25—probably reflects a physical-education requirement in the schools. For the French population *not* in school, only 8 percent of the men and women answered that they were regular participants and 14.9 percent that they participated "irregularly." The inequality among the various occupations was as striking as for the German population, with 10.1 percent of factory workers and 32.3 percent of "free professionals" claiming regular participation. (This portion of the poll did not separate male from female respondents.) In 1970, the nation's sixty-one sports federations had a total membership of 4,043,565 men and 1,192,533 women. The male/female ratio of 3.39 was much higher than the ratios calculated from the general survey because, in most of the federations, the women were involved in authentic sports and not merely in noncompetitive physical activities.[19]

Concentrating on sports (and excluding outdoor activities of a noncompetitive nature), N. G. Vlot demonstrated that less than 1 percent of the Dutch population was involved in "organized sports" in 1900 while over 12 percent were in 1961. In 1900, 19.4 percent of the participants were female; in 1961, 29 percent. Men played soccer; women did gymnastics. It is unlikely that many of the women— even in the sixties—competed in gymnastics matches.[20] Unfortunately for those of us who pine for tidy research, the data reported for 1963 indicated an improbable quantum leap in participation. For that year, it was reported that 38 percent of the Dutch population (over twelve years old) did sports. Of men nineteen and older, 25.6 percent were club members; of the women, only 7.4 percent. Accordingly, the male/female ratio was for club membership in 1963 was

TABLE 12.1.
Regular Sports Participation in France
(In percent)

Ages	14–18	18–22	22–25	25–30	30–40	40–50	50–60
Males	61.8	34.9	26.4	21.2	13.6	8.4	6.9
Females	49.5	19.2	17.8	10.2	6.9	6.5	2.8
M/F	1.25	1.79	1.48	2.08	1.97	1.29	2.46

exactly the same as the male/female ratio for participation in 1961—
3.45.[21]

One expects this ratio to have been lower in Scandinavia, where
Lutheranism rather than Catholicism has been the dominant religion,
where democratic socialism was stronger than elsewhere in Europe,
but Sweden's sports clubs were 87 percent male in 1970 (male/female
ratio = 6.69). Adolescent boys were twice as likely as their sisters to
be involved in sports, and the male/female disparity increased to
more than six to one for men and women aged thirty-five to forty.[22]
Similar figures describe the Norwegian case in these years. In 1962
there were 34,175 women eighteen and older in the national sports
federation. They were 18.9 percent of the total adult membership of
180,850. Eleven years later, the male/female ratio dropped from 4.29
to 2.73. There were 158,824 adult female members of sports clubs,
and they were 26.8 percent of the total membership.[23]

The failure of the Soviet Union and its allies to have fulfilled the
egalitarian promises of Communism has already been discussed in
chapter 11. If reasonably accurate data are available for Southern
Europe in these years, I am unaware of them.

In Great Britain, the most reliable information came from the
General Household Survey. The 1973 numbers indicated that men
were approximately twice as likely as women to participate at least
once a month in outdoors and in indoors sports. This datum fits the
results of a microstudy of Manchester's schools, which found that 70
percent of the adolescent boys did sports outside of school while only
43.3 percent of the girls did. (When asked about the sports, games,
or outdoors activities they expected to pursue after leaving school or
college, 43.8 percent of the girls and 22 percent of the boys wrote
"None.") But when the Household Survey asked about *daily* participation, a different light was cast on the situation. As the figures in
table 12.2 indicate, the male/female ratio climbed to almost ten to
one![24]

In an essay entitled "Sport and Physical Activity in the Lives of
Canadian Women," M. Ann Hall reported that 13.9 percent of women
aged 20–44 participated in sports from one to three hours a week
(compared to 17.7 percent of the men).[25] Although Hall cites this
disparity as evidence of pervasive injustice in a male-dominated society, incongruous data published in the same collection of essays
indicated a far greater gender gap. A 1974 survey of over 40,000
employed men and women found that 10.4 percent of the men and
4.9 percent of the women claimed to be involved in *sports* (as distin-

TABLE 12.2.
Sports Participation in Great Britain
(In percent)

	16–19	20–29	Ages 30–59	60+	All
Monthly: Outdoors					
Male	46	33	22	14	24
Female	20	15	12	6	11
M/F	2.3	2.2	1.83	2.33	2.18
Monthly: Indoors					
Male	27	22	14	3	14
Female	15	9	10	2	6
M/F	1.8	2.44	1.4	1.5	2.33

	orc16–20	21–29	Ages 30–59	60+	All
Daily					
Male	2.8	3.0	1.6	1.1	2.4
Female	—	0.3	0.2	0.1	0.4
M/F		10.0	8.0	11.0	6.0

guished from "physical activities"). This male/female ratio of 2.12 was much more probable than the nearly utopian 1.24 derived from Hall's data.[26]

In Canada and Australia, sociologists documented the apparently universal relationship between social class and sports participation. Their research showed clearly that the strong positive correlation between social class and sports participation grew even stronger when the sampled population consisted of elite athletes. In B. R. Blishen's categorization of occupational ranks, 31 percent of the Canadian labor force fell into the lowest category, but only 16 percent of the male athletes' fathers (and only 9 percent of the females' fathers).[27] The under-representation of lower-class women was crassly evident in a sample of Australian athletes of roughly the same elite calibre. While 34 percent of the total population were semiskilled or unskilled laborers, only 18 percent of the elite male athletes and 14 percent of the elite female athletes had fathers who came from that social stratum. In other words, for elite female athletes, class-gender interactions were intensified. For upper-class women, the disadvantages of gender were minimized. For lower-class women, the disabilities of their class were added to those of their sex.[28]

For the United States in these years, there are no satisfactory studies of adult sports participation. Government surveys asked about sports and other outdoors activities. A frequently cited study of "Daily Participation in Sports Across Twelve Countries" included data from the United States, but "sports" were defined to include not only ballgames but also calisthenics and noncompetitive recreational activities such as a day at the seashore. With this catch-all definition in mind, 5.1 percent of the men and 4.4 percent of the women claimed to do "sports" daily. The resultant male/female ratio of 1.16 obscures the fact that the men were likely to be playing ballgames while the women were sunning themselves at the beach.[29]

It is only when one shifts the focus to adolescence and restricts the scope to interscholastic and intercollegiate athletics that one obtains a realistic picture of girls' and young women's sports participation in the United States. In fact, these data are even better than those on sports-club membership because club membership can be, and often is, totally passive. We can safely assume that team members, whether starters or benchwarmers, are really active participants in their chosen sport. (See table 12.3.)[30] Unfortunately, the longitudinal data which might have allowed us to plot the increase over time in girls' and young women's varsity participation were not systematically gathered before this period (as they *were* for boys and young men).

Generalizations on the basis of such clearly incompatible studies are risky, but it does seem to be incontestably true that women—even in a period of increasing sports participation—were underrepresented in every country for which we have survey data. Furthermore, the women who were said to be involved in sports, either through club membership or as "unorganized actives," were much more likely than men to be counted as participants on the basis of some noncompetitive physical activity.

Whatever the actual rise in the rate of men's and women's active participation was, it was unquestionably related to the dramatic increase in the rate of passive participation, i.e., in spectatorship. In these postwar decades, modern sports, once referred to as the "most

TABLE 12.3.
Participation in Varsity Sports: United States

	Interscholastic (1970–71)	Intercollegiate (1971–72)
Male	3,666,798	172,477
Female	294,000	31,852
M/F Ratio	12.5	5.4

important unimportant thing in the world," threatened to replace traditional religion as a focus of attention and a locus of value. In America, intercollegiate athletics evolved from a diversion for undergraduates to a major branch of the nation's entertainment industry. A profusion of openly professional sports leagues sprang up, fought for a share of the public's attention, merged, expanded, died, and were replaced by new ventures in new sports. Throughout Europe, soccer leagues expanded and faced challenges from newer sports like basketball and team handball. Everywhere, sports and the television industry entered into a marriage of convenience which cut attendance at baseball parks and soccer stadia and, simultaneously, brought the world's great sport spectacles to hundreds of millions, perhaps even to billions, of viewers. Although the female audience for televised sports was generally smaller than the male audience, the "gender gap" for mediated spectatorship was less than for *in situ* attendance. In the United States, in 1978, "only" 75 percent of female television viewers professed an interest in watching sports (compared to 90 percent of the male viewers).[31] In Germany, the comparable figures were 52 percent and 75 percent.[32] In this sports-permeated environment, it was the television viewer's *lack* of interest that needed to be explained.

2. Women at the Olympics

While most of the sports that one was supposed to follow in the print and electronic media were men's sports—soccer in Europe and Latin America, baseball, men's basketball, and football in the United States—but the postwar Olympic Games provided athletic women with a quadrennial opportunity to take their place in the sun and to appear on the tube. Women were 9.4 percent of the athletes who arrived in London for the first postwar games—a slight increase from the 8.1 percent of twelve years earlier.[33] Although many men and women continued to resist the notion of "unfeminine" athleticism for the refined women of the middle classes, track and field has always been central to the games. "Babe" Didrikson and other "muscle molls" of the prewar era had probably reinforced the reputation of track and field as a sport for lower-class women, but the first postwar games, held in London in 1948, heralded the dawn of a new age.

The International Olympic Committee prepared the way when it accepted three new events for the 1948 games: the 200–meter dash, the shot put, and the long jump. (The IOC also added canoe races for women but voted against field hockey and equestrianism.) In the nine track-and-field events, Alice Coachman, who set an Olympic record in the high jump, was the only American woman to win a medal. The headlines went to Holland's Francina Blankers-Koen. She had participated as a fifteen-year-old in the "Nazi Olympics" of 1936 and had placed a respectable fifth in the high jump with a leap of 1.55 meters. She was also a member of Holland's fifth-place 4 x 100–meter relay team. After the war, she returned to competition despite the doubts of her physician husband. Housewife and mother of two, she nonetheless won gold medals in the 100–meter and 200–meter races, in the 80–meter hurdles, and in the 4 x 100–meter relay, the second and third in record time. She became, asserted Ferenc Mező in his history of *Les Jeux Olympiques Modernes* (1956), "the most famous athlete in the history of female athletics." [34] ("Babe" Didrikson fans might disagree.) Blankers-Koen, known as the "flying Dutchwoman," went on from the Olympics to dominate the European championships held at Brussels in 1950. She was then thirty-two years old.

Almost as successful, almost as famous in Europe if not in the United States, was Micheline Ostermeyer of France, who set an Olympic record in the shot put and won a second gold medal with the discus. She came in third in the high jump. Not only was Ostermeyer a very respectable middle-class woman, she was also an excellent pianist who subsequently had a distinguished career on the concert stage. Together, Blankers-Koen and Ostermeyer made an eloquent statement about the future of women's sports.

The statement was heard by some and not by others. Ambivalence about the female track-and-field athlete remained strong. The London *Daily Graphic* had a reassuring headline: "FASTEST WOMAN IN THE WORLD IS AN EXPERT COOK" Blankers-Koen was not celebrated to quite the same extent as Emil Zatopek, winner of the marathon, still a hero forty years later to the people of Czechoslovakia. In 1948, the only female Olympian to rival Zatopek's fame was Barbara Ann Scott of Canada, whose domination of figure skating began in 1945 when she became the North American champion. Although figure skaters train hard, they are schooled to make the difficult look easy so that Scott's considerable strength was seldom noticed. *Time* wrote ecstatically of her "peaches-and-cream complexion" and Canadian newspapers discussed her fondness for dolls. She was not merely likened to a doll; a Barbara Ann Scott doll was successfully marketed in Canada. Like Sonja Henie before her and Peggy Fleming and Dorothy Hamill after her, she was an "athlete in disguise" who skated, with unimpaired femininity, into hearts closed to the likes of Blankers-Koen and Ostermeyer.[35]

None of the women who competed at Helsinki in 1952 proved to be as memorable as those who came before and after them. Collectively, however, they passed a milestone. Amplified in number by the Russians, who participated in their first Olympics, the women were now more than 10 percent of all the competitors. From the perspective of women's history, the most extraordinary team at the 1956 games in Melbourne was clearly the host country's. Although they were only 16 percent of their nation's contingent, Betty Cuthbert, Dawn Fraser, Shirley Strickland, and the other Australian women garnered more than half their team's gold medals and led the way to Australia's amazing third-place finish (behind the United States and the Soviet Union).[36]

The public continued in these years to prefer exemplars of conventionally "feminine" sports. The preference was observable in the careers of two of the Australian stars—Cuthbert, a runner, and Fraser, a swimmer. The latter was a self-described "cheeky kid" from a working-class family who was enticed into her sport after she had taunted some swimmers coached by Harry Gallagher at the Balmain Pool. He challenged her to swim against them and quickly recognized her talent. "He turned out to be my personal Professor Higgens," she recalled. "He took me away from the docks and showed me the world." She won her first Olympic gold medal at the Melbourne games in 1956 at what now seems the advanced age of nineteen. Her time of 62 seconds was a world record for 100-meter freestyle. In 1962, at the trials for the Empire Games, she became the first woman to swim 100 meters in less than a minute. Celebrating her record of 59.9 seconds, she "got quietly drunk on beer that night." In and out of trouble with the Australian Swimming Association, which felt that her fondness for beer detracted from a properly feminine public image, she nonetheless continued to dominate her events through the 1964 games in Tokyo, where she won the last of her eight gold and silver medals, and where she was disciplined with a ten-year suspension. (She marched in the opening ceremony, rather than resting as ordered, and she swam in a nonregulation suit.) Australian officialdom had a much harder time with her than with Betty Cuthbert, who, in these same years, won four gold medals in Olympic track and field, but Fraser's antics, which included an attempt to steal the Japanese flag from Emperor Hirohito's palace, made her seem "one of the girls." She was not at all conventionally beautiful, and some of her detractors hinted that she was either a man or a lesbian, but she appeared "curvaceous" in a swimsuit and the public loved her. Photographs of Cuthbert, on the other hand, revealed sinewy limbs and a face contorted to a breathless grimace. The message was clear: the watery way to a man's heart was preferable to the cinder track.[37]

The aesthetic conventions of Eastern Europe are fairly tolerant of rugged women, but the most popular female athletes produced by the Soviet Union have been the figure skaters and the gymnasts. Like figure skating, women's gymnastics is a sport that requires the appearance of ease. Men's gymnastics have always demonstrated strength, especially on the rings, but the women's events —except for the vault —put the emphasis on grace (even when the strength necessary to appear graceful was far beyond anything possible for most of the world's men). The most successful of the many Eastern European gymnasts at the postwar Olympics was Russia's Larisa Latynina, who accumulated eighteen gymnastics medals at the Olympic Games of 1956, 1960, and 1964. Even she remained relatively unknown outside the Soviet Union.

Olga Fikotova of Czechoslovakia was another exception to the rule that female champions are renowned only in their own country, if at all, but it was her commissar-crossed love affair with Harold Connolly, a hammer-thrower from Boston, that stirred people's hearts. The millions who followed the romance in their daily newspapers would have been hard pressed to say if it was a discus or a javelin that Fikotova threw for an Olympic record of 53.69 meters. Even Connolly, who met Fikotova at the 1956 games in Melbourne, seemed surprised at her combination of beauty and prowess. "I never imagined a girl could be so strong and yet so feminine."[38]

It was also difficult for the all-male International Olympic Committee to imagine this combination of attributes. During the fifties, the IOC moved very slowly to enlarge the women's program. In 1952, the IOC established the present four-event gymnastics contest with medals for individuals as well as for teams. The swimmers' program was expanded by the 100–meter butterfly race in 1956 and the 400–meter individual medley in 1960, the year that the runners were once again, after a lapse of thirty-two years, allowed to race over 800 meters. The vote on the restored 800–meter race was 26–22. In 1960, the canoe-racers and the fencers were also awarded expanded programs.[39] None of these additions came without debate. Whenever a disgruntled member of the IOC complained that the games had become a gargantuan spectacle with far too many events, another disgruntled member was sure to move that the IOC eject the women from the Olympics. There was, however, no retreat.

Unexpectedly, the star of the 1960 games came from track and field rather than from one of the conventionally "feminine" sports. Wilma Rudolph was the first American female track-and-field athlete to catch the world's attention since Didrikson's triumph twenty-eight years earlier. Rudolph was not the first black female athlete to win an Olympic medal (Alice Coahman had done it in 1948), but she was probably the most spectacular. Like Althea Gibson, whose Wimbledon victory three years earlier was read as a symbol of black social mobility, Rudolph seemed destined to represent not a dream deferred but one amply fulfilled.

She was born in Clarksville, Tennessee, in 1940, the twentieth of twenty-two children. Her father worked as a railroad porter, her mother as a cleaning woman. In addition to the handicaps of race and class, Rudolph had to overcome physical disability. As a child, she was stricken by polio and forced to wear a brace on her leg. At twelve, when the brace came off, she began to play basketball and then to compete in track. She dominated the junior division of the AAU championships in 1956 and was the youngest member of the Olympic team that went to Melbourne that year. Eliminated in her 200–meter heat, she watched Australia's Betty Cuthbert win over 100, 200, and 400 meters. Rudolph won a bronze medal in the relays and returned home to a local heroine's welcome. The black community's greater acceptance of physically strong women doubtless enhanced her prestige among Afro-Americans.

In her senior year of high school, she did the typically adolescent thing and fell in love with the school's football and basketball hero. She bore him an illegitimate daughter. Since her family refused to allow her to marry, she turned Yolanda over to her grandmother and went off to Tennessee State University where Edward Temple coached her and other great black runners (like Wyomia Tyus and Edith McGuire). In Rome, at the 1960 Olympics, she had some competition from Germany's Jutta Heine and Britain's Dorothy Hyman, but she seemed to float away from them as she won the 100 meters in what would have been world-record time if the runners had not been wind-assisted. She also won gold medals in the 200 meters and the relay. Her grace and beauty undoubtedly impressed the spectators as much as her strength and speed. The press dubbed her the "black gazelle," a mildly racist epithet which suggested the alleged animality of black people. When she returned to the United States, she was awarded the Sullivan Award as the year's outstanding female athlete, and she was received at the White House by President Kennedy. After competing for another season, she retired, married Yolanda's father, and began a new career in teaching and community relations. [40]

Among the millions who watched Rudolph at the 1960 games, which were the first to be televised throughout Europe, was Irene Kirzenstein, a fourteen-year-old Polish Jew who had been born in a Leningrad camp for displaced persons. Kirzenstein was thrilled by Rudolph's performance. Four years later, in Tokyo, she was on the Polish team that won the 4 x 100–meter relay and she placed second in both the 200–meter race and the long jump. At Mexico City, in 1968, the twenty-two-year-old Kirzenstein won the 200–meter race in the world-record time of 22.5 seconds. By 1974, East Germany's Renate Stecher had lowered the record to 22.1 seconds and was clearly the sprinter to beat. Kirzenstein beat her at the European championships in Rome and set a world record of 49.9 seconds for 400 meters, a mark she lowered to 49.29 before East Germany's Marita Koch overtook her with world records in the 200–meter and 400–meter sprints. None of these women was much noticed in the West, and the same can be said for the Eastern European track and field stars who succeeded them in the 1980s.

Between 1960 and 1972, the IOC continued its slow trudge toward full recognition of women's sports. The swimmers got their 400–meter individual medley in 1964 while the track-and-field athletes were finally granted the 400–meter race and the pentathlon. Volleyball was also introduced that year. Four years later, the swimmers had their greatest breakthrough since their initial acceptance in 1912. The committee authorized the 200–meter and 800–meter freestyle, the 100–meter breaststroke, the 200–meter backstroke, the 200–meter butterfly, and the 200–meter individual medley races. [41] The Soviet bloc's lock on women's field events may have influenced the IOC to increase the number of medals to be won in a sport still dominated by the West.

For 1972, the IOC extended the hurdles from 80 to 100 meters and introduced the 1500–meter race and the 4 x 400–meter relay.[42] (The kayak slalom also made its first appearance.) At the games celebrated in Munich there were great achievements in track and field, and committed fans of the sport will probably never forget the triumphs of Heidi Rosendahl and Ulrike Meyfarth. Competing in Munich against the first officially recognized Olympic team from the German Democratic Republic, Rosendahl and Meyfarth, both representing the Federal Republic, defeated their rivals in the pentathlon and the high jump. Meyfarth's triumph was all the more spectacular because she was only sixteen years old. In swimming, fifteen-year-old Shane Gould of Australia won three golds, a silver, and a bronze. Most famous of all, and best remembered today, was "pixie" Olga Korbut, whose celebrity can well be taken as an indicator of the lingering prejudice against "unfeminine" athletes.

Gymnastics had never been very popular in the United States. The team sent to the 1936 games in Berlin was formed entirely from members of German-American gymnastics clubs. When Czechoslovakia's Vera Cavlaska won the 1968 all-round title in a close contest against Russia's Natalia Kuchinskaya, who was favored, interest was sparked as much by the political symbolism as by the extraordinary performances of the athletes. The Olympics took place only weeks after the tanks of the Warsaw Pact rumbled into Prague to crush the possibility of "Socialism with a Human Face." Caslavska told reporters that she had been unable to prepare properly for the games because Russian forces had occupied her country's sports facilities.[43] Perhaps the political tension stimulated her to rise to the occasion in Mexico City.

In 1972, the individual championship went to Ludmilla Tourescheva. She was a woman of regal poise and stunning beauty as well as the finest gymnast of the day, but her physical maturity and pronounced muscularity proved less exciting to the media and to the public than Olga Korbut's "pixie" charm. When Korbut slipped from the uneven parallel bars, she received a score of 7.5 and burst into tears. Roone Arledge, the mastermind of ABC Sports, immediately ordered the television camera to focus on her tearful face. "Before anyone had heard anything of her background or even knew what her voice sounded like, she was adored by millions."[44] She won hearts unmoved by exhibitions of athletic skill. Finishing third behind Tourescheva and Tamara Lazakovich, Korbut was nonetheless named Sportswoman of the Year by the BBC. When she visited Chicago,

Mayor Richard Daley named March 26th "Olga Korbut Day" and enhanced his own popularity by posing with her in what was later to be known as a "photo opportunity." It was she who smiled from the dust jacket of James Riordan's *Sport in Soviet Society* (1977). When Romanian teenger Nadia Comenici defeated her (and Tourescheva) at Montreal in 1976, it was clear that women's gymnastics had become children's gymnastics, with a premium placed on acrobatic flexibility and an elfin smile.

Korbut and Comanici, and to a much less but still significant extent, Tourischeva and Nelli Kim, were the first female athletes from the Soviet bloc to win real acceptance in the "capitalist" world. There can be no doubt that most of the bloc's runners, jumpers, shot putters, and discus and javelin throwers aroused suspicion rather than admiration. Were these "Amazons" really women? (In the case of Irena and Tamara Press, "no" may have been the correct answer. When sex tests were introduced, Irena and Tamara disappeared from international competition.) If they *were* women, were they the kind of women that *our* girls should want to become? In other words, twenty-five years of athletic achievement by Olympic athletes as various as Francina Blankers-Koen and Olga Korbut had only partially dispelled the conviction, held in unequal amounts by all social classes, that some sports are emininently suitable for women but others are not. Intense competition continued to evoke mixed reactions. The revolutionary breakthrough was still to come.

PART II

The Present State of
Women's Sports

THIRTEEN

Revolutionary Change

1. The United States: Women's Liberation and the Female Athlete

As the second wave of feminism swirled through the United States in the 1960s and 1970s, old attitudes were eroded and washed away. By the early 1980s, women's sports were radically transformed, but sports were *not* a primary concern for most of the angry women who demanded equality at home and on the job. (The enthusiasm of some feminists for karate stemmed originally from the desire for self-defense.) The low priority given to women's sports was matched by the detachment of most female athletes from the goals of women's liberation. Indeed, surveys often found socially conservative attitudes among women who stepped out of conventional roles in order to participate in intercollegiate sports.[1]

A convergence of views occurred in the mid-seventies as many athletes became feminists and many feminists discovered the importance of sports. No one did more to bring about this convergence than Billie Jean Moffitt King, the daughter of a Long Beach fireman. In 1970 she won the Italian tennis championship and received $600 while the men's winner pocketed $3500. When she learned that the Pacific Southwest Championships planned to award a men's prize of $12,500 and a women's prize of $1500, she decided that such gross disparities were no longer tolerable. King called for a boycott to compel tournament sponsors to end the discriminatory treatment. Having dominated women's tennis since her first Wimbledon singles victory in 1966 at the age of twenty-three, she was in a relatively strong position. When the United States Lawn Tennis Association resisted the demand for equality, King helped Gladys Heldman organize the Virginia Slims Circuit, financed by the Phillip Morris Company. Within three years the women's tennis circuit encompassed twenty-two cities and offered prize money of $775,000. (The men played in twenty-four cities for $1,280,000.) An official poster, referring to the players as "Ballbusters," suggested the women's lack of awe at male opposition on court or off. In 1973, the USLTA bigwigs gave way. The U.S. Open equalized its awards for men's and women's singles. Each winner received $25,000.[2]

Although King had defeated every challenger and won a number of championships, her most famous match was an unofficial contest. As the women's game became more aggressive, more like the men's serve-and-volley game, the inevitable question arose just as it had in the days of Lenglen and Wills. Are the women as good as the men? Bobby Riggs, the self-proclaimed "clown prince of tennis," boasted that he, at fifty-five, was ready to defeat the best of the women. Margaret Court, the Australian winner of three Wimbledon and five U.S. championships, accepted the challenge and succumbed to the hype on Mother's Day, 1973. Riggs then bragged that he was "the undisputed number-one male chauvinist in the world."[3] King felt that she had to do something to redeem the situation. On September 20, 1973, she played her notorious comic-opera match against Riggs. There were over 30,000 spectators in the Houston Astrodome and some 40,000,000 TV viewers.

Midgets dressed as dancing bears frolicked near the dugouts, the University of Houston marching band thumped out "Jesus Christ Superstar," a dozen cheerleaders in red hot pants swirled pompons, two dozen women tennis pros in BJK T-shirts lined up along a red carpet.

King entered on "a feathered litter right out of *Cleopatra* carried by bare-chested muscle men." Riggs entered in "a Chinese rickshaw on gold wheels pulled by a gaggle of girls known as Bobby's Bosom Buddies."[4] King's win (6–4, 6–3, 6–3) was a travesty of modern sport and an occasion for New York's inimitable Bella Abzug to make book "with a half-dozen congressmen on the floor of the House of Representatives." It was probably a victory of sorts for feminism. "This absurd match," wrote Adrianne Blue of the London *Sunday*

Times, "became for women's tennis the drop shot and volley heard round the world."[5]

As dynamic off the court as on, King also led in the formation of the Women's Tennis Association (1973). Christine Evert and Martina Navratilova, the women who eventually defeated King on the tennis courts, joined her in the WTA (after initial hesitation on the part of Evert). In 1974, King helped to create the Women's Sport Foundation (with assistance from Donna da Varona, a swimmer propelled by good looks and an Olympic championship into a career in television sports). "Sometimes," commented King in her autobiography, "I feel like a 1930s labor organizer."[6] Another of her ventures was a new magazine: *womenSports* (1974).

This magazine and its successor, *Women's Sports,* were not King's last contributions to the cause of female emancipation. In 1981, when she was sued by a former lover, Marilyn Barnett, King chose to admit her bisexuality rather than to attempt a cover-up. Some commercial sponsors became panicky, others did not. Avon Products, the cosmetics manufacturer, dropped its sponsorship of women's tennis and King estimated that she personally lost a total of $1.5 million in contracts, but NBC television kept her on as the network's Wimbledon announcer. Attitudes changed with such rapidity that a similar admission on the part of Navratilova did little to diminish her popularity except with jaundiced anachronisms like England's Auberon Waugh, who wrote in *The Spectator,* "The sad and beastly truth . . . is that Ms. Navratilova, through no fault of her own, is extremely ugly."[7]

To win the battle for equality in professional tennis was relatively easy. After all, although Navratilova's weight-trained athleticism bothered some traditionalists who preferred more conventionally feminine players like Evert and the Australian champion Evonne Goolagong, tennis has long been considered an ideal sport for women. Optimistic feminists were encouraged by the gains in women's tennis to think that other battles might be won as well, but the wiser souls among them knew that every inch of ground would be contested.

The life and death of the Women's Basketball League is a case in point. In 1943, Chicago Cubs owner Philip K. Wrigley took advantage of the scarcity of male athletes, many of whom were in military rather than baseball uniform, to establish the All-American Girls' Baseball League, which played throughout the Middle West. Although the league's attendance reached nearly one million a year,

Wrigley's interests shifted and he let the organization die in 1954.[8] The memory of Wrigley's successful experiment enticed others. In 1978, William Byrne launched the Women's Basketball League with eight teams playing a thirty-four-game schedule. Salaries were low, ranging from a high of about $15,000 to a low estimated at $5,000 a year, but attendance was so poor, averaging about 1500 a game, that the Dayton and Minnesota clubs expired before the end of the season and all the surviving teams lost money. The Chicago Hustle was the only franchise with a decent television contract. For the 1979–80 season, franchises were placed in San Francisco, Los Angeles, Dallas, New Orleans, St. Louis, Philadelphia, and Washington. Stars like UCLA's Ann Meyers and Old Dominion University's Nancy Lieberman were recruited.

As a student at Old Dominion University, Nancy was named All-America three times, and led ODU to two national championships. At seventeen, she became the youngest member of the silver-winning U.S. Olympic team, the first women's basketball team to . . . represent the U.S. in Olympic competition. As a direct result of Nancy Lieberman and her incredible abilities, the strategy and style of the women's game became comparable to the men's game.[9]

In vain. The league lost money for a second year and the Philadelphia and Washington franchises folded. They were replaced for 1980–81 by Omaha and Tampa, but four more teams collapsed financially in the summer of 1980. "By 1981, only three franchises remained operational, Dallas (with Nancy Lieberman), Chicago, and San Francisco. The rest of the teams either suspended operations completely or were looking for buyers."[10] This was actually the same mixed pattern of success and failure that had marked men's baseball until the successful establishment of the National League in 1876, but the start-up costs for a sports league had risen to dizzy heights. The expenses of the WBL were simply too high, media support was too weak, and attendance was too low for the league to be viable. The WBL collapsed.[11]

There were consolations. The drive to increase women's active participation in sports was far more successful than the discouraging attempt to win spectators and sponsors for the Women's Basketball League. In 1971, female physical educators decided that they needed a new organization to replace the moribund Women's Division and to challenge the male-dominated National Collegiate Athletics Association (NCAA). Representatives from 278 colleges and universities formed the Association for Intercollegiate Athletics for Women (AIAW). Split at first between a minority who accepted men's sports as the model and a reform-minded majority who called for a women's alternative, the AIAW initially opposed national championships and athletic scholarships. The AIAW voted to accept athletic scholarships in 1973, when the ban on participation by scholarship students was struck down in the courts in response to a suit brought by a group of female student-athletes. "After only two years, the AIAW had been forced to 'masculinize' their programs."[12] Opposition to championships was also abandoned. By 1975, the AIAW had them in nineteen different sports (compared to the NCAA's thirteen sports). Inevitably, once the AIAW endorsed highly competitive intercollegiate athletics, it was wracked internally by the same controversies that have marked the history of men's sports. Women accused each other of recruiting violations and other forms of skullduggery. Although AIAW rules strictly prohibited coaches from making off-campus personal recruiting visits, many coaches felt that such visits were indispensable. Upset by the trend, Marianne Stanley of Old Dominion asked plaintively, "What good are rules if you can't enforce them?" That winter, her own university was accused of flagrant violation of the AIAW's recruitment rules.[13]

Whatever one wants to say for or against the AIAW, no one can deny that women's athletic programs began, for the first time in American history, to rival men's programs in the number of contests staged and the amount of publicity received. The success of the AIAW forced the NCAA's hand. At its 1980 convention the NCAA voted to hold national championships for women at its Division II and Division III schools. A year later, the NCAA decided to sponsor national championships for women at Division I schools as well. Tournaments were instituted in basketball, cross-country, field hockey, gymnastics, swimming, tennis, track and field, and volleyball. The members also voted to expand the NCAA Council from eighteen to twenty-two and to enlarge the Executive Committee from ten to twelve. Women were guaranteed at least four seats in the first body and two in the second. Eighteen months later, the AIAW was dead.[14]

If the AIAW failed to provide a permanent alternative to men's sports in its ten-year challenge to male domination, it did encourage wider female participation. In 1971–72, some 31,000 women were engaged in varsity sports; a decade later, there were nearly 70,000. The latest data released by the NCAA, shown in table 13.1, demon-

TABLE 13.1.
Intercollegiate Sports Participation

	1971-72	1981-82	1986-87
Men	172,447	157,404	171,361
Women	31,852	69,096	82,979
M/F Ratio	5.5	2.27	2.04

strate a continuing—if less dramatic—gain. Since these figures truly refer to sports and not to a jumbled assortment of sports and non-competitive physical activities, the male/female ratios are a graphic indication of significant change.[15]

Between 1974 and 1981, the number of institutions offering athletic scholarships for women climbed from sixty to five hundred; the women's share of funding for athletic scholarships soared from 1 to 22 percent of the total. There is also evidence that the attitudes of the scholarship recipients of the eighties were more professional than those of their slightly older sisters who had competed without economic aid. The younger women were more likely to have chosen their school because of its sports program, and they were more likely to admit that increasingly professionalized sports participation tended to diminish their commitment to the classroom.[16]

The numerical increase in interscholastic sports was even more spectacular. The figures in table 13.2 are the result of rapidly rising participation by girls and slowly falling participation by boys. The change in the male/female ratio was extraordinary. In 1971, 7 percent of all high-school girls were involved in interscholastic sports; in 1981, 35 percent were.[17]

The explosive increase in participation is one unmistakable sign of the revolution in women's sports. Another is the expansion in the number of formerly forbidden sports which are now sponsored by mainstream organizations. The International Federation of Body Builders may not be considered mainstream, but who can dismiss the Amateur Athletic Union as a radical or deviant institution? In 1975, the AAU began to sponsor powerlifting for women. In 1978, sixty-eight women competed in the International Women's Powerlifting Championship. A year later, NBC gave national television coverage to their bench presses, dead lifts, and squats.[18]

Although the failure to win a national TV contract from one of the networks was probably the major reason for the Women's Basketball

TABLE 13.2.
Interscholastic Sports Participation

	1970–71	1988–89
Boys	3,666,000	3,418,914
Girls	294,000	1,841,252
M/F Ratio	12.46	1.85

League's economic failure, the boom in women's sports has been accompanied by a minirevolution in sports journalism. Traditionally, women's sports have been ignored in the press and on radio and TV. During *Sports Illustrated's* first twenty-five years, female athletes appeared on only 4.4 percent of the magazine's 1250 covers. In the mid-1970s, representative newspapers like the *Los Angeles Times* and the *Washington Post* pictured female athletes in a mere 8 percent of their sports-page photographs. In a thirteen-month period from August 1972 to September 1973, a minuscule 0.2 percent of NBC's live sports coverage was devoted to women's events. Tennis was the only sport whose female stars appeared regularly on network TV. Feminists have protested about this scanty coverage and the media have gotten the message. Efforts have been made to redress the traditional imbalance. Women began to appear to announce the scores on the eleven o'clock local news and ABC hired Ellie Riger as the first female sports producer and CBS Sports hired Jane Chastain as a commentator (only to replace her with a wholly inexperienced former Miss America).[19]

When distance swimmer Diana Nyad swam around Manhattan Island on October 6, 1975, in the record time of seven hours and fifty-seven minutes, she made the front page of the *New York Times* and was the topic of features in *Sports Illustrated, People, Village Voice, Madamoiselle, Glamour, Seventeen,* and *Vogue.* She appeared on the Today Show and was invited to one of Woody Allen's parties (to which she went in trackshorts, T-shirt, headband, unmatched socks, and sneakers).[20] In general, *Sports Illustrated* has increased its reporting of women's sports and has attempted to avoid traditional sexual stereotypes. Indeed, some of the magazine's writers seem determined to forge new stereotypes. Of Belgian judo champion Ingrid Berghmans, Barbara McDermott wrote,

if some still believe women don't have the right to sweat and win without apology—or sport pumped-up, Nautilus-constructed biceps just like the big boys—she's impressive evidence to the contrary. . . . Ingrid . . . is as much today's female as she is the modern athlete. Big, blonde and beautiful.

On the other hand, the magazine continues to run its egregious "swimsuit issue" with not a pumped-up biceps in sight.[21]

Swimsuits aside, frailty is now definitely out of favor. When young, Marilyn Monroe worked out in secret; Jane Fonda, well into middle age, has gone public. Kodak has run magazine and TV advertisements showing a girl smiling at her well developed biceps. American Express has used a photograph of Evelyn Ashford running in order to remind us not to leave home—even for a race?—without our Gold Card. "The winsome Breck Girl might once have been an ideal," exulted Janice Kaplan, "but now shampoo ads featured Chris Evert and . . . Dorothy Hamill."[22] A few years later, a noticeably muscular Mary Lou Retton was appearing in Wheaties commercials. When *MS* put two female cyclists on its September 1974 cover, there were nasty comments about muscular legs and short hair and the editors heard the issue referred to as "dikes on bikes."[23] A decade later, athletic women modeled for *Cosmpolitan, Seventeen,* and *Vogue,* and there was even a magazine, *Strength Training for Beauty,* devoted entirely to the proposition that physically developed women are not only strong but also beautiful.[24] Positively portrayed female athletes have begun to appear in the work of serious novelists and film-makers. Jennifer Levin's *Water Dancer* (1982) and Robert Towne's *Personal Best* (1982) are perhaps the most distinguished examples of the new interest in women's sports as a dramatic theme.

The revolution in attitudes has occurred north of the border as well. Canadian pentathlete Diane Jones Konihowski, winner at the 1975 and 1979 Pan American Games and at the 1978 Commonwealth Games, was no pixie, but she became "the most photographed Canadian female star since Barbara Ann Scott."[25] Carolyn Cheshire, one of the female body-builders interviewed by Charles Gaines and George Butler for *Pumping Iron II,* concluded that the best defense is a good offense: "There's nothing feminine," she said, "about looking all soft and squishy."[26] Since aesthetic ideals are intensely subjective and vary widely within pluralistic modern societies, individual preference alone will determine whether the sinewy female in her running shorts is more or less beautiful than the bosomy debutante in her evening gown, but expressions of disdain for athletic women seem more and more anachronistic.

Despite the belief that women seriously involved in sports still suffer from stigmatization and role conflict, most recent psychological and sociological studies show that female athletes experience little of either and that they are perceived positively by most men and by most other women. A study of 268 female athletes in nine sports at thirteen universities and colleges found that the athletes *believed* that female athletes suffered role conflict, but they personally had experienced very little of it.[27] Another investigation revealed the identical incongruence. Of 230 intercollegiate tennis players and 391 track-and-field athletes, 41 percent of the former and 42 percent of the latter *felt* their sport bore a stigma, but only 11 percent and 16 percent actually experienced role conflict.[28] A survey of 1682 female members of the Women's Sports Foundation found that 94 percent of their "Romantic companions," 93 percent of their male friends, and 96 percent of their female friends were either "very supportive" or "somewhat supportive" of their sports involvement.[29] Admittedly, not everyone is supportive of women who do sports (or of women who do *anything* unconventional). When a group of male and female athletes and nonathletes were asked to check a list of attributes characterizing "the Woman Athlete" and "the Ideal Woman," there was a positive correlation between the two ideals for male athletes ($+.27$) and a negative correlation for female nonathletes ($-.23$). In other words, the men approved more strongly of athletic women than the nonathletic women did.[30]

The women who have begun to "pump iron," as body builders or as weight lifters, are an extreme case that tests the limits of liberal opinion. When 205 female body builders were queried about other people's responses to their sport, 63 percent of them reported that they had experienced positive reactions. The negative reactions came predominantly from other women.[31] When male and female students at Brigham Young University were shown slides of female body builders and asked to rate the women on their physical attractiveness, the men's ratings were once again significantly higher than the women's.[32] The authors of a psychological study of forty-four female powerlifters, who are the antithesis of china-doll femininity and ought to suffer role conflict if any female athletes do, concluded that the problem had been greatly exaggerated. Only 9.1 percent of the lifters experienced great or very great role conflict.[33] Is it not time to acknowledge that today's female athletes are more likely to be admired than to encounter hostility and denigration?

Has admiration as an athlete been purchased by the sacrifice of femininity? Despite the claims of some psychologists to this effect, the answer must be No. An experiment asked male and female under-graduates to characterize two imaginary women who were identically described except that one of them was were said to be a body builder. The female undergraduates rated the imaginary body builder *more* masculine and *less* feminine than the non-body builder; the male undergraduates, however, thought the body builder *less* masculine and *more* feminine. (The female undergraduates were also much more likely to suspect the body builder of homosexuality.)[34]

Personality tests which routinely discover that female athletes are "masculine" cannot be taken seriously as evidence for the loss of femininity because tests like Sandra Bem's widely used Sex Role Inventory are designed to score typically athletic traits—like compet-itiveness and aggressiveness—as "masculine." This circularity en-sures that a woman who admits to the competitiveness and aggres-siveness associated with sports is automatically classified as "masculine" or (what luck!) "androgynous." When only 13.6 percent of the female runners tested by the Personality Attribute Questionnaire can be described as "feminine," it is time to examine some of the cultural assumptions behind the test.[35]

It may still be a part of folk wisdom that girls and women do sports to compensate for low self-esteem, but most studies have shown, to the contrary, that female student-athletes have a more positive self-image than nonathletes do. In fact, athletic women are more pleased than other women not only with their arms and legs but even with such intractable anatomical details as the shape of their nose. The only reasonable explanation for such results is that sports involvement raises a woman's self-esteem and enhances her body image generally.[36]

Most of these psychological studies of female athletes have been done with undergraduates (who are the experimenters' natural prey). What does the American public at large think about the combination of these once discrepant social roles? Sociologists Eldon E. Snyder and Elmer Spreitzer directly addressed this question in an article entitled "Change and Variation in the Social Acceptance of Female Participation in Sports." Respondents were asked if certain specified sports detracted from or enhanced a girl's or woman's femininity. In Toledo, Ohio, they found that 30 percent of their 1972 sample and only 18 percent of their 1981 sample had negative feelings about women's track. Negative remarks about women's softball dropped from 20 percent to 14 percent (while basketball was unchanged with 21 percent unfavorable responses). More than 50 percent thought swimming, tennis, and gymnastics enhanced femininity, and 19 percent felt the same way about track. When Snyder and Spreitzer put the same questions to Iowans, 23 percent thought track enhanced femininity and only 7 percent thought it detracted.[37] In another mid-Western study, 353 Oklahoma City residents were interviewed to discover their reactions to six provocative statements, including the following: "Women are likely to develop unsightly muscles if they exercise regularly" and "A woman cannot be both a good athlete and a truly feminine person." Only 27.2 percent of the sample agreed with the first statement, only 10.8 percent with the second. As one might have expected, the older and less educated respondents were much more likely to agree with the negative stereotypes. In this, as in most other research, men were found to be more positively disposed to female athletes than women were.[38] Helen Lenskyj's observation that neither the strong, muscular female sprinter nor the slight, graceful male figure skater satisfies the stereotype of heterosexual attractiveness needs to be revised—at least as far as the female sprinter is concerned.[39]

Undeniably, economic motives play a role in the increased interest in and support for women's sports. There are healthy profits to be made from the new vogue for athletic bodies. Tennis camps and aerobics classes cost money. Sports and fitness magazines are full of glossy advertisements for digital chronometers, exercise machines, tennis racquets, surf boards, running shoes, Goretex training suits, food supplements, and work out manuals. In the articles, lovely young females grimace as they set records or work on their biceps femoris. In the advertisements, lovely young females smile as they wield chromium-plated weights or bound about in iridescent leotards. Observing that cosmetics manufacturers have zeroed in on the fitness market, two feminist scholars complain that even Billie Jean King's refurbished magazine, *Women's Sports,* appeals mainly to the "cosmopolitan, affluent, upwardly mobile, young, white, heterosexual woman." Further evidence of this trend appeared in 1978 when Phillip Morris dropped the Virginia Slims Circuit and Avon Products rushed in to pick up the tab (until King's admission of bisexuality frightened Avon away again). On the other hand, the eagerness of companies like Agfa (film), Proxy (shoes), Mizuno (sporting goods),

Mitsubishi (appliances), Toshiba (copiers), and LNJ (toys) to have Florence Griffith-Joyner endorse their products strongly suggests that black women athletes can now compete on nearly equal terms for endorsements. As Brigitte Tietzel remarks in the *Frankfurter Allgemeine Zeitung,* "Times have changed. . . . Atalanta had to pay for her beauty and her swiftness, but, in our time, 'lovely Flo' can cash in on both." [40]

Economic motives also influence the kinds of women's sports which will appear on television. Although bowling and softball are among the most popular participant sports for adult women, bowlers and softball players are disproportionately working-class. Commercial TV depends on advertisers, and advertisers prefer to invest their money in sports attractive to affluent viewers: golf or tennis rather than bowling and softball. Corporate advertisers are also likely to sponsor golf and tennis tournaments, leaving support for bowling and softball leagues to the local used-car dealer. For golfers and tennis players, endorsements have become an important source of extra income. All three of the women among the world's twenty-five most richly rewarded athletes are tennis players—Steffi Graf, Chris Evert, and Martina Navratilova. For the networks, moreover, women's sports are a relatively inexpensive form of programming, much cheaper, for instance, than situation comedies. For the viewers, the sight of women like Evert and Nancy Lopez is an incentive to go and do likewise, preferably with the latest in racquets, clubs, shorts, and shoes. [41]

There is also a legal aspect to the dramatic rise in women's sports participation. It is doubtful that the rate of sports participation was an important consideration in the legislative battles that culminated in the passage of Title IX of the Education Act of 1972, but the increases in participation in women's interscholastic and intercollegiate sports have certainly been abetted by Title IX and other legal instruments. The laws have made discrimination on the basis of gender illegal in all institutions receiving federal support:

No person . . . shall, on the basis of sex, be excluded from participation in, be denied the benefits of, or be subjected to discrimination under any educational programs or activities receiving federal financial assistance.

That the inequalities between men's and women's programs were obscenely gross is undeniable. At a time when Father Edmund M. Joyce, an executive vice-president of Notre Dame University, castigated Title IX as "assinine," his university allotted over $1 million for financial aid to male athletes and not a penny for the women. The Syracuse, New York, school board's 1969 budget for extracurricular sports allocated $90,000 to the boys' teams and $200 to the girls.' When money grew tight, the board eliminated the girls' budget. At the University of New Mexico, the 1970–71 budget for men's sports was $527,000 and for women's sports $9150. In comparison to the University of Washington's pitance, New Mexico's budget seemed like wildly feminist largesse. In Seattle in 1973–74, the men received $2,582,000 and the women $18,000. Title IX (and the AIAW) made a difference. In response to various forms of pressure, the University of Washington increased the women's 1974–75 budget to $200,000. The average expenditure on women's sports for the NCAA's Division I was $27,000 in 1973–74 and $400,000 in 1981–82. The women's percentage of the athletic budget at Division I universities went from 2 percent to 14 percent in just four years (1973–74 to 1977–78).[42]

That Title IX has made a difference can also be seen in the before and after legal judgments. When Susan Hollander of Hamden, Connecticut, sued her school board for the right to run with the boys' cross-country team because there was no girls' team, John Clark FitzGerald of New Haven Superior Court decided against her on the grounds that the salt of athletic endeavor would lose its savor (for boys) if girls were allowed to challenge them. "Athletic competition builds character in our boys," he ruled. "We do not need that kind of character in our girls."[43] In *Gregorio v. Board of Education of Asbury Park* (1971), which was also decided before the passage of Title IX, the Superior Court of New Jersey ruled that girls had no right to join the boys' tennis team merely because there was no girls' team. After the new law came into effect, the U.S. Court of Appeals for the 6th District of Michigan ruled in *Morris v. Michigan Board of Education* (1973) that girls had the right to try out for the boys' tennis team even when there was a girls' team for them to play on. The drive toward equality was temporarily blocked when the Supreme Court decided in *Grove City College v. Bell* (1984) that illegal discrimination within a single department was not grounds for action against an entire college or university. If the geologists refuse to hire women, decreed the court, they are liable to lose their federal grants, but their colleagues in physical education will continue to be funded. In 1988, Congress unambiguously restated its original intent and mandated that the whole institution lose its federal funds if any one department is found guilty of discrimination. President Reagan vetoed this legislation, but Congress overrode the veto.

Although Title IX has forced changes, it has not wrought miracles. Walter Byers of the NCAA lobbied hard against Title IX because it spelled "the possible doom of intercollegiate sports."[44] Three years after the bill had become law, the NCAA fought for Senator John Tower's amendment, which would have exempted the so-called revenue-producing sports, most of which turn out to be men's sports. The NCAA's lobbying, which persisted through 1976, failed, but most athletic departments were—and are—controlled by men; and many continue to resist full implementation of the law.

Even among men and women of good will, debates continue on the meaning of equality. How should the law be interpreted and implemented? The radical view is that parity should be calculated on the basis of the male/female ratio of the entire student body. If 52 percent of the students are women, female athletes should receive 52 percent of the funding. The more moderate view, accepted by the Department of Education, is that the males and females actually participating in sports form the relevant population. If 30 percent of the athletes are female, women's sports should receive 30 percent of the money. Having failed to prevent the enactment of Title IX, the NCAA has been less than Draconian in its support for enforcement of the law. In the spring of 1984, the organization ruled that a school's failure to equalize the number of male and female teams would be punished by a ban on national competition—for the women's teams. One suspects that some NCAA members are poor losers.[45]

Women lost, too, in a way that not everyone had foreseen. As Joan S. Hult remarked, Title IX was "a two-edged sword."[46] The unintended consequence of the sudden increase in the number of women's teams created a demand for coaches that the pool of female physical educators was unable to meet. As the absolute number of female coaches, managers, and officials rose, the women's percentage fell. "In 1972, 90 percent of those coaching in women's intercollegiate athletics were women. By 1987, only 50 percent were women."[47] In Canada, too, the dramatic increase in women's sports participation during the 1970s actually decreased the percentage of female physical-education faculty at thirty-three universities from 26 percent in 1970 to 23 percent in 1978.[48] In a 1989 article on female officers in Canada's national sports organizations, David Whitson and Donald MacIntosh reported that women were 7 percent of the head coaches, 17 percent of the technical directors, 24 percent of the executive directors, and 21 percent of the members of the boards of directors.[49]

The influx of male coaches into the field of women's sports has been accompanied by assertions that the men ask too much of the women (because of male ambitions for a winning team), that they ask too little (because of male stereotypes of female ineptitude), or that the men just don't understand the women. Studying this problem, Elaine Blinde went beyond the demand that male coaches be replaced by females; she concluded pessimistically that female coaches with male values reinforce "the patterns of patriarchal domination . . . in the larger society, including the objectification and domination of women's physicality and sexuality." Blinde, a responsible scholar, admitted that her own empirical study of 482 NCAA Division I athletes revealed only a weak correlation between participation in a "male model" of sports and a sense of alienation. She attempted to retrieve her apparently disconfirmed hypothesis with the suggestion that "the low reported levels of alienation may be due to the inability of females to isolate or identify the source of their disenchantment." Another hypothesis, which Blinde did not entertain, is that female athletes are no more alienated by NCAA Division I sports than male athletes are, which is not to allege that no one is alienated by "big time" sports. This seems a legitimate conclusion to be drawn from a study of 3060 black and white male and female athletes at 42 NCAA Division I schools. The American Institutes of Research found, for instance, that 21 percent of the women and 22 percent of the men were "totally satisfied" with their basketball coaches. Women were also more satisfied with their sports performance. The AIR discovered that women with male coaches were no more likely to report pressure to ignore injuries than women with coaches of their own sex. The study did not refer specifically to "alienation," but the students were asked about feelings of isolation; 22 percent of the female basketball players and 20 percent of the men acknowledged such feelings while 19 percent of the women and 31 percent of the men felt that their commitment to sports made it harder for them to be liked simply for what they were. In short, male and female student-athletes have rather similar reactions to the stress and strain of semiprofessional intercollegiate sports.[50]

Debates also continue about the desirability of women competing against men. Asked to describe a fictional character, "Linda," who was ahead of male runners in a race, the subjects of a psychological experiment conducted by Susan Birrell described Linda as "less popular, less attractive, more aggressive, sadder than the other girls."[51] Her hard lot suggests that some emotionally insecure male athletes still feel their masculinity undermined by women who outperform them, a conclusion corroborated by some remarkable incidents. When middle-distance runner Jan Merrill ran against eight men in a two-mile race in 1979, she defeated four of the men and came in fifth, which so unnerved Fitchburg College coach Jim Sheehan that he cried out, "I'd die before I would ever be beaten by a woman."[52] Of the Auburn University student whom Becky Birchmore defeated while a member of the University of Georgia's men's tennis team, Coach Dan Magill lamented, "It ruined him. I really wish I hadn't done it." Ellen Cornish of Frederick, Maryland, had no chance to ruin the lives of the boys from Thomas Johnson High School. Leading them in a race, she was dragged from the track before she broke the tape.[53] Small wonder that *some* women have curbed their ambitions to excel at sports in order not to jeopardize their relationships with insecure men. Such women, however, have become increasingly rare.[54]

Even if one feels that male athletes defeated by female athletes will have to live with their fates, other questions remain to be answered. Federal law is presently interpreted to mean that girls whose high schools have no girls' tennis team have the right to play on the boys' team, but this interpretation may not be the best solution to the problem. Many of the girls who do play on boys' teams perform at a level below that of their male teammates. Does this cause the girls psychological damage? And what is the equitable solution to the dilemma of boys who want to join the girls' team because their school has no boys' team in their chosen sport? This may seem like a foolish question, but National Public Radio for August 31, 1986, broadcast a report from Annapolis High School, where two boys had requested to be allowed to join the girls' field hockey team.[55]

2. The European Scene: Changing Attitudes

Throughout Western Europe, fitness centers have proliferated and aerobics classes are the mode. In Europe as in the United States, these commercial enterprises advertise with photographs of splendidly developed men and women. Slick magazines like *Paris Match* and *Der Stern* are full of advertisements in which athletic young women intimate that the products they endorse are the key to strength, health, radiant beauty, and a happy home. Women bold enough to seek partners through the "personals" columns of *Die Zeit* describe themselves as athletic sports enthusiasts—just like the women who advertise in the "personals" columns of *The New York Review*.[56] Female athletes share at least some of the live TV coverage and they now appear on the numerous European talk shows where the talk is about sports. Names like Cornelia Hanisch (a German fencer), Ann-Marie Proell (a Swiss skier), and Fatima Whitbread (a British javelin champion) are widely recognized by their countrymen (but no one knows how widely).

One of the most striking signs of liberalization is the *glasnost* that now allows franker discussions of the athletes' sexual lives. In 1970, a spokesman for the Roman Catholic Church affirmed the value of women's sports by opining that a "healthy tiredness resulting from sports can be considered an effective counter to masturbation and premature sexual activity."[57] It is doubtful that many Europeans paid much attention to this half-hearted endorsement. The Church, led by Pope John Paul II, continues to promulgate its traditional message apropos of human sexual behavior, but athletes and sports spectators do not seem to be listening. *Sports International,* the glossy German equivalent of *Sports Illustrated,* recently pictured a smiling Martina Navratilova vacationing with Judy Nelson, described as Navratilova's *Lebensgefährtin* ("life's companion"). The story betrayed not the slightest hint of disapproval.[58]

Unfortunately, European psychologists have done little to document the changes in attitudes toward women's sports. Their emphasis, once fixed obsessively on the question of personality differences among athletes and between athletes and nonathletes, has shifted to studies of motivation and investigations into the relationship between sports and violence. Occasional studies have looked at children's and adults' attitudes toward specific sports, especially in the schools, but the study of role conflict among female athletes and the research on men's and women's responses to athletic women seem, on the whole, to be American specialities. Dorothee Bierhoff-Alfermann is an exceptional empiricist; she has noted and ventured an informed opinion on role conflict, which she thinks has diminished, at least for German track-and-field athletes.[59]

The impressionistic evidence, supported by some sociological studies, is clear enough. Attitudes have changed, and the rate of change varies from country to country and from class to class. John Betjeman, postwar England's most popular poet, was enthralled by muscular female athletes "full of a pent-up strength" ("Pot-Pourri from a Surrey Garden"), "strongly adorable" ("A Subaltern's Love-Song"), striding on the "strongest legs in Pontefract" ("The Licorice Fields at Pontefract"), or standing "in strong, athletic pose" ("The Olympic Girl"). The poet laureate's infatuation was not shared by all Britons. The state-owned BBC has been accused of reluctance to accept women's sports. Media expert Garry Whannell has argued that "muscular development of any kind is continually presented [by the BBC] as aberrant for women." As for the sponsors who purchase time from Britain's commercial Independent Television (ITV), they —according to Adrianne Blue—still prefer "bustlines to biceps." On the other hand, Liz Ferris commented during the BBC's 1984 "Women in Sport" program, "I think there is a change among some people who are now regarding women with well-developed muscles as more acceptable."[60]

Magazines, too, reveal a spectrum of opinions. In *The Observer,* novelist Martin Amis has sneered at the Olympians from Eastern Europe as "breastless, well-hung iron curtain harridans."[61] *The Guardian,* on the other hand, has been enthusiastic. Specifically referring to the East German swimmers, Jill Tweedie wrote,

To wholly admire these female athletes one must appreciate them visually and to do that means readjusting . . . preconceived notions of feminine beauty and worth. What is the Western stereotype at the moment? A sleek, smooth, soft and curving body with not a muscle or tendon in sight, a body that gives only intimations of sexual pleasure, a pliant body willing to pose its limbs as will best please a man, a submissive body that could not defend itself in dark corners on dark nights. A body, in other words, there to be done unto and never to do.

Tweedie, who entitled her essay "Amazon Grace," was, of course, only partly right about "the Western stereotype of the moment."[62]

Attitudes expressed by BBC commentators and *Guardian* columnists need not mirror the attitudes of ordinary folks. In Milton Keynes, one of England's "New Towns," women explained to an investigating sociologist that they had been required to participate in "ghastly games" in "silly skirts" while they were in school, but now, thank

God, they had a choice and meant to avoid sports. Women who overcame their bad memories of grim games mistresses and ludicrous outfits had to deal with their husbands, who were frequently hostile. Said one jogger,

Well first of all I tried going early in the morning but then everyone complained I was making them late by enjoying myself rather than getting on with the breakfast. Then I thought I'd go at lunchtime—but the girls at work laughed at me and anyway I have to shop most days—so finally I decided I'd try the evenings—after we'd eaten I'd wait an hour or so and then go—that was OK in the summer but of course now it's dark I don't feel safe—and Ron . . . doesn't much like me running anyway—he says I'm getting leg muscles and that feminine women don't get all sweaty.

Overweight women confessed that they were reluctant to expose their bodies in public and attractive women were often afraid of the sexual harassment that runners and joggers sometimes encounter.[63]

There were also mixed signals emitted from across the Channel. Georges Dirand and Renaud de Laborderie published *Les Reines du Sport* (1969), a popular celebration of France's internationally successful female athletes. Among the athletes imagined by Guy Lagorce in his short-story collection, *Les Héroïques* (1980), none is more impressive than Claire Plessis, a self-confident fencing champion who proves herself more than a match for a loutish parking-lot assailant. (When he ignores her warning, she runs her rapier through his heart!) Françoise Giroud, formerly a cabinet minister in charge of *la condition féminine*, was firmly but less violently enthusiastic about women's sports. "There's very little that a man can do that a woman of the same age and with the same good health cannot do, if she has developed her musculature." Giroud added, "It's splendid to feel onself independent." She scorned fears of "masculinization" and even accepted the idea of female boxers, "si cela s'amuse." The popular French women's magazine *Elle* proclaimed the new image in its September 1979 issue: "Sports are the best medicine." They "strengthen the heart, sculpt the body," and keep a woman young. At the same time, however, Monique Berlioux, the highest ranking female administrator employed by the International Olympic Committee, was disgusted by the thought of female body builders. That sport she found "atroce. Je n'aime pas l'excès. . . . Je trouve cela abominable."[64]

In Germany, where the vast network of private clubs provides unusually good opportunities for women's sports, where the print and electronic media give considerable attention to stellar performances by female athletes, there is the same gamut of positive and negative responses. Novelist Botho Strauss, who has satirized male body builders in one of his books, has published a story, "Atalante," in which he ridicules a ruthlessly dominant female runner. Writing in Germany's most severely intellectual weekly publication, Die Zeit, a columnist made fun of America's female body builders in an article entitled "Kraft durch Fonda." Another writer, four years later, used the publication of Robert Mapplethorpe's photographs of American body builder Lisa Lyon to be witty about "the worship of the body as an act of naked will" (a pun on "Willensakt"). In still another clever article in the same highbrow periodical, illustrated this time by a lovely young woman drawing a bow, exercising on a slant board, and suspending herself from a pair of gymnast's rings, a third writer was ironic about the modish "sporty woman" who "does Tai Chi in the morning and shoots clay pigeons, from the hip, in the evening." Der Spiegel, a magazine aimed principally at a middle-class audience, adopted a much less haughty tone. In addition to fairly regular coverage of women's sports, the magazine has published sympathetic interpretations of the fitness craze. Der Spiegel's comments on Jane Fonda and her German emulators were a good deal less ironic than Die Zeit's.[65]

While American sociologists and social psychologists have noted the tendency of the print and electronic media to emphasize the physical attractiveness rather than the sports achievements of female athletes, German scholars have documented the phenomenon at greater length and in more detail. The best study is by Marie-Luise Klein and Gertrud Pfister. Their 1985 book, Goldmädel, Rennmiezen und Turnk-ücken (Golden Girls, Running Kittens, and Gymnastic Chicks), scrutinized the coverage of women's sports in Bild, Germany's most popular daily newspaper (nearly 12 million readers). Over 95 percent of the sports reports were devoted to men's sports, mainly soccer. When female athletes were mentioned, the emphasis was on their age and physical appearance (especially hair color). Photographs of women were selected to emphasize their good looks. Women smile ("Sports are fun!") while men wrinkle their brows in concentration ("Sports are serious!"). Emphasizing sexual attractiveness, Bild featured "female athletes with long hair and a slender figure without visible muscular definition." Klein and Pfister do not skimp on quantified data: muscles are clearly visible in 22.4 percent of the women's photographs and 37.1 percent of the men's; 28.9 percent of the pictured women and only 3.3 percent of the men are said to have sexually attractive bodies.[66] *Bild* is designed to appeal to the least literate segment of the German population. *Sports International,* a lavishly illustrated monthly aimed at affluent readers, is far less traditional in its treatment of gender roles. There are glamorous photographs of beautiful women (and handsome men), but there are also respectful reports of women's achievements in various sports.

While, Europeans, like Americans, continue to feel that some sports are more appropriate for men and some for women, the trend is unquestionably toward acceptance of whatever sport a person wants to do. A study of tennis, gymnastics, and soccer clubs in the German *Land* of Hessen, for example, confirmed that the first two sports are considered more appropriately feminine than the third, but fully half the female soccer players practice with the men, which certainly suggests a kind of acceptance by the latter. In fact, only 4.4 percent of the women who play soccer say that their husbands or lovers disapprove. At the same time, however, 26.4 percent of the female gymnasts think that *Fussball* is an inappropriate sport for women and 40 percent of the soccer players long for the opportunity to learn tennis.[67]

The Scandinavians probably have the most positive attitudes about female athletes. At Denmark's special sports schools, like the one at Gerlev, male and female physical-education students live and play together in what appears to be an atmosphere of complete equality (although one of the young women at the Gerlev school declined to join her male friends in the shower when she realized that a presumably provincial American scholar was in there with them). A study of young married Oslo residents found that both sexes looked favorably on both male and female elite athletes. Women were slightly more positive about both the men and the women, but the differences were not statistically significant. As for *literally* looking, Kari Fasting found that 64 percent of Norwegian men and 49 percent of the women watch their country's popular television sports-review. Although this program devotes only 5 percent of its time to women's sports, it nonetheless seems probable that Greta Waitz is better known—at home and abroad—than any of Norway's male athletes.[68]

Iberian culture remains considerably more resistant than Scandinavian to serious sports competition for women. Portugal's Rosa Motta is headline news and Arantxa Sanchez Vicario became a national heroine when she defeated Steffi Graf to win the 1989 French Open, but Motta and Sanchez Vicario are exceptions. Spain's leading sports sociologist, Manuel García Ferrando, found that female track-and-field athletes had to be a psychologically hardy group who tuned into signals from their male teammates and blocked the negative feedback they received from the wider culture. The average señora continues to devote herself to domesticity and the church.[69]

Italian research into attitudes toward female athleticism is not abundant, but Alessandro Salvini's *Identità Femminile e Sport* (1982) is a major contribution. This work is an unusually detailed study of 482 teenaged athletes drawn from all parts of Italy, from rural Sicily as well as from cosmopolitan centers like Milan. The girls' seriousness is proven by the fact that 72.2 percent of them said they preferred real competition to mere recreational activities. Nonetheless, 97.1 percent of them reported that their families were supportive. While many Italians still hold that the female athlete is "an exception or a transgression," only 4 percent of these girls believed that *"attività sportiva"* impedes a girl in her pursuit of "normal social life and emotional experience"; 13 percent thought sports helped. When asked specifically to name the kinds of criticism they encountered, 35.1 percent were unable to think of *any* negative remarks; 24.1 percent had heard people express the fear that sports destroy a girl's femininity. Did that mean that sports are the product of masculine and not of feminine culture? A resounding 92.3 percent of the girls thought not, and 72.4 percent of them averred that a woman can now participate in whatever sport she wished. These committed young athletes were hardly representative of all Italian teenagers. Adolescent opinion, moreover, was unquestionably at odds with that of older Italians. Indeed, 49 percent of the adult women questioned in a Roman survey explained that they avoided sports because sports cause "an irreversible somatic transformation," i.e., masculinization. Still, the young athletes' experience and attitudes are a sign that young Italians are far less negative now about women's sports than they were in the days of the Fascist dictatorship.[70]

3. Europe, Canada, Latin America: Rising Participation

If we had no evidence whatsoever on European attitudes, the dramatic rise in the levels of women's sports participation would be irrefutable evidence of dramatic change. The German data are abundant. A 1976 study asked German women if they were active in "sports"—defined to include strolling and other forms of relaxation. Seventy-six percent indicated that they had participated at least once in the previous twelve months. While the authors of the study rejoiced that the number of female "actives" had increased from the 63 percent reported eleven years earlier, such data tell us little about actual sports participation. To say that one hike a year makes a sportswoman "in the broadest sense" is nonsense. It is somewhat more helpful to learn that 11 percent of the girls and women have earned a badge or certification for their athletic achievements (compared to 19 percent of the boys and men). For the nation's teenagers, the "gender gap" almost disappeared; 38 percent of the boys and 35 percent of the girls acquired the badges.[71]

The information on club membership is—once again—the most illuminating. In 1950, when the *Deutscher Sportbund* ("German Sports Federation") was established, girls and women were 10.1 percent of its members. By 1987, women were 36.3 percent of the organization's 20,043,290 members (male/female ratio = 1.76).[72] In the eleven years between 1965 and 1976, their number increased by 176 percent, a rate of increase more than twice that of the men. In just these years, the female share of the federation's membership climbed from 20 percent to 31 percent.[73] Almost as many women as men said they approved of sports competition (60 percent to 74 percent), but most of the former continued to be personally involved in predominantly noncompetitive activities. Whereas 55 percent of the men engaged in contests, only 18 percent of the female members did.[74]

The stark contrast in social class was almost as evident as in earlier studies. Class and gender continued to interact in such a way that men of the lower lower class were thirty-four times as likely to be sports-club members than women of the same class.[75] "There is scarcely another voluntary organization where the social class of a woman matters as much or where the lowest stratum suffers as much discrimination."[76]

Ethnicity intensifies the disabilities of class. A national study of Germany's minority population—Turks, Greeks, Italians, etc.—found that 42.2 percent of the young women (average age: 21.6 years) claimed to be active in sports and 13.9 percent were club members.[77] A darker picture emerged, however, from research into the situation of West Berlin's ethnic minorities. Fifteen percent of the city's German population were sports-club members, but only 5 percent of the non-German Berliners were. Of the 12,055 foreigners who *were* enrolled in the city's sports clubs, only 10.3 percent were women. The male/female ratio varied enormously: for the Greek minority it was 4.45 and for the Turks it was 13.06. Harsh religious restrictions explain the plight of Turkish women. In Islamic eyes, there is no modest form of women's basketball.[78]

The most intriguing finding may be that women who work for wages are more active in sports than housewives are. "In every type of sport, women employed outside the home are found more frequently [involved in sports] than women not so employed."[79] Most of these "sportswomen" are engaged in dancing, walking, and going to the beach, but those who participate in soccer and in track and field are also more likely to be gainfully employed women—5 percent of them play soccer and only 2 percent of the others; 9 percent of the former are involved in track and field and only 4 percent of the others. Women unemployed in the sense that they wish to work outside the home but have failed to find a position are the least likely, despite their "free time," to be involved in sports. The most likely reason for their noninvolvement is that they fear a further loss of self-confidence as a consequence of poor performance in sports.[80]

The DSB is composed of many national sports federations devoted to a single sport. Some of the figures on specific sports between 1965 and 1976 are striking. Gymnastics have always attracted the lion's share of Central European women, so that an increase from 761,901 to 1,697,253 female members is no surprise; but the number involved in organized track and field nearly doubled from 149,136 to 248,639. The male/female ratio was an amazingly low 1.23.[81] Still more astonishing is the boom in the number of women playing what most of the world still perceives as *the* masculine sport—soccer football. In 1970, the *Deutscher Sportbund* decided officially to sponsor women's soccer teams. National tournaments were inaugurated in 1974. In 1976, 4 percent of all German women were enrolled in the *Deutscher Fussballverband*. The federation had 215,817 female members.[82] By

1985, the number had more than doubled to 441,932 on no fewer than 3443 teams.[83] This figure drastically underestimates the number involved in *Frauenfussball* because some 2 million women are said to play under the auspices of the gymnastics federation and another 500,000 on teams sponsored by the tennis federation. If all the teams in all the federations are counted, the number of players approaches four million![84]

The incredible boom in women's soccer has caused some scholars to rethink the opinions of the Dutch psychologist F. J. Buytendijk. His book on soccer, originally published in 1952, was widely cited in the German translation. "The game of soccer," he concluded, "is essentially a demonstration of masculinity. . . . Women have never been allowed to play soccer." To this historically inaccurate remark, Buytendijk added a coy comment: "Kicking is specifically masculine; whether being kicked is feminine, I prefer not to say."[85] The actual behavior of female soccer players has dispelled some illusions about women's ability to kick and be kicked. When a team of sociologists studied male and female players, they found that, although the men scored higher on various scales of aggression, the women were not far behind.[86] Renate Schröder, a referee for women's soccer, also discovered that *Frauenfussball* was a good deal rougher than *Damentennis*. She complained that the women were even more aggressive than the men: "And they are cleverer about their fouls."[87]

German experience may help American educators answer a question raised by Title IX. Are coeducational sports desirable? During the excitement of the early seventies, when reform if not revolution was in the air, coeducation was seen as the best way to overcome the deficit in girls' and women's sports. Schools in the more progressive *Länder* (like Bremen) integrated their physical education classes while other *Länder* (like Bavaria) hesitated. The experiment has been deemed a success by some and a failure by others. The most recent studies have shown that neither the boys nor the girls are happy about mixed classes. Adolescence is a period of rapid, unsettling physical changes; neither sex seems to want the additional psychological burden of mandatory public physical exposure to the equally suffering opposite sex.[88]

French data are far less extensive than the German, but they show a similar picture with one important difference. In France, age, gender, and education are apparently more important determinants of sports participation than is social class.[89] While one-third of the entire

German population is enrolled in sports clubs, only 16 percent of French men and 4 percent of French women were members in 1974. Twenty-two percent of the men and 14 percent of the women claimed to be athletically active outside the clubs.[90] The increase in both male and female participation, and the changing male/female ratio, can be seen by comparing the figures for 1973 with those for 1981 (see table 13.3).[91] It is obvious that women were almost as active as men in noncompetitive physical activities (calisthentics, jogging), but they were still only half as likely to participate in individual sports and one-fourth as likely to be involved in team sports. The male/female ratio in team sports had, in fact, *increased,* which is quite unlike the German situation. The explanation is that French women have not yet gone in for soccer as German women have.

An excellent volume published by two geographers, Daniel Mathieu and Jean Praicheux, maps the membership in dozens of sports federations in each of the republic's eighty-nine *départements.* One can see in an instant that a traditional game like *pelote basque* is played by some ten thousand Frenchmen, almost all of whom are concentrated in the southwestern part of France. Brittany is clearly the cyclists' paradise. Residents of urban and suburban areas are, as expected, overrepresented in most modern sports. In many of the major sports, the male/female ratio is much lower than the figures given in the survey data presented in table 13.4. For *all* the federations taken together, the male/female ratio is 1.96. While the French data generate male/female ratios comparable to those of German studies, it should be recalled that German participation is much higher in absolute terms.[92]

In sports, the Scandinavian countries resemble Germany rather than France. The sample for Kari Fasting's study of Norwegian women was drawn from the city of Oslo, where the level of engagement is

TABLE 13.3.
French Participation, 1973–1981
(In percent)

	Calisthenics, Jogging		Individual Sports		Team Sports	
	1973	1981	1973	1981	1973	1981
Male	13	18	12	17	11	13
Female	10	17	6	9	3	3
M/F Ratio	1.3	1.05	2.0	1.89	3.67	4.33

TABLE 13.4.
French Sports Federations (1984)

Federation	Total Membership	Male/Female Ratio
Gymnastics	104,447	0.43
Basketball	358,640	1.14
Swimming	89,042	1.18
Volleyball	64,019	1.41
Golf	62,707	1.79
Tennis	1,266,349	1.83
Skiing	792,662	1.86
Team handball	164,946	1.89
Track and field	106,415	2.00
Cycling	64,262	27.57
Soccer	1,493,861	61.50

surely higher than in more rural areas. The women were still far from equal in terms of sports participation. Fifty-four percent of them claimed to exercise at least once a week (compared to 67 percent of the men), but the men were more than twice as likely to be club members (54 percent to 22 percent) and more than six times as likely to have been involved in competition in the previous twelve months (38 percent to 6 percent). The most popular "sports" for women were gymnastics and skiing (presumably noncompetitive for most), but the next most popular were team handball and soccer—both rough games. Women constitute 15 percent of the national soccer federation although it was 1976 before the federation officially recognized the women's game. In Norway as in Germany gainfully employed women are more likely than housewives to join a sports club.[93]

In the most industrialized of the Scandinavian countries, Sweden, 27 percent of the women aged 16 to 74 are enrolled in sports clubs whose male/female ratio is even lower than the German figures: 1.59. (For children under 16, the ratio drops to 1.48.) The survey data for 1989, in table 13.5, reveal that the Swedish population may be the most health-conscious, if not the most sports-oriented, in the world. The numbers refer to a frequency of at least twice a week. That women are more faithful exercisers than men is no surprise, but the male/female ratios for regular sports participation are very unusual; for the first and third age cohorts they are 1.68 and 1.38. The data gathered for a sample of 1,654 thirty-year-old men and women are particularly interesting; 32 percent of the men and 38 percent of the

TABLE 13.5.
Swedish Participation in Calisthenics and Sports
(In percent)

Age:	16–24	25–44	45–64	65–74	75–84	85–
CALISTHENICS:						
Men	18	16	19	22	12	5
Women	22	21	21	23	7	3
SPORTS:						
Men	32	16	9	11	8	2
Women	19	7	7	3	2	2

women are engaged in strenuous physical exercise at least once a week, but only 3 percent of the women (as compared with 18 percent of the men) were involved in "regular, rigorous training (or competition) several times a week." Not even in egalitarian Sweden are young women as intensely committed to sports as are the men.[94]

In August of 1989, the Danish Sports Federation reported a total of 1,541,845 active members in fifty-four different federations. Women accounted for nearly 38 percent of the membership; they numbered 578,224. The male/female ratio was 1.63, lower than the ratios for American interscholastic and intercollegiate teams and for German clubs and almost as low as the Swedish figures.[95] In Finland, some 8 percent of the girls and women aged ten to sixty-four are said to be actively involved in sports, but the nature of the activity is problematical. Ecologists can rejoice that 62 percent of Finnish women walk or cycle to work during the summer months, but sociologists should not count them among the athletically active. Similarly, it has been reported that middle-aged Finnish women are more involved in sports than men are, but the report is based on the nonsensical definition of "sports" to include dancing, strolling, and berry picking. A better picture of involvement and engagement emerges from the facts that (a) women are 29 percent of the membership in the nation's widespread network of sports clubs, (b) a fifth of all Finnish women read the sports pages, and (c) a third of them watch televised sports (as compared to half the men).[96]

As expected, Southern Europe lags behind, but even here the graphs show a rising curve for women's sports participation. If one accepts the accuracy of a survey by the *Istituto Centrale di Statistica,* Italians—especially the men—are quite active in sports. In 1985, some 30 percent of the entire male population told the survey-takers that they did sports. For women, the figure was 14.4 percent, which yields a male/female ratio of 2.11. Predictably, the bright hues darken when one turns from the respondents' self-reported activity to the official membership lists of the thirty-nine sports federations affiliated with the *Comitato Nazionale Olimpico d'Italia*. In 1981, CONI reported that women were 30.4 percent of the membership of seventeen of these thirty-nine federations, but many of the largest federations— like those for soccer and hunting—were not included in CONI's selective calculations. If one adds just these two federations for *calcio* and *caccia,* the overall percentage of female members quickly sinks to about 7 percent. Southern Italy is, moreover, culturally quite different from Northern Italy, which contains such industrial centers as Genoa, Milan, and Turin. The women of the northernmost six provinces are more than twice as likely to be members of sports clubs as the women of the nation's six predominantly rural southern provinces. The picture becomes even clearer when one examines the individual sports federations. Track-and-field athletes were a mere 6,765 in 1966 and 37,191 in 1983. This was a minuscule number compared to the 248,649 women registered in West Germany's track-and-field federation, but it does represent a seventeen-year increase of nearly 600 percent. Basketball players were a pathetic 8975 in 1971 and rose to some 35,225 in 1983. This, too, was a feeble showing compared to Northern Europe. The most hopeful news for promoters of women's sports came from the volleyball courts, where 51.65 percent of Italy's 226,284 organized players are female. Optimists can also point to the *Giochi della Gioventù*. In these games restricted to young people, the number of female participants soared from 179,000 in 1969 to a rather impressive 1,170,000 in 1980. Participation in these games, however, like participation in the government-sponsored Spartakiads of Eastern Europe, is more or less compulsory for schoolchildren. We can conclude from the evidence that Italian women are doing considerably more sports than their mothers and grandmothers did, but they continue to trail behind the women of Northern Europe.[97]

Although its percentages also remain at a lower level than those of Northern Europe, Spain too has had a rapid increase in sports participation. Between 1975 and 1985, the number of self-identified adult actives increased from 22 percent to 34 percent. With the exception of the peasantry, only 10 percent of whom participate "a great deal," Spaniards with very different occupations seem almost equally likely to do (or not do) sports. Education seems to be the best indicator of sports participation. Those with *"Formación Professional"* are more than twice as likely to participate "a great deal" as those with a primary education (30 percent versus 14 percent). Since Spain, like Italy, is an overwhelmingly Catholic country, the weakness of women's sports is no surprise. Table 13.6 shows men's and women's responses to a national survey that asked simply for participation "in some sport." Another study found that women's sports participation had increased from 6.8 percent in 1968 to 17.0 percent in 1980. Since men's participation had risen from 18.3 percent to 33 percent, the male/female ratio had fallen from 2.69 to 1.94. It should be borne in mind, however, that the most popular "sport" for women was swimming. The men played soccer.[98]

In Spain as in other European countries, statistics on club membership reveal more accurate information about actual participation than do the responses to a pollster's ill-defined questions. In 1989, the *Consejo Superior de Deportes* reported that the country's fifty-four national federations have enrolled a total of 1,411,809 men and 372,352 women. The male/female ratio, 3.79, is typical for Southern Europe. It is, however, rather a surprise that the basketball and team handball federations have registered more female members than the tennis federation. Do unregistered tennis players play on their own courts?[99]

Given the long tradition of British feminism, which stretches from Mary Wollstonecraft's *Vindication of the Rights of Women* (1792) through the suffragette movement of the early twentieth century to the polemics of Germaine Greer's *The Female Eunuch* (1970), one might expect British women to have led the way not only in school sports for the elite but also in mass participation. This has clearly not been the case. Although Parliament passed a Sex Discrimination Act in 1975, designed to end discriminatory practices in sports as well as in other areas, although the Sports Council announced in 1982 that there was "clear evidence of a great increase in male and female participa-

TABLE 13.6.
Participation in Some Sport: Spain
(In percent)

	Great	Enough	Little	None
Men	21	25	18	15
Female	13	10	10	10

tion in indoor sport and a growth in outdoor sport among women," the optimism about women's participation has proved to be premature. Nationally, 19 percent of British men and 17 percent of the women say that they do sports, but—as the attentive reader of this book can readily guess—this astonishing approach to male/female parity disguises the fact that the men are playing soccer while most of the women are gardening, walking, going to the beach, or doing their "physical jerks." Some 6,000 British women are active in 278 soccer clubs, a tiny number compared to the 400,000 German women enrolled in the *Deutscher Fussballverband*. Unlike the DFV, the Football Association has not welcomed women's intrusion into the traditional "male preserve." The association's executive council has only one woman. The famed Marylebone Cricket Club does not allow women to play at Lord's cricket grounds and has no female members. Zola Budd has received as much as 90,000 pounds for a single race, but not many British women are racing after her. The General Household Survey found that a mere 3 percent of British men and 1 percent of British women engaged in track and field. The excitement of Football League and the fame of a few record-holders like Sebastian Coe have obscured the dismal state of British sports.[100]

In her study of the town of Milton Keynes, published in 1986, Rosemary Deem concluded sadly that sports played a "very marginal role . . . in the lives of most women. . . . Once women have left full-time education their involvement in sport begins a downhill descent from which it never recovers."[101] A study of 707 Sheffield women aged 18–60 was somewhat more hopeful. The survey found that 32 percent claimed to do sports, broadly defined, at least several times a week, but the distribution was the expected one. Young women aged 18–24 are nearly three times as likely to be involved as women aged 45–59. Single women without children are more active than single parents (36 percent to 15 percent). Those with lower-middle-class jobs are twice as likely to be active as casual workers (35 percent to 17 percent). Those with professional-managerial partners were over five times as likely to be participants as those with lower-class partners (42 percent to 8 percent). As in most other places, the women with full-time out-of-the-house employment were more involved in sports than housewives (29 percent to 12 percent).[102] Quite obviously the common excuse of having "no time for sports" has to be taken with a grain of salt. Within broad limits, people make time for what they most want to do.

Aside from several studies done on Germany's minority population, there are surprisingly few empirical investigations of ethnic differences in sports participation. One exception is a recently published study of British-French differences in Canadian sports. Working with a sample of over 35,000 adults, Philip G. White and James E. Curtis found practically no difference at all in the sports participation, broadly defined, of anglophone and francophone men; 48 percent of the first group and 47 percent of the second claimed to have been involved in "sports" at least ten times in the previous twelve months. For women the numbers were 41 percent for both linguistic groups. When White and Curtis asked about sustained involvement in "competitive sports," i.e., ten or more contests a year, a very different picture emerged. The mostly Protestant sample of anglophones were much more likely than the mostly Catholic francophones to be involved in real sports (as opposed to noncompetitive activities): 20 percent of the anglophone men versus 12 percent of the francophones; 11 percent of the anglophone women versus only 4 percent of the francophones. In other words, the male/female ratio for the English-speakers was a fairly low 1.82 while the ratio for the French-speakers was 3.00. Clearly, French-Canadian women are not yet full participants in modern sports. They lag behind the women of France as well as those of British Canada.[103]

Reliable empirical studies of Latin American sports, almost nonexistent before the 1970s, are primarily devoted to *futból*—the players, the fans, the phenomenon of "football madness," the role of soccer as an instrument of national integration, the corruption of the game as a sign of the decline and fall of hispanic civilization. Women are rarely mentioned. The most extensive study of female athletes seems to be that contained in *Blanco, Mestizo, Negro en el Deporte* (1984), a 530–page book by Caetano Carlevaro Persico and José Laurino, but this tome—despite its title—is concerned mainly with the question of physiological differences between men and women. Throughout Latin America, upper-class women are to be found in the swimming pools and on the tennis courts of exclusive private clubs. This numerically tiny segment of the population has produced a few internationally know athletes. Brazil's Maria Bueno, Wimbledon finalist in 1966, comes quickly to mind. The best-known athletes are, moreover, disproportionately women of European ancestry. Many are the daughters or granddaughters of German immigrants. Chile's Marlene Ahrens and Costa Rica's Silvia Poll are good examples. Ahrens threw her javelin for a gold medal in the Pan American Games and for a silver one at the 1956 Olympics in Melbourne. Poll swam to a silver medal in the 200–meter freestyle at Seoul in 1988. Neither of them nor any other Latin American sportswoman achieved anything like the adulation called forth by soccer stars like Pelé, Garrincha, and Maradona, but attitudes are changing. The 1990 U.S. Open Champion Gabriela Sabatini's tennis has made her "one of the three most popular people in all of Argentina, along with soccer god Diego Maradona and president Raúl Alfonsin."[104]

Only in Cuba and Nicaragua, where Communist governments have made a special effort to democratize sports, have there been signs of a Latin American revolution in women's sports. At the 1980 Olympic Games in Moscow, Cuba's María Caridad Colón cast her javelin the Olympic-record distance of 68.4 meters. This daughter of a rural schoolteacher was the first Latin American woman to win an Olympic event.[105] She and other female athletes from Fidel Castro's Cuba have done very well at the Pan American and the Central American and Caribbean Games. The hemisphere's Marxist regimes have had less success with their programs for recreational sports for women. Comparing the populations of Nicaragua and Belize, Eric A. Wagner reported in 1982 that 33.8 percent of the Nicaraguan women and 23 percent of the women of Belize were participants in sports. Both figures should be treated skeptically. It is extremely unlikely that they refer to *sports* participation. If they are accurate, then poverty-stricken Nicaraguan women are far more involved in sports than the women of wealthier and more highly developed societies. Similarly, Wagner was told by 31.7 percent of the Cuban women he interviewed that they were sports participants. Once again, however, the reader is frustrated by Wagner's failure to indicate exactly what these women meant by "sports." A more extensive study of Cuban sports by a sympathetic German scholar concluded that the island's women were involved, almost exclusively, in some form of calisthenics. In his view, sports remain the "Achilles heel" of the programs devised to facilitate widespread participation. Given our present state of knowledge, we are probably wise to postpone any further summary remarks about women's sports in Latin America.[106]

While it cannot be stated with certainty that the dramatic rise in European women's sports participation has been accompanied by a decrease in the percentage of female coaches and sports administrators, as was the case in North America, there is no doubt that these women are drastically underrepresented in every European country for which evidence exists (and also in the International Olympic Committee, which elected its first female members in 1981). In relatively egalitarian Finland, women chair 27.1 percent of the sports clubs where the emphasis is on recreational fun and games, but they lead only 6.1 percent of the clubs where competition is the chief goal.[107] In the Finnish national sports federations, women occupy 8 percent of the committee seats.[108] In Norway, in 1984, women were 35 percent of the active membership of the nation's forty-one sports federations, but they were only 15 percent of the executive-board members and they coached only 12 percent of the elite teams. Their 50 percent representation on the board of the national gymnastics federation seems like equality until one remembers that they are 85 percent of the membership. In Norway's track-and-field federation, where women came unusually close to parity in membership (41 percent of the total), they were only 8 percent of the governing board.[109]

A British study published in 1983 reported that only two women sat on the twenty-three member Sports Council. Britain's Princess Anne—an equestrian—has been one of the very few women with real influence in an international sports federation; but one suspects that her title adds to her clout.[110]

The most complete data on women's role as coaches and administrators come, once again, from West Germany, where *Sportsoziologie* has long been a major academic enterprise. "In the German sports federations, leading positions are almost entirely taken by men: 91 percent of the voluntary and 88 percent of the salaried administrators are men."[111] Women are some 35 percent of the DSB, but they have only two representatives in the fifteen-member Presidium and are only one-ninth of the committee chairs. Two women sit on the forty-one-member Advisory Board for Elite Sports. The 766,055 women who have flocked to the tennis courts have no representatives at all in the presidium of the *Deutscher Tennisbund*. In the *Deutscher Leichtathletikverband* (for track and field), there are 352,795 women to 435,100 men, yet only one woman has a place in the twelve-member presidium. The presidium of the National Olympic Committee consists of twenty-two men.[112] The dismal picture was more dismal still in the German Democratic Republic. In 1972, none of that country's forty sports federations had a female president (and no woman was represented in the sixteen-member Politburo or in the eight-member secretariat of the ruling Socialist Unity Party).[113]

4. Olympic Glory

For the games held at Montreal in 1976, the International Olympic Committee gave its belated imprimatur to two new team sports for women: basketball and team handball (which is a cross between basketball and soccer). Six events for rowers were also introduced. Women were 20.6 percent of the athletes in Montreal.[114] Russian women won the first basketball and team handball competitions and the rowers, gymnasts, fencers, swimmers, runners, jumpers, and throwers from Eastern Europe threatened to monopolize the victors' platform. Russian women had often bested their American rivals in dual meets in track and field (while the American men had almost always defeated the Russian men by a smaller margin), but the 1976 games were an unparalleled triumph for the women of Eastern Europe. Of the forty-nine gold medals awarded to female athletes, the women of the Soviet bloc won forty-four. The East Germans were especially impressive. In 1968, female athletes from the German Democratic Republic had won one gold medal in track and field (Margitta Gummel's for the shot-put). In 1972, competing for the first time under their own flag and in their own uniforms, the women had won six gold medals. At Montreal, leaving their rivals from West Germany far behind, they won nine gold medals in track and field. (Sports fans from West Germany consoled themselves with thoughts of skier Rosi Mittermeier, star of the winter games at Innsbruck.) Collectively, however, it was the swimmers—even more than the runners, jumpers, and throwers—who shocked the American spectators because the American team was studded with great swimmers and American confidence verged on arrogance. In race after race, the German women outswam the Americans (and everyone else). Nine of a possible thirteen world records were bettered as the Germans reaped their harvest of eleven gold medals. America's Shirley Babashoff was expected to splash her way to glory, but it was Kornelia Ender who emerged from the water as the world's best swimmer. Her four gold and one silver medals, added to the three silver medals from Munich, equalled Dawn Fraser's total and, of course, her times were much faster than Fraser's had been. Babashoff first refused to congratulate Ender and then gave vent to bitter innuendo about broad shoulders and deep voices, the results presumably of steroids. Her implicit accusation was brushed off with the witty rejoinder, "We came here to swim, not to sing," but the question of steroids was not to be dismissed (as we shall see).

In all, the swimmers and the other female athletes from the German Democratic Republic won 56.6 percent of their team's medals. While the women had done better than the men, East German TV spent 61 percent of its time on the men's team. The official newspaper, *Neues Deutschland,* gave the men 71 percent of its coverage. In the Federal Republic of Germany, on the other hand, the women won 15.2 percent of the team's medals and received 34 percent of the television time and 23 percent of the space in the *Frankfurter Allgemeine Zeitung.*[115]

Kornelia Ender's medals and records did not make her the most famous female athlete of the games. The unofficial popularity contest was won, easily, by Romania's Nadia Comaneci. Her charm was so great that she was forgiven her defeat of Olga Korbut, once the idol of the West. Neither Comaneci nor Korbut was as formidably powerful in appearance as the swimmers, which doubtless helps to explain why it was easier to love them. They were everybody's teenage daughter, not "masculinized" symbols of an ideological challenge.

The dominance of Eastern European women may have reached its zenith in the late seventies. Even then, the awesome achievements of the very best female athletes represented the tip of a narrow pyramid. If one looked at the top *one hundred* swimmers and track-and-field athletes rather than at the top five or ten, which is precisely what geographer John Bale did for 1980 and 1982, a somewhat different picture emerges from the one that comes to mind when one contemplates the Olympic medal-count. Beginning with an index based on the world's per capita "production" of elite performers, Bale found that Eastern and Western Europe were both significantly more productive than the "world norm" of 1.00. This was no surprise, nor was it surprising that East Germany accounted for about thirty times its per capita share of women in the top one hundred for their event. The unexpected result, for those who assumed the overwhelming superiority of the Communist bloc, was that "there is very little evidence . . . of an Eastern European bloc of highly productive nations." In track and field, the three most productive nations were

East Germany, Bulgaria, and Romania, but Finland, Sweden, and Switzerland all outproduced the Soviet Union on a per capita basis. In swimming, East Germany was disproportionately productive, but Sweden, Holland, and Norway followed, and Hungary was the only other Communist country to score above the European "norm" on a per capita basis. Despite the humiliating defeats of 1976, there was no reason for American or Western European women to despair.[116]

The American swimmers went home and resolved to train as exhaustively as the Germans and to overcome their repugnance for the weight-training that had obviously been a factor in the Germans' sudden improvement. At dual meets and world championships, they gradually recovered from the débacle. For redemption they had to wait until 1984, because swimmers attract the public's attention—at least the American public's—only in an Olympic year, when nationalism gives them a boost. Jimmy Carter's quixotic boycott of the 1980 Olympics, the ineffectual response of an unpopular president to the Soviet invasion of Afghanistan, did nothing to hasten the day of military withdrawal, but it did keep the swimmers—and all the other athletes—at home.

Without the Americans and the West Germans, who were kept from Moscow by their government's military and economic dependence upon the United States, the women of Western Europe were simply overwhelmed by the athletes of the Soviet bloc. Italy's Sara Simeoni was memorable because her unexpected win in the high jump was one of the few occasions when three Eastern Europeans did not embrace upon the victors' stand. Of the sixty track-and-field medals, for instance, the women of the Soviet bloc took home fifty-one. Eight of the nine medals won by other European women were awarded to the British for two third-place finishes in the relay races.

Increased political pressure on the Olympic Games, which had *never* been wholly free of social purpose and political overtones, had a negative impact on the games celebrated in Los Angeles in 1984. Whatever explanations were offered by the Soviet Union, about environmental pollution, lack of security, or American inflexibility in regard to visas, the underlying reason is best described in children's terms: tit for tat. The boycott was an act of revenge. Like the previous boycott, it damaged but did not destroy the games.

Without significant competition from Soviet women, the Americans seemed to stand in line for their turn to receive their medals. The 1984 Olympics were, moreover, the first for which American media coverage of women's events was comparable both in extent and in tone to that afforded the men's. Taking advantage of the fact that these were the second games to be contested in Los Angeles, Beth Allyson Posnack contrasted the reports of 1932 with those of 1984. She found that the runners and the throwers were no longer photographed in swimsuits at poolside or in high heels and evening gowns, as they had been in 1932.

The American media of 1984 identified . . . female athletes by their achievements—not by their physical attributes. Clearly, the terms "woman" and "athlete" were no longer separate notions in 1984. Mary Decker was an athlete just as Carl Lewis was an athlete. There was no need to remind the reading public that Mary was also a woman who was capable of dressing up and applying makeup.

In both the *Los Angeles Times* and the *New York Times,* women were given some 40 percent of the space allotted to the games.[117]

Of the female athletes whose stellar performances earned them medals and headlines, Joan Benoit was perhaps the most symbolically important because it was she who won the first-ever women's Olympic marathon. That she ran only a few weeks after knee surgery made her triumph even more remarkable. Although Greta Waitz and Ingrid Kristiansen were among the early favorites, Benoit endured the California heat better than the Scandinavians. "I could perhaps have run faster," said Waitz, "I was afraid of dying."[118] Benoit loped to a fairly easy victory. Only a few years earlier, Waitz had won the New York Marathon in world-record time and had not appeared in the live TV coverage. Now the cameras followed Benoit through the forty-two kilometers of the race, not continuously, but persistently enough to make a clear statement about the increased importance of the women's event. The cameras also brought to the world's horrified attention the marathon ordeal of Switzerland's Gabriela Anderson-Schiess. Stricken by dehydration, she staggered towards the finish line and collapsed when she crossed it. Although the officials were denounced for their failure to intervene, the ensuing controversy did *not* lead to cries for the abolition of the event as had been the case after the far less frightening conclusion of the 800–meter race in 1928.

Benoit was not the only female athlete to score a "first-ever" Olympic victory. In addition to a grueling 79.2–kilometer road race for cyclists, won by Connie Carpenter-Phinney of the United States, there were two new events reserved exclusively for women: Tracie

Ruiz triumphed in synchronized swimming, winning the solo event and teaming with another American, Candy Costie, to win the duet as well; Lori Fung of Canada took the first gold medal in rhythmic gymnastics. In the heptathlon, less than a second in the 800–meter run made the difference between Australia's Glynis Nunn and her two closest rivals, America's Jackie Joyner and Germany's Sabine Evert.

More newsworthy still was Mary Decker Slaney. In fact, prior to the games she was the person *most* cited by American respondents when asked to name members of the American team. In the public's consciousness, she loomed larger than Carl Lewis, Edwin Moses, and Greg Louganis.[119] There were doubtless several reasons for this extraordinary prominence. One is that "Little Mary" Decker had impressed track fans by her performance in the middle-distance events and by her perseverence after a series of injuries and operations. A second reason for her fame is that she ran world-record times in an era when the Eastern Europeans seemed to have purloined the record book. More important still was the hoopla that attended the sudden rise to fame of South Africa's Zola Budd.

Slender and almost child-like in appearance, with a name suggesting youth and freshness, Budd sprang into the headlines on January 5, 1984, the day after she set an unofficial world record over 5,000 meters. Her time was five seconds faster than Slaney's. That she ran barefoot added to the image of "natural" talent. Since South Africa had long been barred from the Olympics (because of its policy of apartheid), Budd became eligible to compete in Los Angeles only after a promotional campaign launched by the London *Daily Mail* and some fast legerdemain on the part of the British Foreign Office. Explaining weakly that her grandfather had been a British subject, the authorities whisked her through the naturalization process and declared her a bona fide Englishwoman. Amid swirls of angry protest, the confrontation between Slaney and Budd aroused intense excitement. The dénouement was totally unexpected. In an effort to overtake Budd, Slaney accidently spiked her, tripped, sprawled, and cried out in pain and disappointment. Afterwards, Slaney ungraciously blamed Budd for the mishap, which more objective observers eventually concluded had been Slaney's fault. Budd finished in seventh place, to cries of unjustified derision, while most of the world simply ignored Romania's Maricac? Puica, who won the race. In later contests, Slaney proved herself a better runner than Budd, whose performances were hardly improved by the protesters who dogged her heels and denounced her as a symbol of racial oppression.

Although Ulrike Meyfarth once again surprised track-and-field fans by winning the high jump, as she had in Munich twelve years earlier, she had never been particularly popular outside of West Germany. The chauvinistic American press made the most of Mary Lou Retton's narrow victory in the boycott-ravaged field of women's gymnastics. Had Romania not broken ranks with its Communist allies by sending a team to Los Angeles, the event might have lacked drama, but Ecaterina Szabo was there to challenge Retton and to enhance the sweetness of her victory. Retton's almost madly extroverted personality seemed made for television (and for post-Olympics product endorsements). Although the political symbolism was not emphasized by ABC, which actually made some effort to avoid jingoism, the fact that Retton's coach—Bela Karolyi—had been Nadia Comaneci's coach added further drama. Mistreatment at the hands of petty Communist bureaucrats had driven Karolyi into exile, and from exile he had proven once more that he was the magician who transformed little girls into athletic heroines.[120]

In the stadium, Afro-American runners dominated the shorter distance races. Evelyn Ashford won the 100 meters, Benita Brown-Fitzgerald the 200 meters, and Valerie Briscoe-Hooks the 400 meters. None of the black women, not even Ashford, held the spotlight as Benoit, Decker, and Retton did. They probably received less recognition than the swimmers: Tracy Caulkins, Mary Meagher, Tiffany Cohen. That Wilma Rudolph *had* caught the nation's fancy as early as 1960 suggests that it was a matter of personality as well as residual racism that accounted for the relative neglect of the black runners in 1984.

No reasonable observer can speak of "neglect" in regard to the black women who competed at Calgary and at Seoul in 1988. Debbie Thomas had skated to a world championship and was favored to win the first Olympic gold medal ever awarded to a black figure-skater. Her rivalry with East Germany's Katarina Witt was manipulated into another of those symbolic confrontations that are the essence of representative sports.[121] At Calgary, Witt was not to be halted. Her dance to the music of *Carmen* was an unforgettable athletic, aesthetic, and erotic event. With a silver medal around her neck rather than a gold one, Thomas nonetheless proved that it was the not-so-hidden disadvantages of class and race, not a lack of aptitude for cold-weather sports, that had kept black athletes away from the winter games.

In comparison to the summer games at Los Angeles, the ones celebrated at Seoul in 1988 went smoothly (aside from the uproar caused by unfair decisions in boxing). The sheer number of female athletes implicitly demonstrated that sports were no longer, if they ever had been, a purely "masculine domain." The IOC added a 10,000–meter race for distance runners, the swiftest of whom turned out to be Olga Bondarenko of the USSR. In a curious way, however, the proliferation of women's events, many of them for teams, tended to diffuse the impact of the individual athletes. There were repetitions of a familiar pattern. The athletes from Eastern Europe were supreme in the field events, the fencers from West Germany were superb. (They swept all the medals awarded for foils and defeated the Italians for the team title.) There were also surprises. Portugal's Rosa Motta won the marathon, divers from the People's Republic of China were spectacular. (Xu Yanmei was first in platform diving and Gao Min in springboard diving.) And there was a return to Olympic tennis (with no surprise at all-Steffi Graf won).

Although American television watchers might have had the impression that Janet Evans was the only swimmer in Seoul, East Germany's Kristin Otto won the 50–meter and the 100–meter freestyle races, the 100–meter backstroke, and the 100–meter medley. Except for Evans's victories in the 400–meter medley and the 400–meter and 800–meter freestyle competitions, Eastern European women took home all of the swimmers' twenty-one gold medals.

The brightest star of the games was not a swimmer. Florence Griffith-Joyner outshone Janet Evans (and Carl Lewis and Greg Louganis). Her flamboyant, intensely colorful space-age one-legged track suits and her lengthy, iridescent fingernails had already made her the world's most easily identifiable runner. At Seoul, she had to wear the team uniform, but there was no danger that she might be overlooked. Her fantastic speed won her a victory in the 100 meters, ahead of Evelyn Ashford and East Germany's Heike Drechsler. The 200–meter race was a repeat except that Grace Jackson of Jamaica came in second. Griffith-Joyner's incredible final lap cinched the gold for the American 4 x 100–meter relay team (against East Germany). Meanwhile, her sister-in-law, Jackie Joyner, added to the family's golden harvest by winning the heptathlon. (Sabina John of East Germany was second.) The dominance of black runners was not a theme for extended comment because sports commentators shy away from even the most remote suggestion that black athletes might be genetically advantaged; but no one in the stadium or seated before a television set was unaware of the fact that black women represented not only the United States, where Afro-Americans are some 12 percent of the total population, but also a number of other countries, where blacks are a small minority. Although some radical critics continue to condemn the Olympics as an orgy of racism and nationalism, others, like Jennifer Hargreaves, have become a little more sanguine.[122] "Flo-Jo" 's post-Olympic appearances in Japanese television commercials do seem to indicate a step in the direction of multiracial cosmopolitanism.

FOURTEEN

Three Contemporary Controversies

1. Catching Up with the Men?

Feminists have been understandably sensitive about male-female comparisons which seem "to endorse the doctrine of male supremacy."[1] Physical prowess is, however, what sports are all about, and comparisons between the sexes are probably inescapable. If we must compare, let us at least try to be clear about the physiological evidence, such as it is.

On the average, men are taller, heavier, and stronger than women. They are said by some experimental psychologists to have faster reaction times, more acute vision, and better spatial perception. Although estimates vary, women seem to be about 65 percent as strong as men in absolute terms and about 80 percent as strong when size is held constant. The differences in upper-body strength are far greater than in lower-body strength, which partly explains why female runners are almost as fast as male runners while female throwers lag far behind. The female runner is also hampered by a wider pelvis, which disadvantageously alters the angle of her legs. Male superiority in strength is partly attributable to the fact that men have twenty to thirty times as much testosterone as women. This male hormone also seems to account for some of the difference in men's as compared to women's aggressiveness. Women, on the other hand, are more flexible than men and surpass men at very long distance running and swimming (because they seem to metabolize fat better than men and because they have relatively more fat to metabolize). Natalie Cullimore, for instance, won a 1971 race over 100 miles in a time of 16 hours and 17 minutes; none of the men finished. Susan Butcher won Alaska's 1168–mile dogsled race from Anchorage to Nome—three years in a row. In 1990, she triumphed for the fourth time.[2]

Where men's and women's performances can be compared objectively, the convergence is remarkable. In eight selected track events, the average of the men's times (compared to the women's) was 21.35 percent better in 1927 and only 10.64 percent better in 1977. Between 1956 and 1985, the difference over 100 meters dropped from 11.4 percent to 8.0 percent. The closure of the performance gap in the marathon was spectacular. Between 1972 and 1982, women's records improved by 16.2 percent (to 2 hours, 26 minutes, 11 seconds). For every other distance from 200 to 10,000 meters, the women's records improved far more rapidly than the men's. In the pool as on the track, the women have been catching up. For fifteen swimming events, the difference between the men's and women's records was 12.41 percent in 1936, 11.36 percent in 1956, and 9.27 percent in 1976. By 1980, the difference in the 400–meter crawl had diminished to only 5.2 percent.[3] Clearly, the narrowing of the difference is explicable not by evolutionary changes in the male and the female of the species but by social and cultural factors. More women are involved in sports; they train longer and harder than they did; they are less inhibited than they were by fears of "masculinization," by the stigma of aggressiveness, and by whispered references to suspected lesbianism.

Although today's women are faster than some of the famed male athletes of the past ("The fabulous Weismuller wouldn't make it to the women's finals"), the fact remains that the best men continue to surpass the best women in almost every sport where victory is objectively determined by times and distances. As the derogation of good old Johnny Weismuller implies, many feminists express delight in women's improved athletic performance, which they see as vindication of their claim that women must be freed from cultural constraints in order finally to realize their physical potential. On the other hand, some radical critics of patriarchy are adamantly opposed to sports because of what they see as female entanglement in an essentially masculine web of aggressive competitiveness. "To succeed as an athlete," asserts Paul Willis, "can be to fail as a woman" because the female athlete "has in certain profound symbolic ways, become a man." When, for example, female body-builders flex their "pecs and lats," they betray their submissive emulation of men. It is preferable, from this perspective, for women to swim, run long distances, do gymnastics, and dance. In such suggestions, today's radicalism has an uncanny resemblance to yesterday's conservatism.[4]

With the physiological facts clearly in mind, Jane English has suggested in a widely discussed essay that we "should develop a variety of sports, in which a variety of physical types can expect to excel." If the sports in which women outperform men were as salient in the public's imagination as the sports in which men have the physical advantage, then women would be more likely to be perceived not only as men's physical but also as men's moral equals. Through their superiority in these "alternative sports" women would have an opportunity to gain in self-respect, which English describes as a "basic benefit" of sports that should be available to all women.[5] The argument is questionable and it has been questioned.[6] It is unlikely that made-to-order sports can attain the prestige and popularity of baseball, basketball, football, ice hockey, rugby, soccer, and other male-dominated sports. Even if it *were* possible to promote made-to-order "feminine" sports to the point where women were acknowledged to be as athletic as men, not all feminists would be satisfied. There are some whose sharpest scorn is reserved for advocates of "feminine" sports designed for female abilities: "The image of the youthful, gracious, lithe, subtle female floating gracefully in the water or twirling ribbons to music does little to challenge male power."[7]

Some scholars have stressed the cultural factors behind the physical differentials and concluded that women do not need alternate "feminist" sports because women have the undeveloped physical potential to equal men's performances in the modern sports now dominated by male athletes. "By developing her powers to the fullest," wrote Ann Crittenden Scott in "Closing the Muscle Gap," "any woman . . . can be a match for any man she chooses to take on."[8] Why has this state of athletic equality never been realized? The usual answer given by those who believe in potential physical equality is that women's present physical inferiority is culturally induced by patriarchal domination. Caroline MacKinnon, for instance, argues that men prefer weak women because their "disability" leaves them vulnerable. Weak women are "more easily able to be raped, available to be molested, open to sexual harassment."[9]

MacKinnon's explanation is implausible. It is simply wrong to assert, in the face of all the evidence of admiration for athletic women, that culturally induced debility is still the desired norm—if it ever was. The question remains: *does* culture explain "the muscle gap"?

Radical feminists are certainly correct to assert that socialization rather than genetic endowment explains the sad finding that the average American woman attains her maximum strength in her teens while the strength of the average man continues to increase into his twenties, but it is unlikely that social and cultural factors can account for *all* the observed gender differences in strength and in sports performance. In many sports, women may be potentially the equals or even the superiors of men, but it is improbable that many of the women who play in the National Women's Football League will ever have careers in the NFL or that any female weight-lifter will ever raise a 250–kilogram barbell to her shoulders and then hoist it over-head.[10]

If we accept the fact that men are likely to remain, on the average, superior to women in most sports that require strength and speed, what is to be done? The ideal solution is one that takes into account physical differences only when these differences are truly relevant to athletic performance (as they are, for instance, in football and weight-lifting) M. Ann Hall and Dorothy A. Richardson conclude, after a vigorous attack on inequality in sports, that "Integration in sports competition should take place wherever sex is not relevant to per-formance."[11] This criterion makes separation of men's and wom-en's sports the exception rather than the rule. Mary Anne Warren shifts the emphasis slightly in an essay on justice and gender in education. She begins with the insistence that "all students have an equal opportunity to participate in the school's sports program," but she then admits that male-female competition makes sense only when neither sex has "a distinct physical advantage."[12] Obviously, there will always be controversy over which sports should take into ac-count which "truly relevant" physical differences. Such disputes are inevitable. In most official contests, as opposed to recreational situa-tions, a commitment to equality dictates that—as a general rule—men be matched against men, women against women, but there is no reason why exceptional women should not directly challenge the men if they feel they must. And there is no sport acceptable for men from which women should be barred.

2. Masculinization at Last

The physical differences between men and women, "truly relevant" or not, can be altered by drugs. If the name Florence Griffith-Joyner is one of those most likely to be associated with the 1988 Olympics, the name Ben Johnson is another. His use of anabolic steroids, a synthetic form of the male hormone testosterone, enabled him to win the 100 meters in record time. His faith in his doctor's ability to mask his use of steroids and to prevent detection by the IOC's medical experts lost him the gold medal and made him a symbol of dishonest sports. After he was hustled away from Seoul, in disgrace, rumors circulated. Were all the other winners "clean," or were they simply clever enough to have halted their steroid intake in time for their bodies to eliminate the incriminating evidence? No one knows. Scientific research has done to modern sports what it has done, on a larger and more fearful scale, to modern warfare. In both cases, the consequences of research have been immense and unpredictable. The frantic effort to detect and control the results of research are disturbingly similar.

Users of anabolic steroids recover more quickly from exercise than non-users, which enables them to train longer and harder, but they risk side effects that can permanently damage their bodies. Medical experts differ over the degree of damage, but the consensus is that steroids are dangerous. In addition to the risk of organic deterioration and ungovernable aggressiveness, which all users face, women have the further problem of literal masculinization, the inevitable result of the massive ingestion or injection of male hormones. All women produce, quite naturally, some male hormones, just as all men, equally naturally, produce some female hormones. There have always been women whose muscular development made them seem "mannish." But anabolic steroids can masculinize a woman to the point where the *only* visible evidence of her female identity is her absence of male genitals. This, in a much misused word, does seem unnatural.

Beyond these physical and psychological problems, there is the question of fairness. The epidemic of clandestine steroid use threatens to destroy the ideal of fair play (never the most robust creation of modern sports). Steroids allow some athletes to achieve muscular size and strength greater than that obtainable by the most naturally mesomorphic person following the most intense workout program. Because steroid use is banned, it is secret; and because it is secret, no one knows which performance was achieved honestly and which was not. Did Ludmilla Toureschiva, the strikingly muscular gymnast who defeated Olga Korbut in Munich in 1972, win by ethical means or was she propelled chemically to an unfair victory? Did Florence Griffith-Joyner transform her body by dint of hard work or did she do what Ben Johnson did? The moral climate is such that *everyone* is suspect.

While there are not and cannot be exact data about the extent of the problem, there are strong reasons to believe that steroids may have begun to distort athletic results more than twenty years ago. The list of detected users is already a lengthy one.

The first woman to be caught after the institution of steroid tests was the Romanian shot putter Valentina Cioltan; the banned substance was detected at the 1975 European Cup finals. The first Olympian to fall from grace was Poland's Danuta Rosani, a discus thrower. At the 1977 European Finals in Helsinki, East Germany's Ilona Slupianek, a shot putter, was caught and banned for a year. A year and sixteen days later, she won the European championship at Prague, tested positive, and was disqualified for the second time. At the same meet, Elena Stoyanova of Bulgaria, another shot putter, was disqualified. Ditto for Russia's pentathlon winner Nayezhda Tkachenko. The two shot putters were reinstated in time for the Moscow Olympics of 1980, at which Slupianek placed first and Stoyanova sixth. None of the nearly ten thousand athletes in Moscow was disqualified for steroid use, but Stoyanova was caught again at the 1982 European championships. Meanwhile, back at the testing labs, other women were detected. In 1979, these women were caught and disqualified: Yelena Kovalyeva (USSR, discus), Nadya Kudryavtseva (USSR, discus), Totka Petrova (USSR, 1500 meters), Daniela Teneva (Bulgaria, hurdles), Natalia Marasescu (Romania, 1500 meters), Ileana Silai (Romania, 1500 meters), and Sanda Vlad (Romania, long jump). The last five appealed their disqualifications to the Executive Council of the Internation Amateur Athletic Federation, which divided in an 8–8 vote. IAAF President Adriaan Paulen then broke the tie and allowed the athletes to compete in the Moscow Olympics where, as just noted, all winners were certified as drug-free.[13]

As awareness of the deleterious effects of steroid use became obvious, some women began to resist the pressure to improve their times and distances at the cost of the health and self-respect. East

Germany's Renate Vogel swam the 100–meter butterfly in 59.78 seconds on August 28, 1977. A year later, she confessed to steroid use and charged, "We were all guinea pigs." In 1977, Renate Neufeld, a sprinter for the *TSC Berlin,* took the pills she was given by her coach until she noticed that her legs had become more muscular and had begun to ache. Her voice deepened, she grew a light moustache. When she refused to continue the pills, she was dropped from the Olympic team and brusquely threatened with reprisals: "You'll soon be scrubbing factory floors." She fled to West Germany, where her pills were identified as anabolic steroids.[14]

While most of the disqualified women represented the Soviet Union or one of its allies, athletes from Eastern Europe have not been the only ones to test positive for anabolic steroids. Austria's Karoline Kafer, a sprinter, and Greece's Anna Verouli, the European javelin champion, were also caught and punished.[15] Angel Myers, who swam for Furman University, tested positive and was disqualifed at the 1988 Olympic trials.[16] It is simply assumed nowadays, rightly or wrongly, that female body builders and power lifters require steroids to reach the top of their sports. After Florence Griffith-Joyner's triumph at the 1988 Olympic Games, there were allegations, including one from teammate Carl Lewis, that she, too, had resorted to steroids to transform her body and improve her times.[17]

Suspicions of complicity have also touched officials and coaches in the West. Liesel Westermann, Germany's world-record discus thrower, implied in her autobiography that some members of the *Deutscher Leichtathletikverband,* which controls track and field, looked aside when athletes reached for anabolic steroids. Stephanie Storp, Germany's shot put champion, condemned sports officials who set the qualifying norms so high that only steroid-users had a chance to make the Olympic team.[18] The sad tale of Canadian coach Charlie Francis, who gave steroids to Ben Johnson and other athletes entrusted to his care, is unique only in the amount of publicity it received.

In response to the outcry over steroids and other performance-enhancing drugs, detected users have commonly pointed their fingers at other users and argued that "everybody does it." To refrain is to consign oneself to hopeless mediocrity. A more sophisticated (and sophistical) attempt at justification is one that denies individual responsibility and shifts the entire culpability to society. The emphasis on victory and the frenzied quest for records have allegedly produced a system that legitimates every means to the desired end of athletic fame and fortune. Ben Johnson—it is said—had no choice. He was not the culprit but rather the pitiable victim.

While it is true that we are all socialized to value athletic achievements, most of us are also socialized to cherish other values—like honesty and fairness. No one is an absolutely free agent, but most social actors are more than the puppets of circumstance. Undoubtedly, the cards were stacked against Ben Johnson as they were not against athletes from comfortable middle-class homes, but steroids are not the answer to inequalities of opportunity. The denial of individual responsibility annuls the athletes' glory as well as their guilt.

What, then, should be done? The culturally induced "instinctive" response to the epidemic of steroid use is predictable. Scientists must find a way to put the genie back in the bottle. The techniques of detection must be improved. The resolve of the IOC and other sports administrators must be strengthened so that the guilty are banished for life. Whether these conditions will be met is anybody's guess. Until they are, all athletes—male and female—will train and compete under a cloud of suspicion in an atmosphere of mistrust.

3. Sports and Eros

When Athenian youths ran races or hurled the discus, when Spartan girls wrestled one another by the banks of the Eurotas, everyone seems to have understood that physically trained bodies, in motion or at rest, can be sexually attractive. The erotic aspects of sports, welcomed by most of the ancients, have always been obvious to the *critics* of sports, then and now. Tertullian's complaints, uttered in the second century A.D., were echoed in 1934 by Cardinal Rodrigue Villeneuve of Quebec. He condemned the "pagan" cult of the body as manifested in sports and deprecated the rampant concern for "hysterical strength, sensual pleasure, and the development of the human animal." For centuries, however, lovers of sports, spectators as well as athletes, have discussed their passion as if the sensual pleasure in sports had no connection whatsoever with human sexuality. They have denied rather than defended the association of eros and sports. Whenever, for instance, outraged religious traditionalists have called attention to the erotic appeal of the female body at play, ingenuous progressive reformers have blandly explained that sunlight, fresh air, and unencumbered movement were their only motives. No wonder that the interminable debates over sportswear for women left both sides frustrated and unhappy.[19]

When Protestant clergymen invented "muscular Christianity" in the mid-nineteenth century, when Pope Pius XII decided in 1945 to affirm the value of modern sports, there was no sudden acceptance of what had been condemned, no reconsideration of the erotic element in sports. Quite the contrary. Christian propagandists for sports seemed to become blind to the sexual dimensions that had been anathema to their clerical predecessors. Ironically, once the mainstream churches took to celebrations of the joy of sports, a number of secular critics, mostly Marxists, began to deplore the "sexualization" of women's (but not of men's) sports. We seem now to be in the midst of what Margaret Hunt has aptly termed "the de-eroticization of women's liberation."[20]

While some of the more ascetic Marxist critics seem to have resurrected Tertullian's indictments of sports, social scientists of a more empirical bent seem to have entered into a conspiracy to avoid mentioning (in public) the erotic element in sports. Numerous studies have documented the fact that exercise programs result in an "improved body-image." The implications of this fact are seldom explored. European and American psychologists and sociologists have discussed an array of motivations for sports participation, including an aesthetic dimension. They are reluctant to acknowledge (in public) that "fitness" and "to be in shape" are often euphemisms for the desire to be sexually attractive. Yves LePogam edged closer to candor when he referred in a careful sociological study to the quest for "un corps conforme aux canons de beauté," at which point he, too, seemed eager to drop the epistemological hot potato.[21]

Recognition of simple truths known thousands of years ago is blocked because the topic of eros and sports is obviously, for many people, athletes and spectators both, a taboo, a source of shame and denial. To say this is most emphatically *not* to say that all sports have an erotic aspect or that all athletes are sexually atttractive. The heady rediscovery of the erotic component in sports need not impel one to assert, as Christian Messenger does, that the "presentation of female athletes is . . . always eroticized by the fact that . . . any movement of the female body is erotic."[22] The sad truth is that some men and women will, inevitably, deem some male and female athletes, in motion or at rest, unattractive or even repulsive. Nonetheless, to insist that there is *no* connection between eros and sports is nonsense. Happily, the anxious denial of a connection has become less and less plausible.

When Hollywood stripped Johnny Weissmuller of his Olympic swimsuit, wrapped him in a loin-cloth, and filmed him in the role of Tarzan, the dream-merchants knew what they were doing. Katherine Albert, writing in *Photoplay,* marveled that "a lad who had never been in a picture before, who had been interested in nothing but swimming all his life, and who frankly admits he can't act, is the top-notch heart flutterer of the year."[23]

A generation later, Jean-Claude Killy, the French skier, became an international heart-throb. George Best, the Irish soccer star, joined the Beatles and Mick Jagger as a "teenage 'pin-up.'" Joe Namath marketed his sex appeal almost as successfully as he sold his skills as a quarterback for the New York Jets. Speaking about Canadian football players, anthropologist Robert A. Stebbins remarks mildly that they, too, are "attractive to the opposite sex." Thelma McCormack has anatomized Hollywood prizefight films as a form of "jock appeal." For the benefit of readers who have managed to remain oblivious to their own culture, R. M. Lerner has conducted psychological research in order to prove that women find athletic men attractive.[24]

In regard to female athletes too, there is now somewhat less hypocrisy about sports and eros. Australian sportswriter Keith Dunston confesses, "I think I am turned on by Martina."[25] "Men," remarks American pentathlete Jane Frederick, "go cuckoo for me." She is obviously not offended: "As long as I love my body, everyone else does, too."[26] Noticing that sex and sports are both forms of physical expression, runner Lynda Huey was equally forthright: "Physical strength added to the whole sexual experience. How can anyone want anyone but an athlete? . . . Athletes love physical expression and sex is one of the best forms of it."[27] Ordinary women have admitted that a devotion to sports has done more than improve their cardiovascular fitness. "Sports," comments a thirty-seven-year-old softball player, make "me feel more attractive . . . I feel sleeker, more fit, more feminine. And that carries over to my marriage."[28] Women who play in the National Women's Football League say that their game has transformed them into better lovers.[29]

In the eighties, mainstream women's magazines became explicit about sports and eros. In April 1983, for instance, *Cosmopolitan* crowed that body builders are "shaplier, firmer, *sexier!*"[30] For advertisers who pay large sums for the right to display "Flo-Jo" in full stride, the message seems equally obvious. Of course, the advertisers have never hesitated to lure consumers with beautiful bodies, male as well as female. Documentation of this fact is hardly necessary for anyone alive and well in the 1990s. That newspapers and magazines now have a special penchant for sexually attractive female athletes is equally evident.

Almost as obvious is the way that sports promoters have capitalized on men's desire to observe women's movements (as opposed to the Women's Movement). When the movements are intrinsic to the sport, as was the case when Colonel McCoombs dressed the "Golden Cyclones" in shorts and jerseys, feminist sensibilities are alerted; when the clothing worn and the poses struck are no longer related to the sport in question, the ethical alarm goes off. During the frantic attempt to keep the failing Women's Basketball League alive, promoters marketed posters of Molly Bolin in shorts and a tank top. The posters sold; the tickets didn't.[31] In 1981, the Ladies Professional Golf Association hired Ray Volpe to improve the appeal of women's golf with photographs of Laura Baugh and other beautiful golfers. Australia's Jan Stephenson suddenly appeared in *Fairway*—in bed with a seductive display of leg.[32] *Fairway* followed this tasteless act with facsimile scenes from sexy films. It was "a shoddy way to sell golf."[33] More abysmal yet was *Vogue*'s April 1990 issue, in which Steffi Graf posed in "a black Norma Kamali maillot dress, adjusting her high heel and aiming her décolletage lensward."[34] What the perpetrators of these travesties fail to understand is that the erotic appeal of the female athlete is to a large degree sport-specific. Bolin, Baugh, Stephenson, and Graf are unusually attractive because of the way they move and have moved—*as athletes*. The marvel of their athletic performances eroticizes them as a maillot dress cannot. In fact, an athletic body in an evening gown can cause the same kind of cognitive dissonance as obesity in a track suit.

A number of radical feminists, especially those influenced by Marxism, have waged an energetic and often bitter campaign against the commercial exploitation of the attractiveness which, they allege, transforms women into commodities. European and American Neo-Marxists have sounded variations on themes long familiar to churchgoers (and to mosque-goers too). They have, for instance, condemned the attempt of interested parties to take advantage of the female athlete's "erotic exchange value."[35] Their attack goes beyond the assault on sports promoters, media programmers, and advertisers who use women's bodies to sell tickets, boost ratings, and market products. They also deplore the efforts of women who jog, play tennis, or lift weights in order to brighten their image in the eyes of the opposite sex. Quoting poet Adrienne Rich on heterosexuality as "a beachhead of male dominance," Helen Lenskyj maintains that "a woman's conformity to male-defined standards of heterosexual attractiveness signifies her acquiescence to men's rules. "[36]

While admitting that some women have benefited from sports and from the fitness fad, Nancy Theberge still alleges that programs promising enhanced sexual attractiveness represent, "not the liberation of women in sport, but their continued oppression through the sexualization of physical activity."[37] After warning in an article that sports are potentially voyeuristic, Margaret Carlisle Duncan has written a sharply focussed attack on the alleged "soft-core pornography" in media coverage of women's sports. Analyzing 186 photographs from the 1984 and 1988 Olympic Games, she notes the intense media interest in sexually attractive athletes like Katarina Witt and Florence Griffith-Joyner. Such athletes are portrayed in ways that emphasize the sexual difference between men and women. Witt, for instance, is shown with "her lipsticked lips drawn up in an exaggerated pout" while four Romanian gymnasts are photographed from behind as they bend over to congratulate their Chinese rivals—a pose which, according to Duncan, accentuates the gymnasts' small stature and makes them seem submissive and sexually accessible. "This is a potentially dangerous combination because it sexualizes a child image and gives viewers visual power over that image."[38] Reviewing the film *Personal Best* for *Jump Cut* magazine, Linda Williams approved of the portrayal of female athletes who were both "tough and compassionate," but she was irked that the women were presented "as so many trained seals flexing their muscles to male awe and approval."[39] (What Williams does *not* acknowledge is the film's recognition that women, too, can find athletic women sexually attractive.)

Women who allegedly acquiesce in their own humiliation have not escaped castigation by militant feminists. Margaret MacNeill, for instance, has condemned female athletes who collaborate in the repressions of patriarchal capitalism. Specifically, her ire is aroused less by Florence Griffith-Joyner's iridescent fingernails than by television's treatment of female body builders whose sexuality is accentuated by voyeuristic camera angles. "Patriarchy," she charges, "is thus reproduced in a newly negotiated form that attracts women by the range of narcissistic commodities."[40] Small wonder that anger sometimes builds to the point where modern sports per se are rejected as wholly evil.

What one makes of all of this is obviously related not only to one's analytic powers and mastery of the evidence but also to one's philosophical stance and personal values. The total rejection of modern sports in the name of play, often deemed "feminine" rather than "masculine," is a topic I have discussed more than once.[41] The specific charge that sports are an exploitation of female sexuality requires comment.

I can easily imagine that we might all be better off if advertisements were purely objective statements about the availability of a newly designed automobile, the latest vintage of Beaujolais, or a long-awaited scholarly history of women's sports, but I cannot foresee an austerely rational world in which this kind of advertisement replaces the frantic hype that presently dominates the print and electronic media.

If one understands that advertisements are here to stay and that most advertisements will use physically attractive rather than unattractive models, male as well as female, one can deal with what, for me, is the root question for anyone concerned about the relationship between eros and sports. Why have so many radical feminists condemned the men who have admired physically fit women and their sports performances and why have they sought to discourage women eager for that admiration? Might they not, more logically, have demanded women's right to admire—and even to be erotically stimulated by—physically fit men and *their* sports performances? Although thoughtful scholars are properly leery of efforts to legitimize culture by references to nature, there does seem to be some biological justification for mutual attraction between men and women. Recognition of the legitimacy of this phenomenon need not be tantamount to "compulsory heterosexuality" if we are ready also to recognize, as the film *Personal Best* does, that men and women can also be moved, stirred, excited, and sometimes erotically attracted by athletes of their own sex.

Fears of violence committed against women are certainly involved in the condemnation of an erotic response to sports. Eros, it is argued, is nothing but a fancy name for lust. It motivates men to commit rape and other acts of violence against women. Since the erotic component is ineradicable, this line of argument leads logically to the inescapable conclusion that sports ought to be abolished—along with ballet, modern dance, and most other forms of physical expression. But is there any reason to believe that men who find active women attractive, as dancers or as athletes, are therefore more likely to commit violence against them or against any other woman? I doubt that there is. The undeniable fact that adolescent girls and grown women are sexually attracted to male athletes certainly does not impel *them* to seduce the first hapless male who ambles into their field of vision. The argument that eros drives us to acts of violence reduces us all to the status of Pavlovian dogs.

How can one answer the related argument that men who have erotic fantasies about female athletes are not treating these women as *persons?* The best response is that the charge is often true. The focus on the merely physical *is* partial. But modern societies require partial relationships and differentiated roles as well as the I-Thou relationships celebrated by modern piety. Admiration of Placido Domingo's disembodied voice implies no judgment whatsoever about him as a person. Humanistic philosophers urge us to treat people as ends rather than as means, but do such philosophers really want the clerk at the checkout counter and the attendant at the gas pump to take a serious interest in their personal lives? Civilization is built on civility. Intimacy is for intimates.

Some radical feminists have also, as we have seen, charged that sports spectators and sports reporters who concentrate on the appearance of female athletes neglect their performance. There is considerable truth to this accusation (as there is some truth to the related accusation that moviegoers frequently idolize bad actors with good looks). The television camera that skips over the drama of a sports contest in order to linger over "honey shots" trivializes sports. The spectator who admires the performer and ignores the performance might just as well depart from the stadium and scurry to the burlesque theater. We are not, however, trapped in an either-or situation that forces a choice between the athlete and the performance. Motivations are mixed; responses are complex. The athletic body is an inscription of the sports performance. While it may be trite to quote William Butler Yeats on the inextricability of actor from act, no one has said it better than he. How *can* we tell the dancer from the dance?

Why *should* we? One can gasp at Katharina Witt's skill as a figure skater, admire her courage as a competitor, shiver with delight at the beauty of her movements, and simultaneously be stirred by the erotic appeal of her gliding, whirling, spinning, leaping figure. Why not have it all?

Notes

These notes contain only one abbreviation: *IRSS* = *International Review of Sport Sociology*.

Introduction

1. For a particularly egregious example, see Ruth M. Sparhawk et al., *American Women in Sport, 1887–1987* (Metuchen, N.J.: Scarecrow Press, 1989), p. xiii.

2. Lois Bryson, "Sport and the Maintenance of Masculine Hegemony," *Women's Studies International Forum* (1987) 10:4 350.; Birgit Palzkill, "Between Gymshoes and High Heels," *IRSS* (1990) 25(3):221–32.

3. Stokes: quoted in Maria Kloeren, *Sport und Rekord* (Leipzig: Bernhard Tauchnitz, 1935), p. 65.

4. Henning Eichberg, "Körperlichkeit, Identität und Entfremdung," *Sportpädogogik* (1984) 4:11; Nancy Chodorow, *The Reproductiong of Mothering* (Berkeley: University of California Press, 1978); Mary O'Brien, *The Politics of Reproduction* (London: Routledge and Kegan Paul, 1981); Carol Gilligan, *In a Different Voice* (Cambridge: Harvard University Press, 1982).

O N E : From the Egyptians to the Etruscans

1. Helene P. Foley, "Introduction," *Reflections of Women in Antiquity,* ed. Helene P. Foley (New York: Gordon and Breach, 1981), p. xi.

2. Sigrid Paul, "The Wrestling Tradition and Its Social Functions," *Sport in Africa,* ed. William J. Baker and S. A. Mangan (New York: Africana Publishing Co., 1987), p. 24. See also Peter Rummelt, *Sport im Kolonialismus, Kolonialismus im Sport* (Cologne: Pahl-Rugenstein, 1986), pp. 71–72.

3. Paul, "Wrestling Tradition," pp. 30–31.

4. Hans Kamphausen, "Traditionelle Leibesübungen bei autochthonen Völkern," *Geschichte der Leibesübungen,* ed. Horst Ueberhorst, 6 vols. (Berlin: Bartels und Wernitz, 1972–88), 1:86.

5. Carl Diem, *Weltgeschichte des Sports,* 3rd ed., 2 vols. (Frankfurt: Cotta Verlag, 1971), 1:18.

6. Alyce Taylor Cheska, "Ball Games Played by North American Indian Women," *The History, the Evolution and Diffusion of Sports and Games in Different Cultures,* ed. Roland Renson et al. (Brussels: Bestuur voor de Lichamelijke Opvoeding, de Sport en het Openluchtleven, 1976), p. 39; see also Alyce Taylor Cheska, "Ball Game Participation of North American Indian Women," *Her Story in Sport,* ed. Reet Howell (West Point: Leisure Press, 1982), pp. 19–34.

7. Joseph B. Oxendine, *American Indian Sports Heritage* (Champaign, Ill.: Human Kinetics, 1988), pp. 22–26.

8. Barbara S. Lesko, "Women of Egypt and the Ancient Near East," *Becoming Visible,* ed. Renate Bridenthal et al., 2nd ed. (Boston: Houghton Mifflin, 1987), p. 57.

9. B. G. Trigger et al., *Ancient Egypt: A Social History* (Cambridge: Cambridge University Press, 1983), p. 312.

10. For illustrations of acrobatics and dances, see Vera Olivova, *Sport und Spiele im Altertum* (Munich: Copress, 1985), p. 53; A. D. Touny and Steffen Wenig, *Der Sport im alten Aegypten* (Leipzig: Edition Leipzig, 1969), plates 64–65; Wolfgang Decker, *Sport und Spiel im alten Aegypten* (Munich: C. H. Beck, 1987), pp. 144–54.

11. After a survey entitled "Women in Sport in the Ancient World," Reet Howell conceded that her paper was "a summary of . . . physical activities" rather than sports; see *Philosophy, Theology and History of Sport and Physical Activity,* ed. Fernand Landry and William A. R. Orban (Miami: Symposia Specialists, 1978), p. 308.

12. Decker, *Sport und Spiel,* p. 175; Olivova, *Sport und Spiele,* p. 61.

13. Ricardo A. Caminos, *Literary Fragments in the Hieratic Script* (Oxford: Griffith Institute, 1956), p. 10.

14. Decker, *Sport und Spiel,* pp. 99–100.

15. Touny and Wenig, *Der Sport,* p. 32.

16. Decker, *Sport und Spiel,* p. 122.

17. E. Norman Gardiner, *Athletics of the Ancient World* (Oxford: Oxford University Press, 1930), p. 6.

18. Sir Arthur Evans, *The Palace of Minos,* 4 vols. (London: Macmillan, 1921–35), 4:29–31.

19. Olivova, *Sport und Spiele,* p. 73.

20. Evans, *Palace of Minos,* 3: 227.

21. Vermeule: quoted in J.K. Anderson, *Hunting in the Ancient World* (Berkeley: University of California Press, 1985), p. 13.

22. Ibid.

23. Jacquetta Hawkes, *Dawn of the Gods* (New York: Random House, 1968), p. 121.

24. Ibid., pp. 121–4; Hans Peter Duerr, *Sedna* (Frankfurt: Suhrkamp, 1984), pp. 175–84.

25. Jacques Heurgon, *Daily Life of the Etruscans,* trans. James Kirkup (London: Weidenfeld and Nicolson, 1964), p. 77.

26. Ibid., p. 206.

27. Olivova, *Sport und Spiele,* p. 157; the acrobat is pictured on p. 156.

28. Athenaeus, *The Deipnosophists* [12.517d], trans. Charles B. Gulick, 7 vols. (London: Heinemann, 1927–42), 5:329.

29. Jean-Paul Thuillier, *Les Jeux Athlétiques dans la Civilisation Etrusque* (Rome: Ecole française de Rome, 1985), pp. 529, 535.

T W O : Spartan Girls and Other Runners

1. Xenophon: quoted in J.K. Anderson, *Hunting in the Ancient World* (Berkeley: University of California Press, 1985), p. 47.

2. Sir John Beazley, *The Development of Attic Black-Figure* (Berkeley: University of California Press, 1951), p. 32. A convenient account of the legend and its various versions is Reet A. Howell and Maxwell L. Howell, "The Atalanta Legend in Art and Literature," *Journal of Sport History* (Summer 1989) 16(3): 127–39. For an extended discussion of Atalanta as a huntress, see Giampiera Arrigoni, "Atalanta e il Cinghiale Bianco," *Scripta Philologica* (1977) 1:9–43.

3. Mary R. Lefkowitz, *Women in Greek Myth* (Baltimore: Johns Hopkins University Press, 1986), p. 44; *Lexicon Iconographicum Mythologiae Classicae,* ed. Hans Christoph Ackermann and Jean-Robert Gisler (Zurich: Artémis, 1981), lists 94 representations of Atalanta in Greek and Roman art 2(1):940–48.

4. Pericles: quoted in Thucydides, *The Peloponnesian War* [2.45], trans. Benjamin Jowett, *The Greek Historians,* ed. Francis R. B. Godolphin, 2 vols. (New York: Random House, 1942) 1:653.

5. Eva Cantarella, *Pandora's Daughters* (Baltimore: Johns Hopkins University Press, 1987), p. 47.

6. See Ken Dowden, *Death and the Maiden: Girls' Initiation Rites in Greek Mythology* (London: Routledge, 1989) "Despite the impression that mythology can give, we must guard against the idea that Greek girls or women habitually went hunting" (p. 177).

7. William Blake Tyrrell, *Amazons* (Baltimore: Johns Hopkins University Press, 1984), p. 63.

8. Ludwig Deubner, *Kult und Spiel im alten Olympia* (Leipzig: Heinrich Keller, 1936), p. 25. Manfred Lämmer asserts that the games were, at least in the classical period, "merely a traditional cultic ceremony for local girls"; see

"Women and Sport in Ancient Greece," *Women and Sport,* ed. J. Borms, M. Hebbelinck, and A. Venerando (Basel: S. Karger, 1981), p. 19.

9. Nicolaos Yalouris, *The Eternal Olympics* (New Rochelle: Caratzas Brothers, 1979), p. 78.

10. Pausanias, *Description of Greece* 516, 4 vols., trans. W.H.S. Jones (London: William Heinemann, 1918–35), 2: 473.

11. H.A. Harris, *Sport in Greece and Rome* (Ithaca: Cornell University Press, 1972), plates 42, 45.

12. Thomas Scanlon, "The Footrace of the Heraia at Olympia," *Ancient World* (August 1984) 9(3–4):77–90.

13. Erwin Mehl, "Mütterrechtliche Reste in der olympischen Festordnung," *Carl Diem,* ed. Werner Körbs et al. (Frankfurt: 9:3 Wilhelm Limpert, 1962), p. 76.

14. Lilly Kahil, "Mythological Repertoire of Brauron," *Ancient Greek Art and Iconography,* ed. Warren G. Moon (Madison: University of Wisconsin Press, 1983), pp. 237, 239–40, 243; Lilly Kahil, "L'Artémis de Brauron: Rites et Mystère," *Antike Kunst* (1977) 20:94. See also Angelo Brelich, *Paides e Parthenoi* (Rome: Edizioni dell'Ateneo, 1969), pp. 240–79; Erika Simon, *Festivals of Attica* (Madison: University of Wisconsin Press, 1983), pp. 83–88; Dowden, *Death and the Maiden,* pp. 25–32.

15. Giampiera Arrigoni, "Donne e Sport nel Mundo Greco," *Le Donne in Grecia,* ed. Giampiera Arrigoni (Bari: Editori Laterza, 1985), pp. 127–28.

16. Kahil, "L'Artémis de Brauron," p. 97.

17. Paula Perlman, "Plato Laws 833c-834d and the Bears of Brauron," *Greek, Roman and Byzantine Studies* (1983) 24:123; Christiane Sourvinou-Inwood, *Studies in Girls' Transitions* (Athens: Kardamitsu, 1988), pp. 15–105.

18. Pierre Vidal-Naquet, *The Black Hunter,* trans. Andrew Szegedy-Maszak (Baltimore: Johns Hopkins University Press, 1986), p. 146; the huntress is illustrated in Kahil, "L'Artémis de Brauron," p. 92 (fig. 6).

19. Kahil, ibid., p. 91 (fig. 3).

20. Claude Bérard et al., *A City of Images,* trans. Deborah Lyons (Princeton: Princeton University Press, 1989), p. 92. The krater is reproduced in color on p. 94.

21. Claude Calame, *Les Choeurs de jeunes Filles en Grèce archaïque,* 2 vols. (Rome: Edizione dell'Ateneo e Bizarri, 1977), 2:45–133.

22. Arrigoni, "Donne e Sport," p. 83; Scanlan, "The Footrace of the Heraia at Olympia," p. 90; Scanlan, "Virgineum Gymnasium," *The Archaeology of the Olympic Games,* ed. Wendy Raschke (Madison: University of Wisconsin Press, 1988), p. 201.

23. Xenophon, *The Constitution of the Spartans* [1.4], trans. H. G. Daykins, *The Greek Historians,* ed. F. R. B. Godolphin, 2 vols. (New York: Random House, 1942) 2: 658–59.

24. Plutarch, *Lives of Illustrious Men* [Lyc. 14.2–3], trans. John Dryden et al., 3 vols. (Chicago: Bedford, Clarke, n.d.), 1:79–80. In line with modern scholarship, I have substituted *discus* and *javelin* for *quoit* and *dart.*

25. Ibid.; Degas: illustrated in Daniel Catton Rich, *Degas* (New York: Harry N. Abrams, 1966), p. 35.

26. Arrigoni, "Donne e Sport," p. 66.

27. J. K. Anderson, *Ancient Greek Horsemanship* (Berkeley: University of California Press, 1961), pp. 113, 115.

28. Athenaeus, *The Deipnosophists* [iv.139f], trans. Charles B. Gulick, 7 vols. (London: Heinemann, 1927–42) 2:137, 139.

29. Mary R. Lefkowitz and Maureen B. Fant, eds., *Women's Life in Greece and Rome* (Baltimore: Johns Hopkins University Press, 1982), pp. 23–24. For a more detailed discussion, see Luigi Moretti, *Iscrizioni Agonistiche Greche* (Rome: Angelo Signorelli, 1953), pp. 40–44.

30. Paola Angeli Bernardini, "Aspects Ludiques, Rituels et Sportifs de la Course Féminine dans la Grèce Antique," *Proceedings of the XIIth HISPA Congress,* ed. Manfred Lämmer, Roland Renson, and James Riordan (Sankt Augustin, Germany: Academia-Verlag Richarz, 1989), p. 18.

31. Paul Cartledge, "Spartan Wives: Liberation or License?" *Classical Quarterly* (1981) 31:93.

32. Pindar, *Odes,* trans. Sir John Sandys (London: William Heinemann, 1915), pp. 273, 279.

33. Euripides, *Andromache* [595–600], trans. John Frederick Nims, *The Complete Greek Tragedies,* ed. David Grene and Richard Lattimore, 4 vols. (Chicago:University of Chicago Press, 1959), 3:582.

34. Plato, *The Dialogues* [Rep. V.452, 457; Laws, VII.804], trans. Benjamin Jowett, 2 vols. (New York:Random House, 1937) 1:713, 718; 2:560.

35. Scanlon, "The Footrace of the Heraia," p. 83.

36. Aristophanes, *Lysistrata* [79–83], trans. Douglass Parker (Ann Arbor:University of Michigan Press, 1964), p. 13. On Spartan women's "vivid physical presences," see also James Redfield, "The Women of Sparta," *Classical Journal* (1977–78) 73:146–61.

37. See Frederick Griffiths, "Home before Lunch:The Emancipated Women in Theocritus," *Reflections of Women in Antiquity,* pp. 247–73.

38. Arrigoni, "Donne e Sport," pp. 114, 118; Johann Heinrich Krause, *Olympia* (Vienna:Universitätsbuchhandlung, 1838), p. 214.

39. Clarence A. Forbes, *Greek Physical Education* (New York:Century Co., 1929), p. 231.

40. Lefkowitz and Fant, *Women's Life in Greece and Rome,* p. 24; Arrigoni, "Donne e Sport," p. 101.

41. Arrigoni, ibid.; Sarah B. Pomeroy, *Women in Hellenistic Egypt* (New York:Schocken Books, 1984), p. 20. P.J.Parsons, "Callimachus:Victoria Berenices," *Zeitschrift für Papyrologie und Epigraphik* (1977) 25:45.

42. Lefkowitz and Fant, *Women's Life in Greece and Rome,* p. 24; Arrigoni, "Donne e sport," p. 105.

43. Kostas J. Gallis, "The Ganes in Ancient Larisa," *The Archaeology of the Olympic Games,* ed. Wendy Raschke (Madison:University of Wisconsin Press, 1988), p. 225.

44. Lefkowitz and Fant, *Women's Life in Greece and Rome,* pp. 150–51.

45. *The Poems of Theocritus* [Idyll 18. 22–25], trans. Anna Rist (Chapel Hill:University of North Carolina Press, 1978), p. 164.

46. For the original Greek and a discussion, see Moretti, *Iscrizioni,* pp. 165–69. For a translation, see Rachel Sargent Robinson, ed., *Sources for the History of Greek Athletics,* 2d ed. (1927; Chicago: Ares Books, 1955), pp. 163–64. For the debate, see H. A. Harris, *Greek Athletes and Athletics,* pp. 176–81; Hans Langenfeld, "Griechische Athletinnen in der römerischen Kaiserzeit," *The History . . . of Sport and Games in Different Cultures,* ed. Roland Renson et al. (Brussels:Bestuur voor de Lichamelijke Opvoeding, de Sport en het Openluchtlieven, 1976), pp. 116–25; Manfred Lämmer, "Women and Sport in Ancient Greece," *Women and Sport,* ed. J. Borms et al. (Basel:S. Karger, 1981), pp. 16–23; Hugh M. Lee, "Athletics and the Bikini Girls from Piazza Armerina," *Stadion* (1984) 10:45–76; Hugh M. Lee, "Sig 802:Did Women Compete against Men in Greek Athletic Festivals?" *Nikephoros* (1988) 1(1):104;

47. Arrigoni, "Donne e Sport," 110–11.

48. Lee, "Sig 802," p. 104.

49. Athenaeus, *The Deipnosophists* [13.566e], 6:61.

50. Souliardos:quoted in Arrigoni, "Donne e Sport," p. 109.

51. John Malalas, *The Chronicle of John Malalas,* trans. Elizabeth Jeffreys et al. (Melbourne:Australian Association for Byzantine Studies, 1986), p. 153.

52. Arnaldo Momigliano, "Malalas,"*Oxford Classical Dictionary,* 2d ed., ed. N. G. L.Hammond et al. (Oxford:Oxford University Press, 1970), p. 641.

53. Nonnos, *Dionysiaca,* trans. W.H.D. Rouse, 3 vols. (London: Heinemann, 1940), 3:433, 451.

THREE: Matrons and Gladiators

1. Judith P. Hallett, *Fathers and Daughters in Roman Society* (Princeton: Princeton University Press, 1984).

2. Horace, *Satires and Epistles* [II, ii], trans. S. P. Bovie (Chicago: University of Chicago Press, 1959), p. 104.

3. Cicero [Tusc 2.15.36]; see also Peter L. Lindsay, "Attitudes towards Physical Education in the Literature of Ancient Rome," *History of Sport and Physical Exercise Reflected,* ed. Earle F. Zeigler (Champaign, Ill.: Stipes, 1973), pp. 177–86.

4. Jerome Carcopino, *Daily Life in Ancient Rome,* trans. E. O. Lorimer (New Haven: Yale University Press, 1940), pp. 204–5.

5. Elizabeth Lyding Will, "Women in Pompeii," *Archeology* (September/October 1979)32(5):34–43.

6. *The Poems of Propertius* [3.14], trans. John Warden (Indianapolis: Bobbs-Merrill, 1972), pp. 166–67.

7. Suetonius, *Lives of the Caesars* [Dom. 4.1], trans. J. C. Rolfe, 2 vols. (London: William Heinemann, 1929) 2:349.

8. Hugh Lee, "Athletics and the Bikini Girls from Piazza Armerina," *Stadion* (1984) 10:46; Giampiera Arrigoni, "Donne e Sport," p. 119.

9. J. P. V. D. Balsdon, *Roman Women* (New York: Barnes and Noble, 1983), plate 12 and p. 274n.

10. Lee, "Athletics and the Bikini Girls," p. 64.

11. Ibid.

12. Balsdon, *Roman Women,* p. 267.

13. Cited in Siegfried Mendner, *Das Ballspiel im Leben der Völker* (Münster: Verlag Aschendorff, 1956), p. 96.

14. Tacitus, *Annals* [XV.32.3]; see also Georges Ville, *La Gladiature en Occident des Origines à le Mort de Domitien* (Rome: Ecole française de Rome, 1981), pp. 263–64.

15. Dio Cassius, *Roman History* [LXII.2], trans. E. Cary and H. B. Foster, 9 vols. (New York: Macmillan, 1908–1913), 8:141.

16. Suetonius, *Lives of the Caesars* [Dom.4.1], 2:345, 347; Edith Hamilton, *The Roman Way* (New York: Norton, 1932), p. 195.

17. T. T. Duke, "Women and Pygmies in the Roman Arena," *Classical Journal* (1955) 50:223–24.

18. Statius, *The Silvae* [I, 6], trans. D. A. Slater (Oxford: Clarendon Press, 1908), pp. 73–74.

19. Louis Robert, *Les Gladiateurs dans l'Orient Grec,* 2nd ed. (Amsterdam: Hakkert, 1971), p. 188.

20. Martial [lib.spec.6b]: quoted in Carl W. Weber, *Panem et Circenses* (Düsseldorf: Econ Verlag, 1983), p. 56. My translation. See also Eberhard Mähl, *Gymnastik und Athletik im Denken der Römer* (Amsterdam: B. R. Gruener, 1974), pp. 54–55.

21. Juvenal, *The Satires* [1.22, 6.268–82], trans. Rolfe Humphries (Bloomington: Indiana University Press, 1958), pp. 18, 72–73.

22. Petronius, *Satyricon* [XLV.7], trans. William Arrowsmith (Ann Arbor: University of Michigan Press, 1959), p. 43.

FOUR: The Lady Hunts a Stag

1. Suzanne Fonay Wemple, *Women in Frankish Society* (Philadelphia: University of Pennsylvania Press, 1981), p. 189.

2. Jacques LeGoff, *Medieval Civilization,* trans. Julia Barrow (Oxford: Basil Blackwell, 1988), p. 286.

3. Ibid., p. 239. On the unequal distribution of scarce food in early modern times, see Edward Shorter, *A History of Women's Bodies* (New York: Basic Books, 1982), pp. 19–22. I am assuming that medieval peasants behaved in this respect like their 18th- and 19th-century descendents.

4. The least implausible attempt to find a positive view of sports in early Christianity is Alois Koch's *Die Leibesübungen im Urteil der antiken und frühchristlichen Anthropologie* (Schorndorf: Karl Hofmann, 1965).

5. Caroline Walker Bynum, *Holy Feast and Holy Fast* (Berkeley: University of California Press, 1987), p. 200; Margaret Wade Labarge, *A Small Sound of the Trumpet* (Boston: Beacon Press, 1986), p. 122.

6. Jacques de Vitry: quoted in Shulamith Shahar, *The Fourth Estate,* trans. Chaya Galai (London: Methuen, 1983), p. 59; see also Brenda Boilton, "Vitae Matrum," *Medieval Women,* ed. Derek Baker (Oxford: Basil Blackwell, 1978), pp. 253–73.

7. J. J. Jusserand, *Les Sports et les Jeux d'Exercice dans l'ancienne France* (Paris: Plon, 1901), p. 240.

8. Christine Fell et al., *Women in Anglo-Saxon England* (Oxford: Basil Blackwell, 1984), pp. 54–55, 160.

9. Labarge, *A Small Sound of the Trumpet,* p. 227.

10. Teresa McLean, *The English at Play in the Middle Ages* (Shooter's Lodge, Windsor Forest: Kensal Press, 1983), p. 70.

11. Josef Macek, "Das Tournier im mittelalterlichen Böhmen," *Das ritterliche Tournier im Mittelalter,* ed. Josef Fleckenstein (Goettingen: Vandenhoeck und Ruprecht, 1985), p. 387.

12. Martin Hahn, *Die Leibesübungen im mittelalterlichen Volksleben* (Langensalza: Hermann Beyer und Söhne, 1929), pp. 30–31; Andrea Pulega, *Ludi e Spettacoli nel Medioevo: I Tornei di Dame* (Milan: Cisalpino-Goliardica, 1970); Ulrich Mölk, "Philologische Aspekte des Tourniers," *Das ritterliche Tournier,* pp. 170–71.

13. These illustrations are reproduced in Lilian M. C. Randall's *Images in the Margins of Gothic Manuscripts* (Berkeley: University of California Press, 1966), figs. 61, 706, 708–10, 719.

14. Philippe Verdier, "Women in the Marginalia of Gothic Manuscripts and Related Works," *The Role of Woman in the Middle Ages,* ed. Rosemarie T. Morewedge (Albany: State University of New York Press, 1975), pp. 136–38.

15. LeGoff, *Medieval Civilization,* p. 178.

16. J. J. Jusserand, *Les Sports et les Jeux d'Exercice,* p. 282.

17. McLean, *The English at Play,* p. 7.

18. Thomas Elyot, *The Governor* (1531): quoted in Percy M. Young, *A History of British Football* (1968; London: Arrow Books, 1973), p. 48.

19. Christina Hole, *English Sports and Pastimes* (London: B. T. Batsford, 1949), pp. 52–53.

20. William J. Baker, *Sports in the Western World* (Totowa: Rowman and Littlefield, 1982), p. 48.

21. Shahar, *The Fourth Estate,* p. 247.

22. John Marshall Carter, "Sports and Recreations in Thirteenth-Century England," *Journal of Sport History* (Summer 1988) 15(2):169.

23. Shahar, *The Fourth Estate,* p. 152.

24. Joseph Strutt, *The Sports and Pastimes of the People of England,* 3rd ed. (London: Thomas Tegg, 1838), p. 13.

25. Roger Longrigg, *The English Squire and His Sport* (New York: St. Martin's Press, 1977), p. 16.

26. See Randall, *Images,* figs. 714, 716.

27. Jean Longnon, ed., *The Très Riches Heures of Jean, Duke of Berry,* trans. Victoria Benedict (New York: George Braziller, 1969), pl. 9.

28. Don Morrow, "Sport as Metaphor: Shakespeare's Use of Falconry in the Early Plays," *Aethlon* (Spring 1988) 5(2):122.

29. John of Salisbury: quoted in Shahar, *The Fourth Estate,* p. 152.

30. Cited in Léon Gautier, *La Chevalerie,* ed. Jacques Levron (1884: Paris: Arthaud, 1959), p. 170.

31. Theo Reintges, *Ursprung und Wesen des spätmittelalterlichen Schützengilden* (Bonn: Ludwig Röhrscheid, 1963), pp. 298–99.

32. Jean La Floc'hmoan, *La Genèse des Sports* (Paris: Payot, 1962), p. 46; Jean Verdon, *Les Loisirs en France au Moyen Age* (Paris: Jules Tallandier, 1980), pp. 165–66.

FIVE: A Renaissance for Women's Sports?

1. Joan Kelly-Gadol, "Did Women Have a Renaissance?" *Becoming Visible: Women in European History,* ed. Renata Bridenthal et al., 2d ed. (Boston: Houghton Mifflin, 1987), pp. 176, 197.

2. Karl Lennartz, *Kenntnisse und Vorstellungen von Olympia und den Olympischen Spielen in der Zeit von 393–1896* (Schorndorf: Karl Hofmann, 1974), pp. 18–33.

3. Joachim K. Rühl, *Die "Olympischen Spiele" Robert Dovers* (Heidelberg: Carl Winter, 1975).

4. See, for example, the essays by Arnd Krüger and Peter McIntosh in *Die Anfänge des modernen Sports in der Renaissance* (London: Arena Publications, 1984), pp. 19–42, 43–57.

5. J. J. Jusserand, *Les Sports et les Jeux d'Exercice dans l'ancienne France* (Paris: Plon, 1901), p. 329. I have substituted the past tense for Jusserand's present tense.

6. Baldesar Castiglione, *The Book of the Courtier,* trans. Charles S. Singleton (1528; Garden City: Anchor Books, 1959), pp. 6, 99–100.

7. Henning Eichberg, *Leistung, Spannung, Geschwindigkeit* (Stuttgart: Klett-Cotta, 1978), p. 36.

8. Henning Eichberg, "Geometrie als Barocke Verhaltensnorm," *Zeitschrift für historische Forschung* (1977) 4(1):33–34.

9. Silver: quoted in Christina Hole, *English Sports and Pastimes* (London: B. T. Batsford, 1949), p. 68.

10. Eichberg, *Leistung, Spannung, Geschwindigkeit,* p. 66.

11. De' Bardi: quoted in William Heywood, *Palio and Ponte* (1904; New York: Hacker Art Books, 1969), pp. 165–67.

12. Jacques Thibault, *Les Aventures du Corps dans la Pédagogie Française* (Paris: Vrin, 1977), p. 113.

13. For a discussion of the academies, see Franz Begov, "Sportgeschichte der frühen Neuzeit," *Geschichte der Leibesübungen,* ed. Horst Ueberhorst, 6 vols. (Berlin: Bartels and Wernitz, 1972–88), 3: 145–64.

14. Castiglione, *The Courtier,* pp. 209–10.

15. E. B. English, "Women and Sport during the Renaissance," *Women and Sport,* ed. J. Borms et al. (Basel: S. Karger, 1981), pp. 26, 28.

16. See Sidney Anglo, *The Great Tournament Roll of Westminster,* 2 vols. (Oxford: Clarendon Press, 1968).

17. Juliet R. V. Barker, *The Tournament in England, 1100–1400* (Woodbridge, Suffolk: The Boydell Press, 1986), p. 109.

18. Werner Körbs, *Vom Sinn der Leibesübungen zur Zeit der italienischen Renaissance,* ed. Wolfgang Decker (1938; Hildesheim: Weidmann, 1988), p. 23. As evidence, Körbs cites an 1891 publication by Angelo Golerti.

19. Manuel Piernavieja del Poza, "Spanien," *Geschichte der Leibesübungen,* ed. Horst Ueberhorst, 6 vols. (Berlin: Bartels and Wernitz, 1972–88), 5:207.

20. Philippe Ariès and Jean-Claude Margolin, eds., *Les Jeux à la Renaissance* (Paris: Vrin, 1982), plate 7.

21. Berners: quoted in Marcia Vale, *The Gentleman's Recreations* (Cambridge: D. S. Brewer, 1977), p. 27.

22. Rubens and Cranach: illustrated in Annick Davisse, Léo Lorenzi, and Jane Renoux, *Olympie: La Course des Femmes* (Paris: La Courtille, 1980), pp. 10–11, 28–29.

23. Ibid., p. 27.

24. Robert Scott Fittis, *Sports and Pastimes of Scotland* (Paisley: Alexander Gardner, 1891), pp. 54–56; Kathleen E. McCrone, *Playing the Game* (Lexington: University Press of Kentucky, 1988), p. 166.

25. Strutt, *Sports and Pastimes,* p. 51.

26. Illustrated in Vale, *Gentleman's Recreations,* p. 42 (fig. 5).

27. White: quoted in McCrone, *Playing the Game,* p. 3; Dudley: quoted in Elizabeth Burton, *The Elizabeths at Home* (London: Secker and Warburg, 1958), p. 190.

28. Vale, *Gentleman's Recreations,* p. 28.

29. McCrone, *Playing the Game,* p. 3.

30. Charles Chenevix Trench, *A History of Marksmanship* (London: Ferndale, 1980), p. 18.

31. English, "Women and Sport," p. 27.

32. Hermann Goja, *Die Oesterreichischen Schützengilden und Ihre Feste* (Vienna: Verlag Notring der wissenschaftlichen Verbände Oesterreichs, 1963), pp. 11–12.

33. Joseph Casier, *Chef-Confrerie Royale et Chevaliere de St. Michel* (Ghent: Venderporten, 1921), p. 46; Maurits Sacre and Aime de Cort, *Volkspelen en Volksvermaken in Vlaamsch Belgie* (Merchtem: Sacre-De Buyst, 1925), p. 116;

Josee Moulin-Coppens. *De Geschiedenis van het Oude Sint-Jorisguilde Te Gent* (Ghent: Hoste Staelens, 1982), pp. 173–74.

34. Jusserand, *Les Sports et les Jeux d'Exercice,* p. 219.

35. Eugeen Van Autenboer, "De Vrouw in de Gilde" (unpublished paper, 1985), pp. 12, 15.

36. Klaus Zieschang, *Vom Schützenfest zum Turnfest* (Ahrensburg: Czwalina, 1977), pp. 80–81.

37. Anne Braun, *Historische Zielscheiben* (Leipzig: Edition Leipzig, 1981), p. 108.

38. Autenboer, "De Vrouw in de Gilde," pp. 18–19.

39. Erik de Vroede, "Het Spel van Trou-Madame," *Nieuwsbrief van de Vlaamse Volkssport Centrale* (1988) 8(2):20–23.

40. Carlo Ginzburg, *The Cheese and the Worms: The Cosmos of a Sixteenth-Century Miller* (Balimore: Johns Hopkins University Press, 1980); p. 126.

41. F. K. Mathys, *Die Frau im Sport* (Basel: Turn- und Sportmuseum Basel, 1969), p. 19; Dennis Brailsford, *Sport and Society: Elizabeth to Anne* (Toronto: University of Toronto Press, 1969), p. 115; Siegfried Mender, *Das Ballspiel im Leben der Völker* (Münster: Aschendorff, 1956), p. 62; Monika Heffels, *Meister um Dürer* (Ramerding: Berghaus, 1981), fig. 152.

42. Körbs, *Vom Sinn,* pp. 17–18, 29.

43. Brailsford, *Sport and Society,* p. 113; by far the most detailed and authoritative account of the Cotswold Games is Joachim K. Rühl's *Die "Olympischen Spiele" Robert Dovers* (Heidelberg: Carl Winter, 1975).

44. Brailsford, *Sport and Society,* p. 204.

45. Michel de Montaigne, *Complete Works,* trans. Donald M. Frame (Stanford: Stanford University Press, 1957), p. 946.

46. Körbs, *Vom Sinn,* pp. 17–18; Martine Boiteux, "Chasse aux Taureaux et Jeux Romains de la Renaissance," *Les Jeux à la Renaissance,* ed. Ariès and Margolin, p. 39.

47. Robert Davidsohn, *Geschichte von Florenz,* 4 vols. (Berlin: E. S. Mittler und Sohn, 1927): 4: 297.

48. Guido Reni's *Atalanta e Ippomeno* is reproduced in Cesare Garboli, *L'Opera Completa di Guido Reni* (Milan: Rizzoli Editore, 1971), pl. xxxii–xxxiii.

49. Zieschang, *Vom Schützenfest zum Turnfest,* pp. 82–83.

50. F. K. Mathys, *Spiel und Sport im alten Basel* (Basel: Verlag Cratander, 1954), p. 19.

51. Walter Schaufelberger, *Der Wettkampf in der alten Eidgenossenschaft* (Bern: Paul Haupt, 1972), p. 90.

52. Jacques Rossiaud, *Medieval Prostitution,* trans. Lydia G. Cochrane (Oxford: Basil Blackwell, 1988), pp. 68–69.

53. Werner Meyer, *Hirsebrei und Hellbarde* (Olten and Freiburg im Breisgau: Walter Verlag, 1985), pp. 290–91.

54. Körbs, *Vom Sinn,* pp. 26–27.

55. Ibid., pp. 13–15.

56. Fresco: illustrated in Sally Fox, *The Sporting Woman: A Book of Days* (Boston: Little, Brown–Bulfinch, 1989), facing "January 13–18."

SIX: Cricketeers on the Green and Viragos in the Ring

1. Allen Guttmann, *From Ritual to Record: The Nature of Modern Sports* (New York: Columbia University Press, 1978), pp. 15–55; see also Richard Mandell's classic essay, "The Invention of the Sport Record," *Stadion* (1976) 2(2):250–64.

2. Henning Eichberg, *Leistung, Spannung, Geschwindigkeit* (Stuttgart: Klett-Cotta, 1978), p. 42.

3. Guttmann, *From Ritual to Record,* pp. 57–89.

4. Wray Vamplew, *Pay Up and Play the Game* (Cambridge: Cambridge University Press, 1988), pp. 24–25.

5. Ibid., p. 21.

6. Ibid., p. 28.

7. On this, see Robert W. Malcolmson, *Popular Recreations in English Society, 1700–1850* (Cambridge: Cambridge University Press, 1973), pp. 118–57;

8. A notable exception is Roberta J. Park; see "Stephanie-Félicité du Crest, La Comtesse du Genlis (1746–1831), Early Female Proponent of Physical Education," *Research Quarterly* (March 1973) 44(1):34–45; "Concern for the Physical Education of the Female Sex from 1675 to 1800 in France, England, and Spain," *Research Quarterly* (May 1974) 45(2):104–19.

9. Hall: quoted in Gerhard Schneider, *Puritanismus und Leibesübungen* (Schorndorf: Karl Hofmann, 1968), p. 119.

10. Malcolmson, *Popular Recreations,* p. 19.

11. Anonymous ballad: quoted in Shirley Heather M. Reekie, "A History of Sport and Recreation for Women in Great Britain, 1700–1850," (Ph.D. dissertation, Ohio State University, 1982), p. 61.

12. Malcolmson, *Popular Recreations,* p. 77.

13. *Mist's Journal:* quoted in Maria Kloeren, *Sport und Rekord* (Leipzig: Bernhard Tauchnitz, 1935), pp. 264–65.

14. James Pellor Malcolm, *Anecdotes of the Manners and Customs of London During the Eighteenth Century,* 2d ed., 2 vols. (London: Longman, Hurst, Rees and Orme, 1810), 2:183.

15. *Morning Advertiser:* quoted in Reekie, "History of Sport," p. 63.

16. *Maryland Gazette:* quoted in Nancy L. Struna, "'Good Wives' and 'Gardeners,' Spinners and 'Fearless Riders': Middle- and Upper-Rank Women in the Early American Sporting Culture," *From "Fair Sex" to Feminism,* ed. J.A.Mangan and Roberta J. Park (London: Frank Cass, 1987), p. 239. Despite the promising title, there is little on sports in Reet A. Howell's "Recreational

Activities of Women in the Colonial Period," *Arena Review* (May 1980): 4(2) 3–10.

17. Rowlandson: illustrated in Sally Fox, *The Sporting Woman: A Book of Days* (Boston: Little, Brown-Bulfinch, 1989), facing "June 13–18."

18. LeBlanc and Prevost: quoted in Kloeren, *Sport und Rekord*, p. 264.

19. Ibid., p. 240.

20. Antonia Fraser, *The Weaker Vessel* (New York: Knopf, 1984), p. 183; *Spectator* (September 4, 1711): quoted in Reekie, "History of Sport," p. 70.

21. Musselburgh Golf Club: quoted in McCrone, *Playing the Game*, p. 167.

22. Zacharias Conrad von Uffenbach, *London in 1710*, trans. W.H.Quarrell and Margaret Mare (London: Faber and Faber, 1934), pp. 90–91.

23. *London Journal:* quoted in Kloeren, *Sport und Rekord*, pp. 64–66; Noguè: quoted in ibid., p. 61.

24. Saussure, *Mist's Journal,* and Bramston: Kloeren, *Sport und Rekord*, pp. 56–58.

25. *Daily Post:* quoted in Kloreren, ibid., p. 61.

26. William Rufus Chetwood, *A General History of the Stage* (London: W.Owen, 1749), p. 60.

27. William Hickey, *Memoirs,* ed. Alfred Spenser, 4 vols. (London: Hurst and Blackett, 1913–25), 1:82–83.

28. *Times:* quoted in Reekie, "History of Sport," p. 74.

29. Ibid., p. 76.

30. Guy Jaouen, "Gouren: Jeu et Sport de Lutte," *Körperkultur und Identität,* ed. Henning Eichberg and Jørn Hansen (Münster: LIT, 1989), p. 19; Robert M. Isherwood, *Farce and Fantasy* (New York: Oxford University Press, 1986), p. 39.

31. Joseph Strutt, *The Sports and Pastimes of the People of England,* 3rd ed. (London: Thomas Tegg, 1838), p. 97.

32. Anonymous poem: quoted in Robert W. Henderson, *Ball, Bat and Bishop: The Origin of Ball Games* (New York: The Rockport Press, 1947), p. 72.

33. *Reading Mercury:* quoted in Nancy Joy, *Maiden Over* (London: Sporting Handbooks, 1950), p. 14.

34. Rachel Heyhoe Flint and Netta Rheinberg, *Fair Play: The Story of Women's Cricket* (London: Angus and Robertson, 1976), pp. 14–15.

35. Quoted Joy, *Maiden Over,* pp. 15–16.

36. *Times:* quoted Flint and Rheinberg, *Fair Play,* p. 18.

37. *Sporting Magazine:* Quoted ibid., p. 18; Rowlandson: illustrated in Fox, *Sporting Woman,* facing "August 1–6."

38. Flint and Rheinberg: *Fair Play,* p. 18.

39. Reekie, "History of Sport," pp. 122–23.

40. *Morning Post:* quoted in ibid., p. 126.

41. Reekie, "History of Sport," p. 112.

42. E. G. Heath, *Archery* (London: Faber and Faber, 1978), pp. 75, 97.

43. Illustrated in David Coombs, *Sport and the Countryside in English Painting, Watercolours and Prints* (Oxford: Phaidon, 1978), p. 89.

44. Wedgwood: quoted in Bernard Darwin, "Country Life and Sport," *Early Victorian England, 1830–1865,* ed. George M. Young, 2 vols. (London: Oxford University Press, 1934), 1:295.

45. Heath, *Archery,* pp. 78, 97–98.

46. Michael Hörrmann, "Leibesübungen in der höfischen Gesellschaft," *Sportwissenschaft* 19:1 (1989) 46.

47. P.B.Munsche, *Gentlemen and Poachers* (Cambridge: Cambridge University Press, 1981), p. 19.

48. David C. Itzkowitz, *Peculiar Privilege: A Social History of English Fox-hunting, 1753–1885* (Hassocks, Sussex: Harvester Press, 1977), pp. 21–22.

49. Roger Longrigg, *The English Squire and His Sport* (London: Michael Josephs, 1977), p. 136.

50. Illustrated in Coombs, *Sport and the Countryside,* pp. 32–33.

51. *Sporting Magazine:* reprinted in Carl B. Cone, ed., *Hounds in the Morning* (Lexington: University Press of Kentucky, 1981), p. 199.

52. Reekie, "History of Sport," p. 105; Itzkowitz, *Peculiar Privilege,* p. 49.

53. Coombs, *Sport and the Countryside,* p. 56.

54. Ferdinand M. Bayard, *Voyage dans l'Intérieur des Etats-Unis . . . Pendant l'Eté de 1791* (Paris: Chez Cocheris, 1797), pp. 78–79.

55. Longrigg, *English Squire,* pp. 163–64; Caroline Ramsden, *Ladies in Racing* (London: Stanley Paul, 1973), p. 151.

56. Reekie, "History of Sport," p. 105.

SEVEN: The Victorian Age: Debility and Strength

1. Stephanie L. Twin, ed. *Out of the Bleachers* (New York: McGraw-Hill, 1979), p. xviii.

2. Bram Dijkstra, *Idols of Perversity* (New York: Oxford University Press, 1986), p. 28; Henry Nash Smith, *Virgin Land* (Cambridge: Harvard University Press, 1950), p. 116.

3. Swinburne, *Atalanta in Calydon* (London: Edward Moxon, 1860); Landor, "Hippomenes and Atalanta" (1863), *Works,* ed. S. W. Wheeler, 3 vols. (Oxford: Clarendon Press, 1937), 2:135–38; Morris, "Atalanta's Race" (1870), *Atalanta's Race,* ed. Oscar Fay Adams and William J. Rolfe (Boston: Ticknor, 1888), pp. 116–41.

4. Bruce Haley, *The Healthy Body and Victorian Culture* (Cambridge: Harvard University Press, 1978), pp. 181–82.

5. Moses Coit Tyler, *The Brawnville Papers* (Boston: Fields, Osgood, 1869), p. 194.

6. Clarence King, *Mountaineering in the Sierra Nevada* (Boston: Osgood, 1872), pp. 99, 103, 110.

7. John S. and Robin M. Haller, *The Physician and Sexuality in Victorian America* (Urbana: University of Illinois Press, 1974), pp. 26–27, 84. Carol Smith-Rosenberg expresses a similar view in *Disorderly Conduct: Visions of Gender in Victorian America* (New York: Knopf, 1985), p. 208.

8. Helen Lenskyj, "'A Kind of Precipitate Waddle': Early Opposition to Women Running," *Sport and the Sociological Imagination,* ed. Nancy Theberge and Peter Donnelly (Fort Worth: Texas Christian University Press, 1984), p. 157.

9. Barbara Ehrenreich and Deirdre English, *For Her Own Good* (Garden City: Anchor Books, 1978), p. 99.

10. Jennifer A. Hargreaves, "Victorian Familism and the Formative Years of Female Sport," *From "Fair Sex" to Feminism: Sport and the Socialization of Women in the Industrial and Post-Industrial Eras,* ed. A.J.Mangan and Roberta J. Park (London: Frank Cass, 1987), pp. 134–35.

11. Patricia Vertinsky, "Body Shapes: The Role of the Medical Establishment in Informing Female Exercise and Physical Education in Nineteenth-Century North America," *From "Fair Sex" to Femininism:* pp. 258–59. See also Patricia Vertinsky, "Exercise, Physical Capability, and the Eternally Wounded Woman in Late Nineteenth Century North America," *Journal of Sport History* (Spring 1987) 14(1):7–27.

12. Mitchell: quoted in Sheila M. Rothman, *Woman's Proper Place* (New York: Basic Books, 1978), p. 35.

13. Barbara J. Berg, *The Remembered Gate: Origins of American Feminism* (New York: Oxford University Press, 1978), p. 78.

14. Elizabeth Fox-Genovese, *Within the Plantation Household* (Chapel Hill: University of North Carolina Press, 1988), pp, 197; Sharon O'Brien, "Tomboyism and Adolescent Conflict," *Woman's Being, Woman's Place,* ed. Mary Kelley (Boston: G. K. Hall, 1979), pp. 351–72.

15. Deborah Gorham, *The Victorian Girl and the Feminine Ideal* (Bloomington: Indiana University Press, 1982), p. 93.

16. Roberta J. Park, "The Rise and Development of Women's Concern for the 'Physical Education' of American Women," *Her Story in Sport,* ed. Reet Howell (West Point, N.Y.: Leisure Press, 1982), p. 48; Kathleen E. McCrone, *Playing the Game: Sport and the Physical Emancipation of English Women, 1870–1914* (Lexington: The University Press of Kentucky, 1988), p. 15; *American Farmer:* quoted in Jack W. Berryman and Joann Brislin, "The 'Ladies' Department' of the *American Farmer, 1825–1830, Her Story in Sport,* p. 64; Reet Howell, "American Women, 1800–1860: Recreational Pursuits and Exercise," *Her Story in Sport,* pp. 74–75.

17. McCrone, *Playing the Game,* p. 9.

18. Catharine Beecher, *A Treatise on Domestic Economy* (Boston: Marsh, Capen, Lyon, and Webb, 1841), p. 49; Beecher, *Letters to People on Health and*

Happines (New York: Harper and Brothers, 1855), p. 187; see also Linda J. Borish, "The Robust Woman and the Muscular Christian: Catharine Beecher, Thomas Higginson, and their Vision of American Society, Health and Physical Activities," *International Journal of the History of Sport* (September 1987) 4(2):139–54.

19. Sigourney: cited in Roxanne M. Albertson, "School Physical Activities for Antebellum Females," *Her Story in Sport*, p. 372; Child: quoted in Gorham, *Victorian Girl*, p. 71. For a survey of the period's concern for girls' and women's health, see Roberta J. Park, "'Embodied Selves': The Rise and Development of Concern for Physical Education, Active Games and Recreation for American Women, 1776–1865," *Journal of Sport History* (Summer 1978) 5(2): 5–41.

20. Moncure Conway, *Autobiography, Memories and Experiences*, 2 vols. (Boston: Houghton Mifflin, 1904), 1:332. Conway's use of the term "record" was, as his quotation marks indicated, anachronistic.

21. Edmund Neuendorff, *Geschichte der neueren deutschen Leibesübung vom Beginn des 18. Jahrhunderts bis zur Gegenwart*, 4 vols. (Dresden: Wilhelm Limpert Verlag, 1930), 3:29–30; J.W. von Goethe, *Tagebücher*, ed. Sophie von Sachsen, 13 vols. (Weimar: Hermann Böhlaus Nachfolger, 1887–1903), 11: 225; see also F. K. Mathys, *Die Frau im Sport* (Basel: Turn- und Sportmuseum Basel, 1969), p. 27.

22. Neuendorff, *Geschichte*, 3:542, 4:249.

23. Ibid., 3:120, 238, 419; see also Gertrud Pfister and Hans Langenfeld, "Die Leibesübungen des weiblichen Geschlechts," *Weltgeschichte der Leibesübungen*, ed. Horst Ueberhorst, 6 vols. (Berlin: Bartels and Wernitz, 1972–1988), 3: 485–521.

24. Government rules: quoted in Jacques Thibault, *Les Aventures du Corps dans la Pédagogie française* (Paris: Vrin, 1977), p. 227.

25. Luther Gulick, "Athletics Do Not Test Womanliness," *American Physical Education Review* (September 1906) 11:158–59;

26. Charles E. Strickland, "Juliette Low, the Girl Scouts, and the Role of American Women," *Woman's Being, Woman's Place*, p. 259.

27. "Oxford Blue": quoted in McCrone, *Playing the Game*, pp. 264–65.

28. Rothstein: quoted in Auguste Hoffmann, *Frau und Leibesübungen im Wandel der Zeit* (Schorndorf: Karl Hofmann Verlag, 1965), p. 31.

29. Kloss: quoted in Neuendorff, *Geschichte*, 3: 538; and in Gertrud Pfister, *Geschlechtsspezifische Sozialisation und Koedukation im Sport* (Berlin: Bartels and Wernitz, 1983), p. 61.

30. Arabella Kenealy: reprinted in Twin, *Out of the Bleachers*, pp. 44–45, 48.

31. Kenealy: quoted in McCrone, pp. 208–9. June Arianna Kennard, "Women, Sport and Society in Victorian England" (Ed.D. dissertation, University of Nortth Carolina at Greensboro, 1974), p. 131.

32. Dudley A. Sargent, "Are Athletics Making Girls Masculine?" *Ladies Home Journal* (March 1912) 29(11):71–73.

33. Truth: quoted in Eleanor Flexnor, *Century of Struggle: The Woman's Rights Movement in the United States* (Cambridge: Harvard University Press, 1966), pp. 91–92.

34. Sandra L. Myres, *Westering Women and the Frontier Experience, 1800–1915* (Albuquerque: University of New Mexico Press, 1982), p. 132. Most frontier women, however, returned as quickly as possible to conventional gender roles. See Julie Roy Jeffrey, *Frontier Women* (New York: Hill and Wang, 1979). On Oakley and a number of other working-class women who performed in Wild West shows or competed in rodeos, see Mary Lou Lecompte, "Cowgirls at the Crossroads: Women in Professional Rodeo, 1885–1922," *Canadian Journal of History of Sport* (December 1989) 20(2):27–48.

35. For a sketch of Menken's career, see John Dizikes, *Sportsmen and Gamesmen* (Boston: Houghton Mifflin, 1981), pp. 227–34; for Whitman and Menkin, see Harold Aspiz, *Walt Whitman and the Body Beautiful* (Urbana: University of Illinois Press, 1980), p. 217.

36. Donald J. Mrozek, "The 'Amazon' and the Amercian 'Lady': Sexual Fears of Women as Athletes," *From "Fair Sex" to Feminism,* pp. 290–91.

37. Macfadden: quoted in Jan Todd, "Bernarr Macfadden: Reformer of Feminine Form," *Journal of Sport History* 14:1 (Spring 1987): 68–69.

38. Macfadden: quoted in Helen Lenskyj, *Out of Bounds: Women, Sport and Sexuality* (Toronto: Women's Press, 1986), p. 66.

39. Todd, "Bernarr Macfadden," pp. 61–75; Harvey Green, *Fit for America: Health, Fitness, Sport and American Society* (New York: Pantheon Books, 1986), pp. 242–54.

40. Françoise and Serge Laget and Jean-Paul Mazot, *Le Grand Livre du Sport Féminin* (Belleville-sur-Satne: SIGEFA, 1982), pp. 74, 76.

41. Ibid., pp. 120–22.

42. Cham: illustrated in ibid., p. 107; Courturier: illustrated in Charles Rearick, *Pleasures of the Belle Epoque* (New Haven: Yale University Press, 1985), p. 185; Ibels: illustrated in *Art et Sport* (Mons: Musée des Beaux-Arts, 1984), p. 50; Maillol: illustrated in George Waldemar, *Aristide Maillol,* trans. Dina Vierny (Greenwich, Conn.: New York Graphic Society, 1965), p. 132; Croisé: illustrated in Dijkstra, *Idols of Perversity* (New York: Oxford University Press, 1986), p. 287; photograph: reproduced in Georges Vigarello, *Une Histoire culturelle du Sport* (Paris: Robert Laffont, 1988), pp. 180–81. See also James Riordan, "Tsarist Russia and International Sport," *Stadion* (1988) 14(2):226.

43. Reichel and Viterbo: quoted in Laget, et al., *Le Grand Livre,* pp. 110, 112.

44. Dijkstra, *Idols of Perversity,* pp. 286–87.

45. *Lady's Magazine:* quoted in Linda A. Kerber, *Women of the Republic*

(Chapel Hill: University of North Carolina Press, 1980), p. 199; *DeBow's Review:* quoted in Fox-Genovese, *Within the Plantation Household,* p. 285.

46. Christine Stansell, *City of Women* (New York: Knopf, 1986), p. 59; Laget et al. et al, *Le Grand Livre,* p. 110; Karen Kenney, "The Realm of Sports and the Athletic Woman: 1850–1900," *Her Story in Sport,* p. 135.

47. Melvin Adelman, *A Sporting Time* (Urbana: University of Illinois Press, 1986), p. 242; Steven A. Riess, *City Games* (Urbana: University of Illinois Press, 1989), p. 11.

48. Mathys, *Die Frau im Sport,* pp. 33, 35; Liselott Diem, *Frau und Sport* (Freiburg: Herder, 1980), p. 29; Laget et al., *Le Grand Livre,* p. 294.

49. Coombs and *Cycling:* quoted in Andrew Ritchie, *King of the Road* (London: Wildwood House, 1975), pp. 155–56.

50. Laget et al., *Le Grand Livre,* pp. 292–93; James McGurn, *On Your Bicycle* (New York: Facts on File, 1987), pp. 38, 102, 122; Hans Bonde, "Der schnelle Mann," *Körperkulturen und Identität,* pp. 82–83.

51. *Art et Sport* (Mons: Musée des Beaux-Arts, 1984), p. 160.

52. Lamar Middleton, "The French Renaissance in Athletics," *Outing* 44 (May 1904): 189–201. Laget et al., *Le Grand Livre,* p. 25.

53. Laget, et al., p. 26.

54. Stephen Oettermann, *Läufer und Vorläufer* (Frankfurt: Syndikat, 1984), p. 154; Hanns Glöckle, *Geschichte des Sports* (Munich: Südwest Verlag, 1987), p. 113; Gertrud Pfister, "Abenteuer, Wettkampf und Tanz," *Unter allen Umständen,* ed. Christiane Eifert (Berlin: Rotation, 1986), p. 145.

55. Hajo Bernett, *Leichtathletik in historischen Bilddokumenten* (Munich: Copress Verlag, 1986), p. 170.

56. Dale A. Somers, *The Rise of Sport in New Orleans, 1850–1900* (Baton Rouge: Louisiana State University Press, 1972), p. 119; Harold Seymour, *Baseball: The People's Game* (New York: Oxford University Press, 1990), pp. 454–56.

57. Advertisement and *London Illustrated News:* quoted in McCrone, *Playing the Game,* pp. 145–46.

58. Rachel H. Flint and Netta Rheinberg, *The Story of Women's Cricket* (London: Angus and Robertson, 1976), pp. 25–27.

59. Macfadden: quoted in James C. Whorton, *Crusaders for Fitness: The History of American Health Reformers* (Princeton: Princeton University Press, 1982), pp. 298, 302.

60. Mrozek, "The 'Amazon' and the American 'Lady,' " pp. 282–88.

EIGHT: The Victorian Age: From Swedish Drill
to Field Hockey

1. Beale: quoted in Josephine Kamm, *How Different from Us* (London: Bodley Head, 1958), pp. 222–23.

2. Kathleen E. McCrone, "Play Up! Play Up! And Play the Game! Sport at the Late Victorian Girls' Public School," *Journal of British Studies* (1984) 23:120.

3. Kamm, *How Different from Us*, pp. 220–21.

4. W. David Smith, *Stretching their Bodies* (Newton Abbot: David and Charles, 1974), p. 26. Dove: quoted in McCrone, "Play Up!," p. 123.

5. Roedean School: quoted in ibid., p. 124.

6. Ibid., pp. 126–27.

7. Lawrence: quoted in Sheila Fletcher, *Women First: The Female Tradition in English Physical Education, 1880–1980* (London: Athlone Press, 1984), p. 33.

8. McCrone, *Playing the Game*, pp. 137–41; Jihang Park, "Sport, Dress Reform and the Emancipation of Women in Victorian England," *International Journal of the History of Sport* (May 1989) 6(1):25.

9. John A. Daley, "A New Britannia in the Antipodes: Sport, Class and Community in Colonial South Australia," *Pleasure, Profit, Proselytism*, ed. J. A. Mangan (London: Frank Cass, 1988), p. 166; Ray Crawford, "Moral and Manly: Girls and Games in Early Twentieth-Century Melbourne," *From "Fair Sex" to Feminism*, ed. J. A. Mangan and Roberta J. Park (London: Frank Cass, 1987), pp. 207–8.

10. Davies: quoted in Jihang Park, "Sport, Dress Reform and the Emancipation of Women," p. 23.

11. Kathleen E. McCrone, "The 'Lady Blue': Sport at the Oxbridge Women's Colleges from their Foundation to 1914," *British Journal of Sport History* 3:2 (September 1986): 191–215.

12. Gail Cunningham, Christopher Dodd, "Rowing," *Sport in Britain*, ed. Tony Mason (Cambridge: Cambridge University Press, 1989), p. 298; *The New Woman and the Victorian Novel* (New York: Barnes and Noble, 1978), p. 78.

13. Leena Laine, "The Role of Sport in Replacing the Patriarchal Society by a modern Democracy," *Civilization in Sport History* (Kobe: Department of Physical Education-Kobe University, 1987), p. 184; on Ling and his influence, see Peter C. McIntosh, "Therapeutic Exercise in Scandinvaia," *Landmarks in the History of Physical Education*, ed. Peter C. McIntosh (London: Routledge and Kegan Paul, 1981), pp. 85–111.

14. Bergman-Osterberg: quoted in Fletcher, *Women First*, p. 28.

15. McCrone, *Playing the Game*, p. 113.

16. Taunt and song both quoted in McCrone, ibid., pp. 100, 115.

17. Dioclesian Lewis, "The Health of American Women," *North American Review* (December 1882) 135: 503–10; see also Doris M. Fletcher, "The Pioneer of Genteel Gymnastics for Ladies," *Sports Illustrated* (February 15, 1965) 22:E5–E7.

18. Betty Spears, *Leading the Way: Amy Morris Homans and the Beginnings of Professional Education for Women* (Westport, Conn.: Greenwood Press, 1986).

19. Cindy L. Himes, "The Female Athlete in American Society: 1860–1940" (Ph.D. dissertation, University of Pennsylvania, 1986), p. 87.

20. Roberta J. Park, "History and Structure of the Department of Physical Education at the University of California . . . ," Her Story in Sport, ed. Reet Howell (West Point: Leisure Press, 1982), pp. 405–15.

21. Lynn A. Gordon, "Co-Education on Two Campuses: Berkeley and Chicago, 1890–1912," Woman's Being, Woman's Place, p. 175.

22. Vassar Catalogue: quoted in Margery A. Bulger, "American Sportswomen in the 19th Century," Journal of Popular Culture (1981) 16(2): 11.

23. Alice Katharine Fallows, "Athletics for College Girls," Century (May 1903) 66(1): 61; 28. Françoise and Serge Laget et al. and Jean-Paul Mazot, Le Grand Livre du Sport Féminin (Belleville-sur-Saône: SIGEFA, 1982), p. 25; Harold Seymour, Baseball: The People's Game (New York: Oxford University Press, 1990), pp. 447, 464. For an illustration of women wearing men's letters, see Sally Fox, The Sporting Woman (Boston: Little, Brown, 1989), facing "March 25–31."

24. Gibson: illustrated in Pictures of People by Charles Dana Gibson (New York: J.H. Russell and Son, 1896); Sophia Foster Richardson, "Tendencies in Athletics for Women in Colleges and Universities," Popular Science Monthly (February 1897) 50:519; Harriet Isabel Ballantine, "Out-of-Door Sports for College Women," American Physical Education Review (March 1898) 3:42; Harriet Isabel Ballantine, "The Value of Athletics to College Girls," American Physical Education Review (June 1901) 6(2):151–53. See also Joanna Davenport, "The Eastern Legacy: The Early History of Physical Education for Women," Her Story in Sport, pp. 355–68; Dorothy Ainsworth, "History of Physical Education in Colleges for Women," History of Physical Education and Sport in the United States and Canada, ed. Earle F. Zeigler (Champaign, Ill.: Stipes, 1975), pp. 167–80.

25. Warner and Jewell: quoted in Himes, "Female Athlete," p. 78.

26. Smith Catalogue and Hill: quoted in Catherine E. D'Urso, "A View of American Attitudes toward Femininity: The History of Physical Education for Women and Collegiate Women's Basketball" (unpublished essay, Amherst College, 1989), pp. 33, 51; Stephen and Seelye: quoted in Seymour Baseball, pp. 448–49; See also Gai I. Berlage, "Baseball at the Eastern Women's Colleges during the Victorian Period" (unpublished essay, 1990); Ronald A. Smith, "The Rise of Basketball for Women in Colleges," Canadian Journal of History of Sport (December 1970) 1(2):18–36; Dorothy S. Ainsworth, "History of Physical Education in Colleges for Women," A History of Physical Education and Sport in the United States and Canada, ed. Earle F. Zeigler (Champaign, Ill.: Stipes, 1975), pp. 167–80.

27. D'Urso, "A View of American Attitudes," pp. 47–48, 51.

28. Lynne Emery, "The First Intercollegiate Contest for Women: Basketball, April 4, 1896," Her Story in Sport, pp. 417–23; Paula D. Welch and Harold A. Lerch, History of American Physical Education and Sport (Springfield,

Illinois: Charles C. Thomas, 1981), pp. 234–37; Martha Banta, *Imaging American Women* (New York: Columbia University Press, 1987), p. 90.

29. Goodloe: quoted in Himes, "Female Athlete," p. 92; Jeannette A. Marks, "Outdoor Life at Wellesley College," *Outing* (January 1898) 32:117–24; Catalogue and Yearbook: quoted in Martha H. Verbrugge, *Able-Bodied Womanhood* (New York: Oxford University Press, 1988), pp. 140, 160.

30. Thomas: quoted in Helen Lefkowitz Horowitz, *Alma Mater: Design and Experience in the Women's Colleges from their Nineteenth-Century Beginnings to the 1930s* (New York: Knopf, 1984), pp. 115, 159.

31. Paul Atkinson, "The Feminist Physique: Physical Education and the Medicalization of Women's Education," *From "Fair Sex" to Feminism*, pp. 42–45; Ayres: quoted in Karen Kenney, "The Realm of Sports and the Athletic Woman: 1850–1900," *Her Story in Sport*, p. 109; Berenson and Hill: quoted in D'Urso, "A View," pp. 28, 30.

32. See, for instance, Peter Rummelt, *Sport im Kolonialismus, Kolonialismus im Sport* (Cologne: Pahl-Rugenstein, 1986); André Odendaal, "South Africa's Black Victorians," *Pleasure, Profit, Proselytism*, p. 198; Shinsuke Tanada, "Introduction of European Sport in Kobe," *Civilization in Sport History*, pp. 68–76; Eduardo Oliveros, *Origenes de los Deportes Britanicos en el Rió de la Plata* (Buenos Aires: L. J. Rosso, 1932). Göckle, *Geschichte des Sports*, pp. 54, 78.

33. John A. Daley, *Elysian Fields: Sports, Class and Community in Colonial South Australia* (Adelaide: J. A. Daley, 1982), pp. 82–83.

34. Scott A. G. M. Crawford, "An Emancipation of Sorts," *Canadian Journal of History of Sport* (May 1985) 16(1):46.

35. Eagan and *Young Lady's Book*: quoted in McCrone, *Playing the Game*, pp. 154–55.

36. M. A. Speak, "Social Stratification and Participation in Sport in Mid-Victorian England . . .," *Pleasure, Profit, Proselytism*, p. 47.

37. On Victoria, see Mathys, *Die Frau im Sport*, pp. 8, 41.

38. Reid: quoted in David Park Curry, *Winslow Homer: The Croquet Game* (New Haven: Yale University Art Gallery, 1984), n.p. For the music, see Sally Fox, *The Sporting Woman: A Book of Days* (Boston: Little, Brown-Bulfinch, 1989), facing "September 13–18."

39. Tissot: illustrated in Curry, *Winslow Homer*, fig. 36.

40. "The Immorality of Cricket," *Living Age* (October 15, 1898) 219:200.

41. Curry, *Winslow Homer*.

42. Walters: quoted in Raymond Carr, *English Fox Hunting* (London: Weidenfeld and Nicolson, 1977), p. 174.

43. Mathys, *Die Frau im Sport*, p. 27; Laget et al. et al, *Le Grand Livre*, pp. 88, 90.

44. McCrone, *Playing the Game*, pp. 157–66.

45. Ibid., pp. 166–77; N.L. Tranter, "Organized Sport and the Middle-

Class Woman in 19th-Century Scotland," *International Journal of History of Sport* (May 1989) 6(1):37, 42; Murray G. Phillips, "Golf and Victorian Sporting Values," *Sporting Traditions* (May 1990) 6(2):128–29.

46. *Punch* and *Birmingham Mail:* quoted in McCrone, *Playing the Game,* pp. 143–44, 148.

47. *Cricket:* quoted in ibid., p. 147–48.

48. Ibid., pp. 133–37.

49. Glöckle, *Geschichte des Sports,* p. 92.

50. Henry W. Slocum, Jr., "Lawn Tennis as a Game for Women," *Outing* (July 1889) 14:289–300; Ellen W. Gerber, "A Chronicle of Participation," *The American Woman in Sport,* ed. Ellen W. Gerber (Reading, Mass.: Addison-Wesley, 1974), pp. 27–28; see also Eleanor Waddle, "The Berkeley Ladies' Athletic Club," *Outing* (October 1889) 15:57–63.

51. Charlotte Perkins Gilman, *The Living of Charlotte Perkins Gilman* (New York: D. Appleton-Century, 1935), pp. 64, 67; see also Patricia Vertinsky, "Feminist Charlotte Perkins Gilman's Pursuit of Health and Physical Fitness as a Strategy for Emancipation," *Journal of Sport History* 16:1 (Spring 1989) 5–26.

52. All five of Homer's paintings are reproduced in color in Curry, *Winslow Homer.*

53. Fox, *Sporting Woman,* facing "March 7–12."

54. W.C. Brownell, "Newport," *Scribner's* (August 1894) 16:146.

55. Gilman: quoted in Lois Banner, *American Beauty* (Chicago: University of Chicago Press, 1983), p. 156. Gibson's inspired creation is discussed, along with a multitude of other images, in Martha Banta, *Imaging American Women* (New York: Columbia University Press, 1987).

56. Edith Wharton, *A Backward Glance* (New York: D. Appleton-Century, 1934), p. 46.

57. Edith Wharton, *The Age of Innocence* (1920; New York: Scribner's, 1968), pp. 66, 141–42, 210–11. May's seductively erotic rival, Ellen Olenska, is athletic enough to challenge Newland to an impromptu footrace; see p. 132.

58. Elizabeth Cynthia Barney, "The American Sportswoman," *Fortnightly Review* (August 1894) 52:263–67; see also Donald J. Mrozek, *Sport and American Mentality, 1880–1910* (Knoxville: University of Tennessee Press, 1983), p. 116.

59. Joanna Davenport, "Eleonora Randolph Sears, Pioneer in Women's Sports," *Her Story in Sport,* pp. 266–72; Himes, "Female Athlete," p. 16.

60. Gourlay: quoted in Gerald Redmond, *The Sporting Scots of Nineteenth Century Canada* (Rutherford: Farleigh Dickinson University Press, 1982), p. 234.

61. Margaret Bisland, "Rowing as a Recreation for Women," *Outing* (September 1889) 14:423; Bisland, "Bowling for Women," *Outing* (April 1890) 16:36.

62. Christine Terhune Herrick, "Women in Athletics: The Athletic Girl Not Unfeminine," *Outing* (September 1902) 40:719;

63. Frederick Cozens and Florence Scovil Stumpf, *Sports in American Life* (Chicago: University of Chicago Press, 1953), p. 140.

64. Gerald Redmond, *The Caledonian Games in the Nineteenth Century America*, (Rutherford: Fairleigh Dickinson University Press, 1971), p. 48.

65. Robert Dunn, "The Country Club," *Outing* (November 1905) 47:160–73; H.C.Chatfield-Taylor, "Country Club Life in Chicago," *Harper's Weekly* (August 1, 1896) 40:762; see also John A. Lucas and Ronald A. Smith, *Saga of American Sport* (Philadelphia: Lea and Febiger, 1978), pp. 158–62.

66. Richard Holt, *Sport and Society in Modern France* (London: Macmillan, 1981), p. 38.

67. Monique de Saint Martin, "La Noblesse et les 'Sports Nobles,' " *Actes de la Recherche en Sciences Sociales* (November 1989) 80:25.

68. Laget, et al. *Le Grand Livre*, p. 164. Falguière: quoted in Jeanne L. Wasserman in the exhibition brochure for "Diana in Late Nineteenth-Century Sculpture" (Wellesley College, 1989). For the fencers' aristocratic milieu, see Frederick A. Schwab, "Fencing in France," *Outing* (April 1905) 46(1):105–10.

69. Glöckle, *Geschichte*, pp. 78–79.

70. J. Parmley Paret, "Lawn Tennis on the European Continent," *Outing* (August 1899) 34:470–71.

71. Roland Binz, *"Borussia ist stärker"* (Frankfurt: Peter Lang, 1988), pp. 100–101.

72. Illustrated in color in Laget et al., *Le Grand Livre*, p. 166.

73. Mathys, *Die Frau im Sport*, p. 45.

74. Henning Eichberg, "Sport im 19. Jahrhundert: Genese einer industriellen Verhaltensreform," *Geschichte der Leibesübungen*, ed. Horst Ueberhorst, 6 vols. (Berlin: Bartels and Wernitz, 1972–88) 3: 353; Hans Bonde, "Der schnelle Mann," pp. 82–83.

75. Gertrud Pfister, "Abenteuer, Wettkampf und Tanz," *Unter allen Umständen*, ed. Christiane Eifert and Susanne Rouette (Berlin: Rotation, 1986), pp. 141–47; Glöckle, *Geschichte des Sports*, pp. 54, 78; Gerd von der Lippe, "Frauensport in Norwegen," *Frauensport in Europa*, ed. Christine Peyton and Gertrud Pfister (Ahrensburg: Ingrid Czwalina, 1989), p. 147.

76. Illustrated in Laget et al., *Le Grand Livre*, p. 165.

77. Hans-Georg John, "Das Schwimmfest in der frühzeit des Verbandssports," *Proceedings of the XIIth HISPA Congress*, ed. Manfred Lämmer, Roland Renson, and James Riordan (Sankt Augustin, Germany: Academia Verlag-Richarz, 1989), p. 174.

78. Laget et al., *Le Grand Livre*, pp. 291–94; Richard Holt, "The Bicycle, the Bourgeoisie and the Discovery of Rural France, 1880–1914," *British Journal of Sports History (September 1985)* 2(2):127–39; for Henri de Toulouse-Lautrec, see *Art et Sport* (Mons: Musée des Beaux-Arts, 1984), p. 281.

79. Mathys, _Die Frau im Sport,_ p. 4.

80. Ibid., pp. 49, 53; Glöckle, _Geschichte des Sports,_ pp. 160–62.

81. Sully-Prudhomme and Zola: quoted in Saint Martin, "Les Nobles et les 'Sports Nobles,' " p. 28 n. 31.

82. Jennifer A. Hargreaves, "Playing Like Gentlemen While Behaving Like Ladies," _British Journal of Sports History (May 1985)_ 2(1):43.

83. _Womanhood:_ quoted in: Catriona M. Parratt, "Athletic 'Womanhood': Exploring Sources for Female Sport in Victorian and Edwardian England," _Journal of Sport History (Summer 1989)_ 16(3):153.

84. Fallows, "Athletics for College Girls," p. 61.

85. Helen King, "The Sexual Politics of Sport: An Australian Perspective," _Sport in History,_ ed. Richard Cashman and Michael McKernan (St. Lucia, Queensland: University of Queensland press, 1979), p. 72; Patricia Vertinsky, "God, Science and the Market Place," _Canadian Journal of History of Sport_ (May 1986) 17(1):39.

86. McCrone, _Playing the Game,_ p. 289.

87. Barbara Miller Solomon, _In the Company of Educated Women_ (New Haven: Yale University Press, 1985), p. 104.

88. Anne O'Hagen, "The Athletic Girl," _Munsey's Magazine_ (August 1901) 25:730. It should, however, be noted that sports participation has never been a guarantee that a woman will have generally "liberal" views; see, for example, Eldon E. Snyder and Joseph E. Kivlin, "Perceptions of the Sex Role among Female Athletes and Nonathletes," _Adolescence_ (Spring 1977) 12:23–29.

NINE: Play Days and Muscle Molls

1. Barbara J. Harris, _Beyond Her Sphere: Women and the Professions in American History_ (Westport: Greenwood Press, 1978), pp. 140–41.

2. Catherine E. D'Urso, "A View of American Attitudes toward Femininity" (unpublished essay, Amherst College, 1989), p. 55.

3. For a brief summary, see Laura Robicheaux, "An Analysis of Attitudes towards Women's Athletics in the United States in the Early 20th Century," _Canadian Journal of History of Sport_ (May 1975) 6(1):12–22.

4. _New York Herald,_ April 9, 1922.

5. Judy Jensen, "Women's Collegiate Athletics," _Arena Review_ (May 1979) 3(2):15;

6. D'Urso, "Attitudes toward Femininity," p. 59.

7. Stewart: quoted in Joan S. Hult, "American Sportswomen: 'Go for the Gold' — 1912–1936," _Olympic Scientific Congress 1984 Official Report Sport History,_ ed. Norbert Muller and Joachim Ruhl (Niedernhausen: Schors Verlag, 1985), pp. 34–35.

8. Paula Welch, "American Women: Their Debut in International Track

and Field," *Her Story in Sport,* ed. Reet Howell (West Point: Leisure Press, 1982), pp. 572–78.

9. Richard Korsgaard, "A History of the Amateur Athletic Union of the United States" (Ph.D. dissertation, Columbia-Teachers College, 1952), pp. 285–86.

10. "Athletics for the Girls and Women of America," *Playground* (May 1923) 17:116.

11. Ibid., pp. 116–17.

12. Donald J. Mrozek, *Sport and American Mentality, 1880–1920* (Knoxville: University of Tennessee Press, 1983), p. 156.

13. Mabel Lee, "The Case For and Against Intercollegiate Athletics for Women and the Situation as It Stands Today," *American Physical Education Review* (January 1924) 29(1):14.

14. Ethel Perrin, "Athletics for Women and Girls," *Playground* (March 1924) 17:658.

15. Mabel Lee, "Sports and Games: An Educational Dynamic Force," *Recreation* (July 1929) 23:223.

16. Alice A. Sefton, *The Women's Division National Amateur Athletic Federation* (Palo Alto, Cal.: Stanford University Press, 1941), pp. 8, 82–84.

17. Frederick Rogers, "Olympics for Girls?" *School and Society* 30 (August 10, 1929): 193–94.

18. Laird: quoted in John A. Lucas and Ronald A. Smith, *Saga of American Sport* (Philadelphia: Lea and Febiger, 1978), p. 364.

19. Lee, "The Case For and Against," pp. 16–19.

20. Mabel Lee, "The Case For and Against Intercollegiate Athletics for Women and the Situation Since 1923," *Research Quarterly* (May 1931) 2(2):109.

21. Cindy L. Himes, "The Female Athlete in American Society, 1860–1940" (Ph.D. dissertation, University of Pennsylvania, 1986), p. 188.

22. Lee, "The Case for and Against," pp. 118–19; Helen N. Smith, "Evils of Sport for Women," *Journal of Health, Physical Education, and Recreation* (January 1931) 2:50.

23. Agnes Wayman: quoted in Ellen W. Gerber, "The Controlled Development of Collegiate Sport for Women," *Journal of Sport History* (Spring 1975) 2(1):20; Wayman was for competition, "the very soul of athletics," but against "the highly intense specialized competition" of intercollegiate athletics; see "Competition," *American Physical Education Review* (October 1929) 34(8):469–71.

24. Arthur Ashe, *A Hard Road to Glory,* 3 vols. (New York: Warner Books, 1988), 2:76–78.

25. Otto Mayer, *A Travers les Anneaux Olympiques* (Geneva: P. Cailler, 1960), pp. 163–64.

26. Palmer: quoted in Harold Seymour, *Baseball: The People's Game* (New York: Oxford University Press, 1990), p. 527; M. Gladys Scott, "Competi-

tion for Women in American Colleges and Universities," *Research Quarterly* (March 1945) 16(1):57.

27. Gerber, "Chronicle of Participation," p. 74.

28. On dance halls and other forms of working-class women's amusements, see Kathy Peiss, *Cheap Amusements* (Philadelphia: Temple University Press, 1986).

29. Steven A. Riess, *City Games* (Urbana: University of Illinois Press, 1989), pp. 78, 158, 168; Ashe, *Hard Road to Glory*, 2: 45, 62, 431–32.

30. Riess, *City Games*, p. 86; Glenn: quoted in Seymour, *Baseball*, p. 497.

31. Himes, "The Female Athlete," p. 196; Ellen W. Gerber, "A Chronicle of Participation," *The American Woman in Sport*, ed. Ellen W. Gerber (Lexington: Addison-Wesley, 1974), pp. 39–42.

32. Mildred Didrikson Zaharias, *This Life I've Led*, (New York: A. S. Barnes, 1955), p. 27.

33. William Oscar Johnson and Nancy P. Williamson, *"Whatta-Gal"* (Boston: Little, Brown, 1977), p. 51.

34. Bill Cunningham, "The Colonel's Ladies," *Collier's* (May 23, 1936) 97:28, 60–62.

35. Joan Hult, "American Sportswomen: 'Go for the Gold'—1912–1936," *Olympic Scientific Congress 1984 Official Report Sport History*, ed. Norbert Muller and Joachim K. Rühl (Niederhausen: Schors Verlag, 1985), pp. 36–37.

36. Adrianne Blue, *Faster, Higher, Further* (London: Virago Press, 1988), p.27; Beth Allyson Posnack, "American Women in Sport: A Comparison of Media Reception and Participant Attitudes in the 1932 and 1984 Los Angeles Olympic Games" (unpublished essay, Amherst College, 1985), p. 95.

37. Holm: quoted in Posnack, "American Women in Sport," p. 110.

38. Paul Gallico, *Farewell to Sport* (New York: Knopf, 1938), p. 239.

39. Johnson and Williamson, *"Whatta-Gal,"* p. 85.

40. Ibid., p. 157.

41. Uriel Simri, *A Concise World History of Women's Sports* (Netanya: Wingate Institute, 1983), p. 38.

42. Himes, "The Female Athlete," pp. 226, 228.

43. *Literary Digest:* quoted in ibid.

44. Ederle: quoted in *New York Times*, August 28, 1926.

45. Benjamin Rader, *American Sports* (Englewood Cliffs, N.J.: Prentice-Hall, 1983), p. 237.

46. Himes, "The Female Athlete," p. 233.

47. Gallico, *Farewell to Sport*, p. 236.

48. Gertrud Pfister, "Daughters of the Air," *Civilization in Sport History*, ed. Shigeo Shimizu (Kobe: Department of Education-Kobe University, 1987), pp. 270–91; Gertrud Pfister, "Ikarus' Tochter: Marga von Etzdorf und andere Pilotinnen," *Sozial- und Zeitgeschichte des Sports* (1988) 2(3):86–105.

49. Jerry Seibert, "A Flight to Oblivion," *Yesterday in Sport*, ed. Charles Osborne (New York: TIME-LIFE Books, 1968), p. 155.

50. Judy Lomax, *Women of the Air* (New York: Dodd, Mead, 1987), pp. 68–83; Katherine A. Brick, "Earhart, Amelia Mary," *Notable American Women,* ed. Edward T. James, 3 vols. (Cambridge: Harvard University Press, 1971), 1: 538–41.

51. Earhart: quoted in George Palmer Putnam, *Soaring Wings* (New York: Harcourt, Brace, 1939), p. 76; Lomax, *Women of the Air*, p. 75.

52. Lomax, *Women of the Air*, p. 77.

53. Nancy Cott, *The Grounding of Modern Feminism* (New Haven: Yale University Press, 1987), p. 79.

54. Earhart: quoted in Putnam, *Soaring Wings*, p. 291.

55. Lomax, *Women of the Air*, p. 82.

56. Phillips: quoted in Putnam, *Soaring Wings*, p. 292.

57. Larry Engelmann, *The Goddess and the American Girl* (New York: Oxford University Press, 1988), p. 71.

58. Ibid., p. 77.

59. Ibid., p. 176.

60. Ibid., pp. 299–302.

61. Virginia Wade and Jean Rafferty , *Ladies of the Court* (London: Pavilion, 1984), p. 60.

TEN: The Europeans Take the Lead

1. German clerics: quoted in Liselott Diem, *Frau und Sport* (Freiburg: Herder, 1980), pp. 103–6; see also Edmund Neuendorff, *Geschichte der neueren deutschen Leibesübung vom Beginn des 18. Jahrhunderts bis zur Gegenwart,* 4 vols. (Dresden: Wilhelm Limpert Verlag, 1930), 4:652.

2. Gertrud Pfister, ed., *Frau und Sport* (Frankfurt: Fischer, 1980), pp. 35–36.

3. Eduard Spranger, "Die Persönlichkeit des Turnlehrers," *Leibeserziehung und Sport in der modernen Gesellschaft,* ed. Gottfried Klöhn (Weinheim: Julius Beltz, 1961), pp. 96–101. The essay was originally published in 1929.

4. Homer and Sloan: illustrated in David Park Curry, *Winslow Homer: The Croquet Game* (New Haven: Yale University Art Gallery, 1984), n.p. Gromaire, *Les Bords de la Marne:* illustrated in Françoise Laget, Serge Laget, and Jean-Paul Mazot, *Le Grand Livre du Sport Féminin* (Belleville-sur-Saône: SIGEFA, 1982), p. 332; Gromaire, *Tennis devant la Mer:* illustrated in *Art et Sport* (Mons: Musée des Beaux-Arts, 1984), p. 79; Baumeister: illustrated in Gunter Witt, *Sport in der Kunst* (Leipzig: E. A. Seemann, 1969), p. 101; Zadkine: illustrated in Laget et al., *Le Grand Livre*, p. 175.

5. Henry de Montherlant, quoted in Serge Bressan, *Le Sport et les Femmes* (Paris: La Table Ronde, 1981), p. 35; Montherlant, *Le Songe* (Paris: Grasset, 1922), pp. 19–20, 29–30, 65.

6. Kasimir Edschmid, *Sport um Gagaly* (Berlin: Zsolnay, 1928), pp. 94, 176, 304, 355–56.

7. Larry Engelmann, *The Goddess and the American Girl* (New York: Oxford University Press, 1988), p. 13.

8. Helen Walker, "Tennis," *Sport in Britain,* ed. Tony Mason (Cambridge: Cambridge University Press, 1989), p. 264; William Baker, *Sports in the Western World* (Totowa, N.J.: Rowman and Littlefield, 1982), p. 227.

9. Anaïs Lenglen: quoted in Englemann, *The Goddess and the American Girl,* p. 37.

10. Kasimir Edschmid, "Die französische Meisterin Suzanne Lenglen," *Portraits und Denksteine* (Vienna: Kurt Desch, 1962), p. 161.

11. Adrianne Blue, *Grace Under Pressure* (London: Sidgwick and Jackson, 1987), p. 4.

12. Lenglen: quoted in Engelmann, *The Goddess and the American Girl,* p. 241.

13. Horst Ueberhorst, *Frisch, Frei, Stark und Treu: Die Arbeitersportbewegung in Deutschland* (Düsseldorf: Droste Verlag, 1973); Gertrud Pfister, "'Macht euch frei': Frauen in der Arbeiter- Turn- und Sportbewegung," *Illustrietre Geschichte des Arbeitersports,* ed. Hans Joachim Teichler and Gerhard Hauk (Bonn: J.H.W.Dietz Nachfolger, 1987), pp. 48–57; Sigrid Block, *Frauen und Madchen in der Arbeitersportbewegung* (Münster: LIT, 1987), pp. 188, 275.

14. Fridl Börg, "Die Frau im Arbeitersport" (1929): reprinted in Gertrud Pfister, *Frau und Sport* (Frankfurt: Fischer Verlag, 1980), p. 73.

15. Block, *Frauen und Mädchen,* p. 132.

16. Ueberhorst, *Frisch, Frei, Stark und Treu,* p. 134.

17. Vierke and Köhler: quoted in Block, *Frauen und Mädchen,* pp. 201, 208.

18. Ibid., p. 306.

19. Paul Franken, *Vom Werden einer neuen Kultur* (1930): excerpted in *Sport im Kreuzfeuer der Kritik,* ed. Hajo Bernett (Schorndorf: Karl Hofmann, 1982), pp. 62–64.

20. Poster: illustrated in color in *Illustrierte Geschichte des Arbeitersports,* p. 211.

21. Drechsler: quoted in Block, *Frauen und Mädchen,* p. 333.

22. Leena Laine, "Historische Entwicklung des Frauensports in Finnland," *Frauensport in Europa,* ed. Christine Peyton and Gertrud Pfister (Ahrensburg: Ingrid Czwalina, 1989), pp. 113–31; see also Willibert Strunz, *Der finnische Arbeitersport* (Münster: LIT-Verlag, 1985).

23. Stephen G. Jones, *Sport, Politics and the Working Class* (Manchester: University of Manchester Press, 1988), pp. 92–93, 170; William J. Murray, "Sport and Politics in France in the 1930s: The Workers' Sports Federations on the Eve of the Popular Front," *Australian Society for Sports History Studies in Sports History* (1987) 2:79–80; W. J. Murray, "The French Workers' Sports Movement and the Victory of the Popular Front in 1936," *International Journal of the History of Sport* (September 1987) 4(2):203–30.

24. Arnd Krüger and James Riordan, ed., *Der internationale Arbeitersport* (Cologne: Pahl-Rugenstein, 1985).

25. Mary H. Leigh, "The Evolution of Women's Participation in the Summer Olympic Games, 1900–1948" (Ph.D., Ohio State University, 1974), p. 55; Coubertin: quoted in Louis Callebat, *Pierre de Coubertin* (Paris: Fayard, 1988), p. 192.

26. Paula Welch and Harold Lerch, *History of American Physical Education and Sport* (Springfield, Ill.: Charles C. Thomas, 1981), p. 294.

27. Scott: quoted in Reet Howell, "Australia's First Female Olympians," *Olympic Scientific Congress*, p. 23.

28. Uriel Simri, *A Concise World History of Women's Sports*, p. 34; Dennis Phillips, "Australian Women at the Olympics," *Sporting Traditions* 6:2 (May 1990): 184–85.

29. Brown: quoted in Leigh, "Evolution of Women's Participation," p. 129.

30. Martin-Heinz Ehlert, "Lilli Henoch. Fragmente aus dem Leben einer jüdischen Sportlerin," *Sozial- und Zeitgeschichte des Sports* (1989):3(2) 34–48; see also Gertrud Pfister, "Die Rolle der jüdischen Frauen in der Turn- und Sportbewegung," *Stadion* (1989) 15(1):65–89

31. Carl Diem, *Weltgeschichte des Sports,* 3rd ed. (Frankfurt: Cotta, 1971), p. 635.

32. Liselott Diem, "Rückblick," *Frau und Sport,* ed. Gertrud Pfister (Frankfurt: Fischer Verlag, 1980), p. 54.

33. Françoise and Serge Laget and Jean-Paul Mazot, *Le Grand Livre du Sport Féminin* (Belleville-sur-Saône: SIGEFA, 1982), pp. 27, 216, 233.

34. Hajo Bernett, "Die ersten 'olympischen' Wettbewerbe im internationalen Frauensport," *Sozial- und Zeitgeschichte des Sports* (1988) 2(2):75; see also Mary H. Leigh and Thérèse M. Bonin, "The Pioneering Role of Madame Alice Milliat and the FSFI in Establishing International Trade [sic] and Field Competition for Women," *Journal of Sport History* (Spring 1977) 4(1):72–83.

35. Ibid. (both sources); Laget et al. *Le Grand Livre,* p. 27.

36. Leigh, "Evolution of Women's Participation," p. 164.

37. *Miroir des Sports:* quoted in Bernett, "Die ersten 'olympischen' Wettbewerbe," p. 84.

38. Uriel Simri, *Women at the Olympic Games* (Netanya: Wingate Institute, 1979), p. 25.

39. Uriel Simri, *Concise World History,* p. 53; Laget et al., *Le Grand Livre,* p. 29; Hiroko Seiwa et al., "Review of the History of Women's Sports in Japan," *Olympic Scientific Congress,* pp. 44–53; Gertrud Pfister and Gerd von der Lippe, "Die Olympischen Spiele und der Frauensport in Deutschland und Norwegen," unpublished paper, 1990.

40. Liselott Diem, *Frau und Sport* (Freiburg: Herder, 1980), p. 89.

41. Simri, *Women at the Olympic Games,* pp. 79–80.

42. Betty Spears, "Women in the Olympics," *The Modern Olympics,* ed. Peter J. Graham and Horst Ueberhorst (Cornwall: Leisure Press, 1976), p. 68.

43. Louisa Zerbe, "The 1930 University of British Columbia Women's Basketball Team. . . ," *Her Story in Sport,* ed. Reet Howell (West Point: Leisure Press, 1982), pp. 548–51.

44. Adrianne Blue, *Grace Under Pressure* (London: Sidgwick and Jackson, 1987), p. 148.

45. Kirby and Brundage: quoted in Allen Guttmann, *The Games Must Go On* (New York: Columbia University Press, 1984), p. 59.

46. Brundage: quoted in Leigh, "The Evolution of Women's Participation," p. 161; see also Mary H. Leigh, "The Enigma of Avery Brundage and Women Athletes," *Arena Review* (May 1980) 4(2):11–21; Guttmann, *The Games Must Go On,* pp. 108, 194–96.

ELEVEN: Women's Sports and Totalitarian Regimes

1. James Riordan, *Sport in Soviet Society* (London: Cambridge University Press, 1977), p. 83; see also Norman Shneidmann, *The Soviet Road to Olympus* (Toronto: Ontario Institute for Studies in Education, 1978).

2. Riordan, *Sport in Soviet Society,* p. 103.

3. Ibid., p. 134; H. W. Morton, "Soviet Sport" (Ph.D. dissertation, Columbia University, 1959), p. 232.

4. Riordan, *Sport in Soviet Society,* pp. 289–94.

5. Ibid., p. 337.

6. Ibid., p. 230.

7. Ibid., pp. 232–33; a microstudy of the Siberian town of Krasnojarak in 1963 found that young women spent 4.2% of their leisure time in "physical culture"; see V. Artimov, "Korperkultur und Sport im Zeitaufwand der jungen Arbeiter," *Jugend und Sport,* ed. H. Groll and H. Strohmeyer (Vienna: Osterreichischer Bundesverlag fur Unterricht, Wissenschaft und Kunst, 1970), p. 42.

8. Serge Bressan, *Le Sport et Les Femmes* (Paris: Table Rond, 1981), p. 111.

9. Ladislav Lopata, "The Structure of Time and the Share of Physical Education in the Case of Industrial Workers and Cooperative Farmers in the CSSR," *IRSS* (1968) 3:17–35.

10. Polish Congress and Pasecki: quoted from Barbara Krawczyk, "Social Role and Participation in Sport," *IRSS* (1973) 8:(3–4)47–59. I have corrected some flagrant errors in English.

11. Andrzej Wohl, "Prognostic Models of Sport in Socialist Countries . . . ," *IRSS* (1971) 6:33.

12. Földesiné Szabó Gyongi and Zbigniew Krawczyk, "The Social Role

of Sports Events in Poland and Hungary," *IRSS* (1982) 17(1):23–47; László Kutassi, "Ungarn," *Geschichte der Leibesübungen,* 5: 333–46.

13. Ingeburg Wonneberger, "Die Frau und die sozialistische Körperkultur," *Theorie und Praxis der Körperkultur* (March 1963): 12(3) 195–205; Klaus Ulbrich, "Das Warten der Frau an Olympischen Pforten," *Theorie und Praxis der Körperkultur* (November 1975) 24(11):977–81.

14. For some per-capita comparisons, see John Bale, "Sport and National Identity," *British Journal of Sports History (May 1986)* 3(1):18–41.

15. Ingeburg Wonneberger, "The Role of Physical Culture and Sports in Leisure Pursuits . . . ," *IRSS* (1968) 3:118.

16. Herbert Stündl, *Freizeit und Erhohlungssport in der DDR* (Schorndorf: Karl Hofmann, 1977), p. 31.

17. Riordan, *Sport in Soviet Society,* pp. 316–18; James Riordan, "The Social Emancipation of Women through Sport," *British Journal of Sports History* (May 1985) 2(1):55–56; see also James Riordan, "State and Sport in Developing Societies," *IRSS* (1986) 21(4):287–303. In all Islamic countries taken together, women were 4% of the Olympic teams; see Leila Sfeir, "The Status of Muslim Women in Sport," *IRSS* (1986) 20(4):287.

18. Barbara Wolfe Jancar, *Women under Communism* (Baltimore: Johns Hopkins University Press, 1978), pp. 54–55.

19. Andrzej Wohl, "The Phenomenon of Soviet Sport and Its New Developmental Stage," *IRSS* (1983) 18(3):51–68; Krésmir Petrović, "Trend, Dynamics and Characteristics of the Advancement of Physical Culture of Adults and Seniors," *IRSS* (1982) 17(2): 5–13. See also Heidi Bierstedt, "The Athletic Activities of Citizens of the German Democratic Republic," *IRSS* (1985) 20(1–2):39–50.

20. A. Cotronei and Marinetti: quoted in Felice Fabrizio, *Sport e Fascismo* (Rimini-Firenze: Guaraldi, 1976), pp. 13, 115; on Fascist sport theory see John M. Hoberman, *Sport and Political Ideology* (Austin: University of Texas Press, 1984).

21. Gianni Rossi, "Alla Recerca dell' Uomo Nuovo," *Atleti in Camicia Nera,* ed. Renato Bianda (Rome: Giovanni Volpe Editore, 1983), p. 39.

22. Adolfo Urso, "Il Fascismo e i suoi Giovani," *Atleti,* p. 97.

23. Ibid., pp. 112–13.

24. Victoria de Grazia, *The Culture of Consent* (Cambridge: Cambridge University Press, 1981), pp. 176–77.

25. Felice Fabrizio, *Storia dello Sport in Italia* (Rimini-Firenze: Guaraldi, 1977), p. 112.

26. Rossi, "Alla Ricerca," p. 57; Fabrizio, *Sport e Fascismo,* p. 125.

27. Panti and *Atlética Leggera:* quoted in ibid., pp. 62, 65.

28. Turati: quoted in Urso, "Il Fascismo," p. 98.

29. Rosella Isidori Frasca, *. . . E il Duce le volle Sportive* (Bologna: Patron Editore, 1983), p. 86.

30. Ibid., p. 89.

31. Arnd Krüger, "Sport im faschistischen Italien (1922–1933)," *Sport zwischen Eigenständigkeit und Fremdbestimmung,* ed. Giselher Spitzer and Dieter Schmidt (Bonn: Institut für Sportwissenschaft und Sport, 1986), pp. 221–22.

32. *Deutsche Turnerschaft:* quoted in Horst Geyer, "Stellvertreter der Nation," *Die vertrimmte Nation,* ed. Jörg Richter (Reinbek bei Hamburg: Rowohlt, 1972), pp. 80–81.

33. Bruno Barth, "Englischer Sport—Deutsches Turnen": reprinted in *Der Sport im Kreuzfeuer der Kritik,* ed .Hajo Bernett (Schorndorf: Karl Hofmann, 1982), p. 28.

34. Allen Guttmann, *From Ritual to Record* (New York: Columbia University Press, 1978), p. 63.

35. Elke Nyssen, "'. . . und weil ich Sport eben auch immer gern gemacht habe!': Mädchenerziehung und Sportunterricht im Nationalsozialismus," *Sozial- und Zeitgeschichte des Sports* (1987) 1(3):57–74.

36. Ritter von Halt: quoted in Winfried Joch, "Zur Sportberichterstattung im Jahre 1933 . . . ," *Sport zwischen Eigenständigkeit und Fremdbestimmung,* p. 187; Möckelmann: quoted in Gertrud Pfister, "Weiblichkeitsideologie, Frauenrolle und Frauensport im 'Dritten Reich,' " *Beiträge zur historischen Sozialkunde* (January-March 1983) 13(1):23.

37. Joch, "Zur Sportberichterstattung," p. 182.

38. Knipper: quoted in Hajo Bernett, *Nazionalsozialistische Leibesübungen* (Schorndorf: Karl Hofmann, 1966), p. 96.

39. Jean-Paul Thuillier, "La Nudité athlétique (Grèce, Etrurie, Rome)," *Nikephoros* (1988) 1(1):42.

40. Horst Ueberhorst, *Carl Krümmel und die nazionalsozialistischen Leibeserziehung* (Berlin: Bartels und Wernitz, 1976), pp. 84–85.

41. Regina Landschoof and Karin Hüls, *Frauensport im Faschismus* (Hamburg: Ergebnisse Verlag, 1985), p. 45.

42. Gernot Friese, *Anspruch und Wirklichkeit des Sports im Nationalsozialismus* (Ahrensburg: Czwalina, 1974), p. 96.

43. Landschoof and Hüls, *Frauensport im Faschismus,* p. 100; Hajo Bernett, *Sportunterricht in der nationalsozialistischen Schule* (Sankt Augustin, Germany: Hans Richarz, 1985), p. 34.

44. Hajo Bernett, *Der jüdische Sport im nazionsozialistischen Deutschland, 1933–38* (Schorndorf: Karl Hofmann, 1978), pp. 109–12.

45. Gisela Mauermayer, "Mein Weg zum Olympiasieg," *Frau und Sport,* ed. Gertrud Pfister (Frankfurt: Fischer Verlag, 1980), pp. 267–70. The essay was first published in 1939.

46. Pfister, "Weiblichkeitsideologie," p. 23.

47. On the Jarrett Affair, see Allen Guttmann, *The Games Must Go On: Avery Brundage and the Olympic Movement* (New York: Columbia University Press, 1984), pp. 76–77.

48. Robert Parienté, *La fabuleuse Histoire de l'Athlétisme* (Paris: ODIL, 1978), p. 1032.

49. Coubertin: quoted in Marie-Thérèse Eyquem, *Pierre de Coubertin: l'Epopée Olympique* (Paris: Calmann-Lévy, 1966), p. 234.

TWELVE: Evolutionary Change

1. Mary H. Leigh, "The Evolution of Women's Participation in the Summer Olympic Games, 1900–1948" (Ph.D. dissertation, Ohio State University, 1974), p. 411.

2. *Dagdbladet* (March 6, 1958): quoted by Gerd von der Lippe, "Frauensport in Norwegen," *Frauensport in Europa* (Ahrensburg: Ingrid Czwalina, 1989), p. 153. Yves Brossard, *Sport* (Paris: Flammarion, 1961), p. 103.

3. For studies of girls' socialization into sports, see Susan Greendorfer, "Role of Socializing Agents in Female Sport Involvement," *Research Quarterly* (1977) 48(2):304–10; Susan Greendorfer and John H. Lewko, "Role of Family Members in Sport Socialization of Children," *Research Quarterly* (May 1978) 49:146–53; Susan Greendorfer, "Social Class Influence on Female Sport Involvement," *Sex Roles* (1978) 4:619–25; Susan Greendorfer, "Childhood Sport Socialization Influences of Male and Female Track Athletes," *Arena Review* (May 1979) 3(2):39–52; Susan Greendorfer, "Differences in Childhood Socialization Influences of Women Involved in Sport and Women Not Involved in Sport," *The Dimensions of Sport Sociology,* ed. March L. Krotee (West Point: Leisure Press, 1979), pp. 59–72; George H. Sage, "Parental Influence and Socialization into Sport for Male and Female Intercollegiate Athletes," *Journal of Sport and Social Issues* (1980) 4(2): 1–13; Howard L. Nixon II, "An Exploratory Study of the Effects of Encouragement and Pressure on the Sports Socialization of Males and Females," *Sociology of Sport,* ed. Susan Greendorfer and Andrew Yiannakis (West Point: Leisure Press, 1981): 83–94; Mary A. McElroy, "Parent-Child Relations and Orientations toward Sport," *Sex Roles* (1983) 9(10):997–1004; Lesley Fishwick and Susan Greendorfer, "Socialization Revisited," *Quest* (1987) 39(1):1–8; Maureen R. Weiss and Annelies Knoppers, "The Influence of Socializing Agents on Female Collegiate Volleyball Players," *Journal of Sport Psychology* (1982) 4(3):267–79; Susan Greendorfer, Elaine M. Blinde, and Ana Maria Pellegrini, "Gender Differences in Brazilian Children's Socialization into Sport," *IRSS* (1986) 21(1):51–62; Susan Greendorfer, "Gender Bias in Theoretical Perspectives," *Psychology of Women Quarterly* (1987) 11:327–40.

4. Deborah L. Feltz, "Athletics in the Status System of Female Adolescents," *Review of Sport and Leisure* (Summer 1979) 4(1):110–18. There seems to have been little change in the Eighties. Of 278 girls in high school in eight different cities, 18% wanted to be remembered as athletic stars and 43% as "brilliant students"; see Joel Thirer and Stephen D. Wright, "Sport and Social

Status for Adolescent Males and Females," *Sociology of Sport Journal* (June 1985) 2(2):164–71.

5. Hans G. Buhrmann and Robert D. Bratton, "Athletic Participation and Status of Alberta High School Girls," *IRSS* (1977) 12(1):57–69.

6. *Sport and the Community: Report of the Wolfenden Committee* (London: Central Council of Physical Recreation, 1960), p. 35.

7. R. Berthoumier, "Le sport, question sociale," *Regards Neufs Sur Le Sport,* ed. Joffre Dumazedier et al. (Paris: Editions du Seuil, 1950), p. 55.

8. Raymond Thomas, Antoine Haumont, Jean-Louis Levet, *Sociologie du Sport* (Paris: Presses universitaires de France, 1987), p. 118.

9. Marjatta Marin, "Gender Differences in Sport and Movement in Finland," *IRSS* (1988) 23(4):345–58.

10. Lesley Fishwick and Diane Hayes, "Sport for Whom?" *Sociology of Sport Journal* (September 1989) 6(3):269–77.

11. John P. Robinson, "Time Expenditure on Sports Across Ten Countries," *IRSS* (1967) 2:67–84.

12. Inge Bausenwein and Auguste Hoffmann, *Frau and Leibesübungen* (Mühlehim: Gehoerlosen-Druckerei und Verlag, 1967), p. 91.

13. Ulrike Prokop, "Sport und Emanzipation am Beispiel des Frauensports," *Sport-Kritisch,* ed. Alex Natan (Bern-Stuttgart: Hallweg, 1972), pp. 213–14.

14. Sabine Kröner, *Sport und Geschlecht* (Ahrensburg: Czwalina, 1976), p. 109.

15. Bausenwein and Hoffmann, *Frau und Leibesübungen,* p. 100.

16. Dieter H. Jütting, *Freizeit und Erwachsenensport* (Munich: Ernst Reinhardt, 1976), p. 125; Kröner, *Sport und Geschlecht,* p. 40.

17. Günther Lüschen, "Soziologische Grundlagen von Leibeserziehungen und Sport," *Einführung in die Theorie der Leibeserziehung,* ed. Grupe, p. 124.

18. Bausenwein and Hoffmann, *Frau und Leibesübungen,* pp. 112–13.

19. Joffre Dumazedier, "Sport and Sports Activities," *IRSS* (1973) 8(2):8–32; Yves LePogam, *Démocratisation du Sport: Mythe ou Réalité?* (Paris: Jean-Pierre Delarge, 1979), p. 216; *Sport de France* (Paris: Service de Presse, 1971), pp. 323–24.

20. N. G. Vlot, "'A Sociological Analysis of Sport in the Netherlands," *International Research in Sport and Physical Education,* ed. Ernst Jokl (Springfield, Ill.: Charles C. Thomas, 1964), pp. 198–211.

21. Niels Lommen, "Niederlande," *Geschichte der Leibesübungen,* ed. Ueberhorst, 5: 114–17.

22. O. Halldén, "Schweden," ibid., pp. 31–33.

23. Gerd von der Lippe, "Some Thoughts on the Development of Women's Role in Sports in Norway . . . ," *The History, the Evolution, and the Diffusion of Sports and Games in Different Cultures,* ed. Roland Renson et al. (Brussels: Bestuur voor de Lichamelijke Opvoeding, de Sport en het Openluchtleven, 1976), p. 499.

24. Isabel Emmett, *Youth and Leisure in an Urban Sprawl* (Manchester: Manchester University Press, 1971), pp. 17, 29.

25. M. Ann Hall, "Sport and Physical Activity in the Lives of Canadian Women," *Canadian Sport,* ed. Richard Gruneau and John G. Albinson (Don Mills, Ont.: Addison-Wesley, 1976), p. 174.

26. James E. Curtis and Bryan G. Milton, "Social Status and the 'Active' Society,' " ibid., p. 310.

27. Richard E. DuWors and Maureen Rever Duwors, "Reasons for Participation in Amateur Sport and Educational Status of the Father," *Sociology of Sport/Sociologie du Sport,* ed. Fernand Landry and William A. R. Orban (Miami: Symposia Specialists, 1978), p. 72.

28. G. R. Pavia and T. D. Jaques, "The Socioeconomic Origin, Academic Attainment, Occupational Mobility, and Parental Background of Selected Australian Athletes," ibid., p. 89.

29. John P. Robinson, "Time Expenditure on Sports Across Ten Countries," pp. 67–84. An even lower male/female ratio of 1.18 can be derived from a recent national survey of some 19,000 adults, but the data refer to "physical activity" rather than to sports; see Christine Brooks, "A Causal Modeling Analysis of Sociodemographics and Moderate to Vigorous Physical Activity Behavior of Young Adults," *Research Quarterly* (December 1988) 59:328–38.

30. High School data released by National Federation of State High School Associations, September 15, 1978; collegiate data provided by the National Collegiate Athletic Association.

31. Don Kowett, "TV Sports," *TV Guide* (August 19, 1978), pp. 2–8.

32. Klaus Wehmeier, "Publikum," *Sport und Massenmedien,* ed. Josef Hackforth and Siegfried Weischenberg (Frankfurt: Limpert, 1978), p. 116.

33. Uriel Simri, *Women at the Olympic Games* (Netanya: Wingate Institute, 1979), p. 80.

34. Ferenc Mező, *Les Jeux Olympiques Modernes* (Budapest: Pannonia, 1956), p. 312n2.

35. *Daily Graphic,* August 5, 194:; quoted in Adrianne Blue, *Faster, Higher, Further* (London: Virago Press, 1988), pp. 52–53; *Time,* February 2, 1948; Don Morrow, "Sweetheart Sport: Barbara Ann Scott and the Post World War II Image of the Female Athlete in Canada," *Canadian Journal of History of Sport* (May 1987) 18(1):36–54. Henie won in 1928, 1932, and 1936; Fleming in 1968; Hamill in 1976.

36. Simri, *Women at the Olympic Games,* p. 80; Dennis Phillips, "Australian Women at the Olympics," *Sporting Traditions* (May 1990) 6(2): 195.

37. Phillips, "Australian Women," pp. 189–90; Dawn Fraser and Harry Gordon, *Below the Surface* (New York: William Morrow, 1965), p. 197. Reet and Max Howell, *Aussie Gold* (Albion, Queensland: Brooks Waterloo, 1988), pp. 153–60.

38. Connolly: quoted in Olgla Connolly, *The Rings of Destiny* (New York: David McKay, 1968), p. 149.

39. Simri, *Women and the Olympic Games*, p. 86.

40. Wilma Rudolph, *Wilma* (New York: New American Library, 1977).

41. Simri, *Women at the Olympic Games*, p. 86.

42. Ibid.

43. Walter Gloede, *Sport* (Munich: Goldmann, 1980), pp. 391–92.

44. Justin Beecham, *Olga* (New York: Paddington Press, 1975), p. 7.

THIRTEEN: Revolutionary Change

1. Writing in 1985, Nancy Theberge noted that *Signs* had had one article on women's physical education while *Feminist Studies* and the *International Journal of Women's Studies* had had none; see "Sport and Feminism in North America," *Women in Sport,* ed. Amy L. Reeder and John R. Fuller (Carollton: West Georgia College, 1985), pp. 41–53.

2. Ellen W. Gerber, "A Chronicle of Participation," *The American Woman in Sport,* ed. Ellen W. Gerber (Lexington, Mass.: Addison-Wesley, 1974), p. 130.

3. Bobby Riggs and George McGann, *Court Hustler* (Philadelphia: J. B. Lippincott, 1973), p. 11.

4. Grace Lichtenstein, *A Long Way, Baby* (New York: Morrow, 1974), pp. 232–34.

5. Adrianne Blue, *Grace Under Pressure* (London: Sidgwick and Jackson, 1987), p. 39.

6. Billie Jean King and Kim Chapin, *Billie Jean* (New York: Harper and Row, 1974), p. 7.

7. Waugh: quoted in Blue, *Grace Under Pressure,* p. 44.

8. John A. Lucas and Ronald A. Smith, *Saga of American Sport* (Philadelphia: Lea and Febiger, 1978), pp. 364–66.

9. Danielle Carver, "The Failure of Women's Professional Basketball" (unpublished essay, Amherst College, 1989), p. 44.

10. Ibid., p. 46.

11. For the story of the Women's Basketball League, see ibid., pp. 39–49; Ted Vincent, *Mudville's Revenge* (New York: Seaview Books, 1981), pp. 315–24.

12. Sarah Ann Strauss, "A Locker Room of One's Own: Title IX . . . and Women's College Sports" (unpublished essay, Amherst College, 1988), p. 67.

13. Stanley: quoted in Kent Hannon, "Too Far, Too Fast," *Sports Illustrated* 48 (March 20, 1978): 38; on Title IX and the AIAW, see also Joan S. Hult, "Women's Struggle," pp. 249–61. Anne Ingram, "Origin and Status of a Social Movement," *Sports et Sociétés Contemporaines* (Paris: SFSS, 1984), pp. 231–39; Susan Birrell, "Separatism as an Issue in Women's Sport," *Arena*

Review (July 1984) 8(2):21–29; Donna A. Lopiano, "A Political Analysis of the Possibility of Impact Alternatives for the Accomplishment of Feminist Objectives within American Intercollegiate Sport," *Arena Review* (July 1984) 8(2):49–61; R. Vivian Acosta and Linda Jean Carpenter, "Women in Sport," *Sport and Higher Education,* ed. Donald Chu, Jeffrey O. Segrave, and Beverly J. Becker (Champaign,Ill: Human Kinetics, 1985), pp. 313–25; Linda Jean Carpenter, "The Impact of Title IX on Women's Intercollegiate Sports," *Government and Sport,* ed. Arthur T. Johnson and James Frey (Totowa, N.J.: Rowman and Allanheld, 1985), pp. 62–78; Joan L. Chandler, "The Association for Intercollegiate Athletics for Women," *Women in Sport,* ed. Amy L. Reeder and John R. Fuller (Carrollton: West Georgia College, 1985), pp. 5–17; Christine H. B. Grant, "The Gender Gap in Sport," *Arena Review* (July 1984) 8(2):31–47.

14. Jack Falla, *NCAA: The Voice of College Sports* (Mission, Kansas: NCAA, 1981), pp. 167–74; Strauss, "A Locker Room of One's Own," pp. 75–77.

15. Data from the NCAA's *The Nation's Universities and Colleges: Reports Number 4–7.*

16. Barbara Sinclair Deckard, *The Women's Movement,* 3rd ed. (New York: Harper and Row, 1983), pp. 407–08; Elaine M. Blinde, "Contrasting Orientation toward Sport: Pre- and Post-Title IX Athletes," *Journal of Sport and Social Issues* (Winter/Spring 1986) 10(1):6–14; Elaine M. Blinde and Susan Greendorfer, "Structural and Philosophical Differences in Women's Intercollegiate Sport Programs and the Sport Experience of Athletes," *Journal of Sport Behavior* (June 1987) 10(2):59–72.

17. Data supplied by the National Federation of State High School Associations.

18. Mary A. Boutilier and Lucinda SanGiovanni, *The Sporting Woman* (Champaign, Ill.: Human Kinetics, 1983), p. 38.

19. Ibid., pp. 187, 192, 197–98.

20. Diana Nyad, *Other Shores* (New York: Random House, 1978), pp. 158–61.

21. Barbara McDermott, "Handle at Your Own Risk," *Sports Illustrated* 63 (November 11, 1985): 54. Another laudatory article featured judo expert Rena Glick Kanokogi; see Gary Smith, "Rumbling with Rusty," *Sports Illustrated* 64 (March 24, 1986): 58–70. A two-year study of *Sport, Sports Illustrated, Runner's World,* and *Tennis,* conducted in 1978–80, concluded that these magazines had become less sexist; see James Bryant, "A Two-Year Selective Investigation of the Female in Sport as Reported in the Paper Media," *Arena Review* (May 1980) 4(2):32–44. In an unusually careful study, Jan Rintala and Susan Birrell found that *Sports and Athletes,* a magazine aimed at a twelve-to-twenty-two-year-old audience, was "far less guilty of underrepresentation [of female athletes] and overt misogyny than are other media"; Rintala and Birrell, "Fair Treatment for the Active Female," *Sociology of Sport Journal* (1984) 1(3):247.

22. Janice Kaplan, *Women and Sports* (New York: Viking Press, 1979), p. 6.

23. Boutelier and SanGiovanni, *Sporting Woman,* p. 212.

24. In a survey of fourteen women's magazines investigated in the spring of 1985 and 1988, Mary E. Duquin found that the advertisements rarely portrayed women as "vigorously active," but Duquin does not comment on the kinds of bodies depicted. See "Fashion and Fitness: Images in Women's Magazine Advertisements," *Arena Review* (November 1989) 13(2):97–109.

25. David McDonald and Lauren Drewery, *For the Record: Canada's Greatest Women Athletes* (Rexdale, Ontario: John Wiley and Sons, 1981), p. 230.

26. Cheshire: quoted in Charles Gaines and George Butler, *Pumping Iron II* (New York: Simon and Shuster, 1984), p. 73.

27. George Sage and Sheryl Loudermilk, "The Female Athlete and Role Conflict," *Research Quarterly* (March 1979) 50:88–96.

28. Gai Ingham Berlage, "Women Intercollegiate Athletes' Use of the Apologetic," *Arena Review* (November 1987) 11(2):57–65; for an interesting Australian replication, see Susan A. Jackson and Herbert W. Marsh, "Athletic or Antisocial? The Female Sport Experience," *Journal of Sport Psychology* (1986) 8(3):198–211.

29. *Miller Lite Report on Women's Sports* (Milwaukee: Miller Brewing Co., 1985), p. 8.

30. Pearl Berlin, "The Woman Athlete," *The American Woman in Sport,* ed. Ellen W. Gerber (Lexington: Addison-Wesley, 1974), p. 379. In 1972, Patricia Griffin, performing a very similar experiment at the University of Massachusetts, found a large "semantic distance" between the roles of "Woman Athlete" and "Ideal Woman"; see Patricia Griffin, "What's a Nice Girl Like You Doing in a Profession Like This?" *Quest* (January 1973) 19: 96–101. A study of female athletes and non-athletes at Arizona State University found the former rated female softball players more highly than female dancers, whom the latter preferred; see Joan L. Kingsley et al, "Social Acceptance of Female Athletes by College Women," *Research Quarterly* (December 1977) 48:727–33.

31. Robert W. Duff and Lawrence K. Hong, "Self-Images of Women Body-Builders," *Sociology of Sport Journal* (December 1984) 1(4):374–80.

32. Loren Franck, "Exposure and Gender Effects in the Social Perception of Women Bodybuilders," *Journal of Sport Psychology (1984)* 6(2): 239–45.

33. Maria T. Allison and Beverley Butler, "Role Conflict and the Elite Female Athlete," *IRSS* (1984) 19(2):157–66. Eight of nineteen female karate experts reported that they had been "put down" by others, but only two experienced trouble with boyfriends; see Robert A. Smith et al., "Women, Karate, and Gender Typing," *Sociological Inquiry* (1981) 51(2):113–20. See also J. Anthrop and Maria T. Allison, "Role Conflict and the High School Female Athletes," *Research Quarterly* (1974) 54(2):104–11; Mary M. Bell, Conflict of Women as Athletes . . . ," *Arena Review* (May 1980) 4(1): 22–31;

Gaylene P. Doucetre, Glenna A. Harris, and Kathryn E. Watson, "An Analysis of the Self-Image Differences of Male and Female Athletes," *Journal of Sport Behavior* (July 1983) 6(2):77–83.

34. Harvey R. Freeman, "Social Perception of Bodybuilders," *Journal of Sport and Exercise Psychology* (1988) 10:281–93.

35. On the allegedly "masculine" or "androgynous" female athletes, see Anita M. Myers and Hilary M. Lips, "Participation in Competitive Amateur Sports as a Function of Psychological Androgyny," *Sex Roles* (1978) 4:571–78; Dorothy V. Harris, "Femininity and Athleticism," *Jock,* ed. Donald F. Sabo and Ross Runfola (Englewood Cliffs, N.J.: Prentice-Hall, 1980), pp. 222–39; Sarah M. Uguccioni and Robert H. Ballantyne, "Comparison of Attitudes and Sex Roles for Female Athletic Participants and Non-Participants," *International Journal of Sport Psychology* (1980) 11(1):42–48; L. Chalip, J. Villiger, and P. Duignan, "Sex-Role Identity in a Select Sample of Women Field Hockey Players," *International Journal of Sport Psychology* (1980) 11(4):240–48; Patricia Del Rey and Samona Sheppard, "Relationship of Psychological Androgyny in Female Athletes to Self-Esteem," *International Journal of Sport Psychology* (1981) 12(3):165–75; Ruth Colker and Cathy Spatz Widom, "Correlates of Female Athletic Participation," *Sex Roles* (1980) 6:47–58; Ann Colley, Nigel Roberts, and Anthony Chips, "Sex-Role Identity, Personality and Participation in Team and Individual Sports by Males and Females," *International Journal of Sport Psychology* (1985) 16:103–12; K. P. Henschen, S. W. Edwards, and L. Mathinos, "Achievement Motivation and Sex-Role Orientation of High School Female Track and Field Athletes versus Non-Athletes," *Perceptual and Motor Skills* (1982) 55:183–87; J. Gackenbach, "Collegiate Swimmers," *Perceptual and Motor Skills* (1982) 55:555–58; S. W. Edwards, R. D. Gordin, and K. P. Henschen, "Sex-Role Orientations of Female NCAA Championship Gymnasts," *Perceptual and Motor Skills* (1984) 58:625–26; Arno F. Wittig, "Sports Competition Anxiety and Sex-Role Perceptions *Sex Roles* (1984) 10(5/6):469–73; E. G. Hall, B. Durborow and J. L. Progen, "Self-Esteem of Female Athletes and Non-Athletes . . . ," *Sex Roles* (1986) 15:379–90; H. W. Marsh and S. A. Jackson, "Multidimensional Self Concepts, Masculinity and Femininity as a Function of Women's Involvement in Athletics," *Sex Roles* (1986) 15:391–415.

36. On body image, see Elden E. Snyder and Joseph E. Kivlin, "Women Athletes and Aspects of Psychological Well-Being and Body Image," *Research Quarterly* (May 1975) 46:191–99; Linda Ho and Jon E. Walker, "Female Athletes and Nonathletes: Similarities and Differences in Self Perception," *Journal of Sport Behavior* (March 1982) 5(1):12–27; V. V. Prakasa Rao and Steven J. Overman, "Pyschological Well-Being and Body Image," *Journal of Sport Behavior* (June 1986) 9(2):79–91. Two Canadian psychologists have reported that black female athletes have a more positive self-image than non-athletes but that white female athletes do not. They seem, however, to have

interpreted a high score on the "masculinity-femininity" scale as a sign of a poor self-image; see R. Cochrane and T. Pike, "Self-Image and the Female Athlete," *Psychological and Sociological Factors in Sport*, ed. Peter Klavora and Kirk M. W. Wipper (Toronto: School of Physical and Health Education, 1980), pp. 245–54.

37. Eldon E. Snyder and Elmer Spreitzer, "Change and Variation in the Social Acceptance of Female Participation in Sports," *Journal of Sport Behavior* (March 1983) 6(1):3–8.

38. Robert C. Woodford and Wilbur J. Scott, "Attitudes toward the Participation of Women in Intercollegiate Sports," *Studies in the Sociology of Sport*, ed. Aidan O. Dunleavy et al. (Fort Worth: Texas Christian University Press, 1982), p. 209; see also Howard L. Nixon, Philip J. Maresca, and Marcy A. Silverman, "Sex Differences in College Students' Acceptance of Females in Sport," *Adolescence* (1979) 14:755–64; Susan A. Basow and Jean Spinner, "Social Acceptability of College Athletes," *International Journal of Sport Psychology* (1984) 15:79–87. On the declining approval Among older people, see Andrew C. Ostrow and David A. Dzewatowski, "Older Adults' Perceptions of Physical Activity Participation . . . ," *Research Quarterly* (1986) 57(2):167–69.

39. Helen Lenskyj, "Measured Time: Women, Sport and Leisure," *Leisure Studies* (1988) 7:239.

40. Boutilier and SanGiovanni, *The Sporting Woman*, p. 217; Kenny Moore, "The Spoils of Victory," *Sports Illustrated (April 10, 1989) 70(16):50–55*; Brigitte Tietzel, "Von der Frauen Schönheit, Schnelligkeit und Verführung," *Frankfurter Allgemeine Zeitung,* June 9, 1990.

41. E.M. Swift, "The Most Powerful Man in Sports," *Sports Illustrated* (May 21, 1990) 72(21):98–120.

42. Wiliam H. Beezley and Joseph P. Hobbs, "Nice Girls Don't Sweat," *Journal of Popular Culture* (1981) 16(4):42–53; Jay J. Coakley, *Sport in Society* (St.Louis: C. V. Mosby Co., 1978), pp. 255–57; Boutilier and SanGiovanni, *Sporting Woman,* p. 170; Cheryl M. Fields, "Title IX at X," *Chronicle of Higher Education,* June 23, 1982.

43. Fitzgerald: quoted in Bil Gilbert and Nancy Williamson, "Sport Is Unfair to Women," *Sports Illustrated* (May 28, 1973) 38:95.

44. Walter Byers: quoted in Linda Jean Carpenter, "The Impact of Title IX on Women's Intercollegiate Sports," *Government and Sport,* ed. Arthur T. Johnson and James H. Frey (Totowa, N.J.: Rowman and Allanheld, 1985): p. 63.

45. Patrica L. Geadelmann, et al., *Equality in Sport for Women* (Washington: American Alliance for Health, Physical Education, and Recreation, 1977); Patricia Huckle, "Back to the Starting Lines," *American Behavioral Scientist* (January/February 1978) 21(3):379–92; Michael C. Malmisur, "Title IX Dilemma," *Journal of Sport Behavior* (August 1978) 1(3):130–38; March L. Kro-

tee, "The Battle of the Sexes," *Journal of Sport and Social Issues* (Fall/Winter 1981) 5(2):15–23.

46. Joan S. Hult, "Women's Struggle for Governance in U.S. Amateur Athletics," *IRSS* (1989) 24(3):255.

47. Strauss, "A Locker Room of One's Own," p. 82; see also Blue, *Grace Under Pressure,* p. 132.

48. M. Ann Hall and Dorothy A. Richardson, *Fair Ball: Towards Sex Equality in Canadian Sport* (Ottawa: Canadian Advisory Council on the Status of Women, 1982), p. 70. Females were 14% of all faculty and 40.4% of the students; see also Nancy Theberge, "The Status of Women in Coaching in Canada," *Sports et Sociétés Contemporaines* (Paris: SFSS, 1984), pp. 163–68; Nancy Theberge, "Some Evidence on the Existence of a Sexual Double Standard in Mobility to Leadership Positions in Sport," *IRSS* (1984) 19(2):185–97; Wendy Olson, "A Title IX Paradox: More Female Athletes But Fewer Coaches," *Los Angeles Times,* July 8, 1987.

49. David Whitson and Donald MacIntosh, "Gender and Power," *IRSS* (1989) 24(2):137.

50. Elaine Blinde, "Unequal Exchange and Exploitation in College Sport," *Arena Review* (November 1989) 13(2):120; Elaine Blinde, "Participation in a Male Sport Model and the Value Alienation of Female Intercollegiate Athletes," *Sociology of Sport Journal* (March 1989) 6(1):46; American Institutes of Research, *Studies of Intercollegiate Athletics,* 6 vols. (Palo Alto: American Insitutes of Research, 1988–89), 4: 24, 27, 50. On the advantages as well as the disadvantages of a male coach for a female athletes, see also Gail Whitaker and Susan Molstad, "Male Coach / Female Coach," *Journal of Sport and Social Issues* (Summer/Fall 1985) 9(2):14–25; Robert Weinberg, Margie Reveles, and Allen Jackson, "Attitudes of Male and Female Athletes toward Male and Female Coaches," *Journal of Sport Psychology* (1984) 6(4):448–53; Jean M. Williams and Bonnie L. Parkhouse, "Social Learning Theory as a Foundation for Examining Sex Bias in Evaluation of Coaches," *Journal of Sport and Exercise Psychology* (1988) 10:322–33.

51. Susan Birrell, "Achievement Related Motives and the Woman Athlete," *Women and Sport,* ed. Carole A. Oglesby (Philadelphia: Lea and Febiger, 1978), pp. 157–58.

52. Sheehan: quoted in Anita Verschoth, "She's His Fair Lady," *Sports Illustrated* (February 26, 1979) 50:35.

53. Magill: quoted in Bil Gilbert and Nancy Williamson, "Programmed to Be Losers," *Sports Illustrated* (June 11, 1973) 38:62.

54. Donald Andrews, "Fear of Success and Women Athletes," *Arena Newsletter* (April/June 1977) 1(3–4):5–13; John M. Silva III, "An Evaluation of Fear of Success in Female and Male Athletes and Non-Athletes," *Journal of Sport Psychology* (1982) 4(1):92–96.

55. Among the best discussions of these issues is Christine Grant, "What

Does Equality Mean?" *Equality in Sport for Women,* ed. Patrica L. Geadelmann, Christine Grant, Yvonne Slatton, and N. Peggy Burke (Washington: American Alliance for Health, Physical Education, and Recreation, 1977), pp. 1–25.

56. Allen Guttmann, "Body Image and Sports Participation of the Intellectual Elite," *IRSS* (1989) 24(4):335–43.

57. F. Enz, writing in *Sport im Aufgabenfeld der Kirche* (1970): quoted in Gertrud Pfister, *Geschlechtsspezifische Sozialisation und Koeducation im Sport* (Berlin: Bartels and Wernitz, 1983), p. 79.

58. Martina Navratilova and Andreas Hallaschka, "'Ich weiss nicht, was ich bin,'" *Sports International* (January 1989) 1(1):63.

59. Dorothee Bierhoff-Alfermann, "Die Frau in der Leichtathletik," *Frauenleichtathletik,* ed. Norbert Müller, Dieter Augustin, and Bernd Hunger (Niedernhausern: Schors Verlag, 1985), pp. 143–49.

60. John Betjeman, *Collected Poems* (London: John Murray, 1958), pp. 50–51, 97–99, 180–81, 222–23; Garry Whannel, "The Television Spectacular," *Five-Ring Circus: Money, Power and Politics at the Olympic Games,* ed. Alan Tomlinson and Garry Whannel (London: Pluto Press, 1984), p. 40; Adrianne Blue, *Faster, Higher, Further* (London: Virago Press, 1988) p. 110; Liz Ferris: quoted in James Riordan, "The Social Emancipation of Women through Sport," *British Journal of Sports History* (May 1985) 2(1):57.

61. Amis: quoted in John Hargreaves, *Sport, Power and Culture* (New York: St. Martin's Press, 1986), p. 152.

62. Tweedie: quoted in Riordan, "The Social Emancipation of Women through Sport," p. 54.

63. Rosemary Deem, *All Work and No Play?: A Study of Women and Leisure* (Philadelphia: Open University Press, 1986), pp. 68, 74.

64. Guy Lagorce, "Claire-la-Magnifique," *Les Héroïques* (Paris: Julliard, 1980), pp. 27–50. Martine Anciaux et al., *La Femme d'Aujourd'hui et le Sport* (Paris: Editions Amphora, 1981), pp. 12, 14, 18; Elle: quoted in Catherine Louveau, "La forme, pas les formes!" *Sports et Société,* ed. Christian Pociello (Paris: Vigot, 1981), p. 311.

65. Botho Strauss, "Atalanta," *Niemand Anderes* (Munich: Carl Hanser, 1987), pp. 66–72; Michael Naumann, "Kraft durch Fonda," *Die Zeit,* October 22, 1982; Norbert Denkel, "Robert Mapplethorpe und Lisa Lyons Willens-Akte," *Die Zeit,* March 21, 1986; Volker Lilienthal and Magnus Gerwien, "Ganz Gespannt aufs Hier und Jetzt," *Zeitmagazin* (April 21, 1989): 48–58; Wilhelm Bittorf, "Jede Faser winselt um Gnade," *Der Spiegel* (May 27, 1985), pp.202–11; Ariane Barth, "Im Ambiente eines Ufos," *Der Spiegel* (May 27, 1985), pp. 211–13. For a complicated and rather inconclusive study of the self-image of German body-builders, see Joseph Bednarek, "Pumping Iron or Pulling Strings," *IRSS* (1985) 20(4):239–61.

66. Marie-Luise Klein and Gertrud Pfister, *Goldmädel, Rennmiezen und*

Turnkücken: Die Frau in der Sportberichterstattung der Bild-Zeitung (Berlin: Bartels und Wernitz, 1985), pp. 73–75, 90–91, 129.

67. Angelike Tschap-Bock, *Frauensport und Gesellschaft* (Ahrensberg: Ingrid Czwalina, 1983), pp. 289, 300, 303.

68. Kari Fasting, "Gender Roles and Attitudes towards Top Level Sport for Women and Men," *Sport et Sociétés Contemporaines*, pp. 425–31; Kari Fasting and Jan Tangen, "Gender and Sport in Norwegian Mass Media," *IRSS* (1983) 18(1):61–70.

69. Manuel García Ferrando: cited in Nina Puig et al., "Frauen und Sport in Spanien," *Frauensport in Europa*, p. 108.

70. Alessandro Salvini, *Identità Femminile e Sport* (Florence: La Nuova Italia, 1982), pp. 2, 166–214.

71. Ingeborg Bausenwein, "Die Beteiligung von Frauen am Sport," *Frau und Sport*, ed. Georg Anders (Schorndorf: Karl Hofmann, 1978), pp. 17, 24. For the figures for 1977 through 1981 for school children and young adults, see Gertrud Pfister, *Geschlechtsspezifische Sozialisation und Koedukation im Sport*, p. 116.

72. Helmut Digel, "Schlucken die Kleinen die Grossen?" *Menschen im Sport 2000*, ed. Hartmut Becker and Ommo Grupe (Schorndorf: Karl Hofmann, 1988), pp. 173–74;

73. Waldemar Timm, *Sportvereine in der Bundesrepublik Deutschland II.* (Schorndorf: Karl Hofmann, 1979), pp. 55, 213.

74. Georg Anders, "Die Frau im Sportverein," *Frau und Sport*, p. 65.

75. Ibid., p. 64.

76. Karl Schlagenhauf, *Sportvereine in der Bundesrepublik Deutschland I.* (Schorndorf: Karl Hofmann, 1977), p. 156.

77. Thomas Abel, *Ausländer und Sport* (Cologne: Pahl-Rugenstein, 1984), pp. 78, 102.

78. Thomas Schwarz, *Türkische Sportler in Berlin zwischen Integration und Segregation* (Berlin: Express Edition, 1987), pp. 41, 46.

79. Auguste Hoffmann, "Sportliche Betätigung in Verschiedenen Lebensaltern," *Frau und Sport*, p. 37.

80. Georg Anders et al., *Frau und Sport*, p. 164; see also Klaus Heinemann, "Unemployment, Personality and Involvement in Sport," *Sociology of Sport Journal* (June 1985) 2(2):157–63.

81. Bausenwein, "Beteiligung," p. 20.

82. Ibid., pp. 20–21.

83. Hannelore Ratzeburg, "Fussball ist Frauensport," *Frauen Bewegung Sport*, ed. Sylvia Schenk (Hamburg: VSA-Verlag, 1986), pp. 85–94.

84. Liselott Diem, *Frau und Sport* (Freiburg: Herder, 1980), pp. 97–98; Gunter A. Pilz, *Wandlungen der Gewalt im Sport* (Ahrensburg: Czwalina, 1982), p. 184.

85. Buytendijk: quoted in *Frauen Bewegung Sport*, p. 85.

86. Gunter A. Pilz, "Einstellungen zu sportsspezifischen aggressiven Handlungen," *Sport und Gesellschaft*, ed. Thomas Kutsch and Günter Wiswede (Königstein: Anton Hein, 1981), pp. 153–80.

87. Schröder: quoted in Pilz, *Wandlungen der Gewalt*, p. 235.

88. For arguments that coeducational physical education is a good welcomed by students, see Walter Brehm, *Sport als Sozialisationsinstanz traditioneller Geschlechtsrollen* (Giessen-Lollar: Andreas Aschenbach, 1975); Arnim Brux and Gertrud Pfister, "Koedukation im Sportunterricht," *Sportsoziologie und Erziehung*, ed. Michael Quell (Berlin: Bartels und Wernitz, 1980), pp. 183–205; Gertrud Pfister, *Geschlechtsspezifische Sozialisation*. A more mixed picture appears in Rudolf Engel, *Sportivität und Geschlechtsrolle bei Schulanfängern* (Ahrensburg: Ingrid Czwalina, 1986). Negative judgments predominate in Heidi Scheffel, "Immer ein bisschen weniger . . . ," *Frauen Bewegung Sport*, pp. 95–105. Scheffel concludes that "coeducation, after ten years of practical experience, has brought next to no significant improvements for the girls" (p. 104).

89. Yves LePogam, *Démocratisation du Sport: Mythe ou Réalité?* (Paris: Jean-Pierre Delarge, 1979).

90. Raymond Thomas, Antoine Haumont, and Jean-Louis Levet, *Sociologie du Sport* (Paris: Presses Universitaires de France, 1987), p. 112.

91. Ibid., p. 108.

92. Daniel Mathieu and Jean Praicheux, *Sports en France* (Paris: Fayard/Reclus, 1987); see also Jacques Defrance, "Un Schisme Sportif," *Actes de la Recherche en Sciences Sociales* (September 1989) 79:79.

93. Kari Fasting, "Sports and Women's Culture," *Women's Studies International Forum* (1987) 10(4):361–68; Gerd von der Lippe, "Frauensport in Norwegen," pp. 155, 158; Kari Fasting and J. O. Tangen, "The Influence of Traditional Sex Roles on Women's Participation and Engagement in Sports," *The Female Athlete*, ed. J. Borms, M. Hebbelinck, and A. Venerando (Basel: S. Karger, 1981), pp. 41–48.see also, Kari Fasting and Mari-Kristin Sisjord, "Gender Roles and Barriers to Participation in Sports," *Sociology of Sport Journal* (December 1985) 2(4):345–51.

94. Survey data from Statistika Centralbyran Stockholm forwarded by Lars Magnus Edstrøm (May 17, 1990); data on 30–year-olds from Lars Magnus Edstrøm, "The Process of Socialization into Keep-Fit Activities," *Scandinavian Journal of Sports Sciences* (1986) 8(3):93.

95. Data forward from the Danish Sports Federation by Henning Eichberg of the Danish Institute of Physical Education (March 6, 1990).

96. Arja Laitinen, "Women's Sports—An Overview of Finnish Women's Physical Culture and Physical Activeness," *Contribution of Sociology to the Study of Sport*, ed. Kalevi Olin (Jyväskylä: University of Jyväskylä, 1984), 169–191; Marjatta Marin, "Gender Difference in Sport and Movement in Finland," *IRSS* (1988) 23(4):345–58; ArjaLaitinen, "Finnischer Frauensport in der Gegenwart," *Frauensport in Europa*, pp. 132–42.

97. Comitato Nazionale Olimpico d'Italia, I Numeri dello Sport (Rome: Le Monnier, 1987), pp. 31–32, 45; Salvini, Identità Femminile e Sport, p. 40.

98. Manuel Garcìa Ferrando, "Popular Sport and Sociocultural Change in the Spain of the Eighties," IRSS (1982) 17(3):5–28; Manuel Garcìa Ferrando, Habitos Deportivos de los Espanoles (Madrid: Instituto de Ciencias de la Educacion Fisica y del Deporte, 1986), pp. 40, 67; Nunia Puig et al., "Frauen und Sport in Spanien," p. 106.

99. Data from Consejo Superior de Deportes supplied by Javier Duran Gonzalez, March 14, 1990.

100. Sports Council: quoted in Margaret Talbot, "Frauen und Sport in England," Frauensport in Europa, p. 72; Diana Woodward, Eileen Green, and Sandra Hebron, "The Sociology of Women's Leisure and Physical Recreation," IRSS (1989) 24(2):121–33; Tony Mason, Sport in Britain (London: Faber and Faber, 1988), pp. 7, 11.

101. Rosemary Deem, All Work and No Play: A Study of Women and Leisure (Philadelphia: Open University Press, 1986), p. 26, 73.

102. Woodward et al., "Sociology of Women's Leisure," pp. 121–33.

103. Philip G. White and James E. Curtis, "Participation in Competitive Sport Among Anglophones and Francophones in Canada," IRSS (1990) 25(2):125–38.

104. Carlos Guerrero, Grandes del Deporte (Santiago de Chile: Editora Nacional Gabriela Mistral, 1975), pp. 7–9; Bruce Newman, "Talk About Net Gains," Sports Illustrated (May 2, 1988) 68(18):59.

105. Frank Guiral, Marïa Caridad Colsn: La Jabalina de Oro (Havana: Editorial Cientifico-technica, 1986), p. 71.

106. Eric A. Wagner, "Sport and Participation in Latin America," IRSS (1982) 17(2):29–39; Eric A. Wagner, "Sport after Revolution: A Comparative Study of Cuba and Nicaragua," Studies in Latin American Popular Culture (1982) 1:65–73; Wolf Krämer-Mandeau, Sport und Körpererziehung auf Cuba (Cologne: Pahl-Rugenstein, 1988), pp. 131, 196; Krämer-Mandeau, "Batas, Mani, Corrida und Baseball," Stadion (1988) 14(2):181–220.

107. Kalevi Heinilä, "The Sports Club as a Social Organization in Finland," IRSS (1989) 24(3):240.

108. Laitinin, "Women's Sports," p. 177.

109. Fasting, "Sports and Women's Culture," pp. 363–64.

110. Garry Whannel, Blowing the Whistle (London: Pluto Press, 1983), p. 77.

111. Joachim Winkler, Ralf-Rainer Karhausen, and Rolf Meier, Verbände im Sport (Schorndorf: Karl Hofmann, 1985), p. 89.

112. Sylvia Schenk, "Aus dem Startblock an die Macht," Frauen Bewegung Sport, pp. 8–23.

113. Barbara Wolfe Jancar, Women under Communism (Baltimore: Johns Hopkins University Press, 1978), pp. 215–18.

114. Uriel Simri, *Women at the Olympic Games* (Netanya: Wingate Institute, 1979), pp. 80, 86.

115. Gunter Holzweissig, *Diplomatie in Trainingsanzug* (Munich: Oldenbourg Verlag, 1981), pp. 131–35.

116. John Bale, *Sports Geography* (London: Spon, 1989), p. 193.

117. Beth Allyson Posnack, "American Women in Sport: A Comparison of Media Reception and Participant Attitudes in the 1932 and 1984 Los Angeles Olympic Games" (unpublished essay, Amherst College, 1985), p. 100.

118. Waitz: quoted in Blue, *Grace Under Pressure,* p. 59.

119. *New York Times,* June 6, 1984. A year earlier, *The Miller Lite Report on American Attitudes toward Sports* reported that 80% of their male sample had a sports idol and 2% of this 80% idolized a woman. 63% of the women had an idol and 22% of them idolized a man (p. 164).

120. Mary Lou Retton, Bela Karolyi, and John Powers, *Mary Lou* (New York: Dell, 1986).

121. Both skaters were written up in several *Sports Illustrated* feature articles; see Rick Reilly, "Behold the Shining Star of the GDR," *Sports Illustrated* (January 20, 1986) 54:38–47; E. M. Swift, "Another Miracle on Ice," *Sports Illustrated* (March 17, 1986) 64:58–70; E. M. Swift, "Cashing in on the Collywobbles," *Sports Illustrated* (March 31, 1986) 64:28–35.

122. Jennifer Hargreaves, "Women and the Olympic Phenomenon," *Five-Ring Circus,* ed. Alan Tomlinson and Garry Whannel (London: Pluto Press, 1984), pp. 53–70.

FOURTEEN: Three Contemporary Controversies

1. Claire Louise Williams, Geoffrey Lawrence, and David Rowe, "Patriarchy, Media, and Sport," *Power Play: Essays in the Sociology of Australian Sport* (Sydney: Hale and Iremonger, 1986), p. 222.

2. On the physiological aspects of women's sports, see Waneen Wyrick, "Biophysical Perspectives," *The American Woman in Sport* (Reading, Mass.: Addison-Wesley, 1974), pp. 401–515; J. Borms, M. Hebbelinck, and A. Venerando, eds., *Women and Sport* (Basel: S. Karger, 1981); K. F. Dyer, *Challenging the Men* (St. Lucia: University of Queensland Press, 1982; Norbert Müller, Dieter Augustin, and Bernd Hunger, eds., *Frauenleichtathletik* (Niedernhausern: Schors Verlag, 1985); Jacqueline L. Puhl, C. Harmon Brown, Robert O. Voy, eds., *Sport Science Perspectives for Women* (Champaign: Human Kinetics, 1988).

3. Dyer, *Challenging the Men,* pp. 135, 177; Gerhard Seehase, "Den Männern auf den Fersen," *Die Zeit,* September 19, 1980; K.F. Dyer and T. Dwyer, *Running Out of Time* (Kensington: New South Wales University Press, 1984), pp. 257, 264; Christine L. Wells and Debra Ballinger, "Wom-

en's Performance—the Last Decade," *Sport and Science Perspectives for Women,* pp. 221–31.

4. Paul Willis, "Women in Sport in Ideology," *Sport, Culture and Ideology,* ed. Jennifer Hargreaves (London: Routledge and Kegan Paul, 1982), p. 123.

5. Jane English, "Sex Equality in Sports," *Philosophy and Public Affairs* (Spring 1978) 7(3):275, 277.

6. Raymond A. Belliotti, "Women, Sex, and Sports," *Journal of the Philosophy of Sport* (1979) 6:67–72; Belliotti, "Sports, Sex-Equality, and the Media," *Women, Philosophy, and Sport,* ed. Betsy C. Postow (Metuchen: Scarecrow Press, 1983), pp. 96–114.

7. Claire Louise Williams et al., "Patriarchy, Media and Sport," p. 222.

8. Ann Crittenden Scott, "Closing the Muscle Gap," *MS* (September 1974) 3:89.

9. Catharine A. MacKinnon, *Feminism Unmodified* (Cambridge: Harvard University Press, 1987), p. 118.

10. On the women's league, see John Bridges, "Women's Professional Football and the Changing Role of the Woman Athlete," *American Sport Culture,* ed. Wiley Umphlett (Lewisberg: Bucknell University Press, 1985), pp. 143–58.

11. M. Ann Hall and Dorothy A. Richardson, *Fair Ball,* p. 13.

12. Mary Anne Warren, "Justice and Gender in School Sports," *Women, Philosophy, and Sport,* pp, 14, 24.

13. Uriel Simri, *A Concise World History of Women's Sports* (Netanya: Wingate Institute, 1983), p. 155; Tom Donohoe and Neil Johnson, *Foul Play: Drug Abuse in Sports* (Oxford: Basil Blackwell, 1986), pp. 1–17.

14. Vogel: quoted in "Vertuscht und Vertagt," *Der Spiegel* (1989) 43(29):173–74; German official: quoted in "DDR: Schluck Pillen oder Kehr Fabriken aus," *Der Spiegel* (1979) 33(5):194–207.

15. Donohoe and Johnson, *Foul Play,* pp. 15–16.

16. Steve Wulf, "Scorecard: Failing the Test," *Sports Illustrated* (September 5, 1988) 69:23.

17. Kenny Moore, "The Spoils of Victory," *Sports Illustrated* (April 10, 1989) 70(19):52–53; Craig Neff, "Scorecard: Drugs and Track," *Sports Illustrated* (October 2, 1989) 71(14):25.

18. Liesel Westermann, *Es Kann Nicht Immer Lorbeer Sein* (Vienna: Fritz Molden, 1977), pp. 131–69; Hans Lenk and Gunter A. Pilz, *Das Prinzip Fairness* (Zurich: Interfrom, 1989), p. 96; see also Gunter A. Pilz and Wolfgang Wewer, *Erfolg oder Fair Play?* (Munich: Copress, 1987), pp. 45–46.

19. Villeneuve: quoted in Jean Harvey, "Sport and the Quebec Clergy, 1930–1960," *Not Just a Game,* ed. Jean Harvey and Hart Cantelon (Ottowa: University of Ottawa Press, 1988), p. 74; on the wrangle over sportswear, see Phillis Cunnington and Alan Mansfield, *English Costume for Sports and Outdoor Recreation* (London: Adam and Charles Black, 1969); Judith Elaine

Leslie, "Sports Fashions as a Reflection of the Changing Role of American Women" (Ph.d., University of North Carolina at Greensboro, 1985); Jihang Park, "Sport, Dress Reform and the Emancipation of Women in Victorian England," *International Journal of the History of Sport* (May 1989) 6(1):10–30.

20. Margaret Hunt, "The De-Eroticization of Women's Liberation," *Feminist Review* (Spring 1990) 34:23–46.

21. Yves LePogam, *Démocratisation du Sport* (Paris: Jean-Pierre Delarge, 1979), p. 86. For a more detailed discussion, see Allen Guttmann, "Sport and Eros," ed. Donald G. Kyle and Gary D. Stark (Texas A and M Press, 1990), pp. 139–54; for some tentative empirical explorations of the links between sports and sexuality, see Gordon W. Russell, Veronica E. Horn, Mary J. Huddle, "Male Responses to Female Aggression," *Social Behavior and Personality* (1988) 16(1):51–57; Gordon W. Russell, Sherry L. DiLullo, Dany DiLullo, "Effects of Observing Competitive and Violent Versions of a Sport," *Current Psychology* (Winter 1989) 7(4):312–21.

22. Christian K. Messenger, "The Inscription of Women in American Sports Fictional Narrative," *Heldenmythen und Körperqualen,* ed. Nanda Fischer (Clausthal-Zellerfeld: DVS, 1989), p. 83.

23. Albert: quoted in Donald J. Mrozek, "Sport in American Life," *Fitness in American Culture,* ed. Kathryn Grover (Amherst: University of Massachusetts Press, 1989), p. 39.

24. Richard Holt, *Sport and the British* (Oxford: Clarenden Press 1989), p. 324; Robert A. Stebbins, *Canadian Football* (London, Ontario: University of Western Ontario Press, 1987), p. 157; Thelma McCormack, "Hollywood's Prizefight Films," *Journal of Sport and Social Issues* (1984) 8 (2): 19; R.M. Lerner,"Some Female Stereotypes of Male Bodybuild/Behavior Relations," *Perceptual and Motor Skills* (1969) 28:363–66.

25. Dunstan: quoted from Claire Louise Williams, Geoffrey Lawrence, and David Rowe, "Patriarchy, Media, and Sport," *Power Play: Essays in the Sociology of Australian Sport* (Sydney: Hale and Iremonger, 1986), p. 220.

26. Frederick: quoted in Janice Kaplan, *Women and Sports* (New York: Viking, 1979), p. 77.

27. Linda Huey, *A Running Start* (New York: Quadrangle Books, 1976), pp. 204, 209.

28. Quoted in Judith A. DiIorio, "Feminism, Gender, and the Ethnographic Study of Sport," *Arena Review* (May 1989) 13(1):53.

29. Bridges, "Women's Professional Football," p. 146.

30. *Cosmopolitan:* quoted in Helen Lenskyj, *Out of Bounds* (Toronto: The Women's Press, 1986), p. 135.

31. Ted Vincent, *Mudville's Revenge* (New York: Seaview Books, 1981), p. 322.

32. Brian Stoddart, *Saturday Afternoon Fever* (North Ryde: Angus and Robertson, 1986), p. 155.

33. Adrianne Blue, *Grace Under Pressure* (London: Sidgwick and Jackson,

1987), p. 110; Jaime Diaz, "Find the Golf Here?" *Sports Illustrated* (February 13, 1989) 70:58–64.

34. Alexander Wolff, "Oh La La, Steffi!" *Sports Illustrated* (April 23, 1990) 72(17):45.

35. Christine Kulke, "Emanzipation oder gleiches Recht auf 'Trimm Dich?,' " *Sport in der Klassengesellschaft,* ed. Gerhard Vinnai (Frankfurt: Fischer, 1972), p. 101; see also Jean-Marie Brohm, *Critiques du Sport* (Paris: Christian Bourgeois, 1976), p. 238; Michel Caillat, on the other hand, condemns sports as a bourgeois plot to "neutralize desire and assure the defeat of sexuality"; see *l'Idéologie du Sport en France* (Montreuil: Editions de la Passion, 1989), p. 151.

36. Lenskyj, *Out of Bounds,* p. 56.

37. Nancy Theberge, "Sport and Women's Empowerment," *Women's Studies International Forum* (1987) 10(4):389.

38. Margaret Carlisle Duncan and Barry Brummett, "Types and Sources of Spectating Pleasure in Televised Sports," *Sport Sociology Journal* (September 1989) 6(3):195–211; Margaret Carlisle Duncan, "Sports Photographs and Sexual Difference: Images of Women and Men in the 1984 and 1988 Olympic Games," *Sport Sociology Journal* (March 1990) 7(1):22–43.

39. Williams: quoted in Dorothy Kidd, "Getting Physical: Compulsory Heterosexuality and Sport," *Canadian Woman Studies* (Spring 1983) 4(3):63–64. Thelma McCormck also found the film "a travesty of liberation"; "Hollywood's Prizefight Films," p. 27.

40. Margaret MacNeill, "Active Women, Media Representations, and Ideology," *Not Just a Game,* p. 209. See also Michael A. Messner's fears that the vogue of women's body-building will "replicate many of the more commercialized, narcissistic, and physically unhealthy aspects of men's athletics"; "Sports and Male Domination," *Sociology of Sport Journal* (September 1988) 5(3):204.

41. Allen Guttmann, *From Ritual to Record* (New York: Columbia University Press, 1978), pp. 57–89; Allen Guttmann, "Translator's Introduction" to Bero Rigauer, *Sport and Work* (New York: Columbia University Press, 1981), pp. vii–xxxi.

Bibliographical Note

The history of women's sports is a badly underdeveloped field. There is no comprehensive study of the topic. The closest approach is a collection of essays, not all of which are historical, edited by J. Borms et al.: *Women and Sport* (Basel: S. Karger, 1981). The essays are quite brief and very uneven in quality. Two books have been reviewed as if they were comprehensive histories, but neither is. Uriel Simri's *Concise History of Women's Sports* (Netanya: Wingate Institute, 1983) moves from ancient Greece to the nineteenth century in exactly six pages. Fourteen more pages bring the story to 1900. The book contains useful information about women's sports in the twentieth century. The appendices are excellent. Adrianne Blue's *Grace Under Pressure: The Emergence of Women in Sport* (London: Sidgwick and Jackson, 1987) brings together some of her excellent journalism, but there is very little information on sports earlier than 1900. This same can be said of *Le Grand Livre du Sport Féminin* (Belleville-sur-Saône: SIGEFA, 1982), by Françoise Laget, Serge Laget, and Jean-Paul Mazot, but *Le Grand Livre* is beautifully illustrated with reproductions of art works, ephemera, and a multitude of quite marvelous photographs.

Readers eager to learn more about women's sports in antiquity, in the Middle Ages, during the Renaissance, in early modern times, will be frustrated. Except for a handful of essays on Greek women's sports, practically all of my information was culled from books and essays on topics other than sports history. More often than not, my notes refer to the authors' *only* mention of women's sports. Although I intend to limit this bibliography to published monographs and selected dissertations, a few exceptional chapters and articles require mention. For Egyptian women, the references in Wolfgang Decker's *Sport und Spiel im alten Aegypten* (Munich: C. H. Beck, 1987) are essential. For the Greeks, Giampiera Arrigoni's chapter, "Donne e Sport nel Mondo Greco," is the most detailed discussion; it appears in her *Le Donne in Grecia* (Bari: Editori Laterza, 1985), pp. 55–201. Lilly Kahil, Hugh Lee, and Thomas Scanlon have published excellent essays on Greek and Roman women's sports (see my notes to Chapters 2 and 3). For the period between Roman times and the late eighteenth century, there are scattered discussions of women's recreation but no books or essays that focus on women's sports. Maria Kloeren's *Sport und Rekord* (Leipzig: Bernhard Tauchnitz, 1935) contains more useful information than do most books.

Although *Frauensport in Europa* (Ahrensburg: Czwalina, 1989), edited by Christine Peyton and Gertrud Pfister, includes Pfister's excellent (but very brief) survey of German women's sports from the late eighteenth century to the mid-twentieth century, most of the contributions are very poor and some, like the meager six pages on French history, are a disgrace. Far more impressive is *From "Fair Sex" to Feminism* (London: Frank Cass, 1987), edited by J. A. Mangan and Roberta J. Park. The subtitle, *Sport and the Socialization of Women in the Industrial and Post-Industrial Eras,* is a fair account of the main themes of book, but the focus is somewhat narrower than implied: the analyses, mostly excellent, are limited to the United States and the British Commonwealth.

The situation is not much brighter when one turns to the scholarship on women's sports in the various nations of Europe and the Americas. Auguste Hoffmann's *Frau und Leibesübungen im Wandel der Zeit* (Schorndorf: Karl Hofmann, 1965) is a good introduction with an emphasis on physical education rather than sports. German women tell their own story in an excellent book edited by Gertrud Pfister, *Frau und Sport* (Frankfurt: Fischer Verlag, 1980). Sigrid Block's *Frauen und Mädchen in der Arbeitersportbewegung* (Münster: LIT, 1987) is a good study of women in the workers' sports movement. *Frauensport im Faschismus* (Hamburg: Ergebnisse Verlag, 1985), by Regina Landschoof and Karin Hüls, is weakened by the fact that only two women were interviewed. For women's sport and physical education under Italian Fascism, Rosella Isidori Frasca's *. . . il Duce le Volle Sportive"* (Bologna: Pàtron Editore, 1983) is useful. The French have produced a number of popular works: Georges Dirand and Renaud de Laborderie, *Les Reines du Sport* (Paris: Calmann-Lévy, 1969) and Serge Bresson's *Le Sport et les Femmes* (Paris: Table Ronde, 1981) are good examples of popular collective biography. *Le Femme d'Aujourd'hui et le Sport* (Paris: Amphora, 1981), by Martine Anciaux et al., is a pot-pourri of opinion and analysis. For Great Britain, Shirley Heather M. Reekie's dissertation, "A History of Sport and Recreation for Women in Great Britain, 1700 to 1850" (Ohio State University, 1982), is excellent. A dissertation by June Arianna Kennard, "Women, Sport and Society in Victorian England" (University of North Carolina at Greensboro, 1974), is also well done. A truly outstanding achievement is Kathleen E. McCrone's *Playing the Game: Sport and Physical Education of English Women, 1870–1914* (Lexington: The University Press of Kentucky, 1988). From every point of view—thoroughness, insightfulness, inclusion of visual materials—this is a superb work. Two books provide collective biographies of Canada's female athletes: Jean Cochrane, Abby Hoffman, and Pat Kincaid, *Women in Canadian Sport* (Toronto: Fitzhenry and Whiteside, 1977); and David McDonald, *For the Record* (Rexdale, Ont.: John Wiley, 1981).

There are surprisingly few studies of women in specific sports. Track and field is covered in a work by Annick Davisse, Léo Lorenzi, and Jane Renoux: *Olympie: La Course des Femmes* (Paris: La Courtille, 1980). Visual materials are the book's stong point; a mere twenty pages of text and pictures cover ancient, medieval, Renaissance, and early modern sports. Although there is no history of women's basketball, Harold Seymour's *Baseball: The People's Game* (New York: Oxford University Press, 1990) has ample material (pp. 443–529). Angela Lumpkin's *Women's Tennis* (New York: Whitson, 1981) is a good chronicle. Something can be learned from two books on women's cricket: Nancy Joy's *Maiden Over* (London: Sporting Magazine, 1950) and *Fair Play* (London: Angus and Robertson, 1976), by Rachel H. Flint and Netta Rheinberg. Caroline Ramsden's *Ladies in Racing* (London: Stanley Paul, 1973) also emphasizes the recent past. Highly recommended is Gertrud Pfister's collection of autobiographical accounts by female pilots: *Fliegen—Ihr Leben* (Berlin: Orlanda Frauenverlag, 1989).

There are three useful studies of women at the Olympic Games: Mary H. Leigh's dissertation, "The Evolution of Women's Participation in the Summer Olympic Games, 1900–1948" (Ohio State University, 1974), Uriel Simri's *Women at the Olympic Games* (Netanya: Wingate Institute, 1979), and Adrianne Blue's *Faster, Higher, Further* (London: Virago Press, 1988). Leigh is quite informative but stops in 1948. Simri is best as a presenter of information in tabular form. Blue's book is lively and well illustrated.

Women's sport are at least mentioned in all the major studies of American sports and physical education, but they are usually segregated into a chapter or two. Benjamin Rader's *American Sports* (Englewood Cliffs, N.J.: Prentice-Hall, 1983) is a good example of textbook history. The first section of *The American Woman in Sport* (Reading, Mass.: Addison-Wesley, 1974), written by Ellen W. Gerber, was probably the best historical account available when it was published: "Chronicle of Participation" (pp. 1–176). American women's sports from 1860 to 1940 are well covered in Cindy L. Himes's dissertation, "The Female Athlete in American Society" (University of Pennsylvania, 1986). *Her Story in Sport* (West Point: Leisure Press, 1982), edited by Reet Howell, is very disappointing. The forty-two selections are quite short and vary in quality even beyond what is usually the case in such collections. About half the selections in *Out of the Bleachers: Writings on Women and Sport* (Old Westbury: The Feminist Press, 1979), edited by Stephanie L. Twin, are first-person accounts by nineteenth- and twentieth-century athletes and physical educators.

Needless to say, biographies and autobiographies, including "as-told-to" and ghost-written works, abound, especially for female athletes competing in the United States. Few of them are completely worthless; few of them are very worthwhile—except for the starry-eyed fan. The following strike me as especially notable. For track and field: William Oscar Johnson and Nancy P. Williamson, *"Whatta-Gal": The Babe Didrikson Story* (Boston: Little, Brown, 1977); Olga Connolly, *The Rings of Destiny* (New York: David McKay, 1968); Dorothy Hyman, *Sprint to Fame* (London: Stanley Paul, 1964); David Emery, *Lillian* (London: Hodder and Stoughton, 1971); Lynda Huey, *A Running Start: An Athlete, A Woman* (New York: Quadrangle, 1976); Wilma Rudolph, *Wilma* (New York: NAL, 1977); Liesel Westermann, *Es Kann Nicht Immer Lorbeer Sein* (Vienna: Fritz Molden, 1979). For swimming: Dawn Fraser and Harry Gordon, *Below the Surface: The Confessions of an Olympic Champion* (New York: William Morrow, 1965); Diana Nyad, *Other Shores* (New York: Random House, 1978). For tennis: Larry Engelmann, *The Goddess and the American Girl: The Story of Suzanne Lenglen and Helen Wills* (New York: Oxford University Press, 1988); Althea Gibson, *I Always Wanted to be Somebody* (New York: Harper's, 1958); Billie Jean King and Kim Chapin, *Billy Jean* (New York: Harper and Row, 1974); Martina Navratilova and George Vecsey, *Martina* (New York: Knopf, 1985). I hestitate to recommend any of the biographies of or autobiographies by golfers, gymnasts, skaters, skiers, or basketball players.

There are many references to female spectators in Allen Guttmann, *Sports Spectators* (New York: Columbia University Press, 1986).

The sociological and social-sychological research on women's sports is quite extensive, most of it in the form of scholarly articles rather than book-length monographs or collections intended for non-specialist readers. The articles most useful to me are referred to in the notes to chapters 12–14. Among the best monographs and collections are these: Dorothy V. Harris, ed., *Women and Sport* (University Park: Pennsylvania State University, 1972); Ellen W. Gerber, Jan Felshin, Pearl Berlin, and Waneen Wyrick, *The American Woman in Sport* (Reading, Mass.: Addison-Wesley, 1974); Carole A. Oglesby, ed., *Women and Sport* (Philadelphia: Lea and Febiger, 1978); Liselott Diem, *Frau und Sport* (Freiburg: Herder, 1980); Mary A. Boutilier and Lucinda SanGiovanni, *The Sporting Woman* (Champaign, Ill.: Human Kinetics, 1983); Helen Lenskyj, *Out of Bounds* (Toronto: The Women's Press, 1986); Sylvia Schenk, ed., *Frauen Bewegung Sport* (Hamburg: VSA-Verlag, 1986).

Rather more specialized are Sabine Kröner's *Sport und Geschlecht* (Ahrensburg: Czwalina, 1976), a study of gender and leisure; Angelika Tschap-Bock's *Frauensport und Gesellschaft* (Ahrensburg: Czwalina, 1983), which probes the differences among female athletes; Alessandro Salvini's *Identità Femminile e Sport* (Florence: La Nuova Italia, 1984), which examines motivations and self-perceptions; Marie-Luise Klein and Gertrud Pfister, *Goldmädel, Rennmiezen und Turnkücken* (Berlin: Bartels und Wernitz, 1985), on images of female athletes in *Bild;* and Georg Anders et al., *Frau und Sport* (Schorndorf: Karl Hofmann, 1978), an analysis of participation.

There is a collection devoted to philosophical issues in women's sports: Betsy C. Postow, ed., *Women, Philosophy, and Sport* (Metuchen, N.J.: Scarecrow Press, 1983).

Many journals have published single issues wholly or mostly devoted to women's sports: among them are *Arena Review* (April/June 1977, May 1979, Summer/Fall 1985); *British Journal of Sport History* (May 1985); and *Women's Studies International Forum* (1987). *WomenSport* published frequent essays on "foremothers" in sports. Almost every issue of *The Journal of Sport Psychology* has one or more articles on female athletes. *Sociology of Sport Journal* is another quarterly with a keen interest in women's sports.

Index

Library of Congress Cataloging-in-Publication Data

Guttmann, Allen.
  Women's sports : a history / Allen Guttmann.
    c. cm.
  Includes bibliographical references and index.
  ISBN 0-231-06956-1 — ISBN 0-231-06957-X (pbk)
  1. Sports for women—History. I. Title.
GV709.G85 1991
796'.0194—dc20   90-28692
                                                 CIP

Casebound editions of Columbia University Press
books are Smyth-sewn and printed on permanent
and durable acid-free paper